The Winemaker

The Winemaker

Richard G. Peterson

With my best regards,
Dick Peter—

MEADOWLARK PUBLISHING

CALIFORNIA

Copyright Information

First published in 2015
Second Edition published in 2018
ISBN 978-1-938010-13-2

Book Jacket Photographs

FRONT COVER
The author making his first batch of wine at age 17,
using Concord grapes, Iowa, 1948.
Photo by B.K. Peterson

BACK COVER (TOP)
Magazine advertisement showing the author
inspecting Classic California Dry White,
Monterey County, California, 1979.

BACK COVER (BOTTOM)
Barrel warehouse at Firestone Winery, Santa Barbara County,
California, 1975. Peterson Pallets were not yet invented.
Photo by the author.

FRONT INSIDE FLAP
The author in a promotional photo, E.& J. Gallo
laboratory, Modesto, California, 1959.

BACK INSIDE FLAP
The author with his new steel pallet barrel stacking
system, The Monterey Vineyard, Monterey County,
California, 1981.

DEDICATION

This book is dedicated to my talented editor and collaborator, Sandra Peterson, whose tireless attention to duty turned my hodge-podge ramblings into the book-order chronology I had hoped for.

I simply could not have done it without her.

CONTENTS

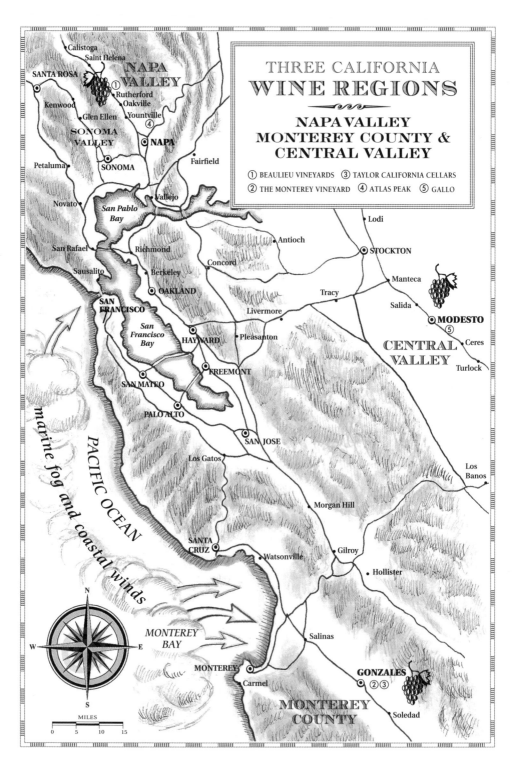

THREE CALIFORNIA
WINE REGIONS
NAPA VALLEY
MONTEREY COUNTY &
CENTRAL VALLEY

① BEAULIEU VINEYARDS ③ TAYLOR CALIFORNIA CELLARS
② THE MONTEREY VINEYARD ④ ATLAS PEAK ⑤ GALLO

Calistoga
Saint Helena
SANTA ROSA
NAPA VALLEY
Rutherford
Kenwood
Oakville
Glen Ellen
Yountville
SONOMA VALLEY
NAPA
Petaluma
SONOMA
Fairfield
Novato
San Pablo Bay
Vallejo
San Rafael
Richmond
Antioch
Lodi
STOCKTON
Sausalito
Berkeley
Concord
Manteca
OAKLAND
Tracy
Salida
SAN FRANCISCO
Livermore
MODESTO
⑤
Ceres
San Francisco Bay
HAYWARD
Pleasanton
CENTRAL VALLEY
Turlock
SAN MATEO
FREEMONT
PALO ALTO
SAN JOSE
Los Banos
Los Gatos
marine fog and coastal winds
PACIFIC OCEAN
Morgan Hill
SANTA CRUZ
Watsonville
Gilroy
Hollister
N
W E
S
MONTEREY BAY
Salinas
MILES
MONTEREY
0 5 10 15
Carmel
GONZALES
②③
MONTEREY COUNTY
Soledad

PREFACE

Parallel snapshots of the California Wine Industry, one taken at the repeal of Prohibition (1933) and the other in 1958, would look almost identical, despite the twenty-five year age differential. Both would show old, moth-eaten wineries buying common grapes and bottling dreary wines – while scrambling to sell them to an uninterested public. Then, something happened.

I entered the wine industry in 1958 to see surprising new beginnings at every turn. New grape varieties were being planted replacing older, non-wine grape vines; soon, new wine types and new labels sprang up on wine shelves (some in grocery stores) without any visible connection to the gloomy past. Unlike a few years earlier, table wines suddenly became worth drinking. They added flavor and complexity to everyday meals; it was a time to eat not merely for survival, but for enjoyment. An aura of excitement, slow to begin, eventually exploded into view until the wines of America were often seen as equals of those in old Europe. Within ten years, a wine sea change had created its own identity as it flowed onto the world stage.

It was fun to be part of it, but that carried an obligation. I began to keep notes, noticing that the wine industry's complex stories were often more interesting than fiction. Twenty years later, I had drawers full of haphazard papers; each was important, but who could sort them into usable order? Each winery had its own story and some were quite fascinating. At the end of one of his visits to Salinas Valley and Monterey, Burgess Meredith, well-known actor and Steinbeck history buff, gave me his personal tape recorder with an order to record my views of wine industry happenings every day. "Get these down on paper, I want you to preserve them," he said. Recordings were more precise than crumpled notes and, most important, they guaranteed that my writing would give accurate accounts of real events, especially since some entries might seem improbable in later years. My assistant at the time, Sharon Archer, typed the recordings into 'RGP Random Notes' in her spare time for me to organize into book form at a future date. Three years ago, my granddaughter, Remi Barrett, was fascinated by the notes and persuaded me that the time to write had arrived. She sorted the random notes into preliminary order and I started writing at breakneck speed.

9

The Road Not Taken

Two roads diverged in a yellow wood,
And sorry I could not travel both
And be one traveler, long I stood
And looked down one as far as I could
To where it bent in the undergrowth;

Then took the other, as just as fair,
And having perhaps the better claim,
Because it was grassy and wanted wear;
Though as for that the passing there
Had worn them really about the same,

And both that morning equally lay
In leaves no step had trodden black.
Oh, I kept the first for another day!
Yet knowing how way leads on to way,
I doubted if I should ever come back.

I shall be telling this with a sigh
Somewhere ages and ages hence:
Two roads diverged in a wood, and I –
I took the one less traveled by,
And that has made all the difference.

ROBERT FROST, 1874-1963

Two true stories took place in parallel between the early 1930s and the 2000 millennium. One was my personal story in wine; the other was a series of events that shaped the California wine industry between Prohibition and the modern era of wine quality worship. The stories remained intimately intertwined throughout the time period, each one affecting the other in significant ways so that, by 2000, each one owed a part of its success and even a little of its personality to the other. This is the surprising story of some of the changes, mistakes and successes of both.

The American wine industry was reduced to a shadow of its former self by the alcohol Prohibition experiment of 1921-1933. By the time Prohibition was repealed, civilized enjoyment of table wine with food in America was essentially dead. Against all expectations, the total banning of alcoholic beverages in the U.S. had led to a culture of alcohol worship rather than the expected denial. People who had enjoyed fine table wine with food prior to 1920 joined the throngs that went to any and all extremes to make and consume alcohol in greater and greater quantities. No longer were great wines recognized, searched for or given a passing thought. Drinkers no longer cared how a wine tasted, what it looked like in a glass or whether the drinker might also be consuming food. It was simply, "Beverage alcohol, Baby, and the more the merrier" – all the time winking at the law, which was powerless to stop or even slow its progress.

Prohibition was repealed, not because of the damage it was doing to American culture, health or economy, but to bring an end to the explosion of violent crime that followed the production, sale and consumption of illegal alcohol, wherever it existed. Moreover, it existed everywhere; no part of America was safe, but big cities were especially dangerous, as illegal alcohol came in from legal producers in Canada and other countries. Illegal importation joined the illegal U.S. production of wine, beer and spirits distilled in homemade machinery, often constructed of poisonous metals soldered together by even more poisonous molten lead. Bootleggers used private trucks, autos, boats, wagons, trains and even occasional pack animals, to deliver their valuable cargo to the speakeasies and 'private' clubs where sales at high prices were a foregone conclusion. Changing from the culture and terror of unlawful alcohol to one of licensing and control would not be easy, and there were those in 1933 who did not believe it could be done at all.

Fast forward a few decades to the Napa Valley Vintners high-end public wine auctions of the 1980s and beyond. Each auction brought, and continues to bring, multimillion dollar sums into Napa Valley for distribution to hospitals, educational institutions and other needy organizations. Wine appreciation groups abound, each seeking the ultimate in superb table wines, judged by worldwide standards and served with the 'ne plus ultra' of fine foods at exquisite events. Wow! What a fantastic change, and all in a few short decades. These are the stories behind some of those changes, as seen through the eyes of one of the intimately involved winemakers of the time. But to fully understand the who's, what's and why's, we have to start at the storyteller's very beginning.......

PART I

~~Poor~~ Rich Beginnings

1931-1958

Nobody Was My Age

I 've never been a city person. I was born in 1931, two miles east of Des Moines, Iowa, and never lived in any city until beginning graduate school twenty-three years later in Berkeley, California. I did spend one complete night in the city jail at age 14, but I don't claim that as living in a city. I entered first grade at a young age 5, and consequently graduated from high school at age 16, a full year younger than most of the other seniors. Later, sometime in my late twenties, it occurred to me that not many kids around me had been my same age – I was always younger. Then, by age 30, I was either younger or older than all my friends and co-workers. That was easy to understand; my birth year was at the bottom of the Great Depression, and U.S. birth rates had dropped to near zero. All my life, it had been rare to find anyone my own age. To my surprise, this rarity had a great effect on what I did, the people I met and the wines I made.

My dad was a coal miner, and I overheard Mom tell someone in 1937 that he earned $18 every two weeks. We were a family of six, and the $18 had to be well stretched. Dad was Victor; I called him Pop – a man who could fix anything. He learned to fix things because he had to. My Mom (Daisy) came from Kansas, and was a high school graduate; this accomplishment made her the family finance manager. She never let us forget that the mortgage carried an interest rate of 2% and had to be paid every month. First born was Martha, the alpha child in charge of the other siblings from day one. Next, me – the oldest son and named for the Baptist preacher who married my parents. The two youngest were Marilyn (nicknamed 'Noy') and Chuck, the baby. Ours was just one of a multitude of poor families throughout America in the 1930s.

Pop's parents had come from the old country, Grandpa Charles from Sweden and Grandma, Bertha Doelz, from Germany. Both grandparents had died by the time I was born, a testament to the hard times they endured all their lives. I never knew much about them. We did know that Grandpa Charles did not have the Peterson last name when he lived in Sweden. Pop told me his father was terrified of the King, and changed his last name, assuming the common name 'Peterson' when he entered the United States. He apparently believed that, if caught, he would be taken back to Europe and put into the Swedish army for life.

He settled outside of Des Moines, married my grandmother, and looked for a house in which to raise his family. He noticed an abandoned wood frame building on three acres that once had been used as a labor camp to house workers for one of the nearby coal mines pock-marking the surrounding neighborhoods. When the local mine closed, he bought the property and settled there. Rock Island Railroad tracks connecting Des Moines with Chicago followed the western edge of the property. Every hobo for miles around knew that the well beside the labor camp building was always full of clean-tasting water; dozens of them got off trains to drink there regularly. In 1890, he moved the old labor camp building about 200 yards away from the tracks to a gravel road and proceeded to make it his home.

After Grandpa's reconstruction, the building had a kitchen, dining room and living room at ground level with stairs to three bedrooms above. It was a simple rectangle with a brick chimney at the middle. The living room took half the first floor space, and the kitchen and dining room split the other half. The pot belly stove between living room and dining room was the primary source of heat, and the kitchen cook stove piped smoke into the backside of the same chimney. Upstairs, each bedroom took up a quarter of the space, the fourth quarter was stairway. The house was simplicity itself.

Pop was born in the house in 1900, joining his older sister and twin brothers. His last sibling, my uncle Carl, was born in 1906. Grandpa Peterson believed that all children had to earn their own living as soon as possible – just as he had been forced to do back in Europe. Pop and his brothers had to begin full-time work in the local coal mines immediately after graduating from the eighth grade. They never got further in school, though all of them were avid readers and continued their educations informally through newspapers, magazines and library books. They never learned to speak Swedish – Grandpa Peterson had learned English as fast as he could and never spoke his native language to them. To this day, we have a sense of loss that we know nothing of the Swedish language or of all those cousins we probably have living somewhere in Sweden today.

Pop's twin brothers were Alvin and Albert. At age thirteen, Albert was plowing with the team of horses when something spooked them. They ran away, dragging Albert behind them to his death nearly thirty years before I was born. I knew my Uncle Alvin only as 'Uncle Pete,' and I don't think he was called by any name other than Pete by anyone. He had no kids of his own and regularly took me fishing in the Des Moines River and to baseball games.

In 1928, after both Grandpa Charles and Grandma Bertha died of pneumonia, Pop bought out the interests of his sister and two brothers to own the house and property. All four of Mom and Pop's kids, including myself, grew up in that house during the 1930s and 1940s. The house was surrounded by farms, but our three-acre piece was too small to be called a farm; still, the only work I knew as a kid was farm work. The dusty gravel road was fifty feet in front. About forty other houses were sprinkled along it and a few other roads, in an area of ten square miles called 'Youngstown.' Mom told me people built houses there to escape the property taxes that would be required if they lived inside the city.

As Iowa was home to layers of soft coal in shallow seams underground, coal was the fuel of choice for both factories and houses in the state's early days of the twentieth century. To store the coal at our house, Grandpa had dug an eight-foot deep oblong hole in the ground about half the size of the footprint of the building, then moved the old labor camp building into place over the hole. The hole became a dirt cellar for storing the coal and kindling wood. An entryway of brick stairs was just outside the kitchen door, and a four-foot square coal chute with a removable cover was at the opposite corner of the house. When a coal truck delivered a load, it dumped the load on the ground at the opening of the chute so that much of the coal fell down the chute and into the cellar. One of my jobs was to remove enough of the coal pieces from around the chute to allow the cover to be put into place. If I failed to get the cover seated properly, cold wind would blow under the house, and we felt it on cold winter nights.

My chores in fall, winter and spring included carrying coal up from the dirt cellar to a spot on the porch just outside the kitchen door. There was room for a large wooden box and five small buckets on the porch. I filled the box with large chunks of coal and the buckets with smaller pieces for easy retrieval at night or in the early morning. Each coal chunk was nearly a foot thick on all sides, and one chunk in the pot belly stove would keep the house warm for many hours in the dead of winter. You could never light a large chunk directly; it had to be ignited by burning wood or smaller pieces of coal under it for about a half hour. The small pieces needed to be half an inch to three inches thick, so we could easily control the fire under any condition.

Breaking up huge chunks of coal into smaller pieces with a small sledgehammer caused some of the coal to shatter into 'slack,' which was the name for finely powdered coal. You had to avoid trying to burn slack without large pieces mixed in. When it was dispersed among bigger coal pieces, it burned successfully, but slack alone didn't put out much heat and didn't last. You could not pile it up because, as a powder, it would spread out into a thin layer over the floor of any container. Every day, it was my chore to go down into the cellar with a flashlight to break up huge chunks of coal into smaller pieces (randomly mixed with whatever amount of slack remained). I can't think of handling coal today without remembering one of Pop's many witticisms: "She must be a coal miner's daughter ...you can tell by the slack in her pants."

Coal was our only source of heat year round, but we cut dry branches from nearby trees to use in starting the fire. Mom's cast iron cook stove used either wood or coal, and whenever a fire burned in the kitchen stove, it heated both the stovetop and its oven. Together the two stoves kept the uninsulated house warm all winter, but I don't think Mom enjoyed cooking there on hot summer days. One of the most exciting things I remember as a kid was getting an electric toaster to replace the old wire contraption Mom had been using to toast bread on the stove top. I thought, Gee! Maybe one of these days we might even get an electric refrigerator, but that had to wait until WW II was over. Until then, the old icebox made do, and we continued to buy 25 lb. blocks of ice from the local ice house or at the supermarket whenever our kitchen ice box ran low. It was routine to place the block of ice on the car bumper for the drive home. It would quickly melt its way into place on the metal bumper, and I never heard of anyone losing a block of ice from their car while driving home.

Chuck and I shared a corner bedroom upstairs and Martha and Noy had another one. Mom and Pop had the third corner bedroom, and all three rooms were served by the stairs from the living room below. The only heat upstairs in winter was whatever drifted upstairs from the pot belly stove. When I was 15, Mr. Barnard, my high school physics teacher, gave me the idea to saw a rectangular hole through the upstairs floor near the outside wall of the dining room. To fit the hole, I bought a sheet metal rectangular grill with a lever that made it easy to open or close. When open, heat from downstairs went directly up to warm the bedrooms on winter nights. At first Mom was wary, but afterwards she thanked me many times. Pop, on the other hand, liked it from the first time he saw it, although he knew I had been lucky not to have sawed through a weight-supporting floor joist!

Coal mining was a major source of employment for local men, including Pop, Uncle Pete and Uncle Carl. From my birth to age 10, Pop worked long, hard days in the mine. When he got home in the evening, he was exhausted and completely black with coal dust all over his body. Only his eyes and mouth were visible. Pop had spent the whole day on his hands and knees in the coal mine – drilling, hammering, scooping, shoveling, lifting, dragging and carrying pieces of coal out of the soft coal seam that was about three feet to four feet in thickness and located between layers of slate, dirt and rock underground. This hand work was typical of the way coal was mined in Iowa in the 1930s.

The first thing Pop wanted at the end of his tiring day was a hot bath.

We kids put an oblong tub with a tight-fitting lid (called a boiler) onto our toy wagon in summer and sled in winter to bring enough water from the far-away 'hobo well' for Pop's nightly bath. It often took two trips to the well to get enough water for Pop's big round tub. Mom had warm water in the round tub ready when he came home at 6 p.m. He sat inside that tub to take his bath indoors during winter, but sometimes moved it outside to the yard in summer. My first job, from about 4 years old, was to wash Pop's back as he sat in the tub of sudsy water. I washed off the coal dust from places he could not reach. He was always glad and plenty relieved to see that each of us had done our share of the family work that day.

Our land certainly saved us during the Depression because we used every inch of it to grow much of our own food. Every spring we planted one full acre of vegetables. Another acre was used to grow field corn, although Pop sometimes planted alfalfa hay to rejuvenate the soil. Another half acre was grapes, fruit trees and berry patches. The rest of the property was pasture, hog pen and range for the chickens. Our garden grew potatoes, carrots, lettuce, celery, squash, onions, tomatoes, spinach, sweet corn, popcorn, radishes, cantaloupe (called muskmelon in Iowa), watermelons, green beans, cucumbers, peas and cabbage. An acre is a lot of garden; most people can't visualize how big an area that is, or what a lot of work it requires. It took that much garden to grow enough food to feed our family of six for the ensuing year. Whatever we couldn't harvest for ourselves was harvested for the animals. Planting was a big job, but planting was only the beginning; after growth started, the garden had to be weeded, cultivated and sometimes sprayed or dusted to keep insects from eating the small plants before they got started. Watching and protecting the new growth was a full-time job until the plants got into their rapid growth stages.

Finally, harvesting the various crops had to be coordinated with Mom's canning. Mom canned applesauce, peaches, pears, sweet corn, green beans, peas, carrots, tomatoes and tomato juice in quart-size jars that were stored in our cave. She got the glass jars, rubber rings and caps sterilized and ready, while we did the picking, cleaning and preparing the crop to be canned. Canning anything was an all-day job, when the crops ripened we often worked at it every day for a week or two at a time. Either Grandpa or Pop and his brothers had dug the cave years before, lining it with bricks and building a brick stair entry. It kept all the canned goods at around 60°F, even on hot summer days. Mom had collected recipes for canning or preserving almost everything we grew.

Every spring, Mom and Pop sat down and planned how much of each fruit and vegetable would be canned during the next summer; that told them how many rows of each crop to plant. The final step was to make a layout of the garden on paper to keep track of when the land was plowed and prepared. Often we'd plant a 'one time only' crop on a whim just to see whether we might want to repeat it in a following year. One year we planted peanuts, another year German black carrots, or celery or different types of lettuce or squash. We planted pumpkins and squash along the near edge of the field corn in the animal food part of the garden. Pumpkin pie was a must every autumn, especially for Thanksgiving and Christmas dinners.

Of course, not all of our food was canned. We constantly picked sweet corn, tomatoes, green beans or peas, carrots and other crops just before a lunch or dinner. Much of our garden was harvested as needed and eaten all summer long. One of my happiest memories is taking a salt shaker to the garden and picking fresh, fully ripe tomatoes and eating them right there. It is no exaggeration to say that a ten-year-old kid can pick and eat seven or eight big tomatoes in one garden trip. (When that happened, it was the only food I ate for that meal.) Some foods never needed much follow-up work – popcorn ears were just picked and dried. We didn't even shell the kernels off the cob until we wanted to pop some. Onions and potatoes had to be dug up by hand, but the potatoes were just rubbed a little to clean them off and placed in gunny sacks for storage in the barn. Our strawberry patch and rows of black raspberry bushes were out near the peach, pear and apple trees along the south edge of the property. Fresh 'black cap' raspberries make the best pie there is. It beats even cherry and peach, though not by much.

We had 50 or 60 Concord grapevines, great for eating fresh grapes or making jelly. Pop had planted the vines and gathered champagne bottles for his own wine, which he began making around 1920. He, like millions of others, had never actually read the written word of any law before the

Volstead Act of 1920. However, after Prohibition was enacted, Section 29 became big news! It permitted any house holder to legally ferment 'non-intoxicating cider and fruit juices for use in his home, up to 200 gallons yearly.' Pop bought local grapes, grape juice and 'grape bricks' from California which he blended with his own Concord fruit as the raw material for his home winemaking during Prohibition.[1]

Grape bricks were made commercially in California by draining the juice from freshly crushed grapes and pressing the drained grape skins into 'dry' bricks. As grape growers knew that most of the color and flavor of grapes is in the skins, not the juice, grape bricks became a convenient way to buy, store, ship and sell grapes (usually referred to as 'Wine Bricks') for home winemaking. Pop had saved one of the labels from a grape brick he'd used for wine in the 1920s. The label had a warning: "Do not break up 5 grape bricks with the enclosed yeast pills and add 5 gallons of water with 10 pounds of sugar, as this might ferment."

Mom canned Concord grape juice in the bottles Pop had originally used for his homemade wine. After heating the juice to boiling, she poured it through a funnel into hot bottles. The bottles were capped with steel beer bottle caps (every family had a simple crown capper in those days). She left the bottles in place until they cooled slowly – if a bottle cooled too fast, it might break. After the juice was cool, we stored the bottles in the cave where the juice would keep for a year or even two. Months later when we ran low on jelly, Mom would open a couple of bottles of juice, add sugar and pectin according to her recipe, boil the mix and pour it into heated jelly jars. She capped them with snug fitting lids with rubberized edges to seal against the glass, screwing the lids into threads on the glass jar. When the jars cooled, a vacuum formed inside the jar, and the jelly would keep at room temperature, until opened. We had Concord grape jelly on the table any time of year.

One of my favorite childhood memories was making our own root beer.

---

[1] During Prohibition, 'home winemaking' stores sprang up here and there, from which an individual could legally buy materials and equipment for making wine at home.

The Hire's Root Beer Company sold small square bottles containing 'Root Beer Extract.' We mixed one bottle of that thick brown stuff into 5 gallons of fresh water and 5 pounds of sugar. Finally, we added a cake of Red Star yeast – the same kind Mom added to the dough when she baked bread. After the whole thing was stirred well, we ladled the liquid through a funnel into Pop's clean champagne bottles and popped a crown cap into place. We stored the bottles on their sides for about two weeks at room temperature to ferment just enough to carbonate the root beer, then moved all the bottles into the cave to remain cool. After that, we had only to open a bottle and pour some terrific root beer into our glasses of ice.

We learned to preserve pickles (dill, sweet and, my favorite, bread and butter) by following the instructions from Mom or an aunt. They would buy or grow the necessary herbs and spices depending on the type of pickles we wanted. Dill always grew in somebody's garden, and I loved picking a handful and chewing it fresh. Making pickles was a fairly easy process: Pick the cucumbers, sort them by size, wash and stuff them into large crock jars, then cover with a brine of saltwater and spices. Finally, place a half-inch thick layer of freshly picked Concord grape leaves in the top of the brine to make a cap over everything and set the jar in the cave for a few weeks to cure. Everybody had a few Concord vines here and there, so the fresh leaves were readily available. After the fermentation had done its magical job, the pickles were crisp and flavorful.

More than two decades later, during graduate school at Berkeley, I noticed an article in the *Journal of Food Science & Technology*. Research microbiologists had discovered a 'mold inhibitor' that exists naturally in Concord grape leaves. The article explained that the old almanac recipe for covering fermenting pickles with Concord grape leaves really worked. The inhibitor in the leaves retarded mold spoilage that otherwise could ruin pickles by softening them, destroying their crispness. Nobody in Youngstown had ever explained that to me in the 1930s. All they knew was that using the leaves seemed to produce crispier pickles.

We had two water wells on the property. The closest one was just at the far corner of the backyard, but Pop stopped using it about the time Martha was born. That well was unusual in that its floor was a thick seam of coal. It gave the water a clean, but slightly sulfurous taste, so Pop went back to using water from the original hobo well near the railroad tracks 200 yards from the house. Water wells in Iowa are rarely deeper than forty feet because the state has enough rainfall to keep the water table high. Because they are shallow, most wells were dug by hand in the 1930s and 40s. Pop helped Art Anderson, the best-known local well driller, as an odd job. I liked watching them work together, standing on opposite sides of the drill hole, pulling and pushing the handles on Art's augur round and round, as they drilled a new well. As the augur filled with dirt, they raised it out of the ground to dump it out and then re-inserted the augur into the hole. When the hole was deep enough to need an extension, they screwed on another length of rod between the augur and the handle, and continued twisting that augur into the ground. Eventually, they found water in a sandy layer on top of something impervious, like clay or rock. After cleaning out as much of the underground bottom sand as possible to 'develop' the well, Art would pronounce the well "dug" and the rod and augur were replaced with lengths of water pipe (with an enlarged intake screen at the bottom). Art then laid a wood plank cover on the ground to protect the new well from cave-ins. He supported the hand pump and water pipe by hanging all of it through a hole in the center of the wood plank cover at the ground surface. It was simple and effective.

Priming the well was a mystery to me, but Art was an expert. He primed the pump by pouring a gallon or two of water into the top while pumping the handle very fast up and down. It was magic. After Art poured and pumped for a minute or two, presto! Plenty of new water started gushing out of the pump with every push down on the handle, and the well was pronounced "finished." After that first priming the pump worked, even many months later, and no further priming would be necessary unless the internal leather seal wore out. We appreciated having a well, but also took it for granted. I didn't understand how a well actually worked until years later when I took Physics in high school.

One of the daily chores I remember most was carrying water by hand to the house from that distant well, one or two buckets at a time. It was a long way and the buckets were heavy, especially when the weather was either too hot or too cold, which was all the time. All three of us older kids had to share the water carrying job. When we were too little to carry regular three-gallon buckets, Mom gave each of us a one-gallon Karo syrup can that we carried by the handle. I was plenty proud the first time I proved I could carry one of those gallon cans of water in each hand all the way from the well. Even with three-gallon buckets, I remember that it was easier to carry two buckets than only one; balance made all the difference. For years after I left Des Moines at age 17, that hobo well continued to provide the family with exceptionally clean water – and it continued to supply random hobos with a cool drink from time to time.

We never had running water or an indoor bathroom at home until after I had graduated from high school. We had only a wooden 'two holer' outhouse at the far end of the backyard. Mom never bought toilet paper; instead, we kept back issues of the mail order catalogs from Sears and Montgomery Ward in the outhouse. It worked well because, in the 1930s, few if any of the pages were printed in color. Black-and-white pages were printed on soft, thin paper (ideal for use as toilet paper) whereas color pages were printed on hard, slick paper – don't try this at home! In winter, we kept a porcelain pot with a lid called a 'Combinette' upstairs in the house at the common corner of the bedrooms. The rule was to use it if you had to in the night, but whoever did 'number two' in the pot had to carry it to the outhouse and dump it as soon as possible the next morning.

We bathed regularly, of course, but not usually in the galvanized metal tub that I helped Pop use when he came home from the mine. That tub took too much water. Most of our baths were taken while standing in the kitchen next to the sink at night while everybody else in the family was in the living room listening to the radio,[2] doing homework, or playing games.

---

[2] The voice of one radio announcer, Burgess Meredith, stood out in introducing programs. He played the character George in my favorite film, Of Mice and Men, which still remains a classic today even though it was made in 1939. Burgess was one of the world's truly outstanding actors, and it would never have occurred to me that he would later become a personal friend. He would even play a role in my writing this book.

We kept a big pan or metal bucket on the stove to guarantee a good supply of warm bath water. The procedure was easy and fairly fast: Fill a large wash pan in the sink with warm water from the stove. Stand there in your underpants and use a wash cloth to scrub from your feet up as far as possible. Next, wash from your head down as far as possible. Finally, drop your underpants and wash 'possible.' Dry off with a warm towel, get dressed and yell, "Next!" to give the dark kitchen to a sibling.

In summer, we went swimming in the creek; it was an easy matter to carry a bar of soap along to use for a bath (with swimsuit on) at the end of a swimming session. To avoid losing the bar in the fast-moving creek, we learned to use Ivory brand soap because it floated in water. In junior high and high school, we got to take showers after gym classes. Those were the first actual showers I ever took.

My chores included feeding the animals their nightly and morning meals, and making sure in winter that all were sheltered away inside the pig shed and cow barn. We had a cow for milk, cream and butter. Buttermilk was a favorite drink, and I grabbed first dibs on it because I was the one who usually churned the butter. Mom saved the excess cream that she skimmed off the tops of milk bottles after they stood around for a while. She poured the cream into a large jar and left it on the kitchen counter with a lid lightly screwed on. No thought was given to refrigeration, since we made butter from either fresh or sour cream – the cream didn't need to be kept refrigerated. We had no refrigerator anyway, only the old ice box in the kitchen for fresh foods. That sufficed for milk, since we got new milk with every morning and night-time milking of Bossie the cow. When we had excess milk that got sour enough to solidify (clabber), we'd just pour it into the hogs' trough with the rest of their food. The pigs loved clabbered milk. Pop told me, "Pigs think it's ice cream."

Part of the acreage was allocated for growing field corn and provided pasture for Bossie, the chickens and hogs. We raised about ten or fifteen hogs every year, and butchered one from time to time. We purchased curing salt to cure our own ham, bacon and 'side meat.' Side meat resembled bacon but did not have that great bacon taste, and the meat portion wasn't as red. Butchering day was quite a procedure. As soon as the hog was shot, his throat was slit, and he was hung from a tree by the hind legs to 'bleed out.' One of my uncles sometimes saved some of the blood to make blood sausage. After skinning, the internal organs were removed, the carcass was washed off and different parts of the body were cut up for ham, steaks, roasts, chops, side meat and bacon. The parts to be salted were put in pans and covered with curing salt. Salting the parts was my job as a kid, and to this day I remember the salt burn on cracks in my hands and under my fingernails. The salted pork cuts were then wrapped in heavy cheese cloth and stored in our cave to cure. Recipes for processing meats were readily available in publications from libraries and various state agencies.

Mom bought 200 newly hatched baby chicks every spring, and we'd feed them cracked corn and mash for the first month or so. The chickens ranged freely all over the property, only coming back to roost at night. They ate everything chickens eat, while sharing the hog pen with pigs and the pasture with Bossie. At night, the chickens roosted on horizontal wooden poles a few feet above ground inside the hog shed, the hogs sleeping on the ground below them. We fed table scraps to the hogs and chickens in addition to their ration of corn. After harvest, Pop stored dry ears of field corn in the corn crib which he'd built inside the barn structure. As there wasn't any household garbage pick-up, we simply used all leftovers for animal feed. We let a small pile of paper trash slowly accumulate in back, and burned it about once a month. Other families did the same; all shared an eroded gully at a far-off bend in the gravel road that served most of the houses. That small 'dump area' served as the final resting place for every family's empty cans and broken glass.

When I got old enough, milking the cow was added to my list of tasks, a job Mom was glad to relinquish. My sisters, Martha and Noy, had their chores as well, but aside from carrying water from the well to the house, their work was almost always inside. Mostly, they helped Mom with washing, ironing, cleaning, cooking, etc. Since my brother, Chuck, was more than six years younger than me, the girls' early chores included helping to take care of him. Household life was simpler in the 1930s, but a whole lot more physical to a degree that is hard to fathom today. Present-day news reports often show that Americans are much heavier today than in the past, and it isn't hard to understand why.

Mom

Every spring like clockwork, Mom went shopping for new wallpaper as the previous winter's fumes from the coal burning stove left last year's paper dingy. She searched the four or five wallpaper stores in Des Moines, as well as mail order stores like Sears, Montgomery Ward and J.C. Penney. With luck, she could count on finding three or four designs that were on sale, or better yet, a close-out. Then she scoured the mail order catalogs for wallpaper designs. Sears and Montgomery Ward were biggest, but Spiegel was often the best place for nicely designed wallpaper at good prices. Spiegel catalogs used more color pages than the larger catalogs, so we never took old Spiegels to the outhouse. Our house had wallpaper covering on the ceilings and walls of every room – wallpaper was literally the only insulation our house had. I counted as many as 14 different layers of old wallpaper in places on some walls, as I removed the loose pieces prior to a new papering job. In Iowa, a winter wind could easily howl through cracks in the walls of a house without wallpaper; with wallpaper, a house was noticeably warmer.

The living room was the largest and most difficult room to satisfy within her budget. The other rooms were smaller, but no two got the same design. Mom had a rule: It doesn't cost any more to make every room different, every year! Sometimes wallpaper shopping took the whole months of March and April, but by Mom's birthday (May 1st) we were always ready. Mom and I started on the first Saturday by stretching out the dining room table with all the expansion leaves, and covering it with three or four layers of old unfolded newspapers. After putty-knife stripping all the loose previous year's wallpaper from the walls, we'd measure the height of the first room's walls with a tape measure. Then we'd unroll and cut successive strips from rolls of the design we wanted for that room. These pieces were stacked on top of each other and then the whole stack was turned upside down so the design was down, and the side to be pasted was up. It was important to make each one a little longer than the measurement because the rooms were never exactly the same height all along their width.

Wallpapers 'without match' were easy but they didn't have any class. One strip of paper didn't have to match the adjoining strip because the pattern was a mishmash of small designs that had no relationship to each other. But *with* a matching pattern, you had to pay attention! Matching papers had a pattern that continued from one strip to the next. You had to cut the lengths so that the patterns matched perfectly. It always wasted paper at the top and bottom of each strip to do so, but Mom knew it was worth the extra cost. A wallpapered wall had to look as if the whole wall was covered by a single large sheet of patterned paper. It surprised me to see how badly out of plumb every wall was! Fortunately, wallpaper stretches a little after being wetted with wallpaper paste; unfortunately, a lot of 'wall flexing' takes place in a room during one year of Iowa weather. If the paper was unduly stretched when applied in May, it was sure to split open on a cold night in December the first time the pot-belly stove heated the room too hot.

We used a scaffold made by extending a plank between two chairs. Mom made a fresh batch of paste by stirring boiling water into a big bucket of powdered starch. It turned a translucent light grey color and then fluffed up to a sticky, pasty mess. I can still remember the good taste of the paste when I licked it off my fingers if I'd gotten sloppy. Using the paste brush, I'd paste the whole underside of the first strip of wallpaper, and then loop the paper back and forth onto itself being careful never to allow it to crease at any of the bends. I handed the loosely folded paper to Mom, who placed the upper end at the top of the wall, and let it all unfold downwards so it stuck at the top but remained loose all the way down to the floor. She used a dry 'spreading brush' to brush the piece onto the wall from the top of the wall downwards to make it stick smoothly, aligning the left edge carefully with the edge of the corner.

Mom and I papered the whole house every spring from the time I was about seven or eight until my last year of college. Noy and Chuck had begun helping her by that time since I was no longer home in May. The job got easier after the mid-1940s when pre-mixed paste became available, but I never liked the taste of pre-mix. One of the skills I have been most proud of as an adult is being able to wallpaper any wall and ceiling of any house quickly, and all alone. For years, I papered at least one wall of most rooms in my house just to show off.

Mom washed all the family's clothes on Mondays. On wash day, we'd put the boiler into our toy wagon and fill it at the well. Martha or I pulled it up to the house in the wagon (with the other one pushing along with Noy's help). We had an electric clothes washer, but the only thing it did was rotate a central agitator back and forth to slosh water over the clothes. Mom put the clothes in, poured in hot water, dropped in small pieces of a bar of laundry soap, skimmed off the soap scum and turned on the washer. When she thought it had sloshed enough, she turned it off and then took the clothes out of the hot, sudsy water by using a short length of broomstick. The water was too hot to reach in and get clothes out by hand. The washer had an attached 'wringer' with two rubber rollers. Wringing the clothes out was done by carefully pushing one edge of a shirt or towel into the tiny space between the two rollers. The rollers grabbed the cloth and squeezed the water out as it went through.

One Monday, when I came home from third grade, Mom was just finishing her all-day washing job and was wringing out one of her last loads. She looked up at me and waved a greeting. Suddenly my two-year-old brother, Chuck, who'd been watching Mom do the laundry, started screaming and I saw the wringer dragging his arm between the two rollers. Mom saw it and quickly hit a lever on top of the roller case to release the upper roller and let go of his arm. Fortunately for Chuck, no bones were broken; the doctor told Mom that his very young bones were too soft to break. Sure enough, within a few weeks, Chuck's arm was as good as new. A day or so after the accident, Mom showed the three of us older kids exactly how the wringer worked and how to hit the lever on top to release the upper roller in case that ever happened again.

Mom's handling of a unique experience I had at age eight had an influence on me for the rest of my life. One afternoon when I was asleep on the grass in the backyard, I became vaguely aware of a melodic, intermittent hissing. There was a subtle pssst for two or three seconds, then silence for

28

maybe five seconds, then another pssst; on and on the hisses alternated with silence. I was aware of it getting louder at first and then slowly diminishing in volume. I was comfortably asleep on my back and must have assumed it was a sound dream of some kind. Finally, I woke up enough to open one eye and saw the long tail of a big bull snake just leaving from my chest. I opened both eyes and could see the tail up close, but the main body was already more than four feet away. Bull snakes were at least five feet long and pretty fat. I wasn't scared because we saw bull snakes regularly all summer; they never bit anyone and were fairly docile, but from the path that snake was following, I figured he had to have crawled directly over my chest. Either that or he might have slithered up to my face for a minute or so and then turned away and went on about his business. He had to have been quite close for me to hear the intermittent hiss as his tongue sniffed the air – that much was certain. I sat up on an elbow in disbelief for a few seconds, then got up and went into the house. I told Mom what had happened, and she told me, "Yes, snakes are sometimes inquisitive." That is all she said, just shrugging it off, but I was unconvinced that I hadn't just escaped a horrible fate. As I think about it now, Mom's shrugging off that snake experience taught me how wise she was never to panic over surprise worrisome events. It was a great lesson.

As if Mom hadn't worked hard enough, she began doing clothing alterations for a department store in downtown Des Moines after all the kids were in school. By her 80s, she had hung out a shingle and was running her own business 'Alterations by Daisy,' working out of her house. I called her from California on her 95th birthday, thinking to add a little humor to her day by reminding her that I would become 65 in another month. I told her that I wanted to retire at some point, but that I didn't feel right about retiring when she was still working 5 days a week. She didn't grab the bait; rather, she just said, "You listen to your mother." I could visualize her shaking her finger at me through the phone mouthpiece. "Don't you ever retire! If you retire, you'll just get old and die."

Two of Mom's four sisters lived with their families close to us, and holiday meals were often held at our house because we had more yard space than our cousins. Mom was a great cook even though hamburger, fried chicken and catfish from the river tended to dominate. Sometimes we'd also catch and eat river carp; small carp were too boney, but when we got a big one it seemed like a treat. It was my job from an early age to catch whatever chickens we needed for the upcoming meal, whether our own supper or a holiday dinner for extended family. I'd hold each chicken by the legs and wing tips in my left hand, and cut the head off with one stroke of the corn knife in my right. I held the chicken so its neck lay on a railroad tie 'chopping block' Pop had placed for that purpose, and my blow with the corn knife was stopped by the tie after the blade severed the neck. I'd learned how to do it by being the 'neck stretcher' when Mom had done the cutting. My mom had lost half of her left little finger at a young age when she had held the chicken's beak to stretch the neck out as her mother used the corn knife. Her mother missed, and cut off Mom's little finger. As Grandma was tending to Mom, they saw one of the other chickens grab the little piece of cut-off finger and run away with it in his beak. After that, everyone used a piece of string to extend the chicken necks out while holding it on the chopping block. Mom taught me to tie a slip knot loop around the chicken's neck and pull the string to stretch the chicken's neck on the railroad tie as she handled the sharp knife.

A corn knife is like a very sharp machete. Its normal use was to cut corn stalks off near the ground for stacking on end to build 'corn shocks.' After Pop picked the corn every fall, he'd go through the field cutting off most of the corn stalks at ground level. At the spot where he wanted a shock, he'd fold two or three uncut stalks together at their middles by wrapping the tops around each other horizontally to make a center structure for a shock. Those few uncut stalks formed a frame to hold the new shock in place. Pop then leaned each new cut stalk against the frame formed by the uncut ones. When he had enough cut stalks standing in place to make the whole shock about three or four feet thick, he'd wrap a piece of twine around the middle and tie the shock together with the twine about three feet above the ground. The twine held all the cornstalks together at their middles and the only part of any stalk to touch the ground was the cut end at the bottom. A well-built corn shock was completely stable in wind, rain or snow, and it preserved the individual corn stalks for feeding to Bossie all winter. It was a great way to store corn stalks in the field for months in any kind of weather.

For the rest of fall and early winter, depending on the weather, we kids would burrow into a shock on hands and knees and hollow it out from the inside by pushing outwards on groups of the stalks. It made a great kid's cave, and we'd take paper bags full of husked and dried black walnuts into our playhouse shock along with a whole brick and another half brick. We'd place the whole brick on the ground, put the black walnuts on it, one at a time, and use the half brick as a hammer to crack them. Black walnuts are very hard, and it isn't easy to crack one without smashing the inner nut meat, but once you caught on, it was easy. All the kids did this, and it was wonderful sitting on the ground inside a corn shock, cracking walnuts and eating them till dinner time. Even in a heavy rain, it stays dry inside a corn shock. Farmers never make shocks anymore; mechanical harvesting now chops the whole stalk into silage for animal feed. I miss seeing them in corn fields as I drive by in the fall. Sometimes I see corn shocks in Halloween displays or picture puzzles, but we never see the real thing in fields anymore. I build a shock every so often in our garden today, whenever we grow enough red popcorn or bicolor sweet corn to do so.

Pop

As a boy, I particularly enjoyed being with and watching Pop. Whenever I saw him working with a machine, he took the time to show me how to operate it and, more importantly, how to stop it. That even extended to the family car, a well-used 1928 Chevy. The car (like most 1928 cars) had an actual trunk on the back. You could unlatch it at the top and allow half the trunk to hinge back to horizontal, in order to carry something too big to fit inside the trunk itself. Pop used the car as if it were a small truck when harvesting field corn in the fall. He taught me to drive it when my legs were not yet long enough to easily reach both the clutch and brake pedals at the same time. I could use one foot to reach either pedal, but not both at once. To stop, I would step on the clutch and move the gear shift to neutral, then quickly switch my foot from the clutch to the brake pedal. My panic 'stop everything' procedure was to forget the clutch, hit the brake and turn off the ignition switch. Cars didn't have keys then, just an off/on ignition switch.

The reason I needed to drive at age eight or nine was so Pop could pick corn by hand and throw the ears into the car trunk as I drove slowly along the outside corn row in the field. He'd pick a few rows at a time, then both Pop and I cut the picked cornstalks off with corn knives, and he'd build two or three corn shocks with the cut stalks. After that was finished, I could again drive the car up close to the next few rows for picking. Pop taught me a carload of things that I couldn't have learned elsewhere.

The Iowa State Fair was usually held the last week or two in August. From about age eight, my cousins and I would walk the two miles to the fair daily, as kids got in free. Pop pointed out that many of the fair visitors bought ice cream bars and just dropped the paper bag wrappers on the ground after removing their ice cream – the fairgrounds area was literally covered with the wrappers by eleven every morning. Pop told me that I could collect those bags and send them in for gifts from the ice cream company. Messages on the bag stated: "Save these bags for gifts," and "Write for catalog of available gifts." I mailed in a postcard asking for the catalog, and spent the next week in great anticipation, checking the mailbox every day. Among the catalog items was a 'ChemCraft' starter set for learning first lessons in chemistry; I could get one by mailing ten ice cream bags with one dollar, or get the set free by sending in one thousand bags. The catalog made chemistry sound so exciting that I just had to get that set. I had never owned a dollar in my life and saw no possibility of ever doing so; my only chance was to collect a thousand bags by picking them up from the ground.

Mom sewed a cloth handle onto a twenty-pound empty sugar sack for me to take to the fair, and over three August days, I collected more than the number of bags I needed. She helped me package them for mailing, and before long I was the happy owner of the world's most exciting chemistry set. That chemistry set was my most prized possession for the next two years. I did every experiment in the manual many times and wanted to play with nothing else for months at a time. The ChemCraft manual was written as a teaching aid, and I learned enough chemistry from that set by age ten to convince me that I would do something involving chemistry as my life's work. The set had ignited my love for science.

People from all over Iowa attended the fair, often showing their animals, fruits, vegetables, art work and many other things. Those showing farm animals slept in dormitories next to, or above, the pens that housed their animals. In the last days of the fair, the exhibitors moved out and often left usable items behind. As we lived only two miles away and knew they didn't charge admission on the last few days, Pop and I would drive to the fair and walk through the abandoned dorm areas above the animal barns. We would find coins, usually pennies, nickels or dimes, but sometimes quarters and even half dollars on the floor! It was not unusual to come home with more than a dozen unopened cans of Coca-Cola or beer, still in their original containers. Pop's rule was never to use food that was out of its original unopened container, but there were almost always plenty of new cans and bottles of soft drinks. Pop sometimes worked at the state fair just before the fair started, and during high school he got me summer jobs cleaning up the fairgrounds. One of my jobs was to shinny up flagpoles, with a rope in my mouth, on the roof of the main amphitheater to replace flag ropes that had broken or blown away during the year. Today when I visit Des Moines, I look up at that building and marvel at how close to the edge of the roof those flagpoles are. How stupid kids are at age fifteen!

Pop would pick a nice weekend in October to bring in the walnuts. Waiting a few days to a week after a windy storm would ensure that the nuts were already on the ground and mostly dry. We drove a few miles to fields that had natural black walnut trees and hickory nut trees growing near the road. Pop knew most of the farmers and property owners in central Iowa and had permission to pick up all the nuts our family needed every fall. We had only to choose the best-looking crop that would be easy to rake up and fill into 'gunny sacks,' burlap bags that had contained chicken feed or cracked grain for hogs. Gunny sacks were like baling wire; you never threw one away because a new use for one was likely to arise at any moment. We kept a stack of folded gunny sacks in a dry part of the barn. When we'd raked up enough walnuts and put them into sacks, Pop carried them to the '28 Chevy and loaded up as many sacks as the trunk could hold.[3]

We often got our year's supply (four or five sacks) on only one trip. After we unloaded the sacks of walnuts onto the porch at home, we had the chore of hulling them by pulling off the outside pieces of green shell. One smack with a hammer knocked most of the hull off the walnut, and you could push the rest off by hand. The hulls oozed tan juice that turned your hands a dark brown after a few hours. The walnut stain lasted for a week or two but eventually wore off. Years later, I learned that diluted walnut hull juice was one of the first things used as an artificial tanning cream by pharmaceutical companies decades ago. After we kids finished hulling, Pop put the nuts back into the gunny sacks, carried them up a ladder, and poured them onto the flat part of the barn roof for drying in the sun. Dried nuts would keep forever when stored in gunny sacks in a dry part of the barn. Hickory nuts were smaller than walnuts and had a different taste, but we loved both in fudge or cookies. To this day I prefer the taste of black walnuts to any other nut in fudge and in most types of cookies. In his later years, Pop cracked Iowa black walnuts and picked out the nut meats for mailing to me in California until his death in 1981. I've always felt sorry for my own kids and grandkids who grew up in California and never developed a taste for Iowa black walnuts. They don't know what they've missed.

I was ten when Pop turned 41 on December 7, 1941. The only news on the radio that day was the Pearl Harbor attack by Japanese carrier airplanes; I didn't know where Pearl Harbor was. Being 41, Pop was exempt from the service by one day. He'd had similar great luck in 1918. He would have become eighteen and eligible for the draft on December 7 of that year, but WW I ended less than one month earlier. Pop's youngest brother, Carl, was the only one directly involved in war. The fighting at Iwo Jima literally de-

---

[3] Non-farmers may not recognize baling wire, the soft iron wire that holds hay bales together. When you use a bale of hay, you're left with loose wire. A farmer never throws away wire; instead, he wraps it around the nearest fence post where it stays until needed. We rolled up our baling wire and hung it on a big nail inside the barn.

stroyed him. Uncle Carl was drafted at age 35 and was sent to Iwo Jima after training as an aircraft mechanic. His unit was attached to the U.S. Marines who took Iwo after a bloody and costly month-long horror. Well before the island was secure, its air strips were used as forced landing fields for damaged B-29 bombers in the midst of ground fire fights. My uncle was in the middle of that, but we knew nothing about it at the time.

He came back after the war, but simply was not the same as before. He lived with us and worked every day in our garden for the first year. It was the best our acre of garden had ever looked and the most productive as well. After the summer, he worked here and there, but drank heavily and could not get his life started again. He took me fishing a few times and often had a faraway pained look in his eye. Many times he said to me, while shaking his head, "That Iwo, Iwo. Iwo, you don't want to know," with tears in his eyes. He cried quietly several times, but I never heard him describe what he'd been through except to just shake his head and say, "Iwo, Iwo."

Uncle Carl's health got progressively worse. He lived with Mom and Pop in my old bedroom for nearly three years, but was hit by several small strokes – just as we were hoping he would recover from one stroke, he'd have another. After his final stroke, he died at age 43 without regaining consciousness. Pop gave me Uncle Carl's favorite necktie, along with his total assets of $50 to help with my college education. Uncle Carl's $50 made a big difference since I had only the money I'd saved from summer farm work to get through my freshman year of college.

As a kid, I had thought we were terribly unlucky because we were so poor. I realize now that I had a wonderful childhood. The prevailing attitude in our house was that each of us was an active partner in the family. Each of us had jobs to do, same as Mom and Pop. Each of us was relied upon to do our jobs and learned that we could count on the others to do theirs as well. We developed self confidence from that, and even today it is one of the major reasons that I believe we were not poor as kids but rich. We had no money of course, but that has nothing to do with being rich. We were rich because we were confident and eager to learn new things and face new challenges. We knew we could rely on each member of our family. Each of us made it our goal to pull our own weight in life because that was our parents' goal. I was taught to enjoy learning how to operate machines, but the real fun was in learning how to repair them if they broke. If I needed a tool we didn't have, I was told to make a new tool out of something. Pop always said, "If a man built it, you and I can repair it." I asked Pop once how he'd learned to fix so many things with baling wire. He told me, "Baling wire is what I had." He showed me how all machinery was held together by nuts and bolts. "Remove the right bolts and the machine comes apart one piece at a time," he explained to me. "Save the nuts and bolts to use when you put it back together. Small devices may use screws instead of bolts, but the principle is the same."

Pop lived by one simple rule, and that rule became embedded in me: **"You can repair anything if you take it apart far enough to understand how it works; that will show you what's worn out or broken, and repairing it will be easy."** He was the smartest man I ever met with only an eighth-grade education.[4]

From Bib Overalls to Levi's

Our homestead wasn't part of an actual town, but the local residents often referred to the whole area informally as 'Youngstown.' All in all, Youngstown might have covered about 10 square miles, but I don't remember more than 50 houses in the entire area. The houses were mostly spaced far apart from each other, and I remember visiting many neighbors who still used kerosene (coal oil) lamps and candles for light. Most families had at least one acre, and a few had thirty or more. There was no particular common design for the houses; this certainly wasn't a housing development. A few were built of brick, but most were simple wood-frame houses without insulation, and no two looked exactly alike. In my whole childhood, I don't remember

---

[4] Digging through Pop's papers, I discovered he had completed a correspondence course in electricity around 1920 (at age nineteen). He told me the coal mine work was rough, and he had hoped to get into wiring houses if the government moved forward with their plan for 'rural electrification.' They did that around 1928, and Pop installed electricity in the house as soon as power lines were installed along our gravel road.

seeing any house getting a new paint job until after WW II. An occasional new house was built here and there in the area, usually to accommodate a new marriage as local kids grew up and married one another.

It became an expected tradition to have a surprise 'shivaree' for the newlyweds a week or two after they moved into their new abode. In the early evening, twenty or thirty neighbors would sneak up to the front door and suddenly begin beating on pans and drums, blowing horns, yelling "surprise!" and making noise until the newlyweds opened their door and came out to receive congratulations and well wishes. Some people brought gifts, but most brought drinks for the whole crowd, and it was a party for the next hour. Finally the crowd would disperse and go back home. We never hear about shivarees any more, even in Iowa.

The only school in town was named Pleasant Hill. It had a large concrete block basement that was used for school programs and some social events. The wooden ceiling of the basement became the main floor above, which had a hallway running down the middle dividing the space into two rooms of equal size. Kids called one the 'Little Room,' which had one teacher for first through fourth grades; the 'Big Room' also had one teacher but for grades five through eight. On school days, we usually walked the mile along Youngstown Road from our house to Pleasant Hill School. A few kids had to walk farther, but most lived closer to the school than we did. All four of us Peterson kids walked both to and from school most of the time. Only in the case of very cold weather were we able to get a ride, at least part way, with some parent.

One of my best friends and classmates, Duane Ellis, lived about half a mile beyond our house; he was one of four students who lived farther away from school than we did. I used to join him, Don Arpy and their two older brothers, Gene 'Red' Ellis and Jim Arpy, when they came walking by on the way to school. We followed the same routine every school day from first through eighth grades. At age five, one morning I awoke to discover that I had wet the bed. It didn't happen regularly, but often enough to cause Mom to make me remove the sheets and hang them outside on the clothes line to dry. I was nearly ready for school and remembered that I still had to hang the sheets on the line. As I did, that group of four kids appeared around the curve in the distance, walking along the road and coming towards our house. I finished hanging the sheets and ran inside to get my lunch sack and then out to the road to join them. Everybody knew that there was only one reason a kid would be outside hanging up bed sheets to dry. They razzed me all the way to school, and I was embarrassed about that for years afterwards. I was so embarrassed that I believe it was the last time I ever wet the bed. Those Ellis and Arpy kids had cured me in the most effective, but worst way, possible.

Youngstown had two small gas stations at its north and south edges. The one at the south edge, near Pleasant Hill School, had an attached one-room grocery store. School kids went there during lunch hour for candy if they had pennies or sometimes even a nickel. Grown-ups often charged grocery purchases there and paid their bills after payday. I didn't go there for candy very often because I had no pennies. One day some second-graders talked me into joining them. I had no money and would not have bought any-thing except that I felt bad about not getting candy along with my friends. I ordered a 1 cent tootsie roll and told Elsie Lovett, the store owner, to "charge it." She smiled and wrote it onto Pop's tab. The next weekend when Pop paid his bill, I became the talk of the town. I had to pay Mom back, of course. Mom told me never to do that again. Without mentioning me by name, teachers reminded their classes that children had no right to buy anything they couldn't pay for. Grown ups, sitting around on benches, drinking beer in front of the gas station and store, laughed and joked about me for what seemed like years whenever I came into sight.

By the third grade we had gotten to know our other classmates well, and one thing stood out in my mind. Duane Ellis, Don Arpy and I usually got the best grades in our class on tests and on our report cards at the end of each semester. I got the highest sometimes, Duane got the highest other times, but it was Don who got the highest grades most of the time. It was always a guess as to which of us would beat the other two, but Don Arpy usually was first and either Duane or I came in second. Their older broth-ers, Jim Arpy and Red Ellis, were three grades ahead of us. Normally, all five of us were friendly, all were thought of as good kids and none was ever a trouble maker. One day when we were walking home from school along the gravel road, the older two decided they wanted Duane and Don to beat me up. I had never fought anyone before and couldn't see any reason to fight either Duane or Don, whom I considered to be some of the very best and least troublesome kids in school.

I was surprised when they kept pushing to get Duane or Don (or both) to fight me. Don didn't want to join Duane in beating me up, so he stood back and added his voice to the older brothers who were pushing Duane to start pounding me. Finally, I realized Duane was going to attack me when he put his books on the edge of the gravel road. While they were adding their final arguments to convince him into action, I saw a rock in the gravel near my feet just the right size to fit into my right hand. I closed my hand around the rock, and it looked like I had made a big fist, but the rock itself wasn't visible. Neither Duane nor I put up our fists in the classic stance of a fighter or tried to protect our faces at all. Duane came over to me and grabbed my left arm. As he did, I raised up my right fist and hit him on the jaw with the rock. I didn't think I'd hit him very hard, but he let out a scream as if he'd been murdered. He grabbed his jaw and screamed at the top of his voice, crying and holding his jaw. The other three huddled over him and tried to calm him down, but he was really sorry he'd ever gotten pushed into trying to fight anybody. I just stood there on the other side of the road, trying not to look as scared as I felt, the rock still hidden inside my right fist. I wasn't sure whether Don or maybe one of the older brothers would come after me, but they would get that rock if they did.

When I was sure none of the others would attack me, I started walking on ahead of them and went into my house while they were still a hundred feet behind me. They were walking huddled around Duane. I didn't walk with them the next morning, but after about three days I joined them on the walk to school as if nothing had happened. Nobody ever mentioned the incident again and within a week all five of us were as good friends as ever. I never told anyone that I'd used a rock in my first (and only) fight. And I never told Mom or Pop why I kept that rock on my windowsill in my bedroom for a few months afterward.

One day in late spring, Uncle Pete came to school and spoke to my teacher. He took me out of my fourth grade class at noon and together we drove twenty-five miles to the small town of Van Meter, just west of Des Moines. The major league baseball pitcher, Bob Feller, had grown up on a nearby farm where he had learned how to pitch by throwing rocks, and later baseballs, at a chalked off 'strike zone' on his dad's barn. He became an ace pitcher for the Cleveland Indians right out of high school and remained an Indian for more than twenty-five years. He had come back to Van Meter with two famous teammates, Luke Easter and Hal Trotsky, for 'Bob Feller Day.' I saw everyone up close. They gave a pitching and hitting demonstration for the crowd. I got to talk to Bob Feller for a long time. I was very excited when he showed me how he held the ball when he threw a fast ball, and how that changed when he threw a curve. I asked Bob Feller why the managers sometimes let a pitcher pitch the whole game and other times they took a pitcher out after only four or five innings. His answer was to have relevance in wine aging that I would not understand for another thirty years: "Sometimes a good pitcher just can't go nine innings." I became a lifelong Cleveland Indians fan from that day forward.

Years later, in 1952, I saw Bob Feller pitch against the Washington Senators in Washington D.C. It was one of his last games in the majors. I was 21-years-old and a new Second Lieutenant in the Marines at Quantico, Virginia, and I drove to the Senators' ballpark alone and full of excitement. I was thrilled to go, but also disappointed that I had no one with whom to share the experience. I drove to Washington just to see the game. I didn't know anybody in the whole city; the only person at the stadium I had ever spoken with was Bob Feller! Nobody would have believed my story. Besides they were all fans of the Senators anyway, so I could not even tell anyone about meeting him and my special experience as a kid. I drove back to Quantico somewhat down in the dumps, but at least Bob Feller had pitched a good game, and the Indians were ahead when my old pal was taken out of the game in a late inning.

One of our favorite winter pastimes, from about fourth grade through high school, was ice skating on Four Mile Creek every winter. I saw a temperature of −20°F only twice in all the years I lived near Des Moines. Most winters were pleasant, with the lowest temperatures between −5°F and −10°F. That was enough to freeze the creek, which was mostly only a foot or two deep, and it was common to have a three-inch thick layer of ice on the surface all winter. Very often, you could look down through a layer of clear ice and see minnows swimming around in the liquid water below. The creek ran along the railroad tracks near our faraway hobo well for about a mile, and eventually emptied into the Des Moines River southeast of the city. Uncle Pete's (and my) favorite summertime fishing spot was near the junction of the creek with the river. People regularly ice skated on the creek from our house to the school and back, especially on moonlit winter nights. Often there might be two or three bonfires here and there along the way where people would stop to warm up.

On weekends during the daytime, we would use snow shovels to clear off a large rectangle of ice. Three small logs were placed at each end to mark off goals, and we used sticks, sometimes old brooms, as hockey sticks and played hockey, using a flat rock as the puck. It was a fun game because we concentrated on getting the puck into the goal. We never attempted to kill or maim the other players with bone-jarring checks as professional teams do today, but it was still a rough sport.

One of my best friends in grade school was Gene Miller. He was two years older and a lot bigger – big enough that I could climb up and sit on his shoulders and hang onto his head while he rode his bike on the gravel road a mile each way to and from school. I enjoyed anything Gene did. He sometimes lived in South Dakota, and elsewhere at other times, and only came back to our grade school every couple of years. I liked Gene a lot, but my sister, Martha, hated him. She didn't speak to him unless it was absolutely necessary, and made it clear to me that he wasn't ever going to be one of her friends. New kids often make quick enemies in new schools, or so it seems. Gene had other enemies in school, and one day in sixth grade he asked me to hold his ring while he and Lloyd Best had a fist fight. Gene knocked him down, and Lloyd got up crying and screaming, "Gene hit me when I wasn't lookin'!" Gene's answer to everybody was, "He was lookin' at me, and I give it to 'im straight!"

Gene was a self-starter who later worked for himself in whatever business he felt like starting. He had been away in some other state for a few years when, one late afternoon in 1949, he drove his new war surplus jeep into our drive. He was about twenty, and I was a sophomore at Iowa State College, home for the weekend. Martha had been working at Meredith Publishing Co. in Des Moines since graduating from East High three years earlier. Gene and I were standing and talking in the front yard, getting reacquainted after a long time apart, when a neighbor's car drove up and stopped in front of our house. Gene noticed Martha get out of the car and watched her walk down the drive and into the house. When she disappeared, he turned to me and asked, "That was Martha, wasn't it?" I answered, "Yeah, she works in Des Moines," and went on with whatever story I was telling him. Two weeks later, I was back in college at Iowa State when Mom told me that Gene had taken Martha out to dinner and a dance. It was hard to believe, but they started dating soon after that. Gene and Martha were married in January, 1950, and have recently celebrated their 65th anniversary! He's still one of my best friends.[5]

One winter night in February, 1943, someone pounded on our front door and yelled, "Schoolhouse is on fire!" When Mom opened the door, the man was gone, but there was lots of activity outside. Everyone was excited, hurrying the long mile towards Pleasant Hill School. We put on our coats, filled the car with empty water buckets, and Pop drove us to the school. The building was encased in smoke, but we saw no flames. The fire appeared

---

[5] One of the first things Gene did was to use his jeep (with trencher attached) to dig a long trench between Mom and Pop's house and the far away well. He installed a water pipeline, pump and electrical wires so that, for the first time, Mom and Pop had an indoor bath and running water. He never charged them a dime for doing the job.

Around 1970, Gene grew a full white beard; he and Martha dressed up as Mr. and Mrs. Santa Claus every year and made it a duty to visit many children's homes and schools during December. They passed out candies and small gifts at their own expense. Only in 2012 did they stop as age began to take its toll.

to be small, high up in the rafters, just under the roof where the furnace chimney met the ceiling. Bigger kids were filling buckets with water and handing them to men who were trying to toss the water from below, half a bucket at a time, up onto the fire. It wasn't working, but no one was brave enough to climb up onto the roof and cut a hole through which to pour water onto the fire.

There were no hoses or pumps at the school, so the men did what they could until the fire trucks could arrive. Several calls had already been made to the nearest fire station. It was located inside the Des Moines city limits, only about two miles away, but they refused to come out to Pleasant Hill School. The school wasn't located inside the city, and the Des Moines fire department wasn't authorized to leave city limits. No amount of pleading helped. Slowly the fire got bigger, and it became more and more a lost cause. Hot embers fell from the ceiling all the way to the basement beside the furnace, and before long the coal in the basement was ablaze. Onlookers couldn't get close to the building once the fire started breaking through the basement ceiling. We had an astonishing sight as we looked in through the classroom windows as the fire burned through the floor directly above the basement.

Mrs. Mahaffey was my 7th grade teacher. Through the windows I watched as thin lines of smoke and fire came up through cracks between the floor boards into the room. Mrs. Mahaffey's heavy desk suddenly disappeared into the fire below, her empty chair left standing alone in front of a gaping hole in the floor where the desk had been. Then the whole classroom erupted in a ball of fire, and we had to move back. There wasn't anything more to do but watch it go. For the next few days, everyone talked about suing Des Moines or at least the fire department. They had, after all, stood by and allowed a nice, well-built school building to go up in flames. A single fire engine could have doused the fire if it had come when first called. It seemed like such a waste, especially in war time, when getting replacement building materials would be slow and difficult. There was talk that the school kids might lose a whole year of classes, maybe two.

Mrs. Mahaffey came to the rescue almost immediately. She lived in a farmhouse near Altoona, Iowa, about 10 miles from Pleasant Hill School.

She had picnic tables and could borrow more from neighbors. She offered to teach the rest of the school year in her yard during good weather and in the house and covered porch when it rained. The parents just had to arrange car pools for the kids. It wouldn't be easy for her since she taught four different grades (5th, 6th, 7th and 8th) in the 'Big Room.' Fortunately, there were only about 25 students in those four grades altogether. Looking back, it seemed to us her plan worked out quite well. All the kids enjoyed exploring her farm during recess, there was lots of space for softball, and the rest of that school year had an air of vacation excitement to it.

The 'Little Room' teacher, Mrs. Foster, held her classes in a similar way, using the small wood-frame church across the road from the burned schoolhouse for 20 or so students in 1st thru 4th grades. After the school year ended, an inside wall was built down the center of the church. One side housed the 'Little Room' grades, and the other side became the 'Big Room' for my 8th grade – my final school year at Pleasant Hill.[6]

It was not until 1946 that a new brick building was built to replace the burned down Pleasant Hill School. Only after the fire did I learn from Pop that he knew exactly how I felt. The school building that I had known all my life had been built in the early 1920s because the original Pleasant Hill School, the one that Pop had attended, had burned down in 1918! The big old bell that was displayed in a small structure on my school grounds was all that was left of Pop's school. All the kids had played around that bell during recesses for years, but none of us had ever been told its history.

I attended 9th grade in Des Moines at Woodrow Wilson Junior High and had to give up the bib overalls I had worn every day at school until then. Summer and winter, bib overalls and a light blue denim shirt was my uniform. I got two new sets every fall just before school started. Those were my new

---

[6] I saw Mrs. Foster again at the celebration of Martha and Gene's 50th wedding anniversary in the town of Pleasant Hill. It was a beautiful day, with dozens of well-wishers. Mrs. Foster was in her 90s, but easy to recognize as she still looked as I had remembered her. She was still quite alert and happy to remember me along with many of her other earlier students at Pleasant Hill School.

clothes for the following year. I wore them all summer after graduating from eighth grade and was increasingly upset as the new school year approached. Martha had told me I'd get razzed and maybe beaten up if I wore that outfit to the new school in Des Moines. Reluctantly, I agreed to wear a pair of Levi's and a non-denim shirt instead. For many weeks, it felt funny to wear only the pants without the bib that I'd become so used to.

One good part of junior high was that I got to ride to school with Duane Ellis and his older brother, Red. Red had a permit and drove to high school after dropping Duane and me off at our school. That's how I got to junior high most days that year. I paid for part of the gas, and it was a good deal for all of us. By the next year, Duane had gotten a permit to drive to and from school, and I often rode with him in his Model T Ford.

Duane's father had operated a garage and did repair work. He specialized on Model T Ford cars and had several in his shop at any given time. Duane had learned to drive a Model T at about fourteen and taught me to drive it as well. (It isn't as easy as one might think, but isn't so hard either.) The Model T had three floor pedals plus a gas 'foot feed,' as well as a hand gas feed and a spark control next to the steering wheel. There was also a hand lever on the left that looked like the emergency brake on later cars of the 1930s. Driving a Model T was nothing at all like driving those cars. There was something you had to know about the Model T. The middle (reverse) pedal overrode the left pedal, so that stepping on the middle pedal immediately threw the car into reverse – even if the car was going forward. That is what Duane and I did on frozen lakes in the winter in Iowa. You could drive forward at maybe 20 miles per hour on the ice and step on the middle pedal, which reversed the rear wheels instantly, spinning the car around and around. Duane and I did that many, many times on all the large ponds we could find when the temperature had been cold enough to freeze the lake hard, but then had warmed up enough to make the ice slippery. Very cold ice is never slippery; ice has to be within a degree or two of freezing to be *really* slippery. Most of the big ponds were less than three-feet deep, so there were ponds with these conditions all over Iowa in winter. Iowa is not flat and has lots of rolling hills; that meant you could find a frozen lake big enough to skid round and round in a Model T almost anywhere you looked.

Skidding in a Model T on a frozen lake is one of life's great memories for me as a stupid high school kid in the late 1940s.

In the summer of 1946, Duane decided to build a new Model T from spare parts in his father's garage. His Model T cars were mostly models from 1925-1927. I helped Duane, and those were my first lessons on what is under the hood of a car. His father had a spare engine and gave it to Duane, and we used an old chassis from a wreck that he had used for parts. The chassis had no body, so we placed 2x6 planks on top of the frame to make a bed, and then nailed wooden boxes on top of that for seats. It ran just fine, but there was nothing comfortable about it. We really needed a car body with seats and doors, but never found one. The system for all cars had changed by 1928, after which there were only two foot pedals on all cars, but none of them had automatic transmissions at that time. All cars had gear shift levers; you pushed the clutch pedal in while you changed gears – something that is becoming rare today, except for farmers who drive tractors with gear shifts.

After a year of junior high, both Duane and I went to East Des Moines High School. We went to football games together, and enjoyed being part of the group of kids that cheered for our classmates on the field. I liked sports in school, and it bugged me that I couldn't play football or basketball in high school. I was jealous of the bigger kids who wore their 'letter sweaters.' It was a serious award when they received their big red and black East High 'E' athletic letter, and they enjoyed being seen wearing one. It no longer bothers me because I was only sixteen when I graduated from high school. How could I have played football? The other kids were eighteen, or nearly so. I stood about 5'6" tall at graduation, nine inches shorter than I am today.

There were big high school rivalries in Des Moines, since the city had four public high schools and one Catholic school. After each of the Friday night games, kids from every school ended up in downtown Des Moines, walking around the same three or four city blocks. The games ended by about 9 p.m. and kids mobbed the city center until around 11, when most headed towards drive-ins for food and soft drinks. The odds were fifty-fifty that there would be a fist fight somewhere in town between two high school bullies who had to see just how tough the other guy was. Kids always rushed in to see who was fighting, and especially who was losing.

One Friday night, Duane and I arrived a little late, around 10 p.m., and had to park about eight blocks away from the center. We walked on the sidewalks towards the noisy, kid-infested area full of excitement and were getting close to the center when we could hear a roar of yelling and lots of activity up ahead. As we got closer, kids began running towards what we assumed was a fist fight. They didn't stay on the sidewalks, but were all over the street, stopping the car traffic. We joined in with the crowd, running down the middle of the street for a couple of blocks. At the end of the block in front of the Katz Drug Store, the crowd suddenly changed direction ahead of us and started running towards us. I couldn't see anything ahead and kept on going.

In an instant, Duane and I found ourselves in the intersection, which was empty of people except for several police with night sticks glaring at the crowd. We hadn't done anything wrong, so instead of running away from the police, we started to walk on into the intersection to go into the store. It was a well-known place where people went to get soft drinks and donuts. I didn't get ten feet further, when I felt a big hand grab the back of my shirt collar and force me over to the police 'paddy wagon' that I hadn't noticed when we arrived. "I told you snot-nosed kids to get away from here," the voice with the hand said to me. "Now get in the truck." He released my shirt, and I was certain I could have run away into the crowd at that instant, but I saw Duane climb up into the police wagon. I remembered that I had no way home that night without Duane, so I climbed in after him. There were a few others in the truck, but I didn't know them, and they didn't look like they'd been fighting. A few seconds later the truck started up, and we were driven to a jail facility somewhere.

We were taken inside and pushed into what I realized was a large cell 'drunk tank.' There were eight or ten obvious drunks in the room, all sitting or lying on steel racks hanging from the walls on all sides. The racks were rectangular beds made of bent pipe with a cross-hatching layer of steel straps woven together to fill in the spaces between the sides and ends of the racks. There were no blankets, pillows or anything else in the room, just those racks around the perimeter of the room. We sat on one of the racks, waiting to ask someone to let us call our parents to come and get us. My parents didn't have a phone, but Duane's parents did. However it did not matter; there was no one there to ask. It was just the two of us and some drunks. No other kids were brought in, and we guessed they had put the other kids in other cells. After an hour or so, a policeman came in and asked if we wanted a cup of coffee. Some of the drunks took some coffee, but most just kept on sleeping on their racks. I was too young to drink coffee, and we asked for a phone to let our parents know where we were. The cop just turned around and left. It wasn't possible to sleep, and after what seemed like another three or four hours, the door opened and a policeman brought in a few more drunks. Again we asked to call and let our parents know where we were, but the policeman simply said, "We will call them for you," and left. The liar couldn't have known whom to call because nobody had even asked us our names.

The whole night passed that way; the door opened occasionally to let in another drunk at intervals, but we were not spoken to, questioned or otherwise acknowledged. Daylight finally came, but it was another hour or two before a man came in and gave each of us a tin cup of coffee and a hard roll. The door closed behind him, and another hour or two passed. Finally, we were taken out of the cell and put into separate rooms. After a while, I was taken to a room where I was made to stand alone in front of glaring lights, preventing me from seeing my questioner. The voice asked me why I had been fighting in Des Moines last night. I told the voice that Duane's parents had a phone, and that we had been asking them to let our parents know where we were. The voice ignored me, but again asked why I had been fighting and causing all that trouble. I told him I never even saw a fight and was just going into Katz Drug Store with my fellow student, Duane Ellis, whose parents had a phone that we'd been asking them to call. He asked over and over again why I was fighting and why I had caused all that trouble in town last night. I told the same story over and over again, and asked to call and let Duane's parents know where we were. Finally they put me back into the same drunk room, and I was told to wait. After a while, Duane came in, and we told each other what had happened. He'd been treated the same way as I.

It was almost noon that Saturday morning when Pop and Duane's dad came to get us. The police let us go with an order that we had to return to court on a certain date with our parents. When that day came, and we went to court, Duane and I had to stand together while a judge told us sternly that he had no doubt there was *some* good to be found in both of us. He warned us that if we kept up our trail of wrongdoings, we would certainly end up behind bars for a long time. It made no difference to him that we had told our true story to all the police we'd seen. He released us without fines or formal charges, and we guessed that they must finally have realized that we'd simply been kids in the wrong place at the wrong time. But I hated, truly hated, the Des Moines police for years afterward. The ones we had met simply didn't know how to deal with kids who weren't bad kids, just kids. Pop told me later, "You were lucky you were white. Black kids would have been beaten for sure." I sympathize with minority causes to this day because of Pop's simple statement.

Iowa State

During high school, I had always gravitated towards kids who liked science classes. They had often talked about going to college, and by senior year most of them were preparing to go. I had loved chemistry since getting that first chemistry set before I was ten, and it seemed natural for me to start believing that I would attend college, too. No one in my extended family had even gone to college, and I didn't know what to expect. I realized that I couldn't afford to move far away to attend school, but fortunately the best state college (meaning cheap tuition) for both chemistry and engineering was Iowa State College located at Ames, only about thirty miles north of Des Moines. Duane's brother, Red, had gone to University of Michigan, and Duane had decided to follow him there. Duane's father had contacts everywhere and had gotten high school summer jobs for us painting walls in various buildings in 1946 and 1947. From the tenth grade on, I had also worked at the Des Moines Register newspaper building from 4:30 p.m. Saturday until 3:30 a.m. Sunday. I was part of a large crew who worked in the mail room. Our job was to insert the various sections together to make complete Sunday papers. I then rode home with a man whose job it was to deliver the Sunday papers not far from Youngstown. I usually arrived home by around 7 a.m. and slept the rest of the day. My starting pay was 62½ cents per hour, which was raised to 65 cents in six months and 75 cents a year later.

I had done farm work wherever I could in previous summers and had saved every dime working for farmers, usually hauling bales of hay from the fields to the barns and hoisting them into the hay lofts using a tractor and winch. Even though I saved all the money I could, my total savings would barely cover my freshman year. Clearly I would not be able to commute through the Iowa winter in 1948-49, but I decided to register for my freshman year anyway and live in a college dorm. At least I would get that far, and maybe I could find some scholarship that would help me in the following years. I was not alone in this – many of my friends were in similar positions and did the same. We felt compelled to make college happen, and would figure out the particulars as we went along. None of us had parents with much money, although WW II had provided better jobs than had been available during the Great Depression. Pop had gotten paid four times as much per hour for painting steel beams at Pittsburgh Des Moines Steel Company during the war than the best wage he had ever received for working in coal mines.

When Duane and I graduated from high school in 1948, we started looking for summer work again. Duane had planned to enroll at University of Michigan in September and needed to save money for college. His father had found him a summer job at the asbestos plant near Winterset, Iowa. I was extremely disappointed that there was only one opening. I did not realize how lucky I was. Duane had begun smoking the year before, but I never liked the smell of tobacco smoke and had tried it only a couple of times, never smoking more than a few puffs each time. The sickening experience made me a lifelong anti-smoking spokesman. Back then, nobody knew that smoking causes cancer or that working with asbestos causes cancer. It was fifty years later that I learned smoking *and* breathing asbestos dust at the same time is a virtual guarantee for dying early. Duane's lung cancer killed him at age forty-two! He had become a good engineer; when he died, the world lost a wonderful person in Duane Ellis.

My grades had been high all through school, but that did not necessarily mean that scholarships were just waiting to be picked up. I quickly learned that the few scholarships available would be only a few hundred dollars on a one-time basis. It would take many of them to fill my need. Fortunately, Iowa State College, as a land-grant institution, offered courses in both Army and Navy Reserve Officer training. The NROTC, or Naval Reserve Officer Training Corps offered two programs to college students, Contract and Regular. Contract Program was a partial scholarship which would pay a nominal amount ($17 per month during my senior year of college). Contract students would go on a three-week Navy cruise between their junior and senior years. After graduation, the student had to accept a commission in the Naval Reserve for two years, but would not have to go on active duty unless there was a national emergency.

The Regular Program was entirely different, and I saw in it a real possibility of getting my college education paid for. Regular NROTC 'Midshipmen' would be paid $50 per month, starting immediately, until graduation. Students would take regular NROTC courses of three or four units every quarter, go on a three-week active duty cruise every summer and be commissioned as Naval officers on active duty at graduation. New officers were then obligated to serve on active duty for three years beginning the day after college graduation. I thought, there's little likelihood of a new war breaking out, WW II is over. I might enjoy being an officer in the Navy. Maybe I'd learn to drive a Cruiser or land airplanes on Carriers…Intrigued, I asked, "Where do I sign?" "Not so fast, kid," Commander Bernard answered. "Only the top 2% of applicants in any state can be put into the Regular Program. The Navy chooses the top 2% after all candidates take a one-day academic test given to Contract students and new high school graduates in April each year." About 7 of us, all graduates of East High in Des Moines, decided to sign up for the Contract Program as freshmen in September 1948, and then later decide whether to take the Regular test in spring, 1949.

I was one of five who took the Regular academic test three months later and Bingo! My name and those of several other friends appeared in the top 2% and we were appointed as midshipmen. I was completely out of money, but wonder of wonders, my college was suddenly assured, and I was elated.

Finest Wine Ever Produced

As a freshman at Iowa State College, I had gotten the idea to make a batch of wine from the Concord grapevines that were still growing on the small acreage where I grew up. I had the recipe from the label of a grape brick that Pop had saved with his champagne bottles in the cave. I went home from college for a weekend, and checked around the neighborhood to see who among our neighbors had grapes still hanging on their vines. Many of our neighbors had been growing Concord grapes, but I'd noticed that they hadn't been picking their grapes for the past few years. They probably wouldn't mind if I added their grapes to mine for my first experiment in winemaking. I got permission before realizing that I didn't have the foggiest notion how to make wine. Pop had made wine as a home winemaker during Prohibition, and he was the only winemaking expert I could ask. Pop had a sense of humor, and his answer to me was, "Smash the grapes all to hell, let 'em spoil with the skins in the mess for awhile, then bottle it without the skins." I said, "Thanks, Pop, I'll check the library." "That's what I said," he answered.

The Des Moines Public Library had a total of just two books on winemaking, a subtle reminder that we lived in the Bible Belt. It reminded me that, at about age ten, I had asked Jim White, our Baptist minister, why everybody considered drinking wine to be a sin when Jesus drank wine all during his ministry. He yelled in my face, "Where in the world did you dig up that stupid falsehood?" "Well, sir," I stammered, "I read it..." He kept yelling, "Where have you been reading...?" "In...the Bible," I finished my sentence. I thought he might have a heart attack as he told me the Bible had intended to say it was grape juice, not wine. Obviously, there had been a mistake in the biblical translation somewhere, probably by one of those... he looked down and almost whispered the word, "Catholics." He told me I ought to be more careful in asking for help in reading my bible. But I was afraid to discuss that subject, or any other subject, with Jim White again.

Winemaking instructions in the library books were sparse, and I realized that Pop's simplified directions had been more or less correct. It wasn't clear just how long to let the 'mess' ferment, because I didn't have a lab hydrometer with which to measure either sugar or alcohol levels. Pop told me, "Watch the fermentation because foam rises in the stone crock while it ferments. When the foam starts to settle back, leave it alone for another three days, then drain the new wine off and use cheesecloth to wring out the rest of the new wine away from the solids. Age it in a wood barrel, then bottle it in my champagne bottles. You don't need a corker; just cap the bottles with regular beer caps, like we did when we used to make root beer." I already said he was an expert.

Bob Peterson, my high school pal and fraternity brother at Iowa State, helped me pick the grapes and then crush them by hand into stone crockery jars with loose-fitting lids. Bob was called B.K. by our friends. I was R.G. to distinguish us from two other Petersons in our Iowa State NROTC classes, I.H. and G.B. Jr. The crockery jars were the same jars Mom had used to ferment cucumbers into pickles in previous years. B.K. found a wood barrel that had been used as a shipper for orange juice concentrate by a local soda producer. It took us the better part of a day to wash, wash, and wash again, thoroughly scrubbing the barrel well enough to remove all traces of orange flavor from the wood. Then, into the barrel our new Concord wine went. Nothing in the books told us how long to age the wine in the barrel, so we settled on one month. I later realized the wine would have been ruined if we had left it in the barrel much longer, or if I had not found some 'meta-bi' crystals in the chemistry lab at Iowa State. Meta-bi becomes SO_2 in solution, which protects the wine from oxidation. The book told me to add 25 ppm, which calculated out to nearly a tablespoonful for the whole barrel. We then bottled the wine and capped the bottles with new root beer caps, which sealed the bottles very well. Now that we'd finished making it and checked our inventory, we realized we probably had a two-year supply of bottled wine. B.K. and I were certain this wine would rank among the very finest wines ever produced by civilized man. We were soon to begin discovering some of the mistakes we had made.

I had bought my first car, a 1937 Ford 60 with my last $150 in order to get to and from Iowa State on weekends.[7] I had no money left for gas, and I drove home with two gallons the salesman had thrown in with the purchase. A gallon of gas cost the same amount as a hamburger at the local drive-in, 18 cents. I still remember that piece of trivia because I skipped the hamburger several times in order to buy gas instead of lunch.

Unfortunately, only a month after the purchase, I left a bottle of my first wine lying on the back seat of my car. When I came back to my car in the hot afternoon, I didn't see the bottle. I opened the car door and immediately was hit by the intense smell of Concord wine. The whole inside of the car had a beautiful odor of Concord grapes, and I saw a large wet stain all over the back seat. Then I noticed all the tiny shards of glass spread around inside the car. Oh, my car, my very first car! What happened here? Bits and pieces of glass were on the seats, the floors, hanging from ceiling upholstery, the inside doors, even the front seats had their share of sharp shards. My bottle of wine, containing lots of dissolved CO_2 gas, had exploded on a hot afternoon inside my locked car while I was gone. In trying the wine a month after bottling, I had noticed the CO_2 (the wine we bottled was now very much like a sweet, yeasty, red Concord champagne). Ten years later, after I became a professional winemaker, I understood that we had bottled the wine too soon – while it still contained residual sugar. The yeast had continued to ferment in the bottles. Because they were sealed, the gas remained dissolved in the wine, and we had unknowingly made a champagne-type sparkling wine. The alcohol content couldn't have been high.

It was only a lucky chance that Pop had used champagne bottles in his winemaking 30 years earlier. We might have put somebody's eye out if we had done that using ordinary bottles. But my first car, why did it have to be my first car? All I could think of was whether my car would ever be the same. I could not even drive it home until I cleaned the glass particles off

---

[7] The '60' designation meant the Ford had an engine of only 60 horsepower. I didn't need more power, Iowa has no mountains, and Ames to Des Moines was just 30 miles; mileage was good and the car suited me perfectly.

the driver's seat. I borrowed some dry cloths and wiped the seat down to remove most of the glass. Finally, I spread a borrowed beach towel across the seat and sat on the towel driving home with the windows open. The good news was that I liked the smell; the bad news was that nobody else did. During the next three years, when I gave someone a lift, most people commented delicately on the smell. I wouldn't have minded if they had commented on the "nice smell of wine," but no one did. All I heard was that my car smelled – like jelly! I stopped giving rides to certain people, but they continued to kid me about jelly anyway. Fortunately, I was either too young or too broke to date girls with that car – getting a girl into that car would have been a waste of time.

B.K. and I started taking bottles of our wine to Iowa State football games surreptitiously. The bottles fit easily, two to a pocket, in the large black Naval officers' overcoats we were issued as NROTC Midshipmen. We wore Navy officers' uniforms to NROTC classes on campus, and the overcoats became a godsend in the Iowa winters. We raised plenty of eyebrows at games, but were generous to neighbors seated nearby, and we never received a complaint over the next two years while the wine lasted. Neither of us was a big drinker. I don't remember anybody ever getting tipsy from that wine. I now believe that most people didn't drink much of it for the same reason that most people don't drink jelly-flavored perfume. Although I had used a vacuum cleaner for hours on the inside of the car to remove glass bits, I continued to find shards of glass in the car for years. Of course, the Concord grape smell in the car remained forever.

NROTC and USMC

I enjoyed the NROTC courses in college. We studied tactics used in the WW II naval battles and in earlier wars. The most unexpected perk I could have imagined happened when I noticed an announcement on the Navy bulletin board. Sign ups for the NROTC rifle team were being solicited. I had hunted rabbits, quail, pheasants and squirrels at home from as far back as I could remember. I carried my BB gun as a small kid while walking with Pop as he hunted rabbits and pheasants. I hunted rabbits on my own using his 12 gauge shotgun from about age eleven. Pop told me to hold the shotgun very snug against my shoulder, or I'd be sorry. I found out what he meant sometime later when I got a badly bruised shoulder from doing it wrong – a 12 gauge shotgun is a big gun for a small kid. We always ate the game we killed, and rabbits were a big source of meat for us during the winters of the 1930s and 1940s. I wondered whether my hunting experience would help me hit targets on the rifle range, so I signed up.

I made the team right away; most of the others were so inexperienced that I was used as the instructor's assistant some of the time. We competed against other NROTC units in various colleges and universities around the country from week to week. Nobody traveled anywhere; the coaches scored their own team members and swapped the used targets for confirmation by mail. I enjoyed doing target practice for two years with various military rifles and pistols, but dropped off the team in my senior year and forgot all about it. Then, that spring, at one of the outside marching drills attended by all NROTC students, the Commander announced an award ceremony. I had no idea what kinds of awards there would be until I was called to the front along with seven or eight other rifle team members. I was presented with an athletic 'letter' from Iowa State College! Unknown to me, the rifle team had been included in the college athletic programs, and I received a red-and-gold Iowa State College 'I' with crossed rifles across it to be sewn onto a letter sweater. "Eat your hearts out East High School football players," I said to myself. "My athletic letter is from Iowa State College!"

The NROTC summer cruise of 1949 was a round trip from San Francisco to Panama aboard the light cruiser Springfield (CL-66). It was my first trip farther away from Iowa than next-door Wisconsin. B.K. Peterson and I went together on the train from Des Moines to Oakland, where we checked in at Treasure Island Naval Base in San Francisco Bay. We went aboard the ship immediately, and the next morning sailed under the Golden Gate Bridge into the blue Pacific. Life aboard a navy ship is highly regimented; every minute of every day is planned thoroughly. We stood four-hour watches and attended classes every day, even weekends. After arriving at Panama, we were allowed a day of liberty, so B.K. and I opted to take a train tour along the canal all the way to the Atlantic. The next day we were sailing again, this time over to the Galapagos Islands and an official crossing of the equator. The ship's captain, F. Moosebrugger, had planned a full day for ceremoniously inducting us 'Pollywogs' across the equator, after which we would become experienced 'Shellbacks.' We had expected some good clean fun, but I was surprised at how brutal it became. Not one minute of it was fun, or even instructive.

We were forced to crawl on our hands and knees along the deck in a specified pathway around the forecastle that seemed as long as a complete trip around the deck of the ship. The part I didn't like was that regular navy Shellbacks walked around carrying two-foot long pieces of heavy canvas strapping, smacking the crawlers on their backs and/or butts as hard as they could hit whenever they wanted to. The blow often knocked a Pollywog flat. The pain was excruciating, and the treatment clearly went much too far. If a Pollywog complained or seemed to be hurt, he would be pulled out of line and placed on the 'operating table' to be cured of whatever ailed him. The 'doctor' jabbed him in the stomach with an unsharpened metal sword which had wires attached to the handle. Sure enough, a spark jumped from the dull blade to the Pollywog, and the poor guy would jump in pain from electric shock. Some hapless Pollywogs were jammed into wooden boxes barely big enough to hold one man, or shackled up in 'stocks.' In the stocks, his head and wrists were locked into holes in a strong plank, while strong hoses blasted him with sea water. The blast was strong enough to knock many of us down, and we were sometimes left hanging by the neck and wrists for a minute or two, gasping for breath. Once out of the stocks, we had to kiss the 'royal baby,' which was some fat-ass sailor's belly that had been painted with raw fuel oil. It was the foulest oil possible, and I vomited several times that day, as did many others.

After a Pollywog made it to the end of the crawling route, he was placed in a barber's chair and given a 'haircut.' The royal barber had a big pair of scissors with which he took chunks of hair off the unsuspecting Pollywog. I had curly hair, which bothered them, and the barber cut big swatches out of it at skin level above my forehead and here and there on the sides and back of my head. After the barber finished, the Pollywog discovered that the barber's chair had hinges at the back two legs, and he was tipped over backwards into the 'swimming pool,' a large canvas tub full of sea water, rotten garbage and crude oil.[8] When you stood up, some bullying Shellbacks would duck you under the water and oil a few times before you could climb out. The worst was still to come, especially for those of us who were sickened by the smell of crude oil. After the ceremony was over, the ship's saltwater showers were restricted for us midshipmen to just two minutes of 'cold water only.' Even though I sneaked back in line to shower more than twice, I never got free of the crude oil smell that night.[9] Salt water soap does not make suds well in cold water, and nobody could get clean in only three two-minute showers that smelled like vomit. Back in our squad bay, we tried to joke with each other that some guys will do almost anything to get a college education. Some years later, I heard that the U.S. Navy had abolished the practice of initiating Pollywogs into the Shellback life when crossing the equator because of what some said was unnecessarily harsh treatment. I wondered why it had taken so long.

On the trip back towards San Francisco, we had gunnery practice at San Clemente Island, not far off the coast from San Diego. The Springfield's main battery was 6-inch guns, which were fired a few times into the island targets. I was assigned to the upper handling room of a 5-inch gun mount, one of the secondary batteries of the ship. My job was to take high explosive projectiles (weighing about 50 pounds each) from an ammunition elevator and deposit them into another conveyor to get them to the guns above. Destroyers came near us to drop depth charges as if there was an enemy sub below. Watching them was interesting, but did not seem like anything new since all of us had seen newsreel movies of depth charges exploding under water,

---

[8] After I returned to Iowa State College, it took more than a year for my hair to grow back enough to look normal. I had to explain it to real barbers and to my fellow college students many times throughout my sophomore year.

[9] Crude oil turned out to be a migraine trigger for me, and I suffered through a severe one for the next three days. I never went to sick bay on that ship for any reason; I didn't want the bastards to know they'd found a weakness that might get me cut from the NROTC program.

raising large plumes of water many feet into the air behind a destroyer. I do not know whether the ship killed any whales or not, but those depth charges could not have done the fish any good. We did not see any floating debris after the exercise was over, and I know that Captain Nemo and his crew survived because I saw them in a movie a few years later.

Just one year later, in June, 1950, the North Korean Army invaded South Korea, triggering a UN police action that would involve U.S. forces in an active war. I had to look on a map to learn exactly where Korea was. Only a week after the invasion, B.K. and I left for our NROTC three-week summer training at the Naval Aviation School at Pensacola, Florida. We found the mood among our fellow NROTC students had changed only a little; the Korean War still seemed a long distance away. We flew in a few different navy planes, and I even got a 15-minute turn at the controls of a Martin Mariner seaplane in the air between Pensacola and New Orleans. I rode in the back seat of a Navy SNJ pilot training plane as the students were practicing formation flying. Their group instructor was the pilot in my plane, and he was all over the sky getting a close look at each student in formation, urging one or another to move in closer or back off a little. From the first day, I knew that the best use of me in the military would be as a carrier pilot. For one thing, I wanted to bomb the foredeck of that goddamn USS Springfield and its pompous ass Captain F. Moosebrugger, who had commanded my unnecessary and stupidly harsh Pollywog hazing at the equator.

Before our senior year at Iowa State, all students had a choice of accepting our commissions in either the Navy or Marine Corps. My reasoning was simple: 20% of Navy officers were pilots; 25% of Marine Corps officers were pilots; both received the same training at Pensacola. I chose the Marine Corps, specifically requesting Aviation as my MOS (Military Occupation Specialty). On graduation from Iowa State in June, 1952, I received my BS in Chemical Technology and was commissioned as a Second Lieutenant in the Marine Corps. After the 6-month Officers Basic Course at Quantico, VA, I was assigned to Artillery, not Aviation. Unbelievably, I was told that my being younger than other officers was the deciding factor! They needed artillery officers in the Korean War and would use me there first. Other officer applicants were up to 24-years-old; I was only 21. Applicants had until age 26 to get in under the maximum age limit for entering flight school. Being younger than my peers was not always a positive. Dang! Dang! Dang!

Dutifully, I went to the Army Artillery School in Ft. Sill, Oklahoma, where we did nothing but fire 105 mm artillery shells for nearly five months. We learned everything you could possibly want to know about artillery. I got so familiar with those guns that I stood about 20 yards in front of a 105 howitzer filming it with my movie camera as the gun fired a shell directly over my head. When I saw the movie I had made, I was stupidly proud that the camera did not flinch a bit as the gun fired a shell over me. That proved that I was as stupid at age 21 as I had been at age 15. As a new graduate of the Artillery School, I became an officer in Battery A, 1st Battalion, Tenth Marines (Second Marine Division), stationed at Camp Lejeune, North Carolina. I was there only two months (just long enough to become competent as a sailor of small 'Lightening Class' sailboats in the harbor at Jacksonville in my spare time).

I was teaching a class on the 105 mm howitzer when a marine messenger interrupted my class to notify me that I was being transferred to Korea on short notice. Within two days, I was on a full troop train heading west. There had not been time to do anything with my car except park it on the street. All the phone lines out of North Carolina were tied up, and I'd had no possibility to call home before the train left. I wrote a letter to Mom and Pop, enclosed the keys, explained where the car was and asked them to take a train to Jacksonville, at my expense, and drive it back to Des Moines. My troop train was at the station in Kansas City before I could reach a phone to call them to further explain what was happening. A large group of marines was being moved to the West Coast. We were on our way to what was becoming a very hot war in Korea. Two of my classmates in the basic officer's course at Quantico had already been killed there by Chinese mortar fire.

Arriving in Camp Pendleton, California, I was transferred to the Third Marine Division and ordered to Japan. Aboard the troopship in mid-Pacific, we got news that a temporary truce had been signed in Korea, and the war was postponed for ninety days. I thought, If I had been just a year older, I might have been caught in some of the hottest fighting of the Korean War.

Instead, after arriving in Japan, we joined the Twelfth Artillery Regiment of the Third Division, which was setting up camp on the shoulder of the famous volcano, Mt. Fuji, an hour or so south of Tokyo. It was a fun experience overall and quite educational to see how large numbers of marines can be moved around the world in a businesslike fashion. Soon we were living in military tents on Mt. Fuji.

Three weeks after our arrival, a typhoon hit us squarely. We sat up all night trying to keep something dry, anything at all. It was no use. A typhoon is a Pacific hurricane and every bit as powerful as an Atlantic hurricane. When daylight arrived, the typhoon moved north, and we emptied all the tents into avenues and walkways to let everything dry out. Three days later most things were dry and secured back inside the tents. Remarkably, the organization was excellent, we recovered quickly from the weather, and no lasting damage was apparent.

Shortly thereafter, a few of us were sent by ship to Okinawa to act as umpires for two practice Marine Corps landings on the island. We were there three weeks, and it was both fun and enlightening. The practice landings were done on a section of the island that would have been difficult if it had been attempted against a hostile foe – it was obvious that the terrain in that part of the island greatly favored the defenders. Wisely, the planners for the actual landings during WW II had chosen a stretch of beach that favored the attackers, and the WW II landing had been only lightly opposed. The Japanese defenders had withdrawn to the southern portion of the island, where the real battle for Okinawa occurred many days after the landing. It was a furious battle, as most Pacific island battles had been.

Shortly after returning to the Third Marine Division in Japan, I received orders to move to Korea, joining the First Marine Division. We were flown to the Seoul military airport and driven north through the almost completely destroyed city, to a position just behind our side of the demilitarized zone (DMZ) near the 38th parallel of latitude. It was clearly a battle area, everything was either destroyed or temporary. I joined Item Battery of the Third Battalion as Executive Officer. Each battery had six 105 mm howitzers and the full complement of marines and equipment to operate such a unit. Our function was to keep our personnel fully trained and ready in case the war started up again. We hooked up our guns to trucks and towed the guns east to an area that had been set up as a practice firing area. We were firing back towards army units that were placed in reserve since they were farther back beyond our shell-impact area. The Chinese side had a similar situation north of us. They could be heard firing regularly in their own firing range, and we used ours routinely as well. During one of our practice firings, an army jeep came driving rapidly into our firing area. A captain got out and told us that a stray round had landed and exploded inside their army unit, and they thought the shell might have come from one of our guns. I ceased our firing immediately. We looked on our maps, comparing the unit's location with our own, and one of the officers noticed that if one of our guns had fired Charge 7 instead of the Charge 4 we had been shooting, then that shell could have passed through a saddle in a mountain range between us and gone as far as the army unit. It was possible that our shell could, indeed, have hit their area. Our investigation later found that the safety officer had failed to notice whether the crew had removed the proper number of powder bags from that shell before it was fired. We believed, therefore, that it was our gun that had fired the shell which exploded within fifty yards of an outside class being conducted by the army unit.[10]

Two days later, the company commander and I took a jeep over to the army unit to explain what we thought had happened. I remember having to step around a very large clerk, whose nametag said 'Martin,' sitting at a small desk. We went in to see the captain, told him that we believed it was our round that had done the damage, and we apologized for the accident. We explained how we thought it had happened and told him the investiga-

---

[10] 105 mm ammunition is made of two parts: (1) the missile and (2) the brass section which contains the gunpowder that drives the missile to the target. The powder is packaged in individual cloth bags, not as loose powder. Each brass section contains seven powder bags held together in a chain of heavy string. Depending on how far we wanted the projectile to travel, we fired the shell with as little powder as only bag #1 and as much as all seven of the bags. Each bag has its number printed on the side for identification. To shoot charge four, for example, the crew would remove bags 5, 6 and 7 from the brass section, then join the projectile to it and load it into the gun.

tion was ongoing. He thanked us and said that there had been only one casualty: one of his men was hit by a small piece of shrapnel in the left wrist, and he was back in a field hospital recovering. We were unable to talk with him and apologize directly, but his commander did not think it would be a serious injury. Not knowing, I worried about him until leaving Korea.

The South Korean people were in dire straits during the war. Once, our first sergeant told me of an occurrence that I thought was quite unusual. He had sent some men to deliver something to a neighboring marine unit. While there, they found a small Korean boy standing completely naked in the road at the entrance to the other unit. They asked the supply people whether they had some clothing that would fit the boy. Locating the smallest uniform they had, they were able to clothe and feed him. The sergeant felt satisfied that they had done the right thing and I agreed, thanking him for helping the boy and telling me. About a week later, the sergeant got a phone call from the other unit. They told our sergeant that the same little boy was outside their entrance, naked and wanting some more clothes! I supposed it was not so unusual an occurrence after all. War is war, and people survive by any means they have.

When the 90-day truce was about over, we were prepared to protect ourselves and kill the enemy in accordance with wartime practice. A few days ahead of time, higher headquarters announced that there had been another 90-day extension, and we resumed our 'watch, wait and prepare' tactics. We were located at the western front of the Korean conflict just behind the Imjin River; Freedom Gate was just beyond the river in front of our unit. Freedom Gate was so named because that was the location where prisoner exchanges were conducted. The war was quiet, but there were intermittent episodes of armed clashes on and around the river every few weeks or so. Korean civilians were caught sneaking into marine tents in the night from time to time to steal things, and the word went out that we could not know whether an intruder was an enemy or only a thief. We were advised to remain armed and watchful, but not to get trigger-happy. The commander did not want any marine killing any of the people we were there to protect. I made sure that our people understood. For my part, I slept with my 45 caliber pistol inside my sleeping bag with no round in the chamber but a full clip of ammo in the magazine. I would be cautious, but ready to load at a moment's notice.

The Korean War stalemated into repeated 90-day truces. After three of these extensions, the Marine Corps decided to cut back on personnel to save money. The battalion commander told us that he had seen this type of thing before, and it was likely that the Marine Corps would cut back on all activities for a time. I asked about flight training, and he told me that it would probably include flight school as well. He also told us that regular officers under a three-year obligation who had served at least 27 months could resign their commissions and go into the inactive Marine Corps Reserve. The category fit me exactly, and I wrote a letter to the Secretary of the Navy, through channels, resigning my regular commission.

Flying back from Korea, I got the surprise of my life when I was discharged at Treasure Island in San Francisco Bay in September, 1954. The discharge officer, Captain Wesley Demmons, told me that I was authorized to receive four years of tuition at a qualified College or University. I told him that the U.S. had already paid for three years of my tuition as an NROTC undergraduate. "That doesn't matter," he said. "The GI Bill neither asks nor cares how you got into the service. You now have an offer of four years of tuition under the GI Bill, should you elect to accept."

I didn't have to think very long. I was young, single and not yet ready to decide what career I wanted to pursue. I wanted to look at other fields than the chemical engineering I'd studied at Iowa State. I knew I would enjoy chemical research of some type, but did not know what my choices were. I looked at booklets in that Marine Corps office and quickly discovered that the University of California at Berkeley was the closest and best school for my needs. My official discharge papers would not arrive for approximately three weeks, so I had to wait with the other officers in the Marines Memorial Hotel in San Francisco. The next day, I went to the chemical engineering department of UC Berkeley and met an outstanding individual, Professor Vermuelen. He told me I had missed the deadline for out-of-state registration by three months. I explained that I had been in Korea for the last year, and asked when I could register for a future semester. He thought a minute and then started making phone calls.

This university, and especially Professor Vermuelen, knew how and when to bend the rules for good reason. I was told I would have to get the transcript for my undergraduate degree in chemical technology from Iowa State College and bring it to UC registration the following Tuesday morning. I was to wear my Marine Corps uniform and bring my newly acquired GI Bill papers. I would be met by a student who would walk me to the front of all lines guiding me through the process for out-of-state registration for classes, which would start within a week! That night I told other marine officers waiting for their discharge papers that I'd have to get my college transcript to Berkeley by Tuesday. Lieutenant 'Wint' Winter told me that his father was a car dealer in Kansas City. He offered to call and ask him to meet me at the Kansas City airport the next day with a car I would be proud of, for the price I could pay. I trusted Wint and told him, "Sure, you're doing me a personal favor."

I got on a flight the next morning. Wint's father met me and gave me the car keys to a nice 1953 Plymouth, and I gave him my check for $1,200, all the money I had saved while overseas. I drove the car to Des Moines that night, then on to Ames Saturday morning where I picked up my college transcript. I drove from Des Moines straight to Berkeley over the weekend with Joe Replogle, another fellow officer, stopping only for gas and meals. One of us drove while the other slept in the back seat until we needed food or gas, then we switched positions. Fortunately, Monday was Labor Day, and I had until Tuesday morning to return to Berkeley for registration. I had the luck of the young one more time. I made up my mind to earn it.

UC Berkeley

I arrived in Berkeley on time, and was met by a nice girl who walked me through the registration lines as promised. I was now a graduate student, having made a rapid choice to be assigned to the food technology department because it included wine studies and another interest of mine, biochemistry. Professor Maynard A. Joslyn was head of the department at UC Berkeley; his was a famous name in the world of food science, as well as in the world of wine. He co-authored (along with Professor Maynard A. Amerine) the classic textbook on wine science and technology titled *Table Wines*. That textbook was nearly 1,000 pages long, and at least one copy of it could be found in nearly every winery in the English speaking world between 1950 and 1990. The bibliography of other books, reviews and research papers listed in *Table Wines* includes no fewer than 36 papers authored by Maynard Joslyn and more than 50 authored by Maynard Amerine.

September 1954 was a time of significant change for the University. The food technology department, previously located on the Berkeley campus, was moved to the Davis campus that summer. Professor Joslyn lived only a few blocks from Hilgard Hall and was planning to retire in three or four years. He refused to move to Davis, so Professor Emil Mrak became the department head at Davis instead of him. Only two years later, Professor Mrak was promoted to become the first chancellor of the UC Davis campus. Such was the expertise associated with Maynard Joslyn in 1954.

Three professors remained in the department on the Berkeley campus: Maynard Joslyn, chairman; Harold McKinney, plant pigments; and Harold Olcott, fishery and seafood specialist. All three continued to teach food technology courses and to carry out research in their fields. For me, it was a highlight that Professor William V. Cruess (Professor Emeritus), one of the pioneers of Food Science, continued to carry on research long after retiring from teaching. Professor Cruess made my day on many occasions when he brought samples from his ongoing research for our evaluation. He was always trying out some new approach to food preservation. He might bring in cans of olives that had been processed in different ways one week and maybe cauliflower the next week. I particularly liked the flavor of his experimental 'acid pack' asparagus. As I remember, the asparagus was bathed in a colorless combination of vinegar and citric acid, and then canned in clear glass jars. The acid caused a leuco-pigment in each of the asparagus 'bracts' to turn red, giving the stalks a mottled appearance – with the stems remaining a normal asparagus green, but each of the bracts along the sides and tips turning quite red. I called it 'canned asparagus with flair.'

I became fascinated with plant pigments and chose an onion project for my MS thesis. Maynard Joslyn had told me that one of the onion packers near Gilroy had wanted to produce an onion puree from Southport White Globe onions to sell in supermarkets. The idea was that a housewife who wanted to add a small amount of onion to her salad could avoid the mess (and tears) caused by peeling and chopping a bit of onion – all she'd need to do was open a jar, add a teaspoon or so of white onion puree to the salad and *voila*! The problem was that when the white onions were pureed with a little white vinegar, and then heat-processed for 'canning,' the puree turned an ugly off-pink color! Over the next year, I made hundreds of pounds of white onion puree, one Waring blender batch at a time, to use in various experiments aimed at identifying the natural component in white onions that reacts with the acetic acid of vinegar to turn pink. The reactions turned out to be more complex than we had assumed, but the 'fix' for the problem was good old heat. Blanching the onions before the vinegar was added solved the problem, but I couldn't elucidate the precise chemistry of what was happening.

I did, however, make a small contribution to pure chemistry. I had tried to isolate what I assumed was an impurity in the vinegar that reacted with some component of white onions to generate the pink or red pigments in the puree. Each batch of vinegar gave different results with the same onions. Since vinegar is simply impure acetic acid, I tried Reagent Grade 'pure' acetic acid instead of household vinegar. I assumed there wouldn't be any impurity in 'chemically pure' acetic. Wrong! The onions turned pink-red again and I got darker pink from some bottles of pure acetic acid than from other bottles. Now the acetic acid people had pissed me off.

I decided to make my own 'absolutely pure' acetic acid. I mixed pure crystals of sodium acetate with a little sulfuric acid and distilled off some truly pure acetic acid. That, mixed with the fresh white onion puree remained a clean white – with no pink pigment forming at all. Holy Smoke! There had to be an impurity in what the world had considered to be 'pure' glacial acetic acid. To make a long story short, I used classic chemistry to identify the impurity. It turned out to be a miniscule amount (parts per million) of formaldehyde that was contaminating the otherwise pure Reagent Grade Glacial Acetic Acid of the J.T. Baker Chemical Co. I published that result in a scientific journal and smugly sent a copy of my publication to the J.T. Baker Chemical Co. I never received so much as a 'thank you' for letting them know. It was the only time I was able to discover, identify and measure a trace amount of anything in pure (non-food) chemistry. I guess I've been going downhill ever since.

A few months after returning from Korea and beginning graduate studies, I met a dental assistant, Diane Brisebois, in San Francisco and we began dating. We were married a few months later and were able to rent a student apartment in the married veteran's village at Albany, about a mile from the Berkeley campus. There, I met a neighbor, Harley Martin, an undergrad studying agriculture at Berkeley.

Harley was very big and athletic, weighing about 260 pounds and was the starting right tackle on the Cal bears' football team. We got together with our wives for a glass of wine one evening, and as we were getting acquainted, Harley told me he had been in an army unit in Korea during the truce periods. I told him I had been there at that time in the Marines Corps. He laughed and said, "The only thing I know about the Marine Corps is that some nut shot an artillery shell into our unit that exploded fifty yards from an outside class we were giving." I remembered the big guy just inside the doorway that I'd had to step around the day I went to see the commander of the army unit, and blurted out, "What a small world, Harley! I was the nut you're talking about. I was the battery exec who gave the order to fire that shell. I remember seeing you at a small typewriter desk in the CO's tent the day we visited your captain."

I asked him immediately about the casualty, the kid who was hit by a piece of shrapnel. Harley said, "It wasn't a bad injury at all. The shrapnel cut the tendons in his left wrist without hitting any bone and the medics were able to fix it very well. Later, the only way you knew he'd been injured was that you could see some small knots in his tendons moving back and forth under the skin of his wrist when he opened and closed his hand." "Wow," I said. "I am so glad to hear that. I've felt bad about not knowing how his injury turned out for two years now." Harley and I remained close friends after we both left the university. He ran a farming operation near McFarland, California, a few miles north of Bakersfield, and I made it a point to stop and see him whenever I was nearby.

A good pal, Al Lukton, a recent PhD recipient under Professor Joslyn, captured me at a dinner and argued all evening that I would be nuts if I didn't go on to get a PhD. I was not sure I could qualify. He mentioned a couple of teachers I'd had in food science courses who weren't good scientists and didn't seem very smart to me. I wondered how they had gotten higher degrees. That was his point: If they could make the grade, how in the world could I miss? He was embarrassed to see them teaching courses, as their incompetence caused students to bad-mouth the university; they weren't good examples of what a PhD should be. I still had two more years of GI Bill tuition if I wanted to use it, but did not want to abuse that privilege. "Nonsense!" Al blared. "If you get a PhD, you'll earn enough to more than pay back the government with higher income taxes over your lifetime." He convinced me in the end, and I told Professor Joslyn what I wanted to do. He said, "Well, I wondered when you were going to see the light. I gave Al Lukton an ultimatum to get you to sign up or else." That was one of the biggest compliments I could have received, and it came from a man I knew to be a giant in both wine and food technology.

On campus I 'lived' in either the food technology lab at Hilgard Hall or in the biochemistry library doing research into wine chemistry. White table wines often had a problem called 'copper casse' (pronounced cass) formation. Copper casse was an unsightly white cloud that sometimes formed in wines during bottle storage. It had been traced to the absorption of small amounts of copper from the brass fittings in wine tanks. The copper combined with certain proteins in the wine to produce the cloud. Professor Joslyn wanted to know exactly how the casse formed, and I decided to use radioactive sulfur to trace how it happened. Because I needed to understand more about radioactive isotopes, I studied nuclear chemistry as well. One course that I particularly enjoyed was taught by Professor Glenn Seaborg, the primary American research scientist for the creation of new transuranium elements and isotope research. I was especially impressed because he did not leave the teaching to a graduate student as so often happens in graduate-level courses. Rather, it was Glenn himself who gave all the lectures and exams and led our class discussions. Glenn became the University of CA Chancellor, and later, Chairman of the Atomic Energy Commission. Today, chemical element 106 is named Seaborgium, after him! From personal experience, I knew that he richly deserved that recognition. His signature appears on my PhD certificate as Chancellor of the UC Berkeley campus. Years later, on November 22, 1981, I saw Glenn in Oakland at the 100th birthday banquet for Professor Joel H. Hildebrand, one of the outstanding academicians of chemistry. I was asked to provide the wines for the Hildebrand dinner at cost and did so gladly. At the dinner I talked with Glenn again and enjoyed a nice reunion with him. I always felt very comfortable in his presence, as I think most people did. He was as famous a scientist as it was possible to be, and yet he remained low key and down to earth. He genuinely enjoyed learning what the universe is all about and had no interest at all in gathering the trappings of fame.

I was equally fortunate to have spent quite a bit of time in biochemistry with Professor Linus Pauling. His many seminars were fascinating, and I always had the feeling that his whole life was living and working at the leading edge of his field. He often spoke on prolonging life through common-sense biochemistry. For example, he told me many times to take as much vitamin C daily as my body would allow.[11] His reasoning combined the basic antioxidant abilities of ascorbic acid with its water solubility. Since vitamin C is water soluble, you almost can't take too much because any excess will always go out in the urine. He pointed out that humans are one of the few mammals that do not produce their own vitamin C, having lost that ability somewhere in evolution. Other mammals have it present, more or less at all times. Nor did he jump to conclusions; he could always back up his suggestions with evidence from recent research. Many mammals keep levels of vitamin C in their bodies that are much higher than the amounts he told me to take every day. To this day, I take 2 grams of vitamin C every morning and another 2 grams at night because he constantly prod-

---

[11] High levels of vitamin C can cause diarrhea in some persons under some conditions. It has never given me a problem in the more than fifty years I've been taking it.

ded me to do so between 1956 and 1958.

He was also interested in sickle cell anemia and the complex biochemistry of malaria; particularly the relationship of various types of hemoglobin to its inhibition. I followed his research on malaria for his last years
at Berkeley and after he moved to Oregon State University. He even came
to Modesto around 1960, when I lived there, to give a seminar on current
work on hemoglobin and malaria. He exuded the kind of scientific, single-
minded interest that you simply could not pass up. Linus Pauling first became famous for his eye-opening work, *The Nature of the Chemical Bond,*
published in 1931, the year I was born. He received two unshared Nobel
prizes in chemistry during his long career.

Looking back, I have often thought that if the Marine Corps had sent me
to Pensacola to become a U.S. Marine carrier pilot, I would have missed
out on knowing two of the most important scientists of my lifetime. Instead, the Corps assigned me to artillery because I was the youngest of the
other aviation applicants. I was a 'career' Marine Corps officer and they
felt I would have plenty of time for the aviation assignment later. Knowing both Professors Glenn Seaborg and Linus Pauling at UC Berkeley was
unimaginably great luck for me. Both gave me enhanced confidence to
seek challenges and develop new approaches to problems I saw in the wine
industry. It certainly was worth my continually feeling 'all alone' at my
age level.

During the 1960s and 1970s, I read that self-appointed do-gooder
groups were picketing land grant colleges and universities trying to get
military units like ROTC and NROTC permanently removed from American college campuses. I detested their short-sighted efforts because ROTC
organizations performed a valuable service to the country by providing
qualified officers for the military. More than that, ROTC organizations had
given me and people like me the opportunity to develop our abilities to a
much higher level than we could have done on our own. Through NROTC
and the GI Bill, the U.S. government paid for much of my college education, both undergraduate and graduate. Without that financial help I doubt
that I could have completed college, much less have gotten a MS in Food

Science and a PhD in Agricultural Chemistry. Al Lukton was right: NROTC and the GI Bill were excellent investments made by the U.S. Government. I certainly have paid the money back through income taxes from increased earnings over my professional years.

Grandpa Peterson, Grandma Bertha, Carl, Pete, Lillian and Pop (*on horse*) in backyard of the Peterson house in Iowa. Pete's twin, Albert, had been killed in a horse accident only months before this picture was taken.

Pop, Lillian, Pete and Carl (*from left*) in 1936. Lillian was on a visit to Iowa from Wisconsin that summer.

Noy, Pop, Dick, Mom and Martha in backyard of the family home in Iowa in the summer of 1936. I was five years old when this photo was taken.

Lined up like stair steps with my sisters and brother in front of the family house in 1939 (*left*). Arranged in age order are: Martha (10), Dick (8), Noy (6) and Chuck (2). Note the well-worn shingle roof; the house was already more than 50 years old.

Mom (*opposite*), in front of the house in 1979, 40 years later. The 'Alterations by Daisy' sign placed outside was illegal – but because of her age, the town of Pleasant Hill allowed her to keep it. Not a believer in the notion of retirement, she continued to work well into her 90s.

Oil painting purchased from a Dutch artist. The scene closely resembles ice skating on Four Mile Creek, two miles east of Des Moines, Iowa in the 1940s.

A typical 'wine brick' offered for sale to American home wine-makers throughout Prohibition. Pop used these in the 1920s. The bricks were comprised of dried and pressed grape skins which, with the addition of sugar and water, would ferment into wine. They dutifully came with specific instructions *not* to let the fermentation occur!

Two different advertisements for the 'Chemcraft Chemistry Set', circa 1940 (*left and below*). I obtained my set free by collecting 1,000 ice cream bar wrappers discarded at the fairgrounds by visitors to the Iowa State Fair that summer. The arrival of my Chemcraft Set started me on a thrilling career in science from an early age.

My first winemaking experience, with Concord grapes (*below*). The grapes came from backyards around Youngstown (now Pleasant Hill), Iowa. Photo taken October 1948 by B.K. Peterson, who shared my belief that we had produced one of the best wines in history. A bottle exploded in my car nine months later.

My athletic 'Letter' from Iowa State College NROTC Rifle team, 1951. I was too small and young to be a high school athlete, so it was great revenge when I earned this sweater monogram in my junior year at college.

The light cruiser USS Springfield CL-66 which took me to Panama, around the Galapagos Islands at the Equator, and then back to San Francisco in 1949.

The Shellback crew of USS Springfield at the Equator, July 1949 (*above*). Captain F. Moosebrugger and these sons of bitches put us midshipmen through a vicious hazing ceremony of crawling on the hard foredeck for two hours while being blasted by strong water hoses (*right*). We also endured spiteful beatings with canvas paddles (*below*). Other insults included having to kiss a fuel oil-covered fat belly, having chunks of our hair cut off and being dumped backwards into a garbage filled seawater 'pool' (*opposite*). The fuel oil caused me a three-day migraine, but I never let those bastards find out.

Korea, 1954: US Marine Corps life just behind the Demilitarized Zone (DMZ), during ninety day truce periods. These repeated truces eventually led to the end of hostilities. Our 105mm guns and crews were kept ready, camouflaged and well-practiced (*below right*). Officers paid an enlisted 'barber' fifty cents for a trim every two weeks.

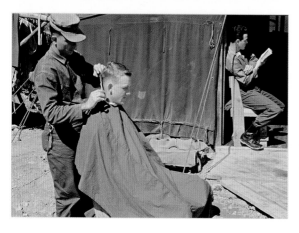

PART II

GALLO

1958-1968

The Visitor

In 1958, I was finishing my PhD thesis at the University of California, when Dr. Robert J. Bouthilet first visited me. He had spoken to Professor Maynard Joslyn about hiring a new PhD graduate for E. & J. Gallo Winery and was invited to Berkeley to meet me. I had a second-floor lab at Hilgard Hall practically all to myself as few food technology students remained at Berkeley – by then most had moved to Davis; the main department had moved there in 1954 as part of a buildup of that campus. UC Davis was a Farm Extension of the Berkeley campus, but was preparing to become a major campus on its own. After that happened, only three food technology professors remained at Berkeley. I was Joslyn's last PhD student; he was winding down his career and had neither reason nor desire to move from Berkeley. I made many trips to Davis doing part of my research work as some of the equipment and all the wines I needed were there.

Bouthilet was as colorful an individual as I ever hoped to meet. He weighed close to 300 pounds, but was only about 5' 10" tall. He was bald on top, but had white-blonde, very curly hair around the sides and back of his head. It was like seeing a bald St. Peter with a ring of long, fuzzy white curls arranged around his face like a halo. His face was cherubic, with rosy cheeks and a big, round smile. Obviously fun-loving, Bob Bouthilet was a real talker (an all-out BS'er, in fact, as I learned later), but his big friendly personality was apparent from the start. He would be a fun guy to work with. Professor Joslyn brought him into the lab where I was working and introduced us. Bouthilet told me that he had been working at the E. & J. Gallo Winery in Modesto as the research director and was looking for help in organizing a new research department.

Until this time, Gallo was more-or-less unknown to me as a wine company. Roma was the nation's largest winery, Italian Swiss Colony was second and Gallo third. I'd seen and heard TV and radio ads from all three and probably had tried their wines as well, but I'd formed no opinion of any of them as their wines all seemed alike. I didn't know at the time that most of the white wines from major wineries in California were primarily made from Thompson Seedless grapes. Thompson Seedless is a table and raisin grape and is not recognized as a wine grape anywhere in the world. It barely made the cut even back in 1958, and its use was driven solely by economics. Thompson Seedless made poor-quality white table wine, but it did not cost much; it had been accepted for winemaking during Prohibition when consumers were not picky.

Fine wine grape varieties had been ripped out of the ground in the early 1920s and replaced by ordinary 'shipping' grapes. Shipping grapes were never thought of in quality terms; they had been planted because the grapes were tough enough to stand shipping from California to the Eastern and Midwestern parts of the U.S. without too much spoilage en route. Fine wine grapes, by contrast, spoiled during shipment. It was a profitable business in central California to grow tough grapes to ship east for the booming homemade wine market and for bootleg Prohibition wine producers.

With the repeal of Prohibition, California vineyard owners found their businesses upside down. In 1934, the now-legal wine producers of the state had to use shipping grapes for their wines until good wine varieties could be planted. The shift was slow; American wine drinkers were not demanding fine table wines, as many had become used to the dessert wines that abounded. High-alcohol dessert wines outsold lower-alcohol table wines by nearly three to one! Intoxication was still the primary reason to drink anything in America, and that included wine. Fine wine had been replaced by AKAB (Any Kind of Alcohol, Baby). As a result, many new plantings in California went to dessert wine grapes and not to table wine varieties. Huge new plantings of coarse varieties like Mission, Tokay, Muscat, Thompson Seedless, Alicante, Feher Szagos and the like dominated vineyards of California from the mid-to-late 1930s up until the 1950s and 1960s.

No real change happened in the first decades after repeal; consequently, most wines of 1958 were not much improved from those of Prohibition. Just as most white wines came from Thompson Seedless, many red wines were blended from cheap Carignane, Aligoté and Alicante with a few other non-descript red grape varieties. There was precious little Grenache grown in California and most of it was used, properly, for rosé wine. Even to my uneducated palate in 1958, Grenache Rosé was central California's very best table wine. Of course, no Central Valley wine could hold a candle to those iconic Cabernet Sauvignons of Beaulieu Vineyard in Napa Valley. Beaulieu wines were in an altogether different league, but were triple the price of Gallo's best, and were not always an easy sell at the time. The culture of wine appreciation in America had a long way to go.

In April 1958, Bob Bouthilet told me that the mood of the wine industry was changing. Most vines planted in the 1920s and 1930s were getting old and needed to be replanted; thus more attention would be paid to new wine types, including finer varieties for quality table wines. He said he was developing a research department for Gallo with the intention of producing new wines and cleaning up many old production practices that wineries were using incorrectly. He reasoned, "Gallo has shown quite a bit of recent growth. Modesto is a nice town, also showing a lot of growth. The wine business is coming to life and, believe me, there is a lot of action at Gallo."

Gallo had developed a real winner less than a year before called Thunderbird. It was a flavored wine, something I had never tasted before. It had an obvious lemon essence, otherwise bland in body and flavor, with high-alcohol and high-sugar content. It was already becoming a huge blockbuster product for Gallo, and they wanted more Thunderbirds to continue their wave of success. Bouthilet wanted his new research department to have some technical competence, which I would bring if I came with them. He had a core group of four or five technicians working there and aimed to greatly expand the influence of science in winemaking.

Professor Joslyn came into the lab the next day to discuss Bouthilet and the Gallo prospect. He showed me an announcement in the April 1958 issue of *Wines & Vines* magazine titled, "New Research Lab for Gallo." It announced that Gallo had just opened a $100,000 Enological Research Laboratory that would be headed by Dr. Robert J. Bouthilet, a nationally known biochemist. He told me that Bouthilet came from a wealthy family and was quite successful in anything he did. He then proceeded to give some examples. He said the guy had a flair for new ideas that might seem crazy at first, but were real money makers. One example: Once when Bouthilet was driving along highways in Minnesota, he noticed little dark, fluffy tufts of something snagged on barbs of the wire fence separating the highway from large pasture areas. He stopped and asked a farmer what those tufts were. The farmer said, "Oh, the cows lean against the fence and scratch themselves against it. The fence barbs pull out little tufts of hair." Bouthilet asked why they itch, and the farmer told him they have mites and other insects that bite them, so the cows scratch where it itches.

Bouthilet thought about the farmer's explanation on his way back home. He had worked for the 3M Corporation and thought this might be a chance to design something to make money while solving a problem. He envisioned a hollow fence post that could be filled with an insecticide. The insecticide would then flow out of the post through horizontal rods, designed like ballpoint pens, that stuck out in all directions. Bouthilet figured the cows would scratch themselves by rubbing against the ballpoint pens; each pen would 'write' with insecticide exactly where it itched, just where the insecticide was needed by the cow. As cows usually follow each other through fields, he would place insecticide fence posts at intervals along cow paths. He sold his design to Shell Chemical Company and made a great amount of money. Bouthilet patented the design and collected royalties on the product, while Shell did all the manufacturing, distribution and sales. Bouthilet just sat back and smiled as the royalties rolled in. Joslyn had a wide grin on his face all the while he was telling me this story.

Another of Bouthilet's ideas was to make instant soda pop by dropping a pill into a glass of ice water. His idea was to sell compressed pills like Alka-Seltzer tablets, containing fruit flavor, color, sugar, citric acid and baking soda. Kids who wanted a quick soda pop could just drop a tablet into their glass of cold water, and it would quickly fizz and give off bubbles of carbonation, turning the water into a fizzy soda pop at the same time. He called the tablets Pop Drops. I told Joslyn I thought the name was as clever as the product itself and he agreed. I tried making them in the lab at Berkeley, just for fun. It worked, but I found it took too much sugar to cover up the taste of baking soda. I would have used an artificial sweetener rather than sugar because it would cover the chemical taste of soda better – at least to my taste. However, I was missing the point: Pop Drops made money in the market; my imagined improvement never hit the market at all.

Bouthilet's clever ideas kept coming. He noticed how people in Minnesota spent a great deal of time working in their yards during summer, spending many hours on their hands and knees, using a small trowel to dig out dandelions from the lawn. That seemed like too much work to Bob Bouthilet (one look at him would tell you that he was against the concept of physical work), so he developed what he called the Killer Kane. The Killer Kane was a hollow green plastic tube just over an inch in diameter, with a small plastic cap on top and a little metal valve at the bottom. You filled the hollow tube with water and dropped in a one-inch 'anti-dandelion' pill. The pill dissolved inside the Killer Kane releasing 'Two-Four-Dee' herbicide into the solution. That herbicide was chosen because it would kill dandelions without affecting the grass. The proud owner of a Killer Kane could simply walk through his yard and wherever he saw a dandelion, he'd put the tip of the cane on it, push down, and a tiny bit of the herbicide solution would squirt out through four little holes at the bottom of the Kane. Herbicide was squirted right onto the dandelion, which promptly keeled over in the next twenty-four hours without leaving a mark on the lawn.

Bouthilet told me later that the spring at the foot end of the Kane had to offer some resistance and make a little noise because if the user just went along and dabbed 'Two-Four-Dee' on each dandelion, he wouldn't get the most satisfaction possible. Full satisfaction came from hearing a little pop or snap and feeling resistance, so the user could feel that he had actively killed that dandelion. He would walk along, place the foot of the Killer Kane on the dandelion and bam! Kill the sonofabitch dead! It was that kind of cleverness that set Bouthilet aside from most other people in developmental work. He had a way of sensing the extra perks that consumers wanted.

Joslyn's great stories about Bouthilet and his inventions convinced me. I decided to go to Modesto, meet the people and consider the possibility of working there. He went with me in May, and by June I had signed up to begin product and process development work for Bouthilet at Gallo for $675 per month. That was double what winemakers were being paid at the time, and I knew I would have to earn my keep. I was anxious to start, but also needed a rest after my heavy schedule at Berkeley. I wanted to take a month off during the summer before moving, as my wife and I wanted to visit my parents and siblings in central Iowa and show off our baby daughter, Heidi, who was just nine-months-old. Gallo agreed and offered to pay my expenses to attend the annual American Society for Enology and Viticulture (ASEV) convention in Asilomar, California, near Monterey, in late June 1958.[1] They said it would be a great place for family, and that I should take my wife and daughter to the convention as well.

The three-day Enology Convention was wonderful. I met active, well-known and experienced winemakers like Eli Skofis, Andre Tchelistcheff and his son, Dimitri, Myron Nightingale, Phil Posson, Mike Nury, Ted Yamada, Philo Biane and many others. I spent time with Charlie Crawford, the production manager at Gallo, who had played a major part in my hiring. Louis P. Martini was president of the ASEV that year, and my wife and I spent a solid amount of time with him and his wife, Liz. Louis and Liz would become two of my very best friends in the industry for the next four decades. I also gained great information about the current promises and

---

[1] The wine society was young – it had been organized in 1950 as the American Society of Enologists (ASE), later changed to American Society for Enology and Viticulture (ASEV). I was elected President of ASEV and served from June 1977 until July 1978. That year, the total membership of ASEV climbed above 2,000 members, and I probably knew 80% of them. Over decades, members of ASEV played major roles in improving California wines and building a thriving professional culture throughout our industry.

problems of the wine industry. It was the best introduction to the industry I could have hoped for. In a single three day weekend, I went from a wide-eyed grad student to a full fledged industry member.

Settling In

I showed up for my job at Gallo on September 3, 1958, my first time to work in an operating winery. Gallo was already crushing grapes full speed, and I got a superb indoctrination by fire. I was met by Charlie Crawford, VP and Production Manager, who handed me off to Bill Lowry, an assistant winemaker who was told to show me everything in the plant and answer my questions. First, we visited the main lab, which was a bee-hive of activity. I was surprised at the number of employees rushing to and fro, bringing samples in and taking samples out. Most were wearing white lab coats covering white shirts and neckties. Some were doing chemical analyses while others were tasting wines. Still others were reading, operating lab equipment or writing in notebooks. It was clear that there were three distinct parts of the main lab: winemaking, analytical and research.

In the winemaking section, there were no chemicals or lab machinery, only white tasting benches with wine samples here and there. Benches were covered with graduated cylinders and beakers of all sizes and shapes. Above the benches were shelves containing tasting glasses and part-full wine bottles. Winemakers in lab coats were busy making trial blends with samples taken from one bottle or another and combined into tasting glasses. After pipetting precise amounts from various bottles to blend in wine glasses, the winemakers and assistants tasted from the glasses; others were comparing some of the wines in bottles by smelling and tasting. Each bench had a large sink along one edge into which tasters were spitting their tasted samples regularly. Occasionally, a winemaker would stick a label onto a sample bottle, fill the bottle from a tasting glass and take it over to the analytical 'in' bench. Samples were left there, which told the analytical people that they were to be analyzed, in accordance with the pencil-checked squares on the label.

In the analytical section, technicians were operating burettes and all types of electronic equipment; each analyst was writing notes or analyses in his notebook or on the paper label of a sample bottle. The large 'in' table was about half full of samples, and someone from the cellar (not wearing a lab coat) brought in trays of new samples and left them on the 'in' bench, or emptied the 'dump' bench samples into a bucket and took it away. Many of the samples were obviously fermenting juice as I could see foam in the upper half of the sample bottles. The whole thing worked like a production line, something I hadn't expected to see in a laboratory.

The research section seemed different from the rest of the lab. Some scientists were reading or discussing things at their desks, while others were making wine blends in the same way I'd seen in the winemaking section. I recognized Dimitri Tchelistcheff working with small stainless steel pressure tanks, and he told me he was experimenting with possible new types of sparkling wines. Gallo had no sparkling wine at the time. I was assigned a small, wooden desk in a corner which had a nice bookshelf that I would have to expand to accommodate my textbooks. It was obvious that this was an exciting, productive lab and I was anxious to get started.

Along with my tour, I got the inside scoop on the winery: Ernest and Julio Gallo had bought the old warehouse building to start their new winery in 1933, when it was clear that Prohibition would be repealed. They added offices on the first floor, and then built the second floor main lab above the offices, just under the roof. They had recently added more space for an expanded research lab for Dr. Bouthilet. The lab was workable, but the whole building was old and not well constructed.

Offices on the first floor were jammed together as a hodge-podge of cubicles, with about half of them assigned to workers in production and the other half to marketing and sales. There was an unmarked, but clearly visible area of demarcation (workers called it 'no man's land') between the two halves of the company. When Ernest and Julio made their decision to start a winery, it seemed natural to them that Ernest, as the oldest, would be in charge of selling while Julio would handle the winemaking. Those titles evolved into Ernest's 'marketing and sales' and Julio's 'production' over the next few years. Both men were strong-willed, competitive and surprisingly jealous of each other's area of responsibility. I was warned that the jealousy extended to employees as well. Julio's managers and lab workers were expected not to wander off into Ernest's territory, and the same was true of Ernest's employees. If one lost soul from production was encountered in Ernest's sales area, he would likely be stopped with the question, "What department do you work for?" Then, before answering, he would be asked, "Why aren't you busy in that department? Aren't you doing anything important over there?" The result was that few of the sales or marketing people got to know many from production and vice versa.

No man's land extended into a large central area towards the rear of the building. It had more than ten large tables with chairs arranged here and there for employees to use on breaks and during lunch hour. Most of the time a table was occupied either by sales people or by production people, but usually not both. With the exception of the few secretaries in the production departments, all Gallo's female employees were in sales and marketing. Only the few 'neutral' departments (personnel, purchasing, legal and government records) became exceptions to the 'Ernest's or Julio's?' rule. All the winemakers and lab workers were male, so the only interaction between unmarried employees took place in the lunch room – and everybody in the company was aware of who was visiting with whom at all times. Modesto was not a large town in 1958, with a population of about 35,000, and most of the employees went out to fast food restaurants or home for lunch.[2] A large stairway extended from the lunch area upstairs to the laboratories; it was big enough to handle foot traffic, four people wide. In my ten years of Gallo employment, I never saw female technicians working in the laboratory at any time. That was Julio's department and the workers belonged to 'his' group.

The big news at the winery was the spectacular explosion in sales thanks to Thunderbird since its introduction to the market the previous year, 1957. Thunderbird was a 'special natural wine,' a category that allowed natural flavors to be added to the wine before bottling. The wine was

---

[2] Only ten years later Modesto's population had grown to more than 100,000 people; in twenty years, the population had grown to over 300,000.

made by using the cheapest and least wine-like grape (Thompson Seedless) and adding a strong lemon flavor along with about 10% sugar (from grape juice or concentrate) and nearly 20% alcohol. It was essentially high-alcohol lemonade, and it sold like hot cakes.

Ripe Thompson grapes contain just under 25% sugar by weight and almost no flavor at all – Gallo didn't want any varietal grape character or body in Thunderbird. Winemakers actually treated the base wine with activated carbon to ensure that, prior to adding lemon. Thunderbird owed its success to the fact that grapes gave nothing at all to the wine except a lot of sugar and a whole lot of alcohol. The wine was essentially clean, blah white wine with plenty of sugar, alcohol and good ol' lemon flavor – just what adult lemonade ought to be. It literally flew out of the winery, on thundering wings, by the truck load.

As successful as Thunderbird was, it was not devoid of problems. Without warning, in the summer of 1957, Gallo suddenly had lots of Thunderbird wine bottles returned because of a serious off-flavor developing in the bottles. The smell and taste of rotten eggs was easy to identify in the lab as hydrogen sulfide (H_2S), but where did it come from? That mystery was easy to figure out as well, and it was one of the things that caused Ernest and Julio Gallo to develop more technical competence in their winery. With the initial success of Thunderbird in the marketplace, stores naturally started setting up large window displays of Thunderbird bottles stacked in front store windows. When wine from those bottles was tasted later, it was awful! Winemakers knew immediately what had happened. Almost any white wine that has been placed in direct sunlight (even for a few minutes) quickly becomes 'sun struck.' Chemically, a few parts per million of the SO_2 that is always present in white wine gets reduced by the ultraviolet of sunlight to H_2S – the dreaded rotten egg smell. The H_2S cannot be removed from wine effectively, except at the winery.[3]

---

[3] Red wine in flint glass doesn't get sun struck, since the red pigment protects the wine from light; however, there are other reasons not to store your red wine in direct sunlight (color loss, etc.).

Gallo guessed correctly that the answer would be to stop bottling Thunderbird wine in clear, colorless 'flint' glass and use instead only dark green glass; dark glass would not allow ultraviolet wavelengths of sunlight to enter and impact the wine. Unfortunately, glass companies could not change over to dark green quickly enough, so Gallo had a problem. They rustled up enough dark glass to get by in 1957, but an accelerated program to build their own adjacent glass plant started immediately. When I visited Gallo with Professor Joslyn to interview about the research job in May 1958, we were allowed to walk into the firebrick lined tank at the glass plant, then under construction. Clean sand, soda and the minerals to give the glass its color would be melted together in that tank. My first day on the job at Gallo in September 1958 included a tour of the newly opened glass plant. I looked into the (now red hot) tank with a dark glass visor to see the molten glass being mixed. Gallo had cleverly named their special glass color 'Flavor Guard,' thereby turning a previous problem into a public relations plus and commercial win. Later, I was involved in a few of the early steps of quality control at Gallo Glass as one of my many tasks.[4]

Bill Lowry showed me every square inch of the winery and told me what all that equipment was for. I saw grapes arriving in trucks from the vineyards being weighed, tested for sugar content and crushed. I watched Billy Joe Williams inoculate fermentation tanks, one by one, with Pasteur yeast. I learned by experience to keep my mouth closed when approaching a swarm of Drosophila fruit flies. I swallowed a whole cloud of them once when I ran up stairs alongside a square concrete fermentation tank with my mouth open at exactly the wrong time. You can't spit all of 'em out, you just have to swallow and forget about it until the next time and always remember to keep your mouth shut. Fruit flies are attracted to wineries by the carbon dioxide (CO_2) that boils up and out of the fermenting tanks.[5]

---

[4] The Gallo glass plant still operates today, and they are the only winery in the world that produces all their own glass. The plant produces more than a billion bottles a year and they sell their glass to other wineries as well.

[5] Twenty years later, I read that mosquitoes are attracted by the same CO_2, which is breathed out by animals and humans.

Wineries have to be careful not to spray for insects when tanks have their lids open because nobody wants wine to smell or taste like fly spray.

One surprise I vividly remember happened in the bottling room. Gallo was bottling their best-selling white table wine. Labels on the bottles said 'Dry Sauternes' which was a common label used by Gallo (and most other wineries) for white table wine in 1958. Bill took me to watch the bottling line, and I was certainly impressed. Empty bottles entered at the left and were conveyed down the line at high speed. They were filled with white wine, then capped with state of the art 'roll-on' pilfer-proof aluminum caps followed by each bottle receiving its label. I touched one of the bottles moving down the line and was surprised how warm it was. Bill told me the method of pasteurization used by wineries at that time was to heat the wine to about 130°F for bottling. The finished bottles of wine were packed into cardboard boxes while warm for storage in the warehouse. It took about 48 hours for the wine to cool to warehouse temperature, which was enough time to kill any residual yeast or bacteria. This was necessary because most table wines were bottled with some residual sugar that would spoil if the wines were not pasteurized. Unfortunately, all table wines picked up a slight baked character from the warm bottling and slow cooling.

Most wineries in California used some type of aluminum or steel caps on the wine bottles in 1958; only a handful of small wineries in the whole state used corks. After capping, the bottles were labeled and then conveyed onwards towards the casing operation. Bottles were collected into groups and dropped into cases, twelve bottles at a time. The cases were then sealed with glue and placed onto pallets at the far end of the line. I was watching with great interest and was impressed by the speed of this modern operation. Then, all of a sudden, everything stopped cold.

I could not see anything wrong; nothing had broken or spilled, and I wondered what had happened. Bill Lowry didn't know, but asked the bottling line supervisor. He mumbled quickly, "label change, no problem." I wondered if I had heard that correctly, but said nothing. As I watched, the line manager took a stack of labels out of a cardboard box he had brought in. He removed the remaining 'Dry Sauternes' labels from the labeler and placed them in a different box. He then filled the space in the labeler with a stack of labels from the new box, stuck his finger in the air and circled it round and round as a signal to restart the line. The line started up again, and it operated identically as before. The whole area went from noisy to deathly quiet to noisy again in less than a minute! I stepped over to the line near the casing operation to look at the finished bottles. The old labels had said 'Dry Sauternes,' but the new labels now said 'Chablis.' Everything else about the bottles, including the wine inside, was exactly the same as before!

Later, someone told me that Ernest Gallo had decided to try a new label in a test market – Houston as I remember. The test would be so successful that Gallo all but stopped using the old 'Dry Sauternes' label within months; the new name for Gallo's biggest selling white table wine had become 'Chablis,' right in front of my eyes, and almost in the time it takes to tell. Nobody could guess why, but the public liked Gallo's new Chablis better than they had liked Gallo's old Dry Sauternes. No statement was ever made about them being identical wines. The same thing appeared to be true for most competing California wineries, since you could no longer find many Dry Sauternes labels on store shelves after about 1960. I remember thinking as I watched that bottling line event, "The first step, changing labels, was easy. I hope I can be a part of the next step – improving the product to make the new label mean something."

On my first day at Gallo, I had inadvertently witnessed the first step in what became a rapid change from Dry Sauternes to Chablis as the primary white wine label from California.[6] Later when better grape varieties replaced junk, wine sales exploded further upwards. I had a million questions for Bill Lowry as he showed me the winery equipment, and I could see

---

[6] Up until the 1960s, the most common white table wines in consumer demand had been labeled Dry Sauternes, Medium Dry Sauternes or Sweet Sauternes. A few small wineries were slowly changing to other European place names like Chablis, Rhine or Burgundy. French wineries hated that American practice, but could do nothing to stop it since the U.S. Congress had failed to ratify the treaty of Versailles after WW I ended. That treaty banned 'calling a wine by a place or regional name' if the wine did not actually come from the place or region stated on the label. Like most treaties, Versailles had good points and very bad points. We now know that the treaty's extreme unfairness to Germany was a direct cause of Hitler's rise to power and the start of WW II.

the relief on his face when high noon finally arrived. We broke for lunch and Bill got to escape from my curiosity for awhile. I learned a great deal that day, including some real eye-openers. More than a few of the stories surprised my wife when I recounted them to her that evening.

I spent the next few days asking the winemakers questions about common wine problems they were having. I knew I would learn what I should work on by that route instead of trying to guess what might be the best use of my time for Gallo's benefit. Observing Dimitri Tchelistcheff was especially beneficial. I had talked with his father, Andre, winemaker at the prestigious Beaulieu Vineyard (BV) in Napa Valley at my first ASEV meeting. Andre was the one winemaker who was universally praised by everyone in the industry, even many who had never met him. The reason was clear: No other winery in the U.S. had consistently produced the superb quality red wines to match those of Beaulieu Vineyard. Knowing Andre, I wasn't surprised to notice that Dimitri stood out as the most accomplished winemaker at Gallo. He was to teach me more about winemaking than all the others in Modesto combined. Students in graduate school don't often learn how to handle wine. They learn that only by doing hands-on work.

I started by spending at least an hour each day following Dimitri's work, as it involved working with natural flavorings and basic wine chemistry. I began tasting everything he was doing and quickly understood why he was doing it. I found it especially enlightening to compare my taste sensations with the actual chemical analyses of each wine. Acidity tasted sour, tannin was astringent or mouth-puckering, even mouth-drying and sometimes bitter. Alcohol tasted hot, but oddly, also a little sweet. Sugar tasted sweet in high concentrations, but when dilute, it only made the wine taste soft and smooth. Sugar also covered and canceled out the tastes of both sour (acid) and bitter (tannin). Carbon dioxide (CO_2) in solution, being acidic, tasted sour, but often CO_2 also made red wine tannins taste bitter. It wasn't long before I could recognize, by smell and taste, what the lab analyses would later show. It was fun to guess a wine's pH (acidity) by its taste, and I still do that fifty years later. Dimitri was already good at tasting pH as early as 1958, but it has surprised me that very few other winemakers, either at Gallo or elsewhere, have made an effort to learn that knack. To this day, I believe tasting the natural chemistry of wine is a primary skill that every winemaker needs to master. Unfortunately, precious few of today's winemakers do this, judging from the crudeness of today's overly alcoholic and flabby wines.

It was especially worthwhile to watch Dimitri handling laboratory wine samples. I didn't need to ask questions; watching was enough. Table wines are delicate foods, easily ruined by heat and air, so you have to protect all wine samples from both air and high temperatures. He kept samples in completely full bottles with no air space under the cap and stored them cool, but not in a freezer. I mimicked Dimitri's care in handling samples of wines and feel lucky to have worked so closely with him for the two years he stayed at Gallo. He was a great teacher by example, and I learned quickly about practical winemaking by following his lead.

During the next two years, Gallo would make significant improvements to table wines. Billy Joe Williams, an Arkansas native who had both a master's degree in microbiology and a good feel for the science, was instrumental in making those improvements. A new company, Millipore, had developed a clever and extremely tight filtration system that would completely remove all yeast and bacteria from table wines immediately prior to bottling. After 'sterile filtration,' table wines could be bottled and stored at cool room temperatures with astonishing results. Suddenly table wines, even sweet wines, tasted cleaner, fresher and lasted longer in the bottle on store shelves.

Billie Joe was already working with Millipore at the time I arrived at Gallo, and they perfected the system on the Gallo bottling lines after only one season of experimentation. There were occasional problems, but the Millipore system of line checks kept track of the bottled wines extremely well. Most bottled wine could be shipped directly off the bottling line, but once in a while, Billie Joe had to place holds on certain pallets of wine until further lab checking could prove that the wine was safe and would not spoil in the bottles as they stood on shelves.

Gallo was one of the first wineries to use the sterile bottling system to avoid heat-treating its table wines, and the success at Gallo gave a great feeling of security to smaller wineries. Within only about five years, most of the wine industry was using Millipore and, as a result, California table wines had made a magnificent leap in quality. Sterile-bottled wines were light-years better than any of the wine produced in America for the first few decades following Prohibition.

Another improvement, equally as effective for improving wine quality, didn't occur in the winery; rather, it was made in the vineyards. Gallo slowly replaced the old and embarrassing Thompson Seedless grapes with much higher-quality white wine varieties like Chenin Blanc and French Colombard. No, it was not yet Chardonnay, but changing from Thompson Seedless to Chenin Blanc and French Colombard amounted to a huge improvement in wine quality. At the time, 1958, there were no more than about 200 acres of Chardonnay planted in all of California, and that was in Napa and Sonoma counties. The grape and wine industry universally believed that Chardonnay would not grow well in the central San Joaquin Valley of California. Having been misled by incorrect guesses of viticulturists in the late 1800s, they thought it might be reasonable to try some Chardonnay in coastal regions, but not in the Central Valley! Only after an additional twenty years had passed did enough Chardonnay grapes become available in central California to allow large wineries like Gallo to further improve their white table wines by blending Chardonnay with their existing French Colombard and Chenin Blanc.

The same thing was true for red table wine varieties. Poor quality grapes like Alicante, Carignane, Aleatico, Aramon, Salvador and Valdepeñas had produced red wine in 1958, but not good-quality wine. As Julio Gallo concentrated on replacing those old vineyards with new clones of Zinfandel, Barbera, Ruby Cabernet and Petite Sirah, the resulting wine quality soared. Increased wine sales followed, with or without creative labeling. All the wineries in California had followed similar patterns in wine labeling at first. All were looking for a sales edge, and all experimented to see what kinds of wine labels the public wanted, or would accept. Most of the sales efforts copied each other then, as they often do today. Many did not recognize that they would never catch the public's attention until they stopped trying to produce quality wines from coarse and flavorless raisin grapes.

First Project: Baking Sherry

One day, Bouthilet sat me down and asked, "Wouldn't it be nice if we could use Thompson Seedless grapes to make sherry? What happens chemically when sherry is baked?" I admitted I had no idea. All I knew was that they heated a fortified wine in a tank to 135°F, often with a little air, and held the wine at that warm temperature in a 'baking tank' for a month or more until it tasted like California baked sherry. "Look at the big picture," he said. "Gallo sells a whole lot of sherry; we use good grape varieties, and it takes weeks to bake the wine and get it ready for bottling. On the other hand, we have a whole lot of Thompson Seedless wine that we don't know what to do with. God knows it can't be used to make good table wine. Why don't you look into the chemistry, and see if it might be possible to make sherry out of Thompson? It's the cheapest grape variety Gallo has, but it makes shitty sherry. Maybe you can figure a way to make Thompson work, Dick. Why don't you look at what happens to wine during the baking process? Maybe you can make a major breakthrough." It was a reference to Karel (Carl) Popper, a fellow researcher, who often claimed that he was on the verge of 'making a major breakthrough' on one project or another.

"I have a separate question for you," he continued. "How can we improve Gallo sherry – with or without Thompson? Julio is always looking for better sherry, and we have to use Grenache and other expensive varieties because of quality." He gave me the goal of adding something "legal, healthy and safe" to a Thompson wine that would cause it to bake quickly into sherry. It would be a lot cheaper if Gallo could make it that way – especially if we could cut the baking time down from weeks to days and avoid using expensive grape varieties.

To start on the problem, I did library research on the various methods used for making sherry. I tried to guess what was making the flavor of sherry develop when wine was held in oxidative conditions for a few weeks at high temperatures. It was well known what winemakers had been doing, but which steps were necessary and which were not? I started by taking wine samples of different grape varieties – Grenache, Thompson Seedless, Palomino and other varieties, setting up parallel experiments where all the flasks were held in a laboratory oven set at 135°F. Every day I would take a small sample out to check the acidity, pH and sugar content; I would smell and taste it, trying to decide whether it was beginning to 'sherrify'. I found that Palomino and Grenache wines sherrified very quickly after baking started (this was already well-known). Thompson Seedless did not; it took on a burned and oxidized flavor, but it was not sherry-like and not even pleasant, at least to my taste.

The next step was to start adding various amounts of different things to those samples before baking. I experimented by adding chemicals that occur in foods, even if never in wines. To study the chemistry, I added chemicals in small amounts to see what each one did. I added tartaric acid, the natural acid in grapes and wine, to some samples. To others, I removed the acid. I added various amino acids and other organic acids – fumaric, citric, and so on. I added vitamins A, B, C, D and anything else that happened to be on the reagent shelf. I added sulfur dioxide, which occurs in wine naturally, and hydrogen peroxide to deliberately destroy all the sulfur dioxide in a different sample. After those additions, I set the oven thermostat to 135°F and turned on the heater. After an oven baking period of a week or ten days, I became convinced that some of the amino acid additions might hold a partial answer. I thought that organic nitrogen might be involved in some way because some of the amino acids gave the wine a slight sherry-like flavor after baking. That was true for most, but definitely not all the amino acids! That seemed like a clue, but what on earth did it mean? Also, lack of SO_2 seemed to be important – the quicker we got rid of SO_2 and allowed the wine to oxidize, the more quickly the wine seemed to sherrify.[7]

With repeated tests, I could not get any one amino acid to give me a clear-cut answer, even though all of them did something; more than half appeared to be moving in the right direction. I suspected that the amino acids

---

[7] I tried oxidizing the wine because the Tressler process had been used to bake sherry in New York for many years by bubbling air through Concord grape wine as the wine was being heated. Air destroys the 'Concord jelly' flavor and produces better sherry than ordinary Concord wine would without oxidation. The Tressler process allowed New York wineries to make good sherry from cheaper wines.

might be breaking down, each at its own rate, under the heat and oxidation of the early stages of baking. If something like that was happening, I figured most amino acids would probably break down into carbon dioxide and, most likely, ammonia. I added a touch of ammonia to one sample, carbon dioxide to another, and left them in the baking oven overnight at 135°F. The next morning, lightening had struck! The carbon dioxide had done nothing at all, but the ammonia sample had darkened and it smelled and tasted very much like sherry!

I could not believe how fast the sample with the ammonia addition sherrified. I had put a small amount of ammonia into Thompson Seedless wine, held it at 135°F and bam! The very next day, it had browned and tasted like sherry. I added a few hundred parts per million of ammonia into other varietal wine samples and heated them overnight once more. Again, every one tasted like sherry the next morning. I thought, son of a gun! this will be easier than I expected. There is a well-known type of reaction in food processing that takes place when cooking certain foods that need to be browned and that seemed to be part of what I had blundered into. That same type of reaction could be used at Gallo to make better and cheaper sherry if I could perfect the process. I knew it was illegal to add any ammonium salt to wine, but any winery could change the regulations by petition. I needed to find a way to add an ingredient that was legal and safe in foods, but that would also break down into ammonia and promote 'Maillard-type' browning reactions early in the sherry baking process.

I checked my textbooks and found that ammonia is only an intermittent and miniscule wine component; only trace amounts occur in some wines naturally. I noticed that the varieties with the highest natural ammonia content (such as Grenache and Palomino) were the varieties that tended to sherrify quickly, while the ones with lower ammonia content (Thompson Seedless) did not tend to sherrify at all. The chemistry fit together perfectly. I went to the trouble of developing a new analytical procedure for the Gallo laboratory. I called it 'Volatile Base' analysis, and it was designed to analyze any wine for natural ammonia content. It was patterned after the well-known 'Volatile Acid' analysis (but using exactly opposite chemistry) and was intended to allow any wine to be adjusted to an exact ammonia content prior to baking into a standardized sherry.

I told production manager Charlie Crawford about the discovery and gave him a small sample to smell and taste. He wanted to make a cellar scale test immediately. He wasn't worried about the wine regulations. Charlie felt that if we could prove that the process would work in the cellar, we could then get approval from the Bureau of Alcohol, Tobacco and Firearms (BATF). The approval request would be to add ammonia 'to correct natural deficiencies in wine' – so that they would then bake properly. Charlie's experience with BATF personnel was that most were surprisingly bureaucratic and completely ignorant about the chemistry of wine. Securing approval from them would be like asking a fence post for a favor. Even if they agreed, it might take many months, but would be published for sure. This secret 'Gallo process' for sherrifying Thompson wine would be all over the industry. I knew the proper procedure would have been to get approval *before* doing it on a cellar scale. Charlie knew that better than I did, but Charlie liked to take short cuts. He was persuasive, and it was a whole lot easier to agree with him than argue with the guy who approves your paycheck. No Gallo employee wanted to give any new process to our United Vintners competitors for free. In the end, Dimitri and I agreed to make a large tank batch in the cellar for him, but he made it clear to us that Jack Fields, cellar superintendant, was not to know, under ANY circumstances. Dimitri later told me the reason (over a glass of wine), and I agreed that Charlie was really taking a chance. Jack would have blown the whistle on Charlie for sure.

Dimitri and I were asked to add the necessary ammonia into a 100,000-gallon tank of Thompson Seedless wine that Charlie had reclassified on the records as sherry material. It would be baked into sherry later through regular cellar orders. I calculated the number of 50-pound bags of pure, crystalline ammonium carbonate to order, and Charlie sent the request to purchasing. The purchasing agent, John Wilson, never asked what it was for, but that was not unusual. The bags came stacked on a wooden pallet, covered by a tarp. Dimitri had it placed beside the tank on a day when we knew Jack would not be present. The cellar crew placed a standard 'pump and tub' setup beside the tank, and it looked to everyone like a standard addition of bags of tartaric or citric acid to the tank. Nobody had any reason to look more closely. Once the ammonium salt was in the tank, I didn't think anyone could figure out what we had done, as it was a small amount that would be not be noticed in routine wine analyses. Dimitri and I came in at eight o'clock that evening and finished the addition within an hour. Charlie baked the tank a day later, and inside of two days Gallo had 100,000 gallons of a nice sherry made from Thompson Seedless wine!

Julio never knew anything about this – as owner of the winery, he could have been put in jail if we had been caught, since it would have been presumed that he had okayed the process. In fact, Julio would have been beyond furious if he had found out, and Ernest would have had Charlie castrated without comment. Charlie, of course, would have sworn it was all my idea, but Dimitri knew better and would have set the record straight.

A week later, when we brought a sample of the latest sherry blend into the tasting lab for Julio to taste, Charlie didn't tell him exactly what we had done. He just said that Dick Peterson had discovered a method that appeared to accelerate the baking process for sherry from Thompson or any other grape. Charlie wanted Julio's impressions of it and thought we might be able to use it in the cellar. He told Julio that it wasn't yet approved by BATF, but we were sure we could get it approved if Julio would accept the process. Julio smelled and tasted it carefully for several minutes. Finally he looked up and said, "Well, it's sherry-like all right, it's got that nuttiness that sherry has, but it's too simple and watery for my taste." I knew what Julio meant: Thompson is always simple, has no vinous character, no mouthfeel, no body, no varietal, no nuthin' – just simple. "It's lacking something," Julio said. "Somehow, it just doesn't have the 'winey-ness' that you look for in a sherry." It was hard to describe, but he wanted some of that baked wine flavor and body that always accompanies baked sherry made from better grape varieties. It was just like we've always known: Thompson Seedless grapes were never good for making normal wine, and now we knew you couldn't even cook with them. There just isn't any way you can use that crap.

My hopes had been too simplistic. I underestimated the complexity of sherry flavor and should have known better. I was disappointed that Thompson couldn't even be used to make sherry – a manufactured wine.

Dimitri expressed it in a different way. He wasn't afraid to use any word in any company at any time, and he was as creative in using English as he was with making wine. He asked the group, "Why is making wine with Thompson Seedless like making love in a canoe?" I knew the answer because he had told me before: "Because it's fuckin' near water."

I learned an important lesson about flavor chemistry that day from Julio Gallo. Our artificial sherry, my Thompson Seedless sherry, did not have complexity. It had the nuttiness, but it did not have the 'winey' component, so Julio turned it down. I was disappointed at first because I thought we could easily blend in enough Grenache or Palomino to make it complex. I had done a pretty good scientific investigation and had come up with something, but it was not perfect. We should not have rushed into production before it was ready. Since Julio didn't want to use it, Charlie now had to use up 100,000 gallons on the sly by dribbling small amounts into larger batches of regular sherry just prior to bottling. He must have asked the sherry winemaker, George Fujii, to add 5,000 to 7,000 gallons of it into each new batch of sherry over the next year until he finally got rid of it. George never mentioned it to me, and I'm sure he never knew where that tank had come from. Julio was always buying and selling bulk wines to and from other wineries, and Charlie probably just told George that this tank was a new one that should be used up a little at a time. I never heard about the subject again. I had done my job and discovered something about sherry flavor through research, but there was no way I could have published the result.[8] My first major Gallo project was a bright and shiny failure.

New Project: Cork Flavor

Bob Bouthilet noticed that most wineries in central California used only screw caps to close wine bottles and none used corks. The same thing was

---

[8] I think it was justice that sales of all types of baked sherry have continued to drop steadily. Twenty years later, long after I'd left Gallo, baked sherry was no longer a factor in wine sales in the U.S. Nobody cares anymore how to bake it, or any of the other particulars, given the insignificance of the product now. I'm happy with the outcome.

true for many coastal wineries as well; most used cheap metal screw caps with cardboard or plastic liners to keep air from leaking in and prevent the wine from leaking out. The few small wineries that stood out on shelves (bottle prices were higher) often used corks instead of caps to seal their bottles. Bob asked each of us whether corks were actually better for sealing, or whether they were just 'window dressing' to make the consumer think the wine was better. Nobody knew. Corks were more traditional, we knew that, but no one knew whether comparison tests had been done in labs. He wanted us to set up tests to compare the leakage of air into bottles with corks versus those with screw caps. Tests like that would take time, but Bob wanted quick results.

While we started setting up the tests, Bob told each of us he wanted to give Julio Gallo an immediate answer. "Julio hired us to give his winery 'pizzazz' and that's what I want to give him. Let's produce a natural cork extract, as a flavored blending wine. If we had cork extract as a blending tool, winemakers could then add a small percentage to Gallo's best table wines to make the wine taste richer." He assumed that corks did something more than just seal the wine in and the air out. He supposed that traces of flavor were leaching from the cork into the wine during long storage or bottle-aging. We would, in effect, produce Gallo wines with screw caps that might taste as if they had been stored in cork-finish bottles. Julio could then give the consumer more for less; everyone would win.

Producing the actual cork extract was easy. Cork is composed of tiny cells, consisting of mostly wax and fiber, with a microscopic bubble of air inside each cork cell and less than about 7% water overall. That meant the cork flavor would not dissolve in water, but it might in alcohol. We ended up grinding fresh, new corks into small pieces and soaking them in a small tank of clean brandy. After soaking for a few days, the liquid was racked off and diluted with clean, white wine. After filtration, this 'wine extract' was used in very small amounts by winemakers to improve the taste of Gallo's best red and white table wines. This secret process was used for about ten years, as I remember. I assume they didn't need it after around 1974, when the company began using actual corks instead of screw caps for their best table blends and varietal wines.

Pop Wines

Dimitri was actively developing new flavored products because Thunderbird was continuing to explode, and sales were climbing every week. We had to make more and more, and then more on top of that. Italian Swiss Colony (ISC) was now Gallo's rival and the largest producing winery in the state. By 1962, Roma, the previous largest winery, had quickly dropped by the wayside and was no longer a competitor in the wine business for unknown reasons. Gallo assumed it was the result of a series of stupid decisions made by the liquor people at Schenley, which had owned Roma. Liquor companies had especially poor records when it came to running wineries; few, if any, succeeded for long. No public explanation was given for Roma's closure, but the rumor was that they had serious labor problems.

In 1958, ISC jumped into the fray with Gallo. ISC was the brand name owned by the United Vintners Wine Company. United Vintners, in turn, was owned by Allied Growers, a giant cooperative of grape growers. Unfortunately for Italian Swiss and United Vintners, most of the grower members of Allied were growing primarily Thompson Seedless grapes. That was a terrible Achilles heel for the Italian Swiss winemakers to bear. They were a bigger wine company than Gallo in both production and sales. Their main winery was located in the town of Asti, north of Santa Rosa, but the company owned many larger old wineries all over the Central Valley. I recall that Gallo was producing about 25 million cases a year at the time, and ISC was doing 29 or 30 million cases.

ISC had just come out with a brand-new flavored wine to compete directly against Thunderbird. The ISC product, called Golden Spur, had a square bottle with a dark label – the package looked like a bottle of Jim Beam Whiskey. Obviously, the bottle shape, glass color, label and every detail was deliberately intended to look like whiskey. Their ad on television was vivid and featured a tough cowboy with six-guns standing in the street ready to draw. The announcer yelled, "Reach!" as the cowboy's hand darted towards his gun, and a close-up showed that he'd grabbed a bottle of Golden Spur by the neck, rather than his pistol. The announcer finished his sentence with just three more words, "for Golden Spur." It was a good competitor for Thunderbird, and Golden Spur was a hot item for a few months in the fall of 1958 and early the next year. I recognized the flavors as ginger and vanilla, combined with a strong bourbon-like oak wood taste. It was not a particularly appealing product in my opinion – it was pretty harsh, and not easy to drink. However, like Thunderbird, it was very high in alcohol and almost sickeningly sweet.[9]

Dimitri was in charge of making all new products at Gallo. He had inherited the project from Ralph Celmer who had developed the formula for Thunderbird a year earlier, but then left Gallo employment. Dimitri's chief input came from two VPs of marketing, Albion Fenderson and Howard Williams, who reported directly to Ernest Gallo. They did not want to copy Golden Spur flavors; rather, they wanted Dimitri to use different flavors that were more familiar to the American taste in soft drinks, yet somehow reminiscent of Golden Spur. They suggested ideas to Dimitri, and he was free to try any flavors he wanted.

He made a product that was similar to a cola soft drink, but easier to drink than Golden Spur. The marketing department named it Eden Roc and used a random group of Roman coins as a logo design on the label. The coins had no connection with either the name Eden Roc or the flavor in the product; nevertheless, Eden Roc was successful and shipments rolled out the door. ISC continued to turn out new flavored wines, but one taste made it clear that all were made from Thompson Seedless base wines. I asked Charlie Crawford once whether ISC made any wines out of Chenin Blanc or Colombard. "Not likely," he said. "Allied Growers grew mostly Thompson Seedless because they thought there was strength in that. Growers figured they could sell their grapes for fresh fruit, for raisins or for winemaking." "Well, they got two out of three right," I said. Charlie laughed and said, "The third choice, wine, will end up ruining their company, just wait and see." He was right on; ISC winemakers inadvertently

---

[9] No cane or beet sugar was added to grape wines; by state regulation, winemakers had to add grape juice when sugar was desired in a wine blend. While federal regulations allow cane or beet sugar in grape wines, California does not.

had their hands tied by their Allied Grower owners. They were forced to try making competitive wines out of Thompson grapes, and it was a sure thing to bet against them. It was obvious to us that Julio's quiet, steady removal of Thompson vineyards and replacement of them with Chenin Blanc and French Colombard would easily kill the Italian Swiss label in the market. It was only a matter of time, and the clock was ticking.

Despite the success of Eden Roc, none of Gallo's newer flavored wines could match the success of Thunderbird, which was already selling around six million cases per year. Most of the next few products could not sell more than a million cases, which told both Ernest Gallo and Howard Williams not to expect the 'pop wine' craze to last long in the public fancy.

Howard Williams, VP of New Product Development, presented a concept that Gallo would follow for the next couple of years. He said the history of flavored wines, with the exception of Thunderbird, was that each new product would have a market life of not more than two years. Sales of a new product would explode upwards and then drop nearly as fast. Dimitri was to have another new product ready to hit the market just as the most recent product was starting to fall off in sales. In that way, Gallo could keep on selling flavored wines at a fast rate even though none of the products was expected to have market longevity. We knew the industry was near the peak of its so-called pop wine bubble, but Ernest wanted to press it as long as it held. People eventually want to be treated like adults, but pop wines were merely alcoholic lemonade. In the lab we called the pop wine concept 'alcoholic Kool-Aid' or 'kid stuff.' Ernest didn't like us saying that: "Never belittle Thunderbird! It brings in tons of money."

For the time being, Dimitri continued breaking new ground with his creations. He made a peppermint-flavored wine that Howard dubbed 'Twister.' They gave the label a distinct candy cane-like appearance, with white and red stripes twisting around a pole. The new dance craze was The Twist, popularized by Chubby Checker. The dance amounted to people twisting their bodies left and right and back and forth, gently crouching down and then rising, while simulating pulling an invisible towel across their backsides left and right. It was such a sensation in 1960 that it seemed easy to cash in on the trend with the Twister wine product.

Dimitri also made a high-alcohol apple wine called Triple Jack, but the reason for this wine had nothing to do with flavor desirability or demand for such a product. The reason was strictly economic. Gallo had a successful and growing brand called Boone's Farm, a line of berry and apple wines that were light, delicate and sweet. Boone's Farm wines included blackberry, loganberry, Concord grape and apple. Julio had apple orchards of his own not far from Modesto that provided the majority of the apples. These were not artificially flavored, but natural wines.

The problem Gallo had was in using up leftover apple wines. Some bottles got returned with scuffed labels and some got old if stock was not rotated on store shelves or in distribution. Those leftover wines had to be distilled to recover the alcohol, otherwise they were a complete loss. Small wineries could not afford to save left over wines, but large ones could. Boone's Farm wine leftovers posed a problem because regulations require that grape wine, if fortified, has to be fortified with grape brandy; apple brandy cannot be used. When Gallo distilled the leftovers of apple fermentations (from Boone's Farm Apple Wine), they got apple brandy. What good was apple brandy when it couldn't be used in grape wine? Gallo had to make a fortified apple wine[10] in order to use up the recovered apple brandy. Triple Jack was Dimitri's answer to that problem.

Dimitri produced every new product by trial and error. He'd try a low-alcohol content, a higher one, an even higher one, lower acidity, higher acidity, low pH, high pH, varying degrees of sweetness and varying amounts

---

[10] Adding alcohol (brandy) to table wines 'fortifies' them turning them into 'dessert' wines, a different tax class. Dessert wines are defined by their higher-alcohol content: If wine contains 14% or less alcohol, it is a 'table wine;' if the alcohol is higher than 14%, the wine is designated as a dessert wine and requires a higher tax. Fifty years later, 14% is still the legal dividing line between the categories of table wines and dessert wines. Something has changed, however; many Syrah, Cabernet, Zinfandel and other red table wines are now being produced at alcohol levels higher than the 14% limit – yet marketed as if they were genuine table wines. I find those high-alcohol wines difficult to drink and impossible to enjoy with food. Others accept them as cocktail wines to drink while standing around socializing.

of added flavors in all these products. He constantly needed a bevy of tasters, and I could expect to be shown new products several times a day when he was fine-tuning. Many lab people were forced to become good wine tasters over time. Each taster was better for certain wine types than others, and we got to know who could be relied upon for which wine types. I found myself working more and more with Dimitri because his flavored wine projects were so much fun. When Dimitri came up with a new product that the tasters thought was good, it was scheduled to go in for Julio Gallo's and Charlie Crawford's approval at the regular evening tasting.

As Julio insisted on tasting every wine ahead of time (if it was scheduled for bottling), his evaluation became a regular event every evening at 5 p.m. Winemakers of Gallo's regular wines usually had their blends tasted first. Dimitri's were new products, with lower priority, and he showed whatever he had after the first 'bottling' tasting. I found myself there more and more often and enjoyed the tastings, not only because it was interesting work, but also because my opinion meant something. I could reliably pick up minor differences and little innuendos in flavor. I was often wrong, of course, (everyone is in tasting), but my record was consistent, so I did it more and more often.

When Ernest had an idea for a new product, he brought Howard Williams and Al Fenderson to the tasting with Julio, Charlie, Dimitri and me; none of the regular winemakers could have their wines tasted that evening. Because of the big tasting load, I often didn't get home before 7 p.m. on weekdays and 1 p.m. on Saturdays. After Julio and the rest of us agreed that Dimitri had samples that were ready for Ernest Gallo and his marketing people to try, it would be scheduled as a separate tasting for Ernest's group.

Any of these tastings could show that some new change should be tried; maybe the wine should be sweeter, maybe lower in alcohol, maybe higher, or maybe less oak flavor. Dimitri would often come out of the tasting room and then immediately start making new samples with the suggested changes for the next day's tasting. Over and over again, these products would be tasted until he got it right. Dimitri worked on them during the day, they would be tasted that afternoon or evening, and then he would go back to work the next day depending on the feedback from the tasting room.

Increasingly I worked with Dimitri on new products, especially sparkling wines, and we became good friends. At some point, we discussed starting our own winery. Dimitri told me he knew of some small wineries that were for sale in Napa Valley and suggested we go and take a look.

Parallel, but unrelated to my job at Gallo, I had become a pilot in the National Guard unit at Stockton only a year after moving to Modesto in 1958. My flying generally took place on weekends and at regular two-week summer camp training sessions at Camp Roberts and Camp San Luis Obispo. Dimitri was a reserve officer, so it was legal for me to take him as a passenger in military planes. Since I had access to army aircraft on short notice from my California Army National Guard unit, I flew him to Napa Valley one Saturday. His father, Andre, met us at John Daniel's Inglenook airstrip on Whitehall Lane, and the three of us drove around looking at possible wineries to purchase. After a few months, we had met with the Cebrian family and were close to an agreement with them to buy the Schramsberg Winery. We had difficulty getting the necessary financing together, and Jack and Jamie Davies bought the winery in the meantime.[11]

We continued to look for another winery over the next several months, but did not find exactly what we wanted. As time passed, Dimitri was becoming increasingly unhappy with some of the marketing people who kept him busy making samples that he knew would not be accepted. He felt that much of his time was being wasted and wanted to get out and become his own boss. He'd made some wonderful sparkling wine out of pineapple 'mill juice concentrate,' and considered moving to Hawaii where he could get a steady source of pineapple juice for wine. After several more months, he took a position with Bodegas de Santo Tomas Winery in Ensenada, Mexico. There, he could make the pineapple champagne as well as making standard table wines. As a side business, he began making pineapple champagne in a partnership on Maui. I visited him at both locations several times over the next few years.

---

[11] The Davies family still owns and operates Schramsberg today. Their story is told in Jim Conaway's book *Napa*, his extensive chronicle of the area and its wine culture pre-1980.

Dimitri called me one day about a month after moving to Ensenada. He asked me to send him a case of Gallo Paisano, which was a very popular table wine made from Zinfandel grapes. I said, "Sure, I'll get it out today as industry samples, but tell me one thing. What's it for?" His answer surprised me at first because I knew Santo Tomas was making some well-accepted wines for the Mexican market. He told me he was trying to clean up the winery. He wanted to improve their sanitation practices, but was having trouble showing why he wanted them to sterilize hoses, pumps and tanks more often. He had told them they would make better wine if sanitation was improved and the wines would contain less volatile acidity (VA), another name for vinegar. Their lack of sanitation was causing their wines to have too much VA content. He wanted to show them what it would taste like, but was unable to find any Santo Tomas wine that had truly low VA. He wanted the Paisano to exemplify what wine would taste like if they would make it cleaner and without noticeable volatile acidity.

I laughed along with the other lab people when we heard what Dimitri was up to. It reminded me of trying to understand why some Greeks actually like a wine they make called Retsina. Retsina is aged in pine wood barrels (instead of oak), and after a short time in those barrels, the wine tastes (at least to me) like turpentine. I think it is truly awful, but the wine sells well in Greece. The explanation, given to wine tasting classes, is that humans will eventually get used to almost any flavor, even Retsina. Obviously, people can also get used to the taste of excessive volatile acidity in table wines.[12]

Big Transitions

After Dimitri left Gallo in 1962, Charlie asked me to take over new product development. Following suggestions from Albion Fenderson and Howard Williams, I made several additional flavored wines. One product was called Champion's Belt (so named by Howard Williams), which Gallo had test-

---

[12] VA is used by the Bureau of Alcohol, Tobacco and Firearms as an index of bacterial spoilage, since it is produced by bacterial spoilage of wine in the presence of air.

marketed in Memphis, Tennessee. Both Ernest and Howard liked the wine a lot, but it failed miserably in that market. The wine emulated a Whiskey Sour in that it contained nearly 21% alcohol, and had a strong whiskey-like oak flavor combined with lemon. It had the highest alcohol content of all the wines Gallo ever produced. The federal legal limit for wine was 21%, and Champion's Belt was barely under that limit. Howard suggested that he had made a mistake in test-marketing the product in Memphis, a strong whiskey area, but Ernest may have had his own reasons for the experiment. Al Fenderson was surprised that Gallo had pissed off the whiskey people, almost on purpose, but Ernest sometimes did exactly that. The tax on wine, even at 21% alcohol, was considerably less than the tax on whiskey, and Gallo was taking advantage of that little quirk in the law. Al figured it was Ernest's way of flipping the finger at the liquor people; I was never sure, but suspected he was right.

This was a difficult wine to taste and especially difficult to assess how it would affect whiskey sour drinkers. Ernest really wanted to know and made an interesting proposal. He asked that I make new samples of Champion's Belt to share with him and Julio the next Saturday morning with no one else present. I remember that morning very clearly. Ernest and Julio came in, and Ernest told us that we had to swallow the wines this time, instead of spitting them out after tasting. He thought we could not effectively evaluate this particular wine without swallowing. Never before had we done any tasting in which the tasters swallowed the wines.

Ernest and Julio began tasting and swallowing, and it became a race against alcohol. I swallowed some with them that morning, but held back because I had already taken samples home for tasting with swallowing a few nights earlier. Each of us wanted to make an evaluation of the overall taste and acceptability of the wine before the alcohol we'd consumed ruined our ability to judge the smell, taste and mouthfeel properly. Within thirty minutes, both Ernest and Julio were red-faced and animated while talking rapidly. I was trying to write notes of their reactions to the taste, but that got more difficult because they began talking at the same time. "I like the lemon flavor level. It might be a little sweet, though. This wine is damn good. I think this one will go over better in the north than in the southern states." It was all I could do to remember what they said and get it down on paper before they came up with new comments. Mostly, I was hoping I could read my own writing later. Both ended up thinking that the flavor balance was exactly right for that product. After a while, Julio put his arm around my shoulder and said, "Pete,[13] you've done a hell of a good job with this one, but I've got to get home. Now you be careful driving home, will you?" I promised to do that if they'd be careful too. The last I saw of them that day, Julio and Ernest were supporting one another, each had one arm around the other's waist as they went, in step, down the long, wide stairs from the lab to the offices below. Their big powerful Cadillacs, Ernest's metallic green and Julio's metallic blue, were just outside, and I was a little worried about each of them driving home alone. I was sure the alcohol effect could only get worse, not better.

Ernest was known for fast driving through town even when absolutely sober. I had ridden with him twice, when Howard Williams and I joined him for lunch to discuss a new product idea. I will never forget those rides. Ernest was so interested in the conversations that he rifled through red lights while talking and driving on the short trip to Minnie's Chinese Restaurant. God only knew how he would drive home on that morning. I knew I could make it OK because I hadn't swallowed nearly as much as either of them and had only a low-speed Chevy station wagon. I stayed long enough to clean up, put the samples away and continue writing notes of their comments in my notebook. It was Monday morning before I knew that they had both made it home safely. I called Dimitri on Sunday, just to tell him about the experience. It was a very enjoyable phone call for both of us, and I still laugh about it from time to time. Neither Julio nor Ernest ever mentioned that tasting to me again.

Within a week or two, the winery bottled the new batch with a new label. This time Howard named the product Sporting Wine, and it was to be test-

---

[13] Julio always called me "Pete," but was the only person in the wine industry ever to do so. It had been a common nickname of mine in college and the Marine Corps, except when there were two Petersons present; then I was "R.G."

marketed in Indianapolis. Again it failed to meet their minimum sales rate so, disappointing as it was, the whole idea had to be abandoned. Julio figured the whiskey people had torpedoed the test markets, but Ernest told us that the market for high-alcohol pop wines may have been fizzling out even while Twister was in the market. "There's only so much we can do with flavors," he said. "Let's concentrate on table wines from now on." After that, new products tended to be made with lower alcohol.

We now know that the whole U.S. market was in transition, but no one recognized how big the transition was at the time. The five-decade boom in dessert wine sales was collapsing while table wine sales were (unaccountably) growing rapidly. It was exactly the change that traditional table wine lovers had been hoping for. Gallo Glass had noticed the change only shortly after Ernest Gallo had, as orders for table wine glass started booming while those for dessert wine glass slackened. Bob Gallo, Julio's son and the glass plant manager, asked me what was going on at the winery; I told him we were moving away from alcoholic flavored wine products towards lower-alcohol wines. The shift explained why the winery had reduced its orders for dessert glass designs, but I did not know that regular (non-flavored) table wines were undergoing a new surge on their own. For no recognizable reason, traditional table wine sales began to surge in 1960, and only Ernest Gallo, alone in the entire industry, knew it ahead of time.

This example of Ernest Gallo's perfect timing was only one of several times I watched him show his uncanny 'feel' for the wine market. I have met no one else who had that extraordinary market touch. Even so, it took another few years before total Gallo sales of table wines passed up their sales of dessert wines for good. The term pop wine was not in use publicly, but we had said it privately during our last two years of marketing high-alcohol, sweet-flavored wines. In about 1966, after Gallo had stopped experimenting with those wines, a new wine company appeared on the scene, using the term 'pop wine' for their own trademark with great fanfare. I don't remember a single wine they attempted to market that was a success. The bubble was over, and the pop wine company went bankrupt as quickly as it had appeared. They learned the hard way that there was only so much a winemaker could do with flavor and sugar in a Thompson base wine.

Another transition was more personal. Julio promoted me to assistant production manager for winemaking, and Jim Coleman, Julio's son-in-law, became assistant production manager for bottling and shipping. Julio was planning for future winery growth and decided to separate the two major functions at the winery. I was placed in complete charge of all Gallo winemaking, while Jim was placed in complete charge of bottling and shipping. Charlie would continue to oversee our jobs, but it prepared the company for Charlie's eventual retirement.

The former 'Julio and Charlie tasting panel' for evening approvals added two permanent members, Jim Coleman and me. Everyone knew that Jim had been moving more and more into a production job role and would eventually take over all of Charlie's position. Since Jim was not trained in the science or technology of winemaking, he would rely on me for the next several years. We all knew that Julio wanted us to lighten Charlie's influence a little without threatening him too much.

Charlie Crawford was VP and production manager at Gallo for the ten years I worked there. I reported to him for most personnel issues and always kept him informed when I worked directly for Ernest or Julio. I had first met him in May 1958, when Professor Joslyn and I visited to explore Bouthilet's new Gallo research lab. We had talked for a considerable period of time that day, discussing winery operations, history, goals and future direction. I could see that Charlie was in charge and that he admired Bouthilet a great deal, but I had also sensed some jealousy, fear or apprehension on his part. I thought Charlie suspected that Bouthilet might take his job, and Charlie was going to be sure to maintain his authority. My impression on that day in 1958 turned out to be pretty accurate.

I learned early on that Charlie suspected that everyone at Gallo was out to get his job. Fortunately, that did not mean that he was difficult to work with or for. In fact, he was usually very pleasant, and I got along with him quite well for the years I worked there. Our families went skiing together in winter and water skiing in summer. We knew his wife (Sallie) and kids (Bob and Judy) like family. The truth is, I never met anyone that I thought could have done his job better than Charlie, and he need not have worried so much about being replaced. He walked his tightrope very well. It was a primary function of Charlie's to explain to Ernest and Julio exactly what was going on in the plant at all times. That was sometimes difficult because we did many things that were far more technical than either of them cared to understand fully.

Charlie tended to oversimplify to the point of not telling them the whole truth, or sometimes actually making up stories. That got him into trouble. I spent a great amount of time with Julio and enjoyed being around him, but I would not have wanted Charlie's job in a million years. I told that to Charlie regularly, especially after Julio promoted me, over Charlie's foot-dragging, only a few years after I began working there. I was involved in so many different projects, it would have been difficult to come up with a single title to cover all the bases. I was given new titles from time to time, but would have preferred the old, more concise title of winemaking director or research coordinator. I always kept one thought in my mind about Charlie: I could enjoy working for him, but should not always believe what he told me. It was an open secret among winemakers that, if a problem appeared, you could bet somebody other than Charlie would be blamed. Fortunately, both Julio and Ernest knew that about him, and I thought the whole operation worked very well. I recognized the superb management capabilities in both Ernest and Julio many times, as they got the most out of their employees while not dwelling on faults.

The older lab guys, Lou Stern and Norm Braskat, had more difficulty in covering their feelings about Charlie. Both had dutifully gone into the Army when WW II broke out. Both told me that by staying out of the service and in Modesto, Charlie guaranteed that he would be their boss at Gallo after the war ended. That had not been the case when the war began. Charlie had been at Gallo only two years when the war started. He graduated from UC Davis in 1939 in the same five-student class as Louis P. Martini. Charlie was to be drafted as well, but managed to get deferred with two claims: first, he said he had a bad back. I never saw evidence of that in all of the skiing and water sports we did together between 1958 and 1968. Charlie was the first skier on the mountain, and the last off the hill at the end of the day. You wouldn't call him a football player, but he certainly didn't have a problem with any kind of physical activity.

The second thing that apparently kept him safe at home was more complicated. Just before WW II, there had been a glut of wine all over California as too much dessert wine had been produced in the 1930s. The public simply couldn't drink all that wine, and it was collecting in tanks everywhere. Gallo had as big a problem as any other producer, even though Ernest was undoubtedly better at selling than most of his competitors. When the U.S. was suddenly thrust into war, the government purchasers started looking around for large supplies of ethyl alcohol. Alcohol was a possible fuel for torpedoes, and the wineries of California were sitting on many, many gallons of it. Gallo had distillation stills that were built for the purpose of making brandy (95% pure alcohol). Suddenly the industry found a way out of its wine glut. Not only would the Gallo Winery distill all its excess wine to make alcohol to sell to the government, but it would agree (for a price) to distill the wines from other wineries as well.

Lou told me that Charlie had taken advantage of this by going to the government agencies and convincing them that his position at Gallo was 'necessary to the war effort.' He told them he was a manager of distillation and was responsible for distilling wine to make the alcohol that the government now needed. When Lou and Norm returned after the war, Charlie was fully in charge of the winery as production manager, having worked at Gallo throughout the war years. Lou Stern died in his late fifties or early sixties, as did Norm Braskat. I heard that story only from them, but they also told it to many others. Both seemed a little bitter about it, so I think there had to be some truth in what they shared.

Table Wine Pizzazz

In the tasting lab one day, Ernest said, "There's a place in the market for a light pink table wine that I want to sell with the name Pink Chablis." That was a typical Ernest idea because it flew in the face of convention. The Chablis region of France had never been known for producing pink wines; by definition, Chablis was a white wine. Everybody agreed that we could make such a wine, and the job was given to Guido Crocci, the regular winemaker for pink table wines. Guido put together a beautiful blend of Grenache with a little Chenin Blanc. Our panel liked it, Julio liked it, and it was sent to Ernest, who approved it. Charlie bottled a small tank, and it went to the test market. It did not sell, and Ernest sent it back to the lab asking us to "correct whatever is wrong." Julio's panel of four tasted it over and over, and none of us could find anything wrong with the wine. The color was attractive and it was delicate, well-balanced and easy to drink. I wondered whether it was the name that was wrong and not the blend; maybe the name Pink Chablis was confusing to the customer. That was a decision for Ernest's department, not Julio's, so I kept my mouth shut and concentrated on tasting. I thought maybe we could solve the problem by making the wine dramatically different. It was a nice wine, but it didn't have pizzazz. "Well, how do we put pizzazz in this wine?" Julio asked. I suggested doing something unexpected, "I'd like to see what happens if we carbonate this wine just a little."

Julio's ears perked up, and he asked, "You mean change the tax class of the wine?" I answered, "No, not at all. I wouldn't make it a sparkling wine. Ernest wants a table wine. I just want to put in a little CO_2 to make it bubble slightly, not a lot. This is a terrific wine as it is, but I think a touch of CO_2 would give it pizzazz." Julio liked the idea, and Charlie agreed that it could be done on the regular bottling line. Charlie scheduled the next bottling which went off with only one hitch – Julio forgot to tell Ernest what we had done. Ernest was busy and hadn't tasted the wine before it was shipped to the test market. Sales exploded immediately. The sales people noticed the small amount of carbonation. It was not champagne, but it had a nice 'spritz.'

The distributor called Ernest to tell him how pleased he was with Gallo carbonating the Pink Chablis. Ernest denied that the wine was carbonated, but the distributor insisted. Ernest was embarrassed, which was just about the worst thing anyone could do to him. He stormed into Julio's office, slammed the door shut and screamed, "Did you carbonate that wine?" Julio said, "Yes, a little. Is it better now?" "That's not the point!" Ernest yelled. "You're my brother and you embarrassed me, you sonofabitch." Julio told him they'd both been busy, adding, "I forgot to tell you, Ernest. We don't usually tell you how we make any of our wines. That's my area. Your area is sales." Ernest said, "In this case, I should have known because the change you made was so big. The market expected me to know what we did, for Christ's sake. I should have known. That distributor thinks I lied to him when I didn't." Julio told Ernest he would call the distributor himself and tell him that Ernest hadn't known about the carbonation. Only then did Ernest calm down a little. He told Julio that the lively Pink Chablis was now a big success and the distributor loved it. "I plan to take it nationwide as soon as possible," he said, and Julio told him we were ready.

Ernest sat down and they started talking like the partners they had always been. "Whose idea was it to carbonate that wine?" Ernest asked. "Pete's," Julio answered. After Ernest left, Julio called Charlie and said he was giving me a raise. Charlie told him he'd just given me a raise two months before, but Julio said, "Give him another hundred a month." Julio asked me to come to his office where he told me the whole story. He was smiling as he told it, and said he thought Ernest was going to suffer a stroke when he first started yelling. "I've never seen him so mad," he said. "It was my fault for embarrassing him." I thanked Julio for the raise and went back to the lab upstairs. I took a bottle of Pink Chablis home for dinner that night.

Personalities

I enjoyed working with Bob Bouthilet, at least for the first year or so. After awhile it became difficult for any of us in the lab to know whether he was telling a true story or just making big talk. There was nothing at all malicious about Bob, it's just that he was hard to handle sometimes. He had 100 ideas every day, and perhaps only a couple were brilliant. The others were of no value at all. He had gotten his PhD from the University of Minnesota, actually doing some graduate work at UC Berkeley under Professor Joslyn. He then finished his degree back in Minnesota – his thesis work was on chicken flavor, especially in developing and perfecting an improved flavor for chicken soup. To my academic point of view, I assumed that meant he was isolating the natural components of chicken flavor, identifying them chemically, and then maybe trying to accentuate some components synthetically so that he could make an enhanced and more refined flavor of what people would call 'chicken soup.'

I could not have been more wrong. His approach was more applied, more practical and it demonstrated Bouthilet's pizzazz. He looked at chicken soup, canned or fresh, and figured out where the flavor was located. Chicken soup, like many other foods, has two distinct phases: oil (or fat) and water. Chicken broth always has a thin layer of fat floating on the top of an aqueous phase below. If you take a sip of the aqueous phase, you will find that it is salty, but really doesn't have much chicken flavor. The fat layer, on the other hand, tastes a lot like chicken, so Bouthilet realized the flavor is mostly fat soluble and not water soluble. His process involved extracting the fatty portion of boiled chicken carcasses and adding a certain amount of this fat into each can of soup as part of the recipe. Because an obvious fat layer floating on top of the water portion in soup would be unsightly, he added an emulsifier to keep the fat layer thoroughly mixed into the water phase, and presto! He had a can of soup with better taste and without any unappealing layer of fat floating on top.

One day I noticed a can of Swanson's chicken soup sitting on the lab counter. It had been there for several weeks and finally I asked Bouthilet what it was. "Oh," he said, "My chicken soup process is in operation, and that is the first can off the production line. They gave it to me when they started using my process." I went over and picked the can up, turned it over and did a double-take. It had a Safeway sticker with a price stamp attached to the bottom of the can! I almost laughed and had to leave the laboratory quickly so he would not see my facial expression.

Gas chromatography was an exciting field at this time, and Bouthilet was friendly with many of the up-and-coming gas chromatograph builders.[14] He bought a gas chromatograph for the lab, one of the first used in the wine industry. Ion exchange was also a big subject by then, and ion exchange for wine stabilization had been installed as a production process at Gallo a year or two prior. Karel Popper, one of the most distinctive personalities

---

[14] Gas chromatography was a relatively new laboratory method for separating tiny amounts of flavor components from a mixture to identify and quantify them.

in the research lab, specialized in ion exchange. However, he got new ideas every few minutes and anything he wanted to do at any time seemed to be all right with Bouthilet.

Karel Popper was a truly unique individual. Born in Czechoslovakia, English was not his first language. Karel's difficult accent, along with a slight speech impediment and natural tendency to mumble, made him particularly hard to understand. Neither Ernest nor Julio had been able to have a conversation with him, despite his seven years of working for them. Karel often appeared to mumble to himself, but then he would look at you expecting an answer, so you knew he had been speaking to you. People often looked at me quizzically when Karel said something to them. After a while I started paying attention and translating for Karel; that's when I finally began to understand some of what he said.

Karel had dark hair with a regular haircut except that the hair on top was always an inch too long. The sides of his head were closely cut, but the hair on top was so long that large crops of it often fell to one side or the other. He was always brushing long hair out of his face, even though his hair was never too long on the sides or back of his head. Dimitri once suggested that Karel's current (third) wife, Aase (pronounced Oh - suh), must be placing a large bowl on his head and then shaving off everything under the bowl. We never knew.

One day, Karel had a particularly weird idea. He leaned back, face beaming, and announced that, "In theory, I could manufacture metallic sodium by boiling off the mercury from a mercury sodium amalgam." It appeared that he'd suddenly had one of those 'bursts of genius' we'd come to expect from him. He asked Bob to order some sodium amalgam, and I don't know why, but Bob did. When it arrived, Karel poured it into a flask, lit a large burner under it and started to boil off the mercury. Karel mumbled to nobody in particular that this major breakthrough would supply us with pure sodium metal. I asked whether he knew that metallic sodium is highly explosive and very dangerous, especially when hot, and he mumbled, "Of course." Somebody else asked why anyone in a winery would want pure sodium metal. Billy Joe Williams, lab bacteriologist, asked him if he understood the dangers of mercury vapor, and Karel's answer to the whole room was that Billy Joe must not have noticed that the apparatus was in the laboratory hood. The whole lab knew that the lab hood was rickety and leaked like a sieve. It may have kept some of the mercury vapor inside, but certainly not all. The hood was also located at the exact spot in the lab that was directly above Ernest's desk on the first floor below. We had discovered that weeks earlier, when some chemical liquid had leaked through the floor and dripped onto Ernest's desk. Bob Bouthilet had put his ass on the line when he went humbly into Ernest's office to apologize. I told Karel that it would be nice if Bob didn't have to do that again.

Billie Joe looked at Karel's experiment, shook his head and said with a grin, "Karel, I don't believe this is going to work, but I sure am rootin' for ya." I liked Billy Joe's sense of humor, but this experiment was so dangerous that it really was not funny. Karel thought that Billy Joe was making fun of what he thought was a stupid idea, but Karel felt sure it would become a major breakthrough. I don't think Karel spoke to Billy Joe for a few days afterward. Karel was curious and probably showing off a little, but it was an absurd thing to try, especially since it was possible that Ernest could get involved. Nevertheless, Karel got this extremely dangerous distillation going and was lucky to get it stopped before he killed us all in the process.

One person I spent a great amount of time with was Don Sanford. Originally, Don was in charge of the analytical lab and was also one of the winemakers. Shortly after I went to work at Gallo, he told me that he had been a P-38 pilot in the Army Air Corps near the end of WW II. I told him I was still pissed that the Marine Corps had repeatedly postponed sending me to Naval Aviation School. Eventually I had given up, resigned my commission, transferred to the inactive Marine Corps Reserve and gone to graduate school at UC Berkeley. Don was still flying in the Army National Guard and flew both airplanes and helicopters out of Stockton field, only 30 miles away. He offered to take me up in both, on the weekend. I met the unit commander, Lt. Col. Bob Stimson, who told me that if I could take a leave of absence from my job at Gallo, he could send me to both fixed-wing and rotary-wing flight schools in the Army. I spoke to Julio about it and then transferred from the Marine Reserve into the Army National Guard

49th Aviation Company in Stockton, California. About a year after joining Gallo, I took my leave of absence and went to the Army flight school at Ft. Rucker, Alabama. At Julio's request, I timed my absence from Gallo so as not to miss any of the grape harvest season. The happy result was that I became an Army pilot and flew Army airplanes and helicopters from 1959 until 1970 – mostly on weekends and for two-week summer camps while being employed full-time at Gallo.

Several times in the ensuing summers, Sanford and I took two L–19 airplanes to the high sierra mountains, making parachute resupply drops to various Boy Scout units who were camping in the high country above Yosemite National Park. The scout mothers had packed the parachute containers with popcorn, steaks, soft drinks, an occasional sweater, and some beer for the scoutmasters. It was tricky flying; the air was thin, and winds were both high and unpredictable, but we had to make the drops close to the scouts to be effective. When we could not see signs on the ground to indicate wind direction, one of us would drop down closer to the trees, while the other watched as each of us made our drops. It was fun flying, very educational and good army training. The Boy Scouts loved us. Other times, Don and I went panning for gold in the lower sierras by helicopter. We looked for sandbars in the Gold Country rivers that were hard to get to on foot. We figured there might be gold there, assuming no one could have been panning at that location before. It was easy to drop in by helicopter and land on a sandbar, but we always got skunked, finding gold dust but no nuggets. We finally realized that the forty-niners lived all over those hills during the Gold Rush days and had not missed any of the serious gold-bearing spots.

Most of my friends were in Julio's side of the winery because we worked together. Employees in Ernest's side of the business tended to be friends with each other and did not know many on our side. A few exceptions stand out in my memory. Besides Gallo's sales and marketing VPs, Albion Fenderson and Howard Williams, I had several other friends on Ernest's side: Legh Knowles, Dick Maher and Charlie Rossi were salesmen working for him. All became my good friends, although I had not worked with them on projects at Gallo; they were outgoing and loved to chat over coffee in the break room. Legh Knowles had been in the music business in a big way. He had played first trumpet in the famous Glen Miller Orchestra during WW II, but wanted to get into a business where he would get stronger, instead of weaker, as he aged. He told me that could never happen in any orchestra, where drinking all night (and wearing out early) is the norm. He left the music business to work with the Wine Advisory Board of The Wine Institute before going to the Gallo sales department. He was a terrific salesman, but left when he was offered the job of sales manager for Beaulieu Vineyard in their San Francisco office. I knew of course, that Andre Tchelistcheff, Dimitri's father, was the winemaker at Beaulieu in Rutherford, Napa Valley.

Charlie Rossi, an outgoing and well-liked salesman, was heading up sales for one of the many Gallo brands at the time we finished developing the Gallo champagne. Julio chose one of the blends that Dimitri had perfected originally and had kept 'on the shelf' for a few years until Gallo marketing was ready for a new product. George Thoukis became head of sparkling wine production, and David Gallo, Ernest's oldest son, worked on marketing it for several years. David tested several brand names: Andre de Montcourt, Andre, Carlo and others before settling on Red Mountain. Sales went slowly at first, and someone told Ernest that the product needed to be more personal; he needed a person's name to associate with Red Mountain to get people's attention. They looked at dozens of made-up names and finally settled on Carlo Rossi's Red Mountain. It sold better than before, but Ernest was still not satisfied. He kept changing the name and finally dropped Red Mountain altogether.

The product had been selling so-so until Charlie Rossi was transferred from another brand to become the Carlo Rossi brand manager. As he was traveling around, it was natural for Charlie to start introducing himself as 'Carlo Rossi.' He had such an infectious personality and had such fun acting like Carlo that it was catching on. Gallo filmed him for a Carlo Rossi TV ad in which he was asked on camera whether he liked talking about Carlo Rossi Champagne. He said, "I like talking about it, but I like drinking it better," then broke into a natural laugh. His affable personality shone through, and history was made. Charlie Rossi actually became 'Carlo Rossi' for the public, and sales soared. I last saw Charlie at Andre Tchelistcheff's memorial ceremony in Napa in 1993. I had a nice visit with him because we hadn't seen each other for several months after he got busy selling champagne. Charlie Rossi died only a few months later.

Oak Chip Espionage

A key function of Gallo research was to produce less costly methods and processes for making wine. One of the more important projects was extracting flavor from oak chips that would make wine taste as if it had been aged in oak barrels. Chips were a by-product from making whiskey barrels and furniture, and were just thrown away or used on the floors of butcher shops. Barrels, on the other hand, were very expensive, so we had to at least try to find a shortcut for oak flavor; the project would be worth money, if we could do it. No one in the industry was using oak chips, and we knew that it could become a big business if we could come up with a method that would work well for using them. I studied the chemistry of oak chips, evaluating catechin, quercetin, other tannin components and lignin that exists in wood, but got nowhere and put the books back on the shelf.

Bouthilet spent little time on it, but he came up with what we now know to be the right answer. Instead of from a scientific viewpoint, he used his practical, empirical method. Bouthilet's approach was to soak some oak chips in wine and then taste the wine. That worked well from the start with dessert wines. Most dessert wines, especially sweet dessert wines, took on a nice oaky flavor when chips were soaked in the wine for a few days, and we did it across the board for nearly all dessert wines. With table wines it was different; sometimes the soaking worked well, sometimes it did not. Bouthilet started smelling and tasting various oak chip treatments as did I, Dimitri, and Karel Popper. Bouthilet thought the very large chips made a different flavor than the smaller chips, but none of us could pin this down exactly. We ended up believing that the larger chips made the same flavor, but less of it. The smaller chips produced more flavor.

As Bob Bouthilet smelled and tasted oak chips, he made a startling discovery. He said there was a difference from one chip to another but couldn't figure out why. He did notice that every time he smelled chips after they had been treated with a strong SO_2 solution, the oak smelled and tasted better than others. He did some direct comparisons by comparing untreated oak chips with chips that had been washed with SO_2 water, and always liked the SO_2 treated chips better. Most of the rest of us thought he was nuts, because SO_2 gas is well-known to have a pungent 'burning matches' smell and taste. SO_2 gas is mean stuff, and it can burn the inside of your nose badly if you aren't careful to sniff gingerly. "How could that taste good?" we asked him. "I don't know, but it does taste better," he insisted.

He set up some Petri dishes with glass covers, and put oak chips in all of them. Then he poured a small amount of SO_2 water into some, but not others. The next day, each of us went by sniffing and tasting the chips. Bouthilet was 100% correct. The treated chips tasted much better than untreated chips, and the good samples seemed to have exactly the kind of 'sweet and vanilla' oak flavor that we wanted in the wines. We didn't smell free SO_2 on the chips at all. All the excess SO_2 had entered the wood or blown away overnight. We were now smelling oak chips after they'd been modified by the SO_2 treatment, and the result was quite good.[15]

Suddenly, we had a process for using oak chips. All we had to do was allow the SO_2 to soak into the wood and dissipate, and the wine would take on the pronounced kind of oakiness we wanted. Bouthilet's theory was that as the SO_2 soaked into the wood structure, it dissolved a little of the wood at the surface of each chip. Since lignin fibers in oak are polymers of vanillin, any that break down would release a little vanilla flavor. Other components of the wood break into molecules having a nice oak barrel taste. The combination was exactly what we wanted. We decided that he probably knew what he was talking about this time, and everybody was impressed. There was no question about the experiment; his treated oak

---

[15] Wineries routinely poured SO_2 water into barrels and closed the bung if those barrels were not going to be used for a few months, as the barrels could be a source of bacterial spoilage if not so treated. When there was a more serious infection, barrel warehousemen blasted a shot of raw SO_2 gas from a small tank into each barrel.

chips gave the wines a very, very good flavor. As before, we all agreed not to tell any competitors in the industry about this. I quietly put my textbooks away, because Bouthilet's intuition had trumped boring old chemistry. The textbooks would never have gotten us anywhere.

The Gallo purchasing department bought a few tons of oak chips from a guy in Oakland and started looking for other sources. We got samples from several dealers at widely varying prices, and Dimitri and Karel both started making wine extracts from the different lots of chips. Unfortunately, no two extracts were alike, even though all samples were treated with Bouthilet's high SO_2 soaking process. Oak chips varied all over the place, but none of us could figure out exactly why. Some had very good flavor, while others were rather paper-like, unpleasant and not at all what we wanted. The best chips came from Tony Baird, a supplier in Oakland, but Baird's price was sky high. He seemed to sense how badly Gallo wanted his chips, and with that in mind, threatened to raise the price even higher.

Julio liked to bargain with people in anything he bought or sold, so he jumped into the fray. He called Tony Baird personally and tried his best to get the price down. The amount of wine we wanted to treat was huge, and we needed many, many tons of good chips. Even with the promised high volumes, Baird was adamant in keeping his price high and wouldn't budge. Bouthilet called him as well, but got nowhere, except for beginning a discussion on exactly how Baird was treating his chips. Baird told Bouthilet that he was making his own chips with his beautiful new stainless steel wood-chipping 'hog' that had to be set just right to get the best flavors out of the chips. He claimed he was buying the best premium Arkansas oak that had to be chipped exactly right in his hog. Bouthilet told him that he had grown up in Minnesota and thought Minnesota oak would be preferable to Arkansas. Tony said he could get Minnesota oak, but at a higher price. We heard Bouthilet's side of the phone conversation from the lab and could tell which way the conversation was going. Karl Popper mumbled to me that the flies on the wall must have enjoyed listening to the two best bullshitters around trying to one-up and out-maneuver each other.

All this negotiation went on for many days. Gallo's purchasing department kept shelling out for Baird's oak chips at up to $300 per ton, and Bouthilet and Julio Gallo kept fuming that wood chips are a by-product and should sell for cheap. How could we let the guy do this to us? Julio called Tony Baird a junk dealer, which was pretty accurate; he just bought and sold anything he could buy and sell at whatever prices he could get. We kept trying oak chips from other sources, but the flavors weren't as good. According to purchasing, most of the sources were selling chips to butcher shops by the fifty-pound bag. Baird wouldn't tell Bouthilet whether he toasted the chips, heated them slightly or actually charred them. He refused to talk about any of that. All he said was that his process was secret, that Baird's were the best oak chips in the world, and that they were useful for flavors in wines. We knew he hadn't charred the chips; we could see that they weren't charred. They looked just like odds and ends of chipped oak wood, with nothing special in their appearance.

I was talking to Charlie Crawford about it one day and brought him one of my very best ideas. I told Charlie that the next time Gallo sent a truck to Oakland for another load of oak chips, I wanted to do some industrial spying. I knew machinery, since my first degree was in chemical engineering, I didn't look very old (I was 28, but could have passed for 21), I knew what a wood hog looked like, had used many types of equipment and thought I would be able to tell exactly what Tony Baird was doing if I could just get in to look around. Charlie thought it was a wonderful idea. He'd get me in the truck as a worker and leave it up to me how I handled things at the plant.

One of the most enjoyable days of my life ensued. To prepare, I didn't shave for three days; it took that long for my beard to start showing because it was light and kind of reddish-blonde, the same color as my skin. I wore gloves and old clothes like a regular worker, and got in the truck with a driver who'd picked up chips before. The Gallo truck driver didn't know who I was or anything about me; we'd kept my mission secret so as to avoid the risk of his inadvertently giving me away. Baird had never seen me before; I was simply 'the labor' to help the driver load bags of chips onto the truck. When we drove in, Tony Baird met us at the gate. He looked us over, but didn't say anything to me; I kept my mouth shut and looked at the ground, trying to look dumb. The driver said, "I've got to pick up some oak chips. Where do you want me to go?"

Baird walked around our large flatbed truck, looking inside and then opened the gate to let us drive in. He directed the driver to a big stack of chips in bags, saying, "These are your bags, load them up." I got out and we started loading. We worked up a pretty good sweat, loading for maybe an hour without saying anything – just minding our own business and stacking fifty-pound bags onto the truck. Tony Baird stood watching us do the loading for nearly all that time, but finally went inside. When we had the truck about half loaded, the driver asked if I wanted to take a break, and I said, yes, I would like a Coke or something else to drink. We went over and asked one of Baird's workers where the Coca-Cola machine was, then went to get a drink. We were standing there when Tony Baird came out and wanted to know why we had stopped. The driver explained that it was heavy work loading the bags, so we'd stopped for a cold drink. Tony Baird nodded and started to go back in to his office, so I asked him where the men's room was. He pointed me down the hall into another area. That was my chance. He went back into the office, and I went further inside to a work area. I looked around, spotting the men's room, but I did not go in. I looked around for equipment, but did not see a wood-chipping hog anywhere. In fact, I didn't see any equipment at all.

There was a block of five or six cyclone separators for separating dust from chips, but nothing else. I spotted a railroad siding where railcars came in, and I noticed a 6- or 8-inch diameter corrugated plastic hose used to blow wood chips around by air. It looked like they were unloading chips from railcars by sucking the chips out of the railcar with air – much like a king-size vacuum cleaner. The other end of the large hose went up to the top of what had to be a cyclone dust separator. It was high up above a funnel that channeled the chips down to a bagging machine where paper bags were filled with chips and then sewn shut. The dust had its own channel, and I could see that the chips and dust were bagged in separate areas. Each 'bagger/sewing machine' was operated by an individual worker. Baird sold bags of chips to us and probably sold the dust to supermarkets and butcher shops for use on their floors. There was no other equipment or machinery.

I concluded that the guy was simply separating chips from sawdust and selling both products separately to different customers according to demand.

I made another trip to the restroom just before we left and looked around again. There was nothing else going on in those buildings. This time, I went over to the open railcar and looked inside. Sure enough, there was nothing in there but loose oak chips filling the whole rail car from floor to ceiling. I found a bill of lading attached to the door from the National Distillers Company in Memphis. That had to be the source of their chips.

I was tired, but very excited when I got back to the winery late that afternoon. I went right to Charlie Crawford's office and told him what I'd found. I said, "They're not using any wood hog, there's no process of any kind going on there; they're simply getting loose oak chips in railroad box cars from National Distillers, unloading by air suction, using a blower system with cyclone separators to separate the chips from the dust, sewing the dusted chips into bags, and selling them to us. He probably sells the dust to butcher shops. It's as simple as that." Charlie laughed for twenty minutes and we both went into Julio's office to relate the story.

I went back to the lab where Karel Popper and Bob Bouthilet were sitting around shooting the bull. I told them what I'd seen and especially what I hadn't seen. I hadn't even finished explaining when Karel interrupted, yelling, "OF COURSE! Strong SO_2 dissolves softwood to make paper and it stinks like hell. You ever visit a paper mill? The SO_2 cannot dissolve chips because they're too big. The dust is easy to dissolve, the chips aren't. Treating oak dust will lead to bad off-flavors; but treating chips will release vanilla, a great flavor." I'd seen him get that sudden flash of genius that Bouthilet so admired several times before, and I knew Karel was right on.

Karel had been exhibiting a surge of sudden, strange impulses lately. Only a week earlier he was at one end of the lab when I was working at a bench at the other end. It was quiet, Karel was sitting there reading, and no one else was in the room. Suddenly, I heard him mumble (a little too loudly), "Jesus, I wish I had a piece of my second wife!" For an instant, I doubted that I had heard him correctly. But I had. I made some stupid comment about maybe you ought to go home early today, and he answered, "You never met my second wife." I answered that I was sorry to have missed her. He said, "Maybe it's best that you didn't know her. We wouldn't be friends today. She'd have tried to run away with you." I said, a little condescendingly, "Karel, it takes two to run away together and I wouldn't be one of them. Whatever happened to her?" "Oh, she ran off with some guy. I never saw her again." I was sorry the conversation had gone that far, but I have laughed about his outburst many times over the years since then.

Before going home that night, I separated some chips from dust using a lab screen and set up some overnight extractions. Next morning I found the expected very nice flavor from the chip portion and a very papery, poorly flavored wine from the dust; another new Gallo process was born. I called National Distiller's in Memphis to arrange a visit to their oak barrel building plant, and went there to see exactly how experts handled oak chips. I wasn't surprised to see that, like Tony Baird, they didn't have any special process either. They were building barrels, mostly for use in aging spirits, but they had sold a few to wineries. They were simply sweeping up dust and chips from the floors at the end of the day and blowing the sweepings into rail cars for shipment out. It was mostly cuttings and various bits and pieces from manufacturing oak whiskey barrels that were left on the floor at the end of a work day. I told them that we preferred to receive less sawdust and more chips in our loads, and the manager said he could steer his workers in that direction. He apparently had dust customers who didn't like chips in their dust, so he would be happy to make as much of an adjustment in that direction as he could. It cost Gallo about $30 a carload (29 tons filled a rail car) as I recall – in contrast to Tony Baird's $300 a ton! I told them they would receive purchase orders from John Wilson or Al Menshew, the Gallo purchasing agents, and that we'd be buying quite a tonnage of chips.

Back in Modesto, I worked with R.L. Nowlin, plant engineer, and Art Caputi, Sr.,[16] maintenance manager, to design and build a new type of wine

---

[16] Art was one of my best friends throughout the years I worked at Gallo (along with his son, Art, Jr.) and the loss was felt by all when Art Sr. got Parkinson's disease and passed away too young.

tank – tank 587. Art Caputi's crew would build much of the structure as doing so would be cheaper than if a contractor did it, and we knew the tank would be better and easier to use. Art did not have a college degree, but he was the best and most accomplished engineer I have ever met. I can't even begin to name all the things he built for Gallo that were perfect for the situation and beautifully designed. Art Caputi Sr. was very much like my Pop, which is a compliment to both of them. We sized Tank 587 to hold one full railcar load of 29 tons of chips without the dust; the tank had to be made of higher-quality 316 stainless steel because of Bouthilet's high SO_2 process. Stainless 316 is more inert chemically – it is not attacked by strong concentrations of SO_2, unlike the cheaper 302 and 304 stainless steels that wineries use for most wine tanks and other equipment.

We built tank 587 standing on stilts to allow a truck to drive under it. It had a cone-shaped bottom half, with a large manhole at the bottom. After extracting the oak flavor from chips, the spent oak chips could be dropped through the manhole into a truck and hauled away easily. By trial-and-error testing in the lab, I found that a seven-mesh screen was the most effective size for quickly removing dust from the chips. Nowlin then mounted a shaker screen above Tank 587 and located the large hose system to move chips from rail cars up and onto the screen. Cellar crews could use suction to pull raw chips from rail cars and move them up and onto the shaker screen. After screening, the dust-free chips would drop into tank 587. We had planned to haul the dust away, but a friendly fight soon developed between Julio, his son Bob, and son-in-law Jim Coleman over who would get the oak dust for their garden. All wanted to spread dust and waste oak chips between shrubs in their gardens, as a ground cover and mulch. Julio told me later that we had done a huge favor for the earthworms; they loved wine-flavored oak chips and multiplied faster than he had ever seen.

After conveying chips into tank 587, it was filled with cream sherry, port, or whatever dessert wine needed oak flavor. After soaking on the oak chips for several days, the wine was drawn off and a second lot of wine re-placed the first. There was so much good flavor in the chips that the cellar crew often got three successive oak extracts from a batch of chips over a three-week period. The extracts were drained into an 'oak concentrate' tank for storage until being used in blends by the winemakers. When a batch of chips was exhausted, the tank was filled with water overnight, then drained the next day to remove any remaining wine from the chips. That diluted wine went to the still for alcohol recovery. Gallo never wasted anything in those days. It was a quick and easy trick to drive an empty dump truck into place under 587, then open the manhole to fill the truck with spent chips for hauling away to family gardens.

Gallo used this process for many years and produced high-quality dessert wines because of it. The process improved many wines and saved the company a great amount of money. We found the flavor of SO_2 treated oak chips to be particularly pleasing in sweet wines, but not so with table wines. The natural bitterness (tannin) of oak extract became exaggerated when combined with high levels of SO_2. That combination was pleasant in sweeter wines, since the sugar covered bitterness very well. However, dry table wines contained nothing to temper the added tannin of high SO_2 oak. Adding oak often spoiled the soft, smooth character of those wines and we had to abandon its use. Gallo table wines were known for having a nice smoothness and soft character, which Julio wanted to preserve, but he would never consider using barrels in the winery because of the horrendous cost of all the necessary hand labor. For a while, we had to avoid the use of oak extract in dry table wines altogether. That had to wait until further experimentation showed that toasting fresh dust-free oak chips to a light brown color could remove much of the harshest tannin. Toasting became the answer.

After the knowledge that Bouthilet's SO_2 discovery would not work for non-sweet table wine, winemakers experimented with toasting fresh oak chips (without SO_2) for perhaps ten years before it became clear that toasted chips could be used to make a wine taste exactly as if the wine had been aged in oak barrels. Once the barrel builders learned the best way to toast chips, the use of chips by wineries exploded. Today, huge tonnages of toasted oak chips, slats, balls and staves (both French and American oak) are used to produce barrel-like oakiness in table wines around the world. Dust continues to be avoided because it always causes a papery off-flavor even without the use of SO_2.

Experimentation

Robert J. Bouthilet had brought a period of great experimentation to Gallo. He fed my incessant desire to produce, deduce and discover, and I loved every minute of it. Except for that one tank of Thompson wine that Dimitri and I made into sherry by adding ammonia for Charlie in 1961, there was never a time when I saw anybody openly break rules of legality in winemaking. Other than that, as far as I know the whole industry ran rigidly 'by the book.' We had numerous projects in the works at all times; many of which never worked out, but all were worthwhile because the good projects easily paid for the whole research effort.

We worked with ion exchange for cold stabilization; Gallo attorneys got two patents issued in my name, but assigned to Gallo, of course. Manny Jaffe was a co-author on one and George Fujii on the other. Manny was the winemaker in charge of Thunderbird and other flavored wines through the early part of the 60's, and George Fujii had been plant manager at the Gallo Fresno plant.[17] He had encountered a labor union problem there – George was a very good winemaker, excellent taster, but also a very rigid individual. He apparently got a bit too authoritative for the union, and they didn't like it, so the only answer for Gallo was to move him back to Modesto. George came back to Modesto to work as a winemaker in the laboratory, a task for which he was very well-suited. He did an excellent job as winemaker for dessert wines over many years.

Many lesser scientific breakthroughs were made in the late 1950s and early 1960s. We worked on chemistry-of-wine-component research, knowing that Julio would never allow our results to be published in scientific journals. I distinctly remember recognizing a flavor component that filled the room with a smell of popcorn after working with a new large-scale gas chromatograph called the Megatherm. The idea was to prepare large enough

---

[17] Gallo's Fresno facility (the old Cribari Winery), even bigger than the Modesto winery, was located near the airport in southeast Fresno. The Fresno plant was a crushing and fermenting winery. All the wines produced there had to be hauled to Modesto to be blended, then bottled, at the Modesto plant.

samples so a significant amount of each flavor component was ejected at the end of a tube. We extracted a great amount of flor sherry with a solvent and concentrated it to about 1 ml of intense flor sherry flavor. When this was injected into the Megatherm, it was not long before the whole laboratory room started smelling exactly like popcorn.

It was very clear what was happening: We smelled pure flavor compounds from flor sherry as they came out of the Megatherm. We found diacetyl, the major flavor component of butter, with chemical homologues[18] like acetyl propionyl, acetyl butryl, dibutryl and so forth. Each homologue had an odor reminiscent of butter, but each one was slightly different from the others. We found and collected more than twenty flavor compounds of that type. I remember that butryl compounds tended to smell like a combination of too-old butter and my Pop's dirty feet after he'd worked all day in the sweaty coal mine. Today's scientist can certainly detect and identify more compounds faster, but there is something about personally recognizing each homologue individually, by nose, that is hard to describe. It's an experience that few chemists take the trouble to enjoy, and I think they are less competent as flavor chemists as a result. I found it fascinating to compare the chemical structure of flavor molecules with what each compound actually smelled like.

I told Professor A. Dinsmore (Dinny) Webb at UC Davis what we had found, as he was the primary professor at Davis who was using gas chromatography to identify flavor components of wine. These homologues were definite components of flor sherry, and nobody was surprised that they were found. Flor sherry does have a butter-like tendency, although it's mostly covered by the predominant piercing smell of acetaldehyde. He told me these compounds had not been reported in the literature before and asked whether I was going to publish it. I said, "No, we aren't allowed to publish by our company, but when you find all those compounds in your research, please go ahead and publish what you find without thinking of

---

[18] Homologues are chemical compounds with similar chemical structure but with different size molecules.

us." I never felt cheated that Julio didn't allow us to publish our discoveries, because that was the business we were in. I've been told that today's Gallo laboratory is even more secretive than it was 'way back when,' but do not know whether that is true. If so, I consider it to be Gallo's business; if the winery pays for the research, it is fair that they own it.

We tested many types of machinery in the winery and those things usually fell into my area. Grapes were always hand-harvested in 1958, but at the Gallo vineyards Ernest and Julio's brother, Joe, was working on a mechanical grape harvester. He built several prototype machines at great expense and had them stenciled with large letters: 'Patent applied for' on multiple sides. My job was to follow the harvesters as they went through several of the Gallo vineyards under test conditions. I kept notes on the plusses and minuses with regard to wine quality, and I reported my feelings on how it was going every day to Julio and Charlie as well as to Art Caputi, Sr. The design was unique, and no other company in the wine industry had yet used this approach.

Each harvester was a giant, self-propelled vacuum cleaner with four large hoses attached to the main tank. At the far end of each hose was a handle which an operator would use to direct the end of the hose towards grapes on the vine. Each machine had a driver and four operators, so that one pass could pick four rows at a time. The vacuum would suck all the grapes from the vine into each hose and convey them through large plastic tubing into the big tank on the main machine. Of course, there was lots of juicing as the grape clusters and individual berries were drawn along the hose towards the tank. It worked well as far as getting all the grapes picked from the vines, but the cloud of dust raised by those giant fans moving all that air was tremendous. They started harvesting early in the morning, and I never had to ask anyone where the experimental pickers were working. I could see where they were from miles away by the mushroom cloud of dust directly above each harvester.

The major problem (and I soon realized it would be insurmountable with this design) was that the vacuum also tended to pull all the leaves off the vines along with the grapes. That didn't hurt the vines, but it was a definite quality issue when all those green leaves became shredded along with the grapes and mixed with the juice. It was impossible to keep the green taste of the leaves from affecting the grape juice (and wine); the resulting wine was impossible to salvage in the winery. The machines were successful in picking the vines clean, but the fact that the machine also picked most of the vine's leaves and mixed them into the fruit eventually killed the design. We did the work only for about a month before everybody gave up.

Other companies were scrambling to try other new designs at the same time. For several years, different harvester designs were being tested in many vineyards around central California. Eventually, the best designs came to the fore, and mechanical grape harvesting became superior to hand harvesting for good reasons. Cost and quality shared the spotlight. Quality was criticized at first, but winemakers began noticing that machine harvesting produced better wines when the harvesting was done at night. Years later, I wrote an article with the title "Tell Me What Time You Pick, and I'll Tell You How Good Your Wine Quality Is." My point was that the fruit gets very hot when picked in daytime, and quality suffers when it takes hours to fill a gondola in the field. Night-time harvesting (which can be done by machine, but not by human pickers) brings the fruit to the winery at cool temperatures, which always makes better wine. Picking by hand misses a large percentage of the grapes. White grapes have a similar color to that of grape leaves and are difficult for tired workers to see at night. Even with black grapes, a large percentage is missed when handpicked. The machines rarely miss any fruit, although early harvester designs tended to lose much of the crop onto the ground because they often removed the fruit from vines a few feet ahead of the harvester.

We tested a huge machine called a diffuser in the Gallo winery at Fresno. A diffuser is designed to extract the sugar from sugar beets by using counter current water flow. The Silver Company from Salt Lake City sent Barney Silver to Gallo for the whole crushing season of 1959, during which time I lived in a motel in Fresno and worked with him to test the approach. We were using the diffuser trying to recover alcohol from grape pomace, as opposed to extracting sugar from beets. Barney and I found that the counter current flow of water extracted alcohol from the pomace quite well, but it lacked the capacity of a small still for removing alcohol from pomace. The diffuser worked, but the economics were better with a still.

I loved running machinery and was fascinated with all the machines we tested. I often did machinery research during grape crushing seasons, but was back in the lab and winemaking for the other ten months. When Julio asked me one day whether I liked doing machinery work in the vineyards, I told him, "Yes, but I do miss inhaling those fruit flies near the fermenters."

Firehouse Research

During this time, I became comfortable with the 'big winery' approach to winemaking, and how to handle the main problems. I also learned to define problems for technical people who were not experienced in winemaking. It occurred to me that I had been misguided, as had Bouthilet, in trying to use the 'pie-in-the-sky' approach of academia for Gallo's research. That would take too long to pay off, if it ever did. He had always said, "Don't let your research department become a firehouse, where all you do is put out fires." However, I came to realize that the kind of research Gallo needed was precisely firehouse research. Gallo had no need for the type of academic research that we brought there when I first arrived in 1958; that is better done at universities. Neither did Gallo have much need for the type of flashy research that Bouthilet brought to the company.

Firehouse research at Gallo was effective, and we paid our way many times over just by solving many costly problems. We introduced new concepts; natural fumaric acid was suggested to us by a food company as a potential acidulant for wine, so we tried it. All the winemakers liked the taste, and none could distinguish its taste from that of tartaric acid (the predominant natural acid in grapes and wine). Its advantage was that it was much cheaper than tartaric acid. Of the many organic acids that occur naturally in fruits, each one has a natural, acidic 'sour' taste, but each also has its own personality. Citric acid tastes like lemons, malic acid tastes like apples or pears and both tartaric and fumaric taste like grapes or wine. Fumaric has a slight disadvantage in that it isn't as soluble as other acids. There was some confusion to using it in the cellar. It dissolved only slowly, and it wasn't obvious to an observer that it really was dissolving – but it always did.

It still tickles me to recall an incident that arose over the matter with Jack Fields, cellar superintendent. Jack was a real loudmouth, antagonistically aggressive to almost everyone he met. Everyone remembered him unpleasantly sooner or later because he was big and loud and tended to bully his way through most encounters. He claimed to have the ability to out-drink everybody else, and he was proud of how he could handle Jack Daniels whiskey. I never doubted him in that, and I never heard anyone have a quiet conversation with him. He hated Charlie Crawford, hated Art Caputi, hated me, and hated all the lab people and all the marketing people. He especially hated anyone who stood up to him, which was about half of us at one time or another. He and Art Caputi Sr. told each other to go f--- himself in loud voices regularly. Jack ruled the unionized cellar people with an iron hand. I assumed this was why Julio kept him in charge of the cellar.

We had tasted fumaric acid in the lab, and Julio liked it when I told him that it was much cheaper than tartaric acid, the natural acid of grapes. I wanted to add fumaric, instead of tartaric, to a tank of wine in the cellar and wrote a work order to do so. I told Jack how much to use in writing and when/how to put it in. Jack Fields had a good method for adding citric or tartaric acid to wine: He placed a 500-gallon tub on the ground beside the huge wine tank and let a little bit of wine run slowly from the tank into the tub (while pumping wine from the tub back into the big tank at the same rate). His crew parked a flatbed truck of citric bags next to the tub, cut open paper bags of citric acid, dumped them, one at a time, into the wine in the tub, and mixed it around.[19] Citric or tartaric acid crystals dissolved immediately in the tub of wine, and the wine being pumped back into the big tank contained the dissolved acid. More wine coming from the tank into the tub would dissolve more acid, and all the acid would quickly end up in the large tank. When using fumaric acid, it didn't look like it was dissolving

---

[19] This is the identical system that Dimitri and I had used to add the bags of ammonium carbonate crystals to Thompson Seedless sherry material back in 1961. The same method is still in general use in commercial wineries today.

as the fumaric acid powder just slurried around in the wine. It got pumped back into the big tank as slurry, and then dissolved on its own (when Jack wasn't looking) during the next hour.

When Jack tried his citric acid addition method with fumaric acid, he thought it didn't work. The fumaric acid powder didn't 'wet' very well, and it sure didn't seem to dissolve in the tub. He screamed bloody murder, raising hell with me at the top of his loudest voice. He said it was going to be a disaster; fumaric acid doesn't dissolve, and it was a stupid-ass Peterson idea. It was one of those lab ideas that we never should have listened to, that Julio should never have allowed, and he was going to have my ass for it, etc, etc, etc. Finally I said, "Jack, the solubility is there. We're only putting in 0.2% and the solubility is 0.3%, so we know it will dissolve. It may not dissolve in the tub, but I guarantee it will dissolve once you get it in the big tank. It WILL dissolve." Jack looked at me like I was crazy. He yelled, "You asshole! That's stupid. You can't tell me it'll dissolve in the tank when it won't dissolve in the tub." I said, "That's exactly what I'm telling you." He said, "Bullshit! You're fuckin' up the wine, we're going to scrape that acid off of the filter tomorrow, and you know where I'm gonna shove it."

I said, "Jack, I'll put $20 on the line, please do what I'm telling you to do, and when you get it in the tank you'll find it dissolves." He said, "I'm going to put that in the tank all right, but I'm going to do it just to cost you your job. I'm going to do it to get rid of you once and for all! We'll put the fumaric acid in that tub, pump it into the tank as a slurry, but then I'm going to filter that fucking tank, and if I find fumaric acid plugging up the filter, that's when I'm going to Julio, and I'm going to have your ass." And I said, "OK, but if you don't find any fumaric acid on the filter, you owe me $20." He nodded very strongly, as if to make the point more violently, but didn't actually say 'okay.' I made a mental note, the SOB ain't gonna pay.

Of course, science was on my side. I knew it would start dissolving once it touched the wine and would be all dissolved in an hour or so. Jack's crew pumped it in one day and filtered it the next day; of course the wine came out perfectly clean, no undissolved powder or crystals on the filter. Wine analysis showed the fumaric acid had dissolved and everything worked out well; the wine tasted exactly right. I did not rub it in and said nothing about it. Jack never mentioned it to me, and I never mentioned it to him, but he knew it had dissolved into the wine, and it grated him. The SOB still owes me $20, and I do not want him ever to repay it, because I want to keep bitching about it forever. I didn't care that I had made a real enemy with that fumaric acid because the enemy was there all along. Jack was not the kind of person who could lose in an ego fight. When he couldn't figure out what had happened to the fumaric acid, it made him boiling mad. He basically declared war from that time on (he had already declared war on most of the lab people anyway). It became a running battle between Jack and everyone else. The fumaric acid brought it to our attention, but fumaric was not the cause of the problem.

Charlie Crawford was always on a tight rope as well. Jack was trying to dump Charlie as much as me or anyone else, and Charlie did an outstanding job of staying above water. He had to do a lot of truth bending and fast talking to get out from under sticky situations, but always survived. Julio didn't understand technology very well, but had seen us do things that were very good for the company. He recognized that Billie Joe's Millipore sterile filtration made a product improvement, my oak chip espionage and Bouthilet's SO_2 process were very useful to the company, and the use of fumaric acid was a good winemaking improvement. All those came out of the research department. He also knew that the various flavored wines all pulled more than their own weight over the years, so he was a cautious believer in what technology could do. He obviously wished Charlie would explain it more clearly when asked, but when he went around Charlie for explanations, Charlie would usually raise hell later with whomever did the explaining. In the lab, we had the feeling that, as Julio had a whole winery to run, and Charlie kept most production operations going OK, Julio had decided it was better to keep the status quo than to start over. Charlie's obvious successor, Jim Coleman, was learning, but wasn't yet ready to replace Charlie. Julio knew that my strong points were science and winemaking, not in running production; I had made it clear to everyone that I had no desire to run any large winery.

Charlie had an additional problem. He tried to maintain his authority against pointed attacks from Jack Fields (and phantom attacks from everyone else), while at the same time, he was anxious to put new methods into practice. Charlie was so eager to see Gallo take advantage of new approaches that he didn't explain things to Julio very clearly. Worse, Charlie oversimplified to the point of not telling the whole truth. Later on, if Julio found out that he had lied to him, as often happened, it made all of us miserable for several days because Julio raised so much hell. He would yell and swear at Charlie, who would often yell right back. Sometimes it became a real battle, but Charlie didn't own the winery, Julio and Ernest did. Once, in the tasting room, Charlie got excited about a product we had made and started expanding its importance, saying, "This will sell here, this will attract attention- -." Ernest looked up and interrupted him in mid-sentence with a loud voice, "Let me see now, Crawford, what department are you in?" Charlie went quiet, but never seemed to realize that he had 'done it again.'

One day, Pat Gardali, Charlie's secretary (later to become Mrs. Joe Gallo, sister-in-law of Ernest and Julio) called me in the lab, asking me to take two visitors from North Carolina on a tour of the winery for Ernest. I dropped everything and went downstairs to meet them. We hadn't gotten more than a few feet into the winery proper when a secretary from Ernest's office caught up with me. I was to see Ernest immediately. I excused myself from the visitors and left them, saying I'd be right back. When I entered Ernest's office he said, "Dick, haven't you got something better to do than to take some bo-hunks (Ernest's exact, exaggerated words) through the winery?" I said, "Of course I'm busy Ernest, you know I am, but when Charlie said you wanted me to take visitors through the winery, I - - ." Charlie suddenly appeared in Ernest's doorway obviously having been running and said, "I did not." I said, "Charlie, when Pat asks me to take visitors on a tour, I know it is you doing the asking; I drop everything and try to do what is - -." Charlie interrupted, "I did not ask you to take them on a tour." Ernest realized what must have happened, and said to me, "Well these guys shouldn't be here, and I don't want to waste your time with them." I said, "OK, I've got things to do," and left them. I didn't need to hear what Ernest was about to say to Charlie, but I knew it wasn't going to be good. I never could feel sorry for Charlie; he got himself into these messes by trying to be everybody's boss at all times. I don't think he ever realized that neither Ernest nor Julio wanted Charlie to assume he could speak for them. They were old enough to make their own decisions, thank you very much.

The lab continued to operate very well. Wine quality depended on the winemakers in the lab, and both Ernest and Julio knew it. I liked the originality we saw coming from both Bob Bouthilet and Karel Popper. Karel Popper was considered by most to be a nutty scientist going off in totally tangential, crazy directions. Like 'Mr. Bumble,' he seemed to be blind and couldn't see the obvious, but he often showed a flash of genius that all of us admired. Bouthilet was the same. He was a great talker, boasting about how much money he'd made, what great ideas he'd had, and how many inventions he owned, but in fact we rarely saw him do any laboratory work. He was present less than half the time. He would walk in most mornings at around 10 a.m., but then put on his hat and walk out by 11:30 a.m. saying he couldn't use the 'shitters' at Gallo. When he had to go to the toilet he'd go home, then come back at 2 p.m., or sometimes later. Bob was always there for Julio's 5 p.m. tastings. He correctly felt he might be needed for advice, and knew that Julio would be more comfortable if he were present.

It was a special kind of cleverness that set Bouthilet aside from most other people in developmental work. He told all of us on many occasions, "Bullshit is the name of the game." At the time, I didn't believe he'd used the right word. Instead of bullshit, I thought the word should have been 'cleverness' or maybe 'pizzazz.' Bouthilet had many clever ideas and he truly had pizzazz. We had no proof that all of these inventions were Bouthilet's own ideas, but that was not important. I was beginning to see what he meant when he told me over and over that he wanted to "put some flair into Gallo winemaking." To my mind, one of the best ideas to have emanated from Bouthilet's lips was when he told me one day that he wanted to make a rifle to use for shooting flies. He said, "Wouldn't it be great to just sit there in your living room and shoot flies buzzing around here and there?" I told him a rifle would be OK if the fly was sitting down, but if you wanted to make a sport out of it by getting them while flying, the gun would have to be more of a shotgun. "Not necessarily," he said. "Just imagine how proud a guy would be if he could pick one off right out of the air." I think it was Art Caputi, Jr. who overheard this discussion in the lab and interjected that he though a laser might be the thing to try for such a weapon. Some years later, I spoke to a laser expert about it, and he told me it would have to be a laser that couldn't be focused by the lens of somebody's eyeball onto the retina because otherwise, there'd be the risk of accidental blinding of a lot of kids. I put the brakes on the whole idea after that. I still think it would be a 'best seller' if that risk of injury could be overcome.

There were occasional tensions in the air from time to time, probably no more than par for the number of personalities and excellent scientific minds working together in a small lab. I look back at that ten-year period with a sense of accomplishment and pleasurable memories. Within that rigorous scientific backdrop, there could have been many personality battles, jousting matches, and ego clashes. In fact, there were very few, and those were of little significance. Knowing and working with people like Bouthilet, Popper, Dimitri Tchelistcheff and Art Caputi, Sr. and Jr., not to mention Ernest and Julio Gallo, was an honor. When Art Caputi, Jr. came back from the military in '62 and joined the staff, he was already well-trained scientifically. He didn't have the kind of flash-of-genius flair that both Bouthilet and Popper had – Art's approach was similar to mine in being more rigidly scientific, thorough, and down-to-earth. My direction tended towards new products and processes, while Art tended towards analytical procedures. He spent most of his time creating and improving analytical methods, not really working in winemaking or new products. I was Art's best man when he and Marti married around 1963, and we've remained close friends.

The Times, They Are A-Changing

My years at Gallo coincided with a major change made by wine drinkers, as the market evolved from high-alcohol pop and dessert wines to more sophisticated, low-alcohol table wines. Dessert wines can get by with lesser wine varieties, but table wines cannot. Most of the wine ads before 1958 promoted high alcohol products like port, sherry, muscatel, tokay, or vermouth, all of which used some combination of four or five poor-quality grape varieties. The period set the stage for a hotbed of wine culture that would explode in the 1960s. Part of that explosion came directly from American consumers. They had increasingly visited Europe since the end of World War II, and the European habit of enjoying fine wines with meals was becoming part of American culture. The other part of the wine explosion was due to Julio Gallo's foresight (and that of a few other growers with a similar vision). As far back as 1959, Julio had begun improving wine quality by a program of replanting old vineyards with quality wine grape varieties whenever a vineyard needed replanting. The Gallo vineyards totaled nearly 20,000 acres at that time, and they were farmed by Ernest and Julio's brother, Joe. Already, a few small wineries were using varietal labels, but that was very few indeed. A handful of 'Pinot Chardonnay,' Folle Blanche, French Colombard, Riesling, Sauvignon Blanc and Semillon white wines were entered in the California State Fair wine judging of 1958.[20] Red varietal names were equally scarce, with an occasional Petite Sirah, Zinfandel, Gamay, Cabernet Sauvignon, Pinot Noir, or Carignane entered. Two other varietal grapes were significant in California, Chenin Blanc and Grenache; Chenin was used mostly in blends to soften the roughness of French Colombard, while Grenache made very good rosé and surprisingly good sherry. Only a few acres of Palomino grapes were planted in the state, and most of them were used incorrectly. They were used for white table wines instead of the time-tested Spanish practice of using Palomino to make the world's finest sherries.

Because Julio tasted wine critically every day, he knew it would be wise to replace the old 'Prohibition shipper grapes' with good wine grape varieties as soon as possible. Competing growers didn't have this foresight: Most of the member growers within the Allied Growers Cooperative continued to plant Thompson Seedless when their old vineyards needed replanting.

---

[20] The California State Fair judging was chaired that year by Professor Maynard A. Amerine, Chairman of the Enology Department at UC Davis, who in 1950 had co-authored (with Maynard A. Joslyn, my advisor) the classic textbook of the time on winemaking, *Table Wines: The Technology of Their Production.*

The seven most well-known Gallo wines in 1959, all in pilfer-proof screw cap bottles (*from left*): **Sauterne** the standard white wine (in a Burgundy bottle); **Sherry** a baked wine (in a Bordeaux bottle); **Vin Rosé** made mostly from Grenache grapes and sold in a unique half gallon bottle (Gallo's best wine at the time I thought); **Thunderbird** a flavored wine made from Thompson Seedless grapes (which paid all the bills); **Paisano** our proprietary red wine made from 100% Zinfandel grapes (in a common half gallon bottle); **Burgundy** made from Zinfandel with some Ruby Cabernet, Petite Syrah and other red varietals (in a hock bottle); and **Rhine Garten** a Muscat-flavored sweet wine (in a similar bottle to Vin Rosé).

A promotional photo taken in 1959 at the Gallo Winery laboratory. This shot was used to promote the fact that science was used at Gallo to ensure all their wines were excellent and well-made products of superior quality. The same photo was later used on the cover of a glass industry magazine.

Captain Richard G. Peterson departing from one of the 49th Aviation Battalion Army National Guard H-37 Sikorsky helicopters in Stockton, California after a training flight. I was a 'Weekend Warrior' pilot from 1959 to 1970, while working full time in the wine industry.

This wine storage tank at Gallo had 105,000 gallons of capacity (left).Other outside tanks at the Modesto, California winery held 200,000, 300,000, and 600,000 gallons each. The largest, (Tank 1M), held one million gallons.

Ernest (*left*) and Julio Gallo pose for a tasting organized for a company advertising booklet in 1959.

Dimitri Tchelistcheff (*below*), the best taster and most accomplished winemaker at Gallo in the late 1950s and early 1960s. Dimitri created several of Gallo's best-selling flavored wines between 1958 and 1961.

The Gallo Winery was unique in that it had its own bottle making plant (*left*). This action shot, taken for a promotional booklet in 1959, shows the distinctively shaped Vin Rosé bottles being made. Gallo's proprietary green glass color was cleverly named 'Flavor Guard.'

They could harvest 16 tons per acre every year (good wine varieties often yielded less than 7 tons). That became unfortunate for United Vintners and their Italian Swiss Colony wine brand. United Vintners had to use whatever grapes their owners (Allied Grape Growers) grew. By 1965, Julio had access to a huge tonnage of quality wine grapes (Chenin Blanc, French Colombard, Barbera, Ruby Cabernet, Petite Sirah and Zinfandel), whereas United Vintners had mostly Thompson Seedless. Julio did not use Thompson at all, except for Thunderbird wine.[21]

Something else of importance was going on in the grape and wine industry. Julio had become the dominant grape buyer of California since Gallo sales had been growing by leaps and bounds. By about 1963, whenever Julio announced the grape prices he would pay for the current year, the big news was followed by every grower and winery in the state. Very often the prices Gallo offered were assumed to be valid for everyone; the net result was that Gallo's announcement tended to set prices for the whole industry, with only minor local adjustments.

I think it was 1966 when Julio decided to push this advantage against his competitor, United Vintners. The price for Thompson Seedless had been in the $60 to $70 per ton price range in the previous few vintages. In early July, when Julio announced his prices for that season, he set Thompson Seedless at an astounding $105 per ton! The members of Allied Grape Growers were tickled pink. They knew United Vintners would have to match the price; they had no choice. When individual growers called Julio asking to sell their grapes to Gallo, Julio was friendly and asked for a list of their projected tonnage. Those who had only Thompson were told that Julio had already signed up all the Thompson from their area in the state that he needed for the year. If a grower had only a small amount of Thompson, but a good amount of Barbera, Chenin Blanc, Colombard or other good wine grapes, Julio would agree to take his few tons of Thompson at $105,

---

[21] Not many years later, Gallo dropped using Thompson Seedless grapes altogether. In later years, Thunderbird was made from apples or pears, whichever was cheaper.

along with the good wine grapes that he did not want United Vintners to get.

When the smoke cleared for the season, Julio had bought little or no Thompson, but United Vintners was forced to pay $105 per ton to all their vast number of grower members. It was a devastating blow to United Vintners to pay so dearly for junk grapes while Julio added to his already growing list of good wine variety growers. Julio had paid only slightly above the $105 for quality grapes like Chenin Blanc and Colombard; these grapes made excellent quality wine, as opposed to the trash that United Vintners had to swallow. Gallo passed United Vintners in annual wine sales by 1960 and was producing more wine annually by 1966-7. By the early 1970s, Gallo was selling double the number of cases as Italian Swiss Colony! Gallo had exploded in size as well as wine quality, while United Vintners collapsed to join the crowd of 'also-rans' far below the clear leader.

United Vintners had to sell itself off, and did so in 1969 to Heublein, Inc. At the time, it was clear to most of the industry that Heublein had made one of the worst possible investments in the California wine business. Who on earth, I wondered, could have been stupid enough to advise that big corporation to make such a blunder? I was to discover the answer soon, in 1969. I didn't know anyone at Heublein in 1968, but would get to know most of the major managers quite well, including the chairman of the board, a year later.

One Last Negotiation

Throughout the 1960s, it was often joked that the old Gallo office and lab building might just fall down by itself 'one of these days.' Finally, a new office building was constructed nearby, and all of Ernest's people and many of Julio's moved to the new building in late 1966 and early 1967. Only the laboratory and winemaking employees remained in the old building. To have more space, I moved into Ernest Gallo's old first floor office which was located directly below the research part of the lab on the second floor. Some of the lab managers and other winemakers also took over abandoned offices on the first floor. It was especially nice to have a quiet space in which to write reports or make phone calls without the noise and commotion that had been a constant problem in the lab.

For several years, Mas Ueda, one of the research scientists, had taken periodic measurements of the vertical distance from one painted bolt on a roof joist straight down to the laboratory floor. His measurements showed that the roof was sagging, and probably had been for the past decade. Clearly the whole building had been settling under its own weight. The problem increased the urgency to build a new lab building, as well as the new office digs.

Art Caputi Jr. was the primary designer for the laboratory layout, although Gallo, of course, used a licensed architect for the structure. Art must have spent nearly 100% of his time for many months designing that new lab. He was the perfect designer, since he knew more than anyone else what functions the lab needed to perform, and how much space each section of the lab would require.

After the new laboratory was built and occupied, it was time to demolish the old building. It never did fall down on its own accord, proof of the old adage that weeds don't die, you have to remove them forcefully. It was flattened by a single caged bulldozer, but not before one last serious negotiation involving Julio Gallo. Negotiations between Julio and the contractor who was hired to demolish and clean up the old office and lab building took an interesting turn. Julio wanted to use the former site to install new wine tanks, and he wanted to get them built in time for the upcoming crush season. After the agreement was made to destroy and remove the old building, Julio introduced a new negotiation: He wanted a guarantee that the job would be done on time. He asked for a penalty of $2,000 per day for every day that the contractor was late in finishing the job. The contractor thought this over, and then said he would agree if Julio would agree to pay him a $2,000-per-day bonus for every day that the contractor finished the job ahead of time. Julio smiled, but had to agree that the contractor's counter offer was fair. After a little more dickering, the deal was made and the start day was agreed upon.

It was the Gallo cellar superintendant, Jack Fields, who called and told me the story: That morning Julio stood with his stopwatch in hand and punched the pin as the contractor's cat drove right up the front concrete stairs and pushed the outside wall into Julio's old office. The driver was protected by a steel cage on all sides of the cat and wore a large dust mask that allowed him to continue under almost any dusty condition. The cat disappeared into the building and started turning round and round, smashing the interior walls left and right. The roof fell in quickly, and Julio was amazed at how easily that big cat demolished the old building. By afternoon, big loaders were picking up huge gobs of wreckage and loading it into giant dump trucks. The trucks lined up so that as soon as one was loaded and had departed for the appointed dump site, another truck was in place to pick up the next load. When Julio saw them continue working past 5 p.m., he walked over and asked the contractor how late they would work that day.

The contractor answered Julio with a new question in return, "Who says the day ends with darkness?" He had big spotlights set up, and the job continued all night. Julio was smiling and shaking his head all the way home. When he returned the next morning, he was surprised to see that most of the rubble was already gone. All the demolition was finished, and the job was now reduced to hauling the rest of the chunks away. "My God," Julio said. "He's going to finish the whole job in one f---ing day!" Julio was close, but not exact in his evaluation. The job wasn't completely finished in one day, because some piping, electrical conduit, wires and foundation materials were hard to get out. They were all out of the way before dark that night and the contractor had brought in his leveling crew. Their job was to smooth out the ground after leveling it.

By the next morning, only 48 hours after the work began, Julio was satisfied that the whole job was complete. He hadn't stopped shaking his head since the first day, even though he knew the contractor had gotten the best of him. Julio said later that he never had so much fun losing a bet. The original deal allowed the contractor 15 days to complete the job. He had done it in just two! Julio paid $26,000 in bonus money to the friend he'd made in that contractor. It was said that Ernest was pissed that Julio had wasted twenty-six grand. The story was that he gave Julio hell for not knowing exactly how long the job should have taken. I know that does sound like Ernest, but I prefer not to believe it. Rather, I give Julio great marks for enjoying the humor in the last negotiation ever done in or around that building.

Graduation Day

The wine industry was still small in late 1967, when Andre Tchelistcheff decided once and for all that he was going to leave Beaulieu Vineyard. Dimitri and I had stayed in touch by phone, and he knew that I hadn't enjoyed having to fight with Jack Fields over mundane issues, and that Charlie often wasn't supportive. When Dimitri asked me, on behalf of Andre, whether I would consider leaving Gallo for BV, I first asked why he didn't do that himself. Dimitri told me he wanted no part of Madame de Pins, the owner of Beaulieu Vineyard. He said he already knew he couldn't put up with her personality, but he thought I might be able to. I didn't know what he meant exactly, but I couldn't imagine any lady being so obnoxious that I wouldn't be able to work with her. I would do my best job as winemaker for her – not become a close friend. Andre had made the position of winemaker at BV very desirable; that was a prize anyone would at least seriously consider.

Eventually, I told him, "Yes, I will move to Napa Valley if Andre wants me to. If Andre decides to leave Beaulieu, I would be proud to be considered as his replacement." Dimitri told me months later that Andre had interviewed many candidates and had made up his mind to offer me the job. When Andre called in late 1967, it wasn't a surprise. He knew all about the work that I'd done with Dimitri, and wanted me to consider the job.

I drove to Rutherford and spent a whole day with him. We tasted many of his wines, and he explained how he had made them. I noticed differences immediately from Gallo winemaking. Beaulieu used very different grape varieties, smaller size equipment and wine lots, and greatly increased aging, both in oak barrels and in bottles prior to shipping. The primary difference (and the one that really sealed the deal in my mind) was that I would do all the farming of grapes as well as making the wines. To a farmer from Iowa who had been missing the farm life, this last difference was like manna from heaven. I had spent time in the Gallo vineyards, of course, but I was never in charge of their farming. I hadn't farmed grapes since leaving Iowa, and was anxious to resume what I'd left a decade before. He showed me the vineyards and winery at Beaulieu, and I made up my mind that I would do whatever it took to make Andre happy about his choice.

When I spoke to Julio, I had second thoughts, of course. I had felt fulfilled working for Julio and had really enjoyed my ten years there. Ernest had never raised his voice at me, even once, which alone made me one in a hundred. Even when he told me not to waste my time giving those 'bohunks' a winery tour, his voice was friendly. But the fact that my name was not Gallo told the tale. I could not advance any higher in the company because I was already in charge of all the winemaking. I certainly did not want Charlie Crawford's job and would not miss his juggling and dancing around every question. Julio understood completely when I told him I was looking forward to working with Andre Tchelistcheff. He wished me well and promised to stop to see me whenever he found himself in my neighborhood. He did that many times over the next twenty years. The last time was 1989 when he and his son, Bob, stopped in to see me at Atlas Peak in Napa Valley. They were out looking at vineyards in the Gallo helicopter and called to see whether I was in. I was, and gave them a tour of the new caves we were digging for Atlas Peak. Julio died in a hillside jeep accident only a few years later and I was devastated; Bob remains one of my close friends today.

A designation was given to professional people who had worked at Gallo and then moved on to positions of authority in other wineries. I don't know how it started, but it was said they had 'graduated from Gallo University.' Looking around the wine industry, dozens of Gallo grads could be found. Most had worked for Ernest in sales and advertising, but I was one of the few who had worked directly for Julio. Among Ernest's grads were Legh Knowles, Dick Maher, Dan Solomon, George McCarthy, Terry Clancy, Bruce Macumber, Dick Witter and dozens of others. Julio's grads included Robert J. Bouthilet, Professor Dinny Webb, Philip Togni, Brad Webb, Walter Schug, Jerry Luper, Bill Bonetti, Doug Davis, Dimitri Tchelistcheff and Karel Popper who, after getting his PhD awarded from UC Davis, moved on to do research at the Western Regional Research Laboratory (USDA) in Albany, California. Karel and I enjoyed periodic phone conversations for another ten years, until he died of a heart attack at age 61.

During my decade at Gallo, it was technology, technology, technology: Make table wines better, cleaner, fresher; make wines to be served with food, but keep the price affordable. Let the snobs go to hell – we paid no attention to glamour, snobbish articles or PR hype. At Gallo, winemaking was a production business; we made the best product we could from the grapes we had, but the price had to be kept low.

Although Gallo passed Italian Swiss Colony to become the nation's biggest winery in 1967, they did not lead in one important measurement. In the field of snob wines, Gallo's name was not on the same page as those who were considered to lead in pricey wines. The perceived 'snob' image of overall wine quality by world standards didn't include Gallo. The list of leaders in that group was short, including only Inglenook and Beaulieu along with Louis Martini, Wente and Charles Krug. In addition, there were three or four other wineries which were perceived as producing outstanding quality, but these were thought of only as 'hobby' wineries. They were so small that they weren't included in discussions because their combined total production amounted to only a few hundred cases. This group included Spring Mountain, Chalone, Zellerbach and a few others.

I had spent ten years helping Gallo bring scientific competence into everyday table and dessert wines. It was all science and engineering, no art and no salesmanship. "Frightfully lacking in bullshit," Bouthilet had said. We paid strict scientific attention to doing a better winemaking job at Gallo, but I really didn't know much about the PR aspect, and paid it little attention. I always thought that research at Gallo in those years was well rounded. We were effective in doing our job, and Gallo not only made money, but also gained a great deal of prestige from our research department having been there. Gallo led the industry in technology, grape tonnage crushed, cases sold, vineyard acreage and dollar volume as well as just about all the other measurements reported. It had, indeed, been ten years of cutting edge technology and I was proud to have been a significant part of it.

PART III
Beaulieu Vineyard
1968-1974

A Pair of Immigrants

N apa Valley in 1968 gave the impression that the U.S. wine world was finally coming back to life after the many dark years of Prohibition, but it was a slow rebirth. During Prohibition, fine wines were nearly destroyed in favor of cheap alcohol; consequently, by 1933, there was little or no acreage of fine wine varietals left in the whole state of California. Vineyards needed to be replanted, but the process was expensive and there was no guarantee that it would be worthwhile. A vineyardist had to cultivate and develop grapevines over the first three or four sterile years before he could see his first crop, and after fermenting the wine, he had to wait another year to see whether his efforts might pay off with better wine. That outcome was not certain by any means at the time the vines were planted. California had begun to study winemaking methods through trial and error in the 1930s, but it had been difficult for two reasons: a lack of true wine grapes with which to work, and a lack of new students wanting to study the science of winemaking.

The situation in France was entirely different: no European country had tried Prohibition, and wine had remained a major field of study throughout the American Prohibition experiment. In France, one of these students was a young Russian named Andre Tchelistcheff. Andre had almost died twice:

once of an infection contracted in infancy that kept him bedridden until age four and later when he fought in the White Army against the Reds during the Russian Revolution. Andre's father was Chief Justice of Russia's Court of Appeals and had always opposed the autocracy. He favored revolution as did other liberal intellectuals, but they were not prepared to take and hold power. Authority was seized from them early in the revolution by the Bolsheviks who proclaimed Andre's father an outlaw. While he was in hiding, Andre's mother was ordered to take her children to Moscow, as their country estate was being taken over by the Red Army government. Civil war was flaring up everywhere. His father secretly joined the family, and they escaped to the south to join White Army sympathizers.

 After an exhaustive trip involving intrigue, false passports, payoffs and fictional identities, they crossed the Soviet border into German-occupied Ukraine. Border guards were stealing anything of value, but Andre's aunt saved enough for the family to survive by swallowing family diamonds and rubies before being searched at the border.

In Kiev, his father had political connections and got permits to travel south from Ukraine. Most of Russia was dominated by the Red Army, but the Crimean Peninsula was a White Army stronghold. Andre's father got him a commission as a second lieutenant, and he was involved in major battles during the next two years. His last battle ended with his unit mostly wiped out by machine guns; he had crawled away, passed out, and was assumed to be dead. Cossacks retrieving dead from the battlefield noticed that he was alive and revived him; Andre was only twenty-one years old. The family's nightmare ended with their evacuation by ship to Algeria, after which Andre went to Bulgaria.

He spent the next few years in agricultural schools and working in southeastern Europe. He married Katherine, the daughter of an exiled Siberian lawyer in 1929, and they moved to France. His son Dimitri was born in Paris in 1930, while Andre was studying wine at the Pasteur Institute. He was also teaching and working at the National Agronomy Institute. In 1938, he was introduced to Georges de Latour and his son-in-law, Henri Galcerand de Pins. They had arrived from California, hoping to locate a wine-making specialist to replace the retiring Leon Bonnet at Beaulieu Vineyard.

Georges de Latour was born in France in 1856, and moved to California sometime between 1883 and 1889. He was a chemical engineer who started a cream of tartar business in the late 1880s, buying argols[1] from old wine tanks for his raw material. He became a U.S. citizen in 1896, married Fernande, a French woman living in San Francisco, and they moved to Healdsburg where he operated his cream of tartar business. In 1900, he bought a house and some land near Rutherford and moved there from Healdsburg to set up a new tartar building. When he found the tartar business was slackening, he sold the business in 1901 and immediately planted Zinfandel and Petite Syrah vines on the Rutherford property. He incorporated the brand name Beaulieu Vineyards in 1904.[2] He sold his grape crops to others for the first several years and started buying and selling bulk wines here and there. His first bottled white wine for sale was called Sauternes, and was made for him by Wente near Livermore.

He bought the old Seneca Ewer Winery near Rutherford, and made his first wine on that estate in 1911. He built a new cellar (or added onto Ewer) in 1916, running the business as a negociant, buying and selling wines in bulk and bottling small amounts to satisfy demand. Georges was a very successful salesman and realized before most others that Prohibition would likely become a money-maker. He bought large amounts of cheap, sweet wine, stored it in his winery, and then sold it at greatly elevated prices just after Prohibition began (wineries were allowed to sell off their inventories for a few months immediately after Prohibition started). Through his friendship with the Catholic hierarchy of San Francisco, he developed significant sales of 'altar wines' to the church for sacramental use. Wine sales

---

[1] Argols are large chunks of cream of tartar crystals that slowly accumulate in wine tanks over time.

[2] Beaulieu ('beautiful place' in French) was near impossible for Americans to pronounce correctly. It was necessary to trademark the initials 'BV' as a brand name to give consumers enough confidence to ask for the wine. The acronym solved a big marketing problem, but it became a challenge to defend the initials as a trademark. The mark was successfully defended by Beaulieu against Buena Vista's claims on the BV initials, and by the Heublein Corporation's attempt to represent their Black Velvet whiskey brand as BV.

for sacramental use were legal during Prohibition, and he operated his winery the whole time. In 1933 (at repeal), his Beaulieu Vineyard brand was perfectly positioned to begin expansion of bottled wine sales to consumers, but he could not find a competent winemaker in California. Prohibition had all but eliminated the occupation in America. He would have to go back to France in search of the right man. There, Georges de Latour and his son-in-law were introduced to Andre Tchelistcheff, who was then working at the National Agronomy Institute. Andre appeared to be everything Georges was looking for, and after considerable discussion, he hired Andre to become winemaker at Beaulieu.

In Andre's mind, it was an enticing time. His work was going well in France, but Georges de Latour made California sound exciting. Prohibition had been repealed, and America seemed on the brink of a wine re-awakening. Georges told him there were endless possibilities in California – the only thing lacking was winemaking competence: "The soils are right, the climate is right, I have friends everywhere who want to buy good wine. Andre, I can sell the wine. What I need is someone like you who knows how to make the best wine. Come with me to California." Georges was an excellent salesman, Andre could see that. "I decided to go," Andre told me more than thirty years later.

On Andre's arrival at Rutherford, Georges de Latour surprised him with a dinner that he could have only dreamed about. Never in his life had he ever taken part in such an extravagant event. It began with native crawfish from the de Latour private stream, followed by Georges handing Andre a net with which he was to skim his own selected trout from the stream near the de Latour backyard. The meal was served by girls in uniform and there was even a butler. Andre could see that Georges enjoyed living the good life and was raising his family in that same spirit.

At the winery, Andre immediately organized a huge cleanup campaign. Georges' Beaulieu winery was filthy. It was managed by Joseph Ponti, an easy-going Italian immigrant who had known (and worked with) Benito Mussolini in Italy. The winery smelled strongly of vinegar, and many of the wooden tanks were so badly infected by mold and bacteria that Andre had to use a strong oxidizer, potassium permanganate, to sterilize them prior to re-use. Once, Andre had seen a rat swimming in a tank of white wine (the rat apparently had fallen in and was not yet ready to give up and drown). He decided to leave Beaulieu at the end of the year, but Georges talked him out of leaving by sheer salesmanship. Andre had seen Georges giving tours to guests and potential bulk wine buyers from other wineries. They would walk past a large wooden tank, which Georges would slap with his open hand and announce, "Full with Sauvignon Blanc" or "Full with Riesling." Andre knew that the tank contained ordinary white wine; nevertheless, Georges sometimes stopped and drained samples from a tank into glasses for them to taste, and the guests always seemed appropriately impressed. Over time, Andre finally got the wine tanks as clean as he wanted and could begin to implement the winemaking procedures he had learned in France. As a result, in a few years Beaulieu wines slowly became the standard by which all table wines in California were judged by wine officialdom.

In 1940, only two years after Andre's arrival, Georges de Latour died. For the next twelve years, Andre reported directly to Georges' widow, Fernande. After Fernande died in 1952, their daughter Hélène became his new boss. Things had run smoothly with the transfer from Georges to Fernande, but it was another story when their daughter Hélène took over. Hélène de Latour had married Count Henri Galcerand de Pins, making her Countess de Pins. After the Count's father (the old Marquis de Pins) died, the Count was elevated to the rank of Marquis, making Hélène 'Marquise de Pins.'

Madame Hélène de Pins truly believed she deserved an aristocratic lifestyle – hadn't her father taught her that? Her composure said royalty, people treated her as royalty, and she lived a royal life. Her bearing, her attitude, her overall lifestyle, and the lifestyle of everyone around her, proclaimed her as royalty – she would not have accepted anything less. It's something you read about in the Old World, but rarely see in America. Imagine a family matriarch living as if her own wishes were all the world cared about, out of touch with what's going on around her, totally inward-looking without regard for anything that didn't touch her personal life. Madame was not snobbish in the standard American 'uppity' vein at all. Her snobbishness made a higher level statement than that. She was not upper class, she was not merely an aristocrat; she was true royalty!

The Marquis and Marquise de Pins had one child, a daughter named Dagmar. She and her husband, Walter Sullivan, lived in San Francisco where Walter had a successful commercial real estate business. Andre told me that Dagmar loved to cook and gave an example of this royal family attitude. When Dagmar was cooking, she might open a stick of butter to use a table-spoonful in a certain recipe. When she had finished that recipe and began to set up for a different dish in the same meal, she would open a fresh stick of butter rather than use the remaining butter from the stick that she had opened minutes before. Of course, she threw away the remainders of both.

After 1952, with Hélène de Pins as boss, Andre continued to enjoy farming the vineyards and making the wine, but he always knew that if something needed repairing in the winery he had to do it without spending visible money. He was told repeatedly by Hélène de Pins, "Your job is to keep operating the winery so it can keep money flowing to me according to my needs. I will not put any more money into that winery; that winery has the job of providing money for me. My father gave me his solemn promise."

Fifteen years later, Andre decided to retire in 1967, but Madame de Pins would not let him go until he provided her with a competent replacement. He did that in November 1967, when he called and asked if I would con-sider leaving Gallo to go to Beaulieu. He told me he knew all about the work I had done with Dimitri, and he very much wanted me to take this job. I spent an entire day with him in Rutherford where he showed me the complete operation. We discussed Madame de Pins, and Andre's descrip-tions of how she demanded the winery operations be dependent on her personal lifestyle were very helpful, though unexpected. He said I would have to exercise a huge amount of flexibility in operating the winery so as to support her lifestyle. "Sometimes, my dear sir," he said, "when you are re-pairing something in the winery with Bill Amaral (maintenance manager), if Madame wants Bill to change a light bulb in her house or fix a door lock, you got (sic) to drop everything and send Bill up to her house. Bill can do the winery job later." He'd shake his head and say, "That's all you can do, my dear sir. In this job I'm asking you to search your inner feelings to decide whether you can operate Beaulieu in this way." I had made up my mind by this time and told him I understood and would do my best. It was only a coincidence that I'd consumed most of the bottle of Beaulieu Blanc de Noir Champagne Andre had opened in late afternoon and needed to stop for a nap in my car at a supermarket parking lot on my way back to Modesto. I admired Andre greatly and wanted to continue his legacy at BV.

Andre spoke his own unique English and that was part of his likability. I will never forget his phone call to me in December, 1967. He said, "Deek, I put my finger on you. When can you transport your family to Beaulieu for the purpose of assuming the important position of enologist?" I had some unfinished jobs at Gallo and needed to complete an active duty helicopter course at Ft. Rucker, Alabama for the California Army National Guard. We agreed that I would begin work at Beaulieu on April 1, 1968. Andre had good reason for insisting that I start with the new growth cycle of the grapevines in early spring. He wanted to spend one full year with me in every phase of each of the five vineyards I would be farming. A few days after Andre's phone call, Marquise Hélène de Pins called and invited me to come to dinner at her Nob Hill apartment in San Francisco. She wanted to hire me, and we were to discuss the details over a private dinner.

Madame de Pins was one elegant lady! She exuded a confidence and style that I'd only read about. I was dining and discussing personal subjects with Catherine the Great, Queen Elizabeth, Isabella of Castille. This was as close as I would ever come to grasping what ancient European aristocracy was like. As owner of Beaulieu Vineyard, she lived alternately in three different locations. She and her husband, the Marquis, spent a couple of months each year in their apartment on Nob Hill and maybe four months in what she called 'the country' house in Rutherford, near the winery. The other six months or so were spent in Montbrun, France, but that time period varied from year to year. Some years she might spend four months in each place; it depended on her mood at the time.

She expected me to keep her fully informed on all phases of winery operation, and especially wanted to know my opinions of each vintage and each of the wines Andre had made. Keeping the company's superb image shared first priority with producing the income upon which her family depended. I offered to write weekly reports to her about all the current goings-on. She laughed and said, "Oh, I don't want to read that often, once a month is enough. I expect to sit down with you for lunch every week or two when I am in the country. But, when I'm in the city, one report a month will be fine. When I'm in Montbrun, you can hold your reports for me to read on my return." She told me that I had received Andre's highest marks, and she was pleased to put me in charge of the winery. Her father had developed this winery to rank with the First Growths of Bordeaux, and she was confident that I would continue that goal. I assured her that it was my goal as well, and that I wanted her to be as proud of Beaulieu in the future as she had been in the past.

Only one thing surprised me: she never mentioned the vineyards. When I asked whether she wanted to be kept up to date on vineyard work as well as the winery, she said the vineyards were of little interest to her. I do not remember her precise words, but her attitude confirmed what Andre had told me earlier. In her mind, wine quality ranked first, the winery was next (it produced and housed the wine), and vineyards ranked last (she did not equate vineyards directly with wine quality). I came away thinking that she believed vineyards were important only because the grape varieties grown would determine which wine types Beaulieu could make. She did not appear to realize that the way we farmed vineyards would have a direct effect on the quality of the wines we produced. I made a mental note to explain that to her in future meetings. We parted on the most gracious of terms.

Rebirth: Becoming a Winegrower

Moving to Napa Valley in 1968 was a rebirth for me because I was introduced to a totally new approach to winemaking. On April 1, 1968, at six in the morning, I met Andre at Beaulieu with a new notebook and pen in hand. I had left Modesto two hours before for the drive to Rutherford. We toured all five Beaulieu vineyards, totaling 750 acres. Andre described each one, giving me its size, grape variety, general history, and the good points and bad points of each vineyard and block. We talked with the Mexican managers of each block and discussed the specific jobs that Andre wanted done that week. I logged everything we discussed in my notebook. I had to learn the minutest details about each vineyard block and also about each of the vineyard managers. My Iowa background made it an easy task. After day one, I continued meeting Andre at six every work morning to do the tour. We discussed the work to be done with each of the vineyard managers, and Andre made sure that I knew the precise reasons for each job. I was not surprised that he was an excellent teacher.

The thing that did surprise me in that first week was the discovery that Andre considered himself to be primarily a winegrower, rather than a winemaker. During my ten years at Gallo, I had believed (as did most others in the California Wine Industry) that Andre was primarily a winemaker.[3] At Beaulieu, I suddenly understood the French concept of 'winegrower' which recognizes that each grape variety can produce different styles of wines depending on the methods of farming, the amount and timing of irrigation, ripeness level at harvest, and crop load on the vines. These were considered to be much more important than 'simple winemaking' (using different methods of fermentation and aging in the winery). Only under unusual circumstances would the French attitude accept winegrowing to include one person managing the viticulture and another managing the winemaking. Only if they worked together towards making the same style and personality of wine could they consider themselves to be 'winegrowing' – and there might even be some argument about that.

Andre was a blue-ribbon winegrower par excellence, managing both the viticulture and the winemaking. During my Gallo years, I had never seen winegrowers, and none of the Gallo competitors considered themselves winegrowers either. There were growers and there were winemakers, but

---

[3] Some time later, Jack Fields called and told me in his friendliest voice, "You are doing what I always dreamed of doing – working directly with the great winemaker Andre Tchelistcheff at Beaulieu Vineyard. You are being granted a genuine privilege to work with that guy." I was astonished. Jack continued to call me from time to time, and our conversations were always on the friendliest of terms.

nobody did both jobs at the same time in the Central Valley in the 1960s. Grape growers thought their job was to produce the highest quantity of grapes they could as long as their grapes ripened fully. Winemakers took whatever grapes they received, and made the best wine they could from that fruit. Among winemakers in California, only a few winegrowers existed in 1968 and all were in Napa or Sonoma Counties. I became one of them in my first weeks at Beaulieu.

One theme was uppermost in Andre's mind as we went through the vineyards each morning from six to ten-thirty or eleven, stopping at Oakville Grocery for coffee around eight-thirty. Many of Napa's vineyard managers appeared there at the same time every morning, and it was a fun, if gossipy, stop. It became a regular occurrence for Andre to ask himself (and me) what effect our vineyard activity would have on the wines produced from those grapes. Answering that question took up much of our discussion time, and I made some important decisions based on those discussions. It was the primary difference between winegrowing on the one hand and just farming grapes for the highest profit on the other.

I made an absurd statement to Andre one day that I later wished I could take back many times. Andre had been farming eleven different grape varieties in vineyard #3 (located near the Silverado Trail, a mile from the winery) and all eleven were still there in 1968. These included some mediocre varieties that I thought should have been removed long ago, such as Aligote, Sauvignon Vert, Burger and Melon. None of these varieties could produce quality wine, and I told him they should have been replaced by better varietals, like Chardonnay and Cabernet Sauvignon. Vineyard #3 was not very big, and it was difficult to farm those small lots separately. Unfortunately, I had used the word "stupid" somewhere in my statement, and Andre may have thought I was criticizing his choice of varietal grapes (as if he was the one who had planted them). He thought a minute about my statement, then turned to me and said in a deliberate voice, "My dear sir, when *I* first came to Beaulieu, *in 1938,* there were *thirty-three* varieties of junk grapes growing in vineyard #3!" He said those words slowly and I wished that I had kept my stupid mouth shut. How difficult it must have been over the years for Andre to milk money out of various vineyard budgets to slowly replace all those mediocre grape varieties with the Cabernet, Chardonnay, Sauvignon Blanc and Semillon that he now had growing next to those leftovers in 1968.

Napa Valley was a friendly place in 1968, and Andre and I often stopped to shoot the bull with other winemakers and winegrowers. Bob Mondavi had bought the piece of land between two Beaulieu Vineyard blocks (#2 and #4) along the west side of Highway 29 in Oakville, and was in the process of building the Robert Mondavi Winery buildings. He was always on his property supervising construction, and often noticed Andre and me as we drove through on our daily inspections. Bob made it a point to intercept us, and we stopped to chat with him for ten minutes about three mornings a week. I was quite impressed with Bob's vigor and drive. Already in his mid-50s, he was just starting his own winery, but he exuded the excitement of a teenager.

Later, Andre told me, "There is only one person in California who has the possibility of catching Beaulieu – that man is Bob Mondavi. But, he has a weakness. He is neither grower nor winemaker; he's a salesman with a scattered life. One minute he focuses on grape varieties, the next minute he concentrates on changing a wing of the winery building, then at the same time, he's concerned with whether to position his Cabernet to compete with Rothschild or Haut-Brion."

Good winemakers can always be hired of course. Bob asked me in April 1968 (outside of Andre's earshot), "Can you give me the name of an upcoming winemaker whom I might talk to about helping me in my winery?" I recognized his unspoken question, but ignored it as I told him he already had as good a winemaker as there was in Warren Winiarski. You had to talk with Bob only a few minutes to realize that he would not allow any winemaker to get credit for wine carrying the Robert Mondavi label – Bob was always going to take that credit. He was pleasant and interesting to talk to, but why would a winemaker want to work for him long-term?

By June, we had good vine growth and the early varieties were already blooming. Periodically, we noticed symptoms of disease here and there in grape vines, especially in vineyard #3; a few bright yellow leaves stuck out in several vines in one area near the creek. The leaves had typical color pattern symptoms of yellow mosaic virus, and Andre told me he suspected the culprit was the nursery where Georges de Latour had sourced the rootstocks. Only a few vines were affected, and I made a note to replace those vines with new bench-grafted vines the following year. Bench grafts were more expensive than 'field budding' for vine propagation, but since fewer than twenty vines were affected, I thought bench grafts were worth the money. We wanted to avoid spreading the virus to nearby vines during pruning, and I knew Andre had the crew sterilize their clippers with chlorine after pruning each individual vine in that part of the vineyard.

We found good examples of most common diseases in one vineyard or another: vineyard #3, the oldest vineyard, was the worst. We found large patches of oak root fungus (Armillaria) here and there, as well as leaf roll virus throughout. The whole vineyard needed replanting rather badly, but Madame de Pins hadn't allowed Andre to spend the needed money. She had told him, "I choose to continue receiving money for the fruit each year rather than pulling the vines and stopping that income for four years until the new vines begin to produce." Andre's answer, "the newly planted vineyard would produce at least double the tonnage after it matured" fell on deaf ears. She told him, "I'll take the bird in hand rather than hoping to get two in the bush after four years." As we drove away, he mumbled something else in Russian/English under his breath that I did not hear exactly. I do know that one of his words was "stupid."

One disease became quite educational and very interesting for me: oak root fungus. Andre remembered that George de Latour had removed some scrub oak trees from one of the areas, and a larger oak tree from another. He had then replanted this area of the vineyard without fumigating the ground to kill the residual fungus. As a result, we could clearly see a pattern on the ground where the original oak tree had been – an uneven, roundish shape in the vineyard containing no vines at all. Oak root fungus had killed all the grapevines in the exact pattern where the tree's roots had been. Andre told me bare spots of that size and shape in vineyards were often diagnostic for Armillaria damage, especially in coastal California. No other disease could be followed so visually from year to year. Professor Bill Hewitt from UC

Davis had explained this to him years earlier.

Andre and I soon found fungal evidence in other smaller voids in the vineyard. When we dug into vine roots that were infected, we could often smell the definite mushroom-like odor of the disease. When humidity was high, we often saw actual mushrooms around those areas. Armillaria can remain in the ground under an oak tree for the lifetime of the tree; after the tree is removed, the fungus can remain alive in the soil for many years, existing on bits of wood and roots. Later, after replanting, the Armillaria can kill new vines and continue to move through an area, spreading from diseased roots to uninfected roots nearby.

The following weekend was a National Guard drill weekend for me. On Saturday, I flew an Army L-19 observation plane from Stockton to the Rutherford locations of BV vineyards #1, #2, #3 and #4, circled around at two hundred feet taking pictures of each vineyard through the open window, and got the film developed in Stockton that evening. That type of plane is especially well suited for air observations and photography; indeed, it was part of my early military pilot training. On Monday, I brought the prints to Andre. He was thrilled to see air views of the problem areas he had previously seen only from the ground. I photographed Beaulieu vineyard #5 near Carneros on another flight, and the air photos helped us decide how to correct some of the problems we found. I continued to photograph the BV vineyards during June for the next two years to watch year-to-year progress of the diseases. I had never heard of anyone using air photos to diagnose vineyard diseases before. Perhaps Andre and I were the first – thanks to my requirement to fly a minimum number of practice hours in Army National Guard aircraft every month of the year.

I took a great number of air photos of other vineyards in Napa Valley over the next year. On one flight, I noticed a seam of white rock running along the ridgeline next to the hillside vineyard of Schramsberg, near Calistoga. I took air photos and gave them to Jack Davies, the owner of Schramsberg. I couldn't tell from the air whether the white rock was quartz or limestone, and asked Jack which it was. He answered, "I didn't even know there was white rock up there. I'll climb up and check it out one of these days."

My interest in the type of rock was not only casual. One of my hobbies during the ten years I'd spent at Gallo was weekend panning for gold in the Sierra Mountains. Another Guard pilot, Don Sanford, and I flew in by helicopter to land on sandbars in streams running along the old Mother Lode of California, not far from Stockton. It was fast and easy to access by chopper, whereas the hike in and out would have taken many hours. We had assumed that we might pan out big nuggets in some hidden spot, but we quickly learned that the old forty-niners had scoured every square inch of every stream. Don and I never found any big gold pieces. I had hoped that the white seam at Schramsberg might be quartz, in which case it might be worthwhile to hike up there and search around for outcroppings containing gold. Unfortunately, Jack Davies told me a few weeks later that the rock was limestone. Unlike quartz, limestone is almost never a good place to look for geological gold residues, but it is very good for growing grapevines. Jack went on to use this fact in his PR releases. His sparkling wine vineyard was planted around a limestone outcropping, similar to so many of the finest vineyards in the Champagne region of France.

In the Winery

After the morning tour of the vineyards, Andre and I returned to the winery each morning around eleven. We would go over the day's plan for cellar workers with Theo Rosenbrand, the cellar supervisor. Andre would then disappear for lunch, and I assumed, a nap. He would come back later in the day, and we would taste samples of all tanks that were in process or might be ready for either barreling down or bottling. I made winemaking, barreling, aging and bottling plans one month in advance, and each decision depended on whether each wine was ready for its next operation. I made determinations by tasting with Theo and Andre, while keeping the sales plans of Legh Knowles, the sales manager, in mind. I spent afternoons with various managers inspecting the cellar, bottling, warehouses and champagne facility. BV sparkling wine was called 'Champagne' on the labels and the warehouse was located about a quarter of a mile away, near Madame de Pins' country house on vineyard #1.

Theo, Andre and I tasted and discussed one BV wine or another nearly every day during 1968. After a few months, I had a good memory of most of the wines from previous vintages not only by analyses, but also by their appearance, smell and taste. It was fun and educational to watch the changes taking place in the wines during aging, especially the reds. The 1964, 1965 and 1966 Cabernet, for example, all had similar tastes except that it was easy to discern one from another by their ages. Each additional year of age added a noticeable softness to the taste and color, so I could tell them apart by how young or how old they looked and tasted. Andre told me that he, too, had to use that trick when the wines were less than four years old.

Some vintages had special problems, and those problems were easy to spot. For example, 1967 was a cool year with early rain, so the later varieties (Cabernet, Mondeuse and Gamay) failed to ripen fully before the November rains arrived. Andre had been forced to fortify the Cabernets of that vintage with a little brandy to bring the wine up to his minimum standard of alcohol content (12.5 to 13%). All of us could identify 1967 in blind tastings by the subtle smell and taste of brandy – only after the 1967 was aged ten years did the taste clear, the brandy flavor dissipating over time as the wine aged in the bottle.

Andre also added small amounts of water to some grapes in fermenters to control the final alcohol content of the wine.[4] In 1968, we decided to begin harvesting the de Pins Vineyard Cabernet (vineyard #1) on October 2nd. The weather turned warmer at just the wrong time, and by the time we finished picking that vineyard on October 8th, the grapes were arriving at the crusher with sugar contents higher than the desired 24%. Andre did not hesitate. He told me to have Theo bring a trailer tank of water from the clear spring behind Madame de Pins' house; we would use that to rehydrate

---

[4] Cabernet grapes harvested at 24% sugar from Rutherford vineyards usually produce wine with 13.9% alcohol. The legal limit for table wines in America is 14%. If wines contain more than 14% alcohol, they are not legal 'table' wines, but 'dessert' wines and must pay a higher tax. Worse than that, most wines containing well above 14% alcohol lack varietal flavor, have a hot taste and do not enhance meal enjoyment. Higher alcohol wines are enjoyed by some people, but most often as 'cocktails' or 'walk around' wines, not as dinner wines.

those last loads of grapes that had suffered field dehydration while waiting to be harvested. This was allowed by both federal and state wine regulations (although the state rules were poorly written). Added water was limited to the amount it would take to reduce the average sugar content of grapes to 22% sugar. We never lowered the sugar content of Beaulieu grapes below 23%, as Andre had learned over the years that keeping the average sugar well above the 22% minimum produced superior wine. His rule of thumb was to keep the average sugar content of Cabernet grapes between 23% and 24.5% to produce the best wine. Tasting the wines over the next few years showed me the correctness of his judgment.

For some reason, wineries often hid the use of water in winemaking from both government regulators and from the public. It seemed odd to me that Charlie Crawford always denied the fact of water use when asked publicly and in meetings with other winemakers, as if he believed Gallo was doing something wrong when they used water. He misinterpreted the regulations as meaning, "no water use is permissible except the minimum necessary to move grapes and their associated stems and skins through the wine processing equipment." However, Gallo was not doing anything wrong, as a careful reading of the actual regulations would show; in fact, judicious use of water under the law when grapes suffer undue field dehydration makes better table wine, not worse. California regulations were clarified decades later; the re-statement made it very clear that there is no reason to cover up any part of legally regulated winery operations.

The year 1968 was undoubtedly Beaulieu's vintage of the century. I didn't recognize it during 1968 because it was my first vintage at Beaulieu, and I had no other weather patterns with which to compare. Andre knew the summer weather was quite good, but also that we would not be able to confirm just how good the vintage would be for at least another five years. After the end of the 1968 season, I noticed something quite unexpected that, as far as I know, no one else experienced. It happened to me only with the 1968 BV Beaumont Pinot Noir, and with no other wine at all. Whenever I tasted that particular Pinot Noir, I noticed an odd sensation in my nasal cavity. My nasal membranes felt like they were swelling inside, as if they were becoming slightly inflamed. It felt a little like the beginning of a head cold, only it happened much more quickly than it would have if I were catching a cold. The sensation began only a minute or two after I tasted the wine, and lasted for twenty minutes after I spit out the last sip. Afterwards, my nose felt normal again. I asked Andre and Theo whether they got the same sensation, but both said, "Not at all." I ended up deciding that I must somehow be sensitive to some component of that vintage Pinot Noir, but who knew what or why? I could not believe that anyone could develop an allergy to only a single vintage of a single wine, but those were the symptoms I experienced. For months afterwards, I watched for the signs whenever I tasted wines, but they never appeared unless I tasted the 1968 BV Beaumont Pinot Noir. Once, immediately after the sensation appeared when I drank a small glass of 1968 Pinot, I sprayed an antihistamine into my nostrils, and almost immediately the sensation stopped. That's the only evidence I saw, but I never identified the component to which I was sensitive. That '1968 allergy mystery' remains in my mind to this day, and I never found any real explanation.

In the day-to-day winery operations at Beaulieu, I remembered what Bouthilet had said many times, "Bullshit is the name of the game." In complete opposition to Gallo, it seemed that promotion and public relations were 90% of the game at Beaulieu. There was no question that the wines were good, and were very different in style from those I had worked with before. Beaulieu table wines were made from individual grape varieties that were not grown in Modesto's Central Valley at all. The only Cabernet Sauvignon, Merlot, Pinot Noir and Chardonnay in all of California were found in Napa (with a little in Sonoma). The wines were produced in much smaller lot sizes and aged in barrels. (Chardonnay was even fermented in barrels.) This was a uniquely different style from the wines at Gallo, or any other low-priced brand of table wine. Few, if any, Central Valley wineries marketed wines with varietal grape labels. Their wines were blends of whatever grapes they had, and the labels copied general areas of France – suggesting to the public that each wine would be similar to generic Chablis, Burgundy, Sauternes, Rhine, or Champagne.

By contrast, Beaulieu and a handful of other coastal wineries, stood out as producers of varietal wines – named for the single grape variety that was used in making the wine. Varietal wine producers usually entered their wines into the L.A. County or California State Fair judgings, while most others (including Gallo) did not. By 1968, only these two 'large' wine competitions were well known, with a handful of small local judgings appearing at a few county fairs. Even so, these larger judgings would later seem miniscule by contrast with those that would become routine by the year 2015. A total of nine white wine varietal grapes and six red wine varietals made up the whole list of varietal wine categories at both the CA State Fair and Los Angeles County Fair in 1958. By 2015, the totals would explode to more than thirty-five red and twenty-five white wine varietal categories in most of the dozens of competitions that had arisen. No professional wine person in 1968 predicted that level of growth.[5]

I could see that Napa Valley wines were not made in any technologically superior way at all. As a matter of fact, Gallo clearly had the superior technology (except that Gallo had never used oak barrels). Wine snobs of the day would not have believed this statement. They assumed that Beaulieu must be using the very best, time-tested wine tanks and machines because the wines were obviously superior. The whole wine industry knew that Andre was the clear leader in wine quality, but I was perhaps the only one who also knew that he lacked proper equipment. I believed in 1968, and I believe today, that Andre can never get enough credit for what he did at Beaulieu.

---

[5] The most common red varietal wine entered would become Cabernet Sauvignon, with Pinot Noir a close second; more than three hundred individual wines of each of those varieties were entered in each of the largest competitions of 2015. The same thing is true of the major white varietal wines: more than three hundred individual Chardonnay wines were entered in each of the largest competitions, some of which reported more than 5,000 entries in all. The largest (named for the San Francisco Chronicle newspaper which sponsors the event and publishes the list of winners) reported nearly seven thousand wines entered in that year. That explosion in varietal wines is easily related to the magnificent increase in wine quality that ensued from the dumping of table and raisin grapes (prohibition grapes) in favor of classic wine varieties from old Europe.

He produced superb wines at a time when nobody else in California was doing so, and he did it with antiquated equipment held together by baling wire and glue. Beaulieu's lack of equipment was a deeply glossed-over secret. Many details about Beaulieu's equipment at the time were frankly appalling. Andre was embarrassed by it, but neither of us told anyone outside the company. We resolved to change the situation as soon as practicable. Both Andre and I were smart enough never to discuss Beaulieu winemaking details with the public.

Gallo had sanitation. Beaulieu lacked sanitation almost everywhere. It is a tribute, not only to Andre but also to the basic superiority of the Cabernet Sauvignon grape, that this winery could make such great wine in spite of its antiquated 1960s equipment. For example, there were no stainless steel wine tanks at Beaulieu in 1968, nor was there sufficient refrigeration. Winemakers knew that to make the best white wine, one secret was to ferment the best grapes cool and in very clean tanks. Stainless steel makes the best fermentation tank because it is easy to keep clean, plus it allows good heat transfer making it easier to keep wine cool. Wood tanks have a natural insulating quality (the thick wood tends to hold heat in), and it is nearly impossible to keep the liquid cool during fermentation. Wood being porous, it is equally impossible to get a wood tank really clean and free from bacteria, which can hide inside the pores and be difficult to reach with heat or chemical sterilizing agents. Even the white wines at Beaulieu were routinely fermented in redwood tanks in 1968, which made me shudder.

I thought the red wine fermentations were even worse. When Andre first showed me his red fermenters that day back in late 1967, I saw what had to be done. Andre already knew, of course. He had been fermenting all Beaulieu red wines in open-top redwood tanks that were all about the same size (8 feet tall and 8 to 12 feet in diameter) and housed inside an extension of the main winery building. That building extension had a wooden truss roof, which was enclosed by light-weight walls on three sides, with multiple sliding doors to close off the fourth side. Birds could easily fly in and out of the fermenting room, and the first thing I spotted were nests in the wooden rafters under the roof and just above the open top fermenters! My first goal would be to get rid of those birds.

Andre was apologetic and told me he'd been trying to get approval to seal the fermenting room from birds for at least ten years, but Madame de Pins wouldn't hear of it. "Oooh that winery," she'd say. "You always want me to put money into that winery. That winery has an obligation to me and to my family. Those fermenting tanks served my father very well, and they can certainly serve you." I remembered that Andre told me shortly after I was hired that, of all the applicants he had interviewed, I was the one who he thought was both competent and able to work with Madame de Pins without getting mad and quitting. Legh Knowles once told me to keep one thing in mind about our jobs at Beaulieu: our duty was simply to keep Madame and her family living in the style to which they had become accustomed. We were to use the winery as necessary to provide that, and he recognized correctly what his mission was as dictated by her.

Our Queen

It would be impossible to describe Madame de Pins with words alone. Ordinary Americans might occasionally come into brief contact with an aristocrat, but never with true royalty. Those of us who worked for her can remember many occasions in which we found ourselves at a loss for words. Those who never knew her could not possibly imagine what we saw.

There was an old stone building, part of the original Ewer Winery, which had long since become dilapidated and susceptible to earthquake damage. The stones themselves were beautiful, so when the old structure was torn down, the stones were kept for use in a new visitor center. It must have cost a fortune to clean those stones by hand and reuse them for the new building. This was done because that's how Madame de Pins did things – it was 'genuine.' She wanted to tell the world that they used the exact same stones that were from the original building, and any other stones simply would not do. There were millions more stones of the same type and size available at lower cost from the same Napa Valley quarry, but that would be unthinkable. Only the 'genuine' stones taken from the original building could be used. No other decision could be made.

It was the same thing when choosing vegetables for dinner. Madame's garden produced a multitude of baby carrots–miniature carrots not more than an inch and a half long. However, if the carrots were pulled out of the ground too early in the day, that just would not do. The carrots had to be pulled up within an hour or so of dinner, washed immediately and cooked. If they had been stored in the refrigerator for three hours, they were pronounced inedible. It was not a question of checking to see whether they might still have an acceptable taste, it was more dogmatic, "How long have they been out of the ground – four hours? Well, four hours is too long; out they go." Moreover, this 'spoiled food' was never given to any of the servants, it was flushed down the garbage disposal. It was not a question of they're not being fit for de Pins consumption, but perhaps suitable for servants; rather, they were not fit for human consumption at all. Madame and her family simply did not understand how anyone could consider eating vegetables that had been out of the garden for more than an hour or so. Those butter-covered baby carrots certainly were good, I must admit. I ate them on several occasions at Madame de Pins' table, and never expect to eat so well again; on the other hand, none of us feared death if we had eaten 'old' baby carrots that had been out of the ground for two hours and twenty minutes.

Her feelings were the same when it came to wine vinegar. Madame de Pins felt strongly about every bit of food that was destined for her table, or the tables of her friends and family. Madame would not consider buying ordinary commercial wine vinegar. She had required Andre to make her own private wine vinegar for as far back as he could remember. I asked him what wine he used for that project, and he said, "Well, my dear sir, what wine would you guess she might specify?" I said it should be one of the lesser red wine varieties, maybe Carignane or Early Burgundy. The flavor of vinegar is so strong that it would overwhelm the varietal flavor of almost any wine grape, so it would be a waste to use a top variety. I thought either of those grapes might make nice wine vinegar. Since they did not stand out as wine varieties, the winery could afford to 'waste them on vinegar.'

"No sir, you aren't thinking like a true connoisseur. Try again," Andre said. I moved up a notch in wine quality, and this time I guessed either Mondeuse or Napa Gamay. These grapes formed the backbone of Beaulieu Burgundy, and both could supply plenty of color and body, as well as a nice 'winey' character. "My dear sir, please be serious," Andre looked down his nose at me as he sneered. "Oh gosh," I stammered, "Not Cabernet Sauvignon?" "Not Cabernet Sauvignon," he agreed firmly. "Not ordinary Cabernet Sauvignon, that is. Nothing will do, but 100% Private Reserve Cabernet Sauvignon from Beaulieu vineyard #1. To use a lesser wine would be unthinkable," he said in a very serious tone of voice.

After a minute to settle my shock, I said, "But Andre, won't the flavor of Private Reserve Cabernet wine get totally lost under the pungent flavor of that vinegar?" Andre answered immediately, without hesitation, "Well my dear sir, perhaps for your taste, and for my taste that would be true – but for Madame's taste, only perfection is acceptable. I have followed orders for many years, and you will follow the same orders as follows: when Madame gives the order, you will remove two barrels of Georges de Latour Private Reserve Cabernet Sauvignon from the winery aging cellar, and transport them to Madame's cellar number one, located closest to her country house. There, you will conduct the acetic acid fermentation, and turn that wine into the finest Private Reserve Cabernet Wine Vinegar. I have left detailed instructions as a recipe for you at the vinegar end of the warehouse. Have you made wine vinegar before?" "No," I replied apologetically. "I've always taken all possible steps to avoid vinegar fermentations." Andre continued seriously, "As you will continue to do in the winery. However, in Madame's wine vinegar cellar, you must follow my instructions. Theo Rosenbrand knows the procedure very well."

I later learned that Madame was particularly proud of her Private Reserve Cabernet Sauvignon Vintage wine vinegar. She often presented bottles of it as gifts, including departing gifts to guests who stayed in her guest houses from time to time. One of the first things I had learned about Madame de Pins was that she had a long list of famous people as close friends. Ernie Pyle, the world famous war correspondent from World War II was one example. Maurice Chevalier had been a close friend of Marquis de Pins for most of his life. Movie stars, high-ranking ambassadors, and many European titled persons (including royalty) were among her friends. It was clear that only genuine Private Reserve Cabernet Sauvignon would be acceptable for her wine vinegar.

Madame de Pins had a full-time gardener from Switzerland named Hans Guestner, who kept all the gardens at the 'country estate' at Rutherford in spotless condition. He grew all the vegetables as well as the flowers that would be used when the de Pins family 'summered in the country.' Most people Madame employed seemed to be European. Nothing about her lifestyle was 'modern American' by any stretch of the imagination, and she seemed more comfortable dealing with Europeans. Hans spoke with a suitable German accent, and was a reasonably good worker. I always enjoyed being around him as he had a great sense of humor, although we did not often see it shine through; he was always rushing between his list of dozens of projects that all had to be completed that day.

Every spring, Madame wanted him to put poison out beyond the garden to kill any rattlesnakes that might come into the area. Hans came to the winery each April or May, and Mike Grgich, Beaulieu's lab technician, would mix a concentrated water solution of potassium permanganate to be diluted and left in little trays in various places outside her yard area. The idea was that snakes might come down from the dry Mayacamas hills looking for water. They would drink the potassium permanganate solution, get sick and die. I do not know whether it worked, but it always satisfied Madame de Pins that something was being done. Hans dutifully reported finding dead rattlesnakes near the garden from time to time.

One day in 1968, Hans had gotten his bottle of the potassium permanganate concentrate, with an old copy of Andre's instructions of how much water to add for proper dilution at the garden. I believe it was the winery office secretary, Dorothy Andrew (later Mrs. Andre Tchelistcheff) who yelled at Hans as he was going out the door, "Hans, Andre says not to forget that we want to keep dogs and cats away from the poison. Be sure and put signs out so everybody knows what's in the trays." Hans, without batting an eye, came back a few steps towards the office, looked around, and said in his heavy Swiss accent, "Vaat langvage do da dawgs read?"

This life belonged to another time, another world. On any given night, if Madame had trouble sleeping, and woke up at two in the morning, she might get up and go to the living room to read for a while. She would read for maybe thirty minutes, and then decide she needed something to drink.

She would pick up the small servant bell from the lamp table and shake it vigorously. She would ring the bell loudly enough so that the butler would eventually hear it, get out of bed, put on his robe and come to ask her what she wanted. She would tell him, "I want a Coke." He would then go to the refrigerator, get the Coke, pour it over ice, bring it in and serve it to her on the usual tray. Needless to say, by 1968, this behavior had become a problem with some of the servants, even though Madame did not display it all that often. After a time, it got harder for her to keep servants in her employ. They would no longer accept requests their predecessors did not question. I do not believe Madame understood fully why they complained to Andre or me. She was genuinely pleasant and nice in her every day treatment of the servants, was usually soft-spoken, but also very definite about what it was she wanted. The reason she had servants was to serve her – in the same way servants had served royalty for centuries. She was living her life as French royalty in spite of her present location and the year, almost 1970.

With Madame's insistence that her own needs came first, trying to maintain the winery in good working order was tricky. I used to dread it when some piece of winery equipment broke, and we needed the maintenance people immediately. Bill Amaral, winery maintenance chief, was an excellent fix-it man. He could fix literally anything and was a diligent worker with two equally hard-working helpers, José and 'Chops.' My problem was that Bill's crew spent more than half of the time working at Madame de Pins' house doing window screens, structural repair, driveways, and various odd repairs (some of them major jobs). When not working at the winery, Bill was working on the house doing miscellaneous carpentry work, replacing beams or rotted floor joists, wallpapering, replacing window glass, anything you could think of that could go wrong with an old house. When something went wrong at the winery, if a motor burned out or if something broke, we'd have to go up to Madame's house to get Bill, a scenario that would likely lead to loud words at a minimum. If Madame de Pins was having dinner guests that evening, it made no difference what the winery emergency was, it had to wait because Bill couldn't leave Madame's work when she needed him. She would scold me, "Oh, you always talk about that damn winery.

The winery needs this, the winery needs that. I have needs, too, and I'm going to use Bill whenever I need him. Is that clear?" I'd always say, "Yes, Madame, I understand" and that would be the end of it.

I was the indirect recipient of Madame's wrath during one incident. From his first days at Beaulieu, Andre wanted to age the red wines in 60-gallon French oak barrels because they were traditional; however, 50-gallon American oak whiskey barrels were less than half the price. In young wines, the two oaks have natural tastes that are distinctly different, although both have a high vanilla content which is quite pleasing. French oak has a bland taste in young red wines when compared with the more aggressive 'bourbon-like' taste of American oak, and it is often preferred by wine lovers. However, the taste of American oak becomes softer after red wines are well aged – after aging, most people don't notice differences between French and American oak aged wines.

Because of cost, Andre was forced to use American oak barrels exclusively at Beaulieu. These barrels could be treated with soda ash to remove the harshness, and Andre found he could use treated American oak barrels to get a nice oak character into wine after a year or two of aging. Fortunately, after aging, American oak's bourbon-like taste tends to marry well with the natural flavor of Cabernet wine and can be quite pleasing, even when the oak flavor is recognized as American.

Our usual procedure for preparing new oak barrels was to wash and then season them with soda ash before using them to store wine. We would fill a barrel with soda ash solution and let it stand overnight; carefully drain it to remove most of the soda ash, rinse with fresh water, rinse a second time with dilute citric acid to neutralize any remaining soda ash, and finally burn a sulfur wick inside the barrel to ensure sterilization of the wood. The barrels could then be stored empty, or if needed immediately for wine, we would simply rinse them out with fresh water, drain thoroughly, and then fill the drained barrels with wine.

We stored barrels in an old warehouse building used for champagne production; it was an unfortunate coincidence that this warehouse was closer to the de Pins house than it was to the winery, and right in plain view from Madame's garden. One time, the cellar workers had dumped the spent soda ash solution from some of the barrels into the driveway in front of that warehouse, and the soda ash solution ran off into the shrub area. It killed three or four of those little green and yellow speckled plants that are so common in California yards. When she saw those dead plants, Madame de Pins was on fire. She was absolutely irate, so upset about Dick Peterson killing her plants that she did not even want to speak to me. Instead, she had raised all manners of hell with Andre. The truth is, the cellar workers hadn't reported it to me, and I hadn't seen it yet, but Andre had taken his ass chewing like a gentleman. Andre came down to the winery from Madame's house with his ears still ringing. He had been given a verbal thrashing by Madame because "Dick Peterson burned up my shrubs."

He walked in and explained to me what had happened, and told me that I would have to go to a nursery and buy identical new plants and get them replanted immediately. I said I'd do it without delay, but that I really didn't know anything about what had happened until he told me. He then shrugged his shoulders as he walked away, "Too bad it wasn't five acres of Pinot Noir vines, she wouldn't have noticed that. The only important plants on the property are the plants around her house."

I don't want any of this to sound as though we were unhappy with Madame de Pins. In fact, I enjoyed working for her very much. She was a very lovable lady, and though demanding, she did so in an otherwise nice way. She was not, after all, an ordinary upper-class citizen; she was our queen. She carried it off so well that we truly thought of her as royalty. Whenever she wanted something that was so unreasonable as to be ludicrous, we somehow did it without even noticing how ridiculous it might sound. I replaced those little plants without any difficulty, and did not use winery funds to buy them. I think it cost me less than twenty-five dollars, but it bothered me that she was missing something of importance: It was the winery that was supporting her, and she should have been a better protector of the winery. I was always amazed that she kept a beautiful apartment in San Francisco and the well-furnished house in the country even though each one was seldom used. Paying servants year-round to keep everything looking lived-in must have been a tremendous expense. (She used the same servants for Rutherford and San Francisco, they moved with her.) It's no wonder that the winery was under constant pressure to deliver more and more money to her family for the maintenance of her lifestyle.

Andre and I knew that preserving the winery was the way to preserve that lifestyle. She, on the other hand, felt competitive towards the winery. Her father promised that the winery would take care of her, but we kept asking for money to put into that damn winery. She wanted no part of that – her father promised her, and that was that. "I don't give a damn about that winery, do you understand? That winery only takes from me; it doesn't give what it's supposed to give." We watched as she milked the winery thoroughly. Would she eventually bleed it dry, and then sell the carcass to some huge company when there was nothing more to be milked from it? I hoped not, but it made me a little uneasy to see just how far the bloodletting from this old winery had already gone.

The Best Dressed Man

It was fun getting to know Marquis de Pins. It was no surprise that his wife, Hélène, wore the pants in the family in the expected way of a powerful queen. The Marquis argued with her, grumbled about it all the time, and did a lot of frowning. He gave me the impression that he had always had an aristocratic title but lacked money. His wife had the money first and got the title, thanks to him, afterwards. The Marquis had represented Beaulieu touring America in the 1930s and 1940s as BV vice president. He didn't enjoy the travel because he never liked American food, and I suspect he was not happy in that position. Andre told me he had been recognized as the best dressed man in America one year, and I'm sure he deserved that honor. I really enjoyed discussing things with the Marquis. His point of view, as French nobility, sometimes astonished me, but was always fascinating. He visited me at the winery many times, and I felt like I was talking to a close friend who, like me, had never had money as a child even though, unlike me, he held titles. I am not sure whether that was really true, but that was the impression I had. He obviously enjoyed talking with me, and yet if we walked through the winery, most of those visits ended with him yelling and trying to civilize me into becoming French. Marquis never seemed to be comfortable in California. In the six years I knew him, I do not believe he ever said anything complimentary about America, or anything American.

I had an ongoing friendly battle of sorts with him over my cleanup campaign. I was careful never to downgrade wine quality or change anything regarding wine style. At the same time, I wanted to clean up some of the bacterial traps that existed in every corner of the winery buildings. For example, there were whole rooms in the winery that had dirt floors (complete with rats). Concrete 'sidewalks' ran down the middle of aisles, and tanks were built on top of small concrete pier blocks that rested directly on dirt floors on either side of the central sidewalk. It was traditional in France and probably began as low-cost expedient; later it became chic. The idea was that dirt floors kept moisture in and the humidity constant, but in my life, I've never seen a winery that wasn't kept very humid inside by the constant hosing down of tanks and cleaning of floors after pumping or filtering operations. Humidity is always present inside wineries, dirt floors or not. Marquis de Pins must have told me at least twenty times, "Wineries always have dirt floors, if you put in a concrete floor, you don't have a winery anymore." Nevertheless, I wanted to clean up that mess. I wanted to get the rats, black widow spiders and cobwebs out and give the interior some semblance of sanitation. For one thing, the law required it.

I forged ahead with the cleanup program, slowly but surely. In one room at a time, one block at a time, Bill Amaral's maintenance crew cleaned out each dirty area and poured new concrete over the dirt floor. It looked much cleaner, and suddenly we had less to fear from state sanitation inspectors. The inspectors had thanked me many times. Still, Marquis used to grumble about it and hated the modernization. He did what he could to stand in the way of progress, but the dirt floor areas kept shrinking, little by little. He hated having concrete floors in the winery and never gave up trying to convince me of that. I have often thought that Marquis de Pins must have spent most of his later life trying to recover the lost, glorious past. Here was a down-to-earth aristocrat from 16th century France, hopelessly lost in time. Trapped in 20th century California, the Marquis never gave up trying to bring back the old life. To his credit, he never seemed to dislike me for sanitizing the dank cellar; he only despaired of his inability to make me see the light. I had been born in 20th century America, where we ate 'crackers and cheese.' He knew that had been an accident of time, and I could not be blamed. However, I once used that phrase in telling him about my early life in Iowa. "No, No, No, No, NO!" He screamed. "Mon Dieu! Not crackers and cheese, it's bread and cheese. Don't you understand? Bread! BREAD!" Then he walked away mumbling something about America ruining the world, and I was truly sorry. I had ruined his day again.

Actually, we rarely saw either Marquis or Madame de Pins inside the winery. I suppose the Marquis de Pins came inside about once a month, but I do not remember seeing Madame de Pins walk all the way through the winery – not even once. She did come in as far as the office a few times, but in all the years I worked directly for her, I probably saw her in the winery only five or six times, for just a few minutes. Now, years later, I still find it amazing that the de Pins' attitude was to keep their house clean enough to pass a Marine Corps white glove inspection at all times, while insisting that the winery be kept filthy.

Baling Wire and Duct Tape

My attitude from the time I first arrived at BV was to preserve the quality image of Beaulieu Vineyard. My approach was to keep up with technological advances and make the winery more efficient so that we could remain competitive and ahead of others in overall quality. I now knew that I was going to have to wrestle for every dollar the winery needed. Longtime operations had taken a toll on winery equipment that had not been repaired or replaced when necessary. New technology was exploding in the wine industry, but none had been implemented at BV: there were no centrifuges, no stainless valves or fittings (only old brass which allowed copper to dissolve into the wine causing oxidation problems). The winery was more or less held together by baling wire and duct tape – all the processing equipment had been worn out with the passage of time.

Beaulieu had a pitifully small amount of refrigeration and only outdated winemaking equipment. The outdated equipment gave us a serious problem on my first day of crush, September 3, 1968. We hauled the first grapes in from the fields (expensive Chardonnay from vineyards #1 and #4), dumped them into the white hopper, then fed the mass into the white crusher. As the crusher whirred and started spitting out stems and grape must, a terrible fact became obvious – precious Chardonnay juice was running directly out onto the ground! This will surprise today's winemakers, but the whole white grape hopper and juice conveying system was made not of stainless, or even a lesser metal, but of wood. We used a wooden board drag conveyor that looked (and was) home-built by Bill Amaral. The design was a simple 18 or 20 inch wide plywood board lying flat, to act as a bottom, with wooden walls 4 or 5 inches high along each side. The whole thing acted like a long, wooden trough sloping up from the crusher to the press on the second floor level. Inside the trough, moved a drag conveyor which was an iron chain with cross-cleats of wood that fitted in place like a moveable ladder. The motor pulled this chain, dragging the wood cleat 'ladder' up inside the board trough, so that the wooden cleats dragged the freshly crushed grapes (called 'must') up and into a funnel-like hopper that dropped the must down into the press.

The wooden boards had dried out and cracked over the long ten months between harvest seasons. Some of the first and most expensive grapes that we crushed in the fall were wasted, because some of the juice was lost through the cracks. Several days of water soaking had been necessary to get the boards to swell up and expand to seal the cracks, just prior to crushing grapes, but even so, that fall we lost some of the first Chardonnay juice because some of the boards had not sealed completely. It seemed to me a terribly jerry-rigged operation. Unfortunately, Dagmar de Pins Sullivan, Madame's daughter, was on hand to see that first crush of the season. You could bet that Madame de Pins would hear about it, and soon. Imagine my shock when I first saw it, having come from Gallo, which was a highly modern front runner of new developments and equipment. The crusher operator would not dare lose one drop of cheap Thompson Seedless juice. Gallo grapes were some of the least expensive in the state in 1968, but a big loss of juice would have caused somebody's head to roll. Now, here I was at magnificent Beaulieu Vineyard, where we were crushing some of the most expensive grapes in the state – Chardonnay from the Beaulieu estate. We lost maybe ten gallons of juice per ton of the first grape load crushed, all because of the dilapidated equipment and the unbelievably antiquated methods we were forced to use. Napa winemakers normally expected about 160 gallons of juice from a ton of freshly crushed grapes. (Gallo got more than 180 gallons from a ton of Central Valley grapes.) The juice loss at Beaulieu must have eaten up all the profit from that first 1968 wine.

It was too late to build a better system, and we went through the rest of the season making do with what we had. Luckily, the climate in 1968 was the best in years, and 1968 Beaulieu wines were some of the best in all of California history despite our equipment. The weather that summer was beautiful for grapes – cool in the mornings and warm, but not hot, in the afternoons. It rained 0.82 inches on August 18 at Rutherford that year, which was a godsend because we did not have enough water to irrigate properly without it. Normal rainfall for the whole month of August is zero, so we felt lucky. We had some heat during September and early October, and it rained a full two inches on October 12th. The vineyard crew had to use a small diesel caterpillar to pull the wagons of grapes out of vineyard #3, the most difficult vineyard we had. In the fermenting room, red fermenters often reached more than 95°F and a few above 100°F during October! Theo kept the refrigeration unit busy, and we ran it all night many times. He did a good job of always cooling the warmest tank (>100°F) down to 95°F, then he'd move to the next warmest tank. In this way most of the Cabernet tanks reached 95°F to 100°F, but only for a few hours. That is not optimal winemaking, but we did the best we could with what we had. Most importantly, we avoided any stuck fermentations.[6] I was astonished to taste the wines months later and recognize how good they were. It is truly a tribute to the Cabernet variety that it can take a beating, and still produce top-notch wine, year in and year out.

One day during the 1968 crush, when we were discussing refrigeration, Andre told me how Georges de Latour had cooled his red fermentations in 1938. He had no ammonia refrigeration but used the very same open top

---

[6] Fermentations that stop prematurely are said to "stick" or "get stuck."

fermenters I was looking at for making red wines. Andre said, "When the temperature in the fermenters approached 100°F, de Latour sent a horse-drawn wagon to Napa to pick up a load of 50-pound blocks of ice. The horses pulled the wagon right here (he showed me) alongside the fermentation tanks, and the driver just kicked six or eight blocks of ice off the wagon into each tank." I was appalled, but saw the humor in it at the same time. Since the melting ice would dilute the wines as it cooled them, I wondered whether Georges might have 'corrected that' by also dumping cane sugar into the tanks from time to time. I never asked Andre; the truth is I didn't want to know. It is never legal to add sugar to fermenters in California; however, adding sugar to grape must is legal in France because some varieties don't ripen fully in 'off years.' If they had not added sugar, they wouldn't have made drinkable wines in those years.

After that 1968 season, I went to work trying to devise a better conveyor system for grapes and an improved method for handling barrels. I had never handled oak barrels at Gallo, and I believe no other winery in California's Central Valley had used barrels either. I was astonished when I first saw how Theo handled them at Beaulieu. Empty barrels were moved by horsing them around by hand, rolling a little and rocking back and forth, one barrel at a time. A man could roll empty barrels from one location to another very fast, one at a time, if he knew how. You could either roll it on the ground or tilt the barrel and roll it on one edge, by keeping the barrel leaning as you rolled it sideways on edge. Both flat ends of an oak barrel are called heads. Empty barrels could be flipped end for end by grabbing the closest edge at the barrel head and smoothly slamming that head down towards the ground. Barrels have rounded shapes, and the motion followed the barrel's own curvature until the former top edge met the ground. The momentum of the flipping action continued, and the bottom head finished its acrobatics by ending up as the top. Even if the flipping went smoothly, a cellar man became pretty tired flipping barrels by the end of a day.

Full barrels were rarely moved without first emptying them. After all, a 50-gallon oak barrel full of wine weighs 500 pounds and nobody moved a full barrel very far, if at all. If a full barrel had to be moved, three men could (with difficulty) jockey it onto a wooden pallet, standing it on its head, and then one would carefully move the pallet by fork lift while two more men walked alongside holding the barrel to keep it from falling off. There simply was no reasonable way to handle wine in full barrels, and it would become a huge problem if wineries were ever to use large numbers of them.[7]

To wash barrels, the cellar supervisor, Theo Rosenbrand, placed 4 x 4 wood beams 18 inches apart along the ground to act as rails for the barrels to roll on. He placed the next set of beams end-to-end to make the rails as long as needed. The barrels were channeled by the beams, which made it easy to roll all the barrels to where we wanted them. He had a specific area for washing the insides of barrels so that the rinse water ran out directly onto the ground or into a rain water drain. After washing the barrels, they were drained, and the empties returned to wooden racks inside the winery. Finally, the barrels were filled with red wine, one at a time, from a tank through a small hose. It was time-consuming work. All that hand work seemed to me like double drudgery. I could not see how we could continue using all that hand labor successfully as the winery got bigger. In wineries without wooden racks, the barrels were stacked on their sides using small wooden wedges to hold the barrels in place, keeping them from rolling away. I made a vow to change all that by designing a rack or pallet that would allow wood wine barrels to be handled by fork lift. There had to be a better way.

My main goal was to get away from stacking barrels by hand because I thought it was dangerous. They were stacked empty, and then a worker filled the barrels with wine from a hose as he climbed over and around the barrel stacks, another dangerous job. I got the idea to build some type of barrel pallet so most of the barrel handling could be done using power rather than by hand. I called whiskey people to see how they handled barrels. They were using ordinary flat wooden pallets, standing barrels upright on their heads, which worked okay for whiskey, since it wasn't sensitive to either air or bacteria. However, standing wine barrels on their heads would not work because I knew a small amount of wine would seep out of each

---

[7] French oak barrels commonly hold 59 or 60 gallons and the weight is close to 600 pounds. Nobody could move a full French barrel without help.

barrel through microscopic pores in the wood. After a time, there would be an empty air space at the top, and head staves would dry out and crack, leaking air into the barrel. As air quickly spoils table wine, storing wine barrels on their heads could never work, and the idea was abandoned. I continued studying the problem for the whole six vintages I remained at Beaulieu, but did not come up with a good solution until my next wine-making adventure, in 1974.

There was a group of about fifty or sixty 1000-gallon redwood tanks, all very old, located in rooms A and E of the winery. Andre told me that some were more than 80 years old. Georges de Latour had bought them *used* in the early 1900's! Most were badly rotted, and all leaked to one degree or another. Ten tanks leaked so badly that Andre had long since stopped using them; they were only filling space, sitting unused on concrete piers above the dirt floor. Those tanks could not possibly be used to store wine or any other liquid. Even if the winery could afford the huge loss due to constant leakage, the stored wine could not have withstood the rapid seepage of air into tanks, as oxidation would have destroyed it.

Along with my program of covering the dirt floor areas by pouring concrete over them to make nice, smooth, easily cleanable floors, I wanted to replace the dilapidated redwood tanks with new ones. Redwood had long since become a bad word in California wineries because of the off-flavors usually imparted to wine that was stored in them for more than a few months. It was an industry joke that wineries which continued to use redwood bragged about it, because they did not know what else to do. They could hardly admit that storing wine in redwood tanks was spoiling the wine, yet they could not hide the tanks from public view either. The best way out was to assume the public would not know, and to be proud of their redwood. To complicate the matter, winemakers knew that very large redwood tanks were more inert than small tanks. Large redwood tanks were probably okay to use for red wine storage; that is, the redwood did not do the wine any good, but then it did not hurt so much either. In any case, when old redwood tanks exist in a winery, the savvy winery owner is not going to tell the world that redwood is a poor wine tank material.

I always found it a clumsy question to answer when customers or writers asked whether we used redwood at Beaulieu. The short answer was yes, but I went into great detail, explaining that only the larger, more inert redwood tanks were used while the smaller ones were just taking up space, empty. That always brought up further questions "Why do you have the tanks here if you don't use them?" I was not going to be critical of my boss, Madame de Pins, so I just said, "We're in the process of repairs" or something equally non-committal. I wanted to replace those old redwood tanks, and the obvious wood to replace them with was oak. American white oak or European oak tanks, built about the same size and shape as the leaky redwood, would do nicely if only we had the funds to buy them.

I remember thinking, "Gee, it's a shame we can't put small stainless steel tanks here in room B. Stainless steel tanks would be so much better than redwood; they'd probably be even more useful than oak tanks since we produce more white wine than red." We never wanted to age BV white wines in oak, with the exception of Chardonnay, so we really needed stainless steel instead of more wood. Both Andre and I wanted to add stainless steel tanks to that section, replacing the redwood, but we felt that the stainless appearance would destroy too much of the glamorous 'old cobweb-lined cellar' image that Beaulieu was built on. We made a facetiously serious (and short-lived) plan, extremely secretive and tentative, to order new stainless tanks just a little smaller than the old redwood tanks. The idea was to dismantle each redwood tank into staves, install a stainless tank in place, and then rebuild the redwood tank around the outside of the stainless tank! We figured the Marquis and Madame would be none the wiser; we would have the best wine tanks for quality and everybody would win.

Andre said, "Well, if they're dumb enough to think that redwood is good, it will serve them right to keep the redwood in here." We laughed about it, but our hidden stainless scheme was not really feasible. The fact is, we could not have put big enough stainless tanks in place, and the end would not justify the effort. It didn't seem worth the price to pay for such a small volume of stainless steel tank space.

One day I was surprised to receive an order from a priest in Alaska for 50 gallons of Beaulieu Port Altar Wine, to be shipped in one 50-gallon oak barrel. I wondered how to do it. Andre told me that Bob Branch,[8] shipping supervisor at Beaulieu, had done it many times before, and knew all the details. The barrel is laid on its bilge on a wooden pallet and strapped down so that it cannot come off. The bung is hammered into position, then covered by a metal strap screwed tightly to the bung stave. The package is handled at all times during shipment by a fork lift, and there had never been any failure of the packaging in Bob's memory. Shipments always arrived in good condition. Bob told me Beaulieu had shipped one barrel a year to this priest as far back in time as he could remember. They supposed that 50 gallons was the exact amount necessary to provide communion wine for his parish for one full year, as well as 'a wee drap o' port after dinner on a cold night in Alaska' for the priests and their guests. Part of the flavor of port is natural oxidation, and the wine would survive for a year in a part-full barrel just fine. Only dessert wines like port, muscatel, tokay and sherry could be handled in that way. It could never have been done with Cabernet Sauvignon or any other table wine. We never fermented port wine at Beaulieu because the best port grape varieties were not grown in Napa Valley. Rather, we bought it in bulk from Phil Posson, an excellent winemaker in Tulare, California, aged it in barrels at Beaulieu, then bottled it as BV Port Altar Wine or BV Tawny Port as Legh Knowles needed it for the market.

When discussing barrel wine shipments, Andre told me that in 1942, they had received an order for 50 barrels of Cabernet to go by ship to New York for bottling. His shipping crew needed to get the full barrels delivered to the dock in San Francisco on a certain day for loading aboard the ship. It happened to be a busy time for the winery workers and they were scrambling to get the barrels of wine delivered in time and had fallen behind schedule. Finally by working into the night, they got the barrels filled and delivered the truckload to the dock at the last minute. The ship was loaded, and it sailed the next morning. Everyone at the winery forgot about that

---

[8] Bob Branch, warehouse and shipping manager, had been a young sailor in the U.S. Navy and was on duty at Pearl Harbor when the attack happened on December 7, 1941. He knew the whole story from firsthand experience.

shipment until being notified two weeks later that the ship had been torpedoed by a German submarine and sunk along the Atlantic coast on its way to New York. Beaulieu was directly affected by the war only that one time.

Wearing the Beaulieu Hat

Because of Gallo's success and position of leadership in the California wine industry, I had gained a reputation among winemakers between 1958 and 1968. Even though we were quite secretive and close-mouthed about our scientific approach to winemaking, many in the trade thought of me as one of wine's technological leaders. That was especially true after Bob Bouthilet left Gallo in 1963. When I moved from Gallo to Beaulieu in Napa Valley, I was somewhat embarrassed to see the term 'Rocket Scientist' beside my name more than once in articles written by authors who covered wines and wineries. One article was shown to me by Ren Harris, a good friend and wine grower, who had just started a new winery, Paradigm Vineyards, in Napa Valley. I shrugged and said, "C'mon, do I look like a rocket scientist?" He answered, "How would I know? You're the only rocket scientist I've ever met."

Merely by moving to Beaulieu as winemaster caused me to be seen by wine lovers in a different light, and I was more surprised than anyone. After only a few weeks at Beaulieu, I started getting phone calls from writers, asking for appointments to interview me for various wine magazines. I had not received any such calls while at Gallo, as there was not any reason for writers to interview ordinary employees like myself. Ernest Gallo retained control over advertising and public relations, and he did not want any employees talking to outside writers. Gallo didn't encourage visitors to the winery at any time, didn't offer tastings to the public, and gave tours of the winery only when Ernest had a specific purpose in mind. I was surprised to be asked for interviews until I remembered that I now wore a Beaulieu hat and Beaulieu thrived on public relations.

Two weeks after I started working at Beaulieu, a news item appeared in the *San Francisco Chronicle* stating that Andre Tchelistcheff had appointed me to the position of winemaster of Beaulieu Vineyard at Rutherford in Napa Valley. It was accompanied by a picture of Andre and me seated at a work table, and stated that Andre would continue as technical director at Beaulieu. A similar announcement, with the same picture appeared in *Wines & Vines*, the most prominent news magazine of the wine industry. Both had been submitted by Legh Knowles, sales manager at Beaulieu. Ernest Gallo's wife, Amelia, saw the picture in the *Chronicle*, and asked Ernest (who had been away on a sales trip) about it. He immediately jumped on Julio, who explained that Andre Tchelistcheff had made me an offer that he couldn't match, which was true.

Wine writers, wine collectors and connoisseurs of rare and high-quality wines suddenly wanted to meet this 'new, hot young winemaker who came out of nowhere' to replace the great Andre Tchelistcheff at Beaulieu. After ten years at Gallo, I had not considered myself to be new, hot or young in any sense of the words. No announcement mentioned that I had been a winemaker elsewhere in the industry before moving to Beaulieu. I had felt a certain importance in my jobs at Gallo, but at Beaulieu none of the writers were giving Gallo any mention at all. None! It was as if they believed Gallo had never existed. Whatever time I had spent at Gallo didn't seem to count as winemaking experience; I might as well have moved from the position of bank teller to become the new winemaster at Beaulieu! I soon realized that connoisseurs of fine wines prided themselves in the belief that wineries the size of Gallo were not in the real wine business. 'Genuine wine' was produced by small wineries, never the size of Gallo, and started at retail prices far above those of Gallo. However, judging wine quality by high price alone is an over-simplification. Connoisseurs are not defined by who can pay the most for a wine (a phony definition); rather, they are proud of limiting themselves to the world's most unique examples of fine wine at any price. Gallo did not qualify, not because their wines were too cheap, but because their wines were too universally available.

High price in wine is always related to small quantity, but only sometimes to high quality. Why do savvy wineries fall all over themselves claiming, "our wine comes from one small corner of a hidden vineyard that produces special wine only in one year out of four?" Because the story allows them to get triple price for the wine, and it greatly massages the owner's reputation – and ego. Why did Robert Mondavi carefully nurture the myth that his wines were made in miniscule quantity, while he sold millions of cases for big bucks? The answer is: "Because he was a smart marketer."

Among the many types of wine consumers, two stand out in contrast to each other: those who collect and drink the world's scarcest wines that taste good, regardless of price; and those who drink readily available wines and look for the best wine at the lowest price. People in the first category go to great lengths to pay high prices for scarce wines that nobody else gets a chance to taste. They tend to treat food as they do wine; trying to eat specialty, unusual and gourmet foods. Their use of wine is as an accompaniment to these unusual foods, and they pay high prices for both food and wine. They try different vintages or brands on different nights, and do not expect the same taste on succeeding dinners; they sometimes even ooh and aah over minor differences from bottle to bottle, and attribute the differences, often correctly, to varying storage conditions.

Those in the second category drink everyday wines with everyday food. Surprisingly, they are often more discriminating than the first group, but not in expecting their wine to match whatever food they are having for dinner. This group often drinks the same brand of wine every day, and if the winery changes something in different batches, it is noticed (and complained about) by the drinker. For that reason, wineries often receive fewer complaints from the first group than the second. I don't rank one group above the other; each adds to the character of wine and the bottom lines of wineries. My personal goal has always been to make wines that go well with meals, as opposed to drinking wine as if it were a cocktail. That can be attained with both small lots and larger lots. Scarcity has nothing to do with whether a wine goes well with or without food.

Over the years, my wife and I attended a great many dinners with wine and food connoisseurs. Many were members of wine and food groups who enjoyed each other's company over monthly dinners at which the highest quality French 'First Growth' wines were served along with superb foods to highlight those wines. Beaulieu winemaking became my introduction to the best French wines, as I had known little about them previously. In trial comparisons, I had tasted expensive French wines at Gallo only a few times over the ten years I was there. Now, we were members of all the best food and wine groups in cities all over the country, and I needed to keep private notes about tasting various wines just to begin understanding them. Over the next decades of fine eating and drinking, I do not remember anyone ever asking me what job I held before being chosen by Andre as his replacement at Beaulieu Vineyards. They simply didn't want to know.

Within a few weeks of the announcement that I had become winemaster at Beaulieu in the spring of 1968, I received invitations to judge wines at several commercial competitions. The rules for each competition varied somewhat, but every competition required that all the wines be judged 'blind.' Wines entered by various wineries a few weeks ahead of the competition were received by workers in a back room, where they were categorized and given individual numbers. The identities of all the wines were recorded, and no one outside of the preparation room saw the identities of any of the entries. Later, at the competition, judges sat at small tables in a large room, and servers placed groups of 8 to 12 glasses in front of each judge (each glass marked with the random number of the wine it contained). Judges evaluated the wines by sight, smell and taste, writing their score for each of the wines on an official score sheet.

After discussing, debating and arguing among the four judges of each panel, a decision was made for each category, and the wines were awarded Gold, Silver, Bronze, Honorable Mention or No Award.[9] Only after the whole judging was over, and the scores were entered into the record, did the judges learn the identities of the wines. Often that was many days after the judging. Most of the competitions lasted two, three or four days and were usually operated quite professionally. Bernard (Barney) Rhodes, M.D. and his wife Belle were prominent judges in several of the larger competitions in 1968. Other judges included managers of large wine shops or sales organizations, members of various wine and food societies, writers

---

[9] Some competitions don't include Honorable Mention; some don't even include Bronze. Wineries often pay no attention to these lower awards, seeking only Gold.

for wine magazines, professors teaching wine science at universities, and a few winemakers from small, high-image wineries. Barney and Belle Rhodes were both experts and experienced in evaluating the best wines of the world, having organized competent wine appreciation groups for decades. Their two most prominent organizations were Northern California's 'Medical Friends of Wine' and the SF Bay Area's 'First Growth Group,' both of which comprised professional people who met at private dinners on a regular schedule. The host would match each food course to the finest wines of a specific sub-region of the wine world, and guests often were shown the wines blind and had to guess the identities of them before the food was served. I accepted most wine evaluation invitations for two reasons: I wanted to learn as much as possible about the current level of quality being produced, and I wanted to do my part to ensure that the best wines entered would be the ones that received the highest medals. That still holds true today, fifty years of judging later.

In 1972, Barney and Belle Rhodes invited Louis Martini and me to their home high in the Oakland hills to join them in their monthly First Growth dinner. Louis and I drove together and arrived to greet the other ten members, who were just beginning to pour the initial bottles of fine French Champagne. After the Champagne and hors d'oeuvres, the group was seated around two tables, and Barney brought in eight bottles, each wrapped in a numbered brown paper sack that was taped at the top to keep the capsule and label covered. Eight wine glasses were arranged in a curved row in front of each taster, and each wine was poured into a glass, numbered one through eight, from left to right. The twelve tasters, including Barney and Belle, began smelling and tasting the unidentified wines in their glasses. When all had made notes about each of the wines, Barney asked us to make guesses as to the identities of the wines.

The more outspoken judges oohed and aahed over "these great French Burgundies" and gave their opinions about vintages and producers. Some named Clos Vougeot, La Tache, Echezeaux, Richebourg and even Romanée-Conti among well-known and highly-prized Burgundies; vintages were guessed at between 1963 and 1970. Barney pulled three bottles out of their paper sacks as the group had guessed correctly, but the other sacks still contained mystery wines. I remained silent because I didn't know enough about any of those wines to open my mouth. I recognized that all the wines were Pinot Noirs (the finest French Burgundies) and none were Cabernets, i.e. this was a Burgundy dinner and no Bordeaux wines would appear.

As I tasted and re-tasted sample #5, I noticed that my nasal cavity started to feel puffy inside, as if it were swelling up a little. It was similar to the experience I had been noticing with the BV 1968 Beaumont Pinot Noir, although the taste of sample #5 seemed clearly French, and not Californian. I was excited because I thought finding that this French wine gave my nose the same reaction as the 1968 BV could give me a clue as to what wine component was giving me the sensitivity reaction. As I was mulling that over, Barney called on me directly for the first time. He said, "Dick, we've got guesses from most of the others, but you haven't said a word. What do you think #5 is?" I decided to tell the group about my stuffy nose experience with both this #5 French wine and the BV 1968 Beaumont Pinot Noir.

I said, "Well, Barney, I really don't know what this wine is. Frankly, I'm a little bit confused. I realize that all this evening's wines are great French Burgundies, but if I didn't know that, I would have sworn that # 5 was the BV 1968. I - - ." Barney interrupted my sentence by dropping his jaw and blurting out loudly, "My gawd, what a palate!" He reached out and pulled the bottle from bag #5. It was BV 1968 Beaumont Pinot Noir! Belle started to clap her hands gently, and was joined by the others, so I stopped talking. I thought to myself, "Barney, you son of a gun, you baited me and I got lucky, not by being a great taster, but by having a simple allergy." I was smart enough not to say another word. I never did tell Belle or Barney how I managed to recognize my own wine that evening, when all the odds were against it. Over the next several years, I noticed many times that Barney did this with guest winemakers, and very few could recognize their own wines when mixed in with others under circumstances that made it difficult to imagine that their own wine would be in the tasting.

One feature of this group, and all other 'First Growth Wine Appreciation' groups in America at the time, was that the members invariably concerned themselves with red table wines. There were occasional evaluations of highly-prized dessert wines, such as the only great wine produced anywhere in the world in the 'off year' of 1931 – the Quinta do Noval Port wine from Portugal. I drank that wine with Belle and Barney's group at the home of Walter and Frances Peterson in 1973. It was (and is) still superb. Walter had served it because he knew that 1931 was my birth year, and I felt very honored by his selection. That wine was truly superb, the obvious standout of that particular evening.

At dinners like this, an occasional white wine – a Chardonnay from Burgundy, for example – would be discussed, but primarily these groups were concerned with reds. If you were to ask them about white Burgundies the answer would be, "Most vintages of Le Montrachet really aren't very good. You sometimes find one that is outstanding, but that is a rare occasion, and it isn't worth the trouble. Red Burgundies are where the greatness is."

Red Wine / White Wine

In the history of bottled wines at Beaulieu Vineyard from the time of World War I (and the altar wines Georges had bottled during Prohibition for the church) up until 1968, the company had neither produced nor sold more red wine than white wine in any given year. BV was primarily a white wine producer, yet no consumer in 1968 would have believed that statement. BV was known for only one wine: Georges de Latour Private Reserve Cabernet Sauvignon. Everybody who knew wine knew BV Cabernet, and it was clearly, year in and year out, one of the two best wines of the state. Inglenook, a much smaller winery, was prized along with Beaulieu, but Inglenook had much less distribution, and was not as well known. Either winery routinely was called 'The' wine of California from time to time. Few writers even noticed Beaulieu's white wines even though Beaulieu had produced more white than red wine in every one of those years!

BV continued to produce, bottle and sell altar wines after the repeal of Prohibition. In 1968, my first year as Beaulieu winemaster, we bottled approximately 5% of our wines with altar wine labels, 90% of which were white or dessert wines, not red. One would think that communion wine, representing the blood of Christ, would be red. In fact, the vast majority of our altar wines were always white. Priests told me the reason was to avoid unsightly red wine stains on the cloths used for drying the chalice after communion. One would also think that altar wines might have been made differently from our regular BV table wines. In fact, we had no separate recipes or procedures. As an example, we bottled and sold 'BV Burgundy Altar Wine' to the church, and we sold 'BV Burgundy' to regular consumers through regular distribution. When we bottled Burgundy fifths, we labeled a small percentage of the bottles with altar wine labels (as needed), and all the rest with regular BV Burgundy labels. It was no different from Gallo using both Sauternes and Chablis labels on bottles of the same wine on my first day in the wine industry a decade earlier!

Collectors of high-quality Cabernets had long noticed that there were just two wineries that normally ranked first and second in competitions. 'Inglenook and Beaulieu, Beaulieu and Inglenook' was commonly said. At a dinner party in the late 1960s, Professor Maynard Amerine was asked what it took to make a great Cabernet. Maynard was famous for clever answers, and never missed a chance to answer a wine question with a clever play on words. He said, "In my opinion, you need one thing to produce great Cabernet; you need Rutherford dust on the grapes." The group knew very well that he was referring to the well-known 'Beaulieu and Inglenook twosome,' both of which were located at the Rutherford intersection of Highway 29, right in the heart of Napa Valley.

Maynard's clever answer was completely misconstrued in the decades following. About twenty years after Maynard's dinner remark, I was quite surprised when I overheard a neophyte wine lover tell someone (with a certain snobbish flair) that he could 'taste the Rutherford dust' in the BV wine he was drinking. The wine was BV Beaufort Chardonnay, which made me grab my sides with laughter. Chardonnay is not similar to Cabernet in any flavor aspect of which I am aware. All BV wines were filtered and there could have been no dust of any kind in the wine. No serious flavor chemist would believe that there could be enough dust in the bloom on grape skins to make the eventual wine taste like dust, especially after aging for some years. Neither does the taste of dust enter vine roots and travel up to the crop and lodge itself inside grapes; biochemistry does not operate that way.[10] On my hands and knees, I have smelled and tasted vineyard dust from Beaulieu vineyard #3 near Rutherford and Beaulieu vineyards #2 and #4 on Highway 29 in Oakville. No taster can tell the difference and, of course, the idea is ludicrous. Not wanting to be asked for an explanation of why I was tasting vineyard dirt, I did so when Andre Tchelistcheff was not around. He wouldn't have understood any explanation I offered.

Interestingly, the tannin in Cabernet table wines bottled at 13% alcohol, pH 3.55 and free SO_2 of 30 parts per million (typical in 1968) sometimes gives a subtle 'powdery mouthfeel' or mouth-drying impression, and that is still true today. It is possible that some tasters could refer to that mouth-drying impression as dusty, but it would be a stretch to say he is tasting dust from a particular type of soil. That taste sensation happens with many Cabernet wines from many different soil types, including Cabernet wine blends grown in France. However, to claim that one is actually tasting dust is to be arrogant, if not a keen bullshitter. There are a lot of such individuals in the wine industry, as most wine lovers have noticed.

In my time at Beaulieu, we never changed the red wines – to do so would have been crazy. We did stop birds from building nests (and even flying into the area) around the red wine open-top fermenters. There simply wasn't any competitor for BV red wines in those days; the only previous competitor, Inglenook, was already losing favor. For decades Inglenook had been, in Andre's memory, 'The Classic Chateau' of California. Historically, it was much smaller than Beaulieu Vineyard, even though Beaulieu, at 150,000 cases, was not considered very big. Inglenook had been in the 18 to 20,000 case range when John Daniel owned it. However, John Daniel sold Inglenook to United Vintners in 1964, and the Inglenook image headed downhill almost immediately as writers noticed that the winery no longer produced great wines of the type made under John Daniel. In 1968 and 1969, I saw John regularly as Inglenook and Beaulieu wineries were located directly

---

[10] Bloom is the name given to a thin, waxy, dust and yeast-covered coating that exists on the skins of all grape berries on a grapevine. It is best seen after wiping a finger across the grape, leaving a clean path where the finger rubbed off the 'bloom.'

across Highway 29 from each other. After the sale, John no longer had control of Inglenook winemaking. The Heublein Corporation[11] bought control of United Vintners in 1969, and quickly removed all remaining doubt about the ensuing expansion of Inglenook. It seems that whenever a large company buys a small winery, the big one automatically wants to jump into a program of 'helping' the little winery grow. If Inglenook had set to work helping United Vintners focus on paying more attention to quality, both companies might have been better off, but that isn't what happened. Inglenook was selling more than a million cases only a year later. The million were sold at greatly reduced prices and, of course, they were totally different wines sold to totally different customers.

Prior to 1968, the closest competitor which could be spoken of in the same tone of voice as Beaulieu might have been Louis Martini or Peter Mondavi's Charles Krug. Joe Heitz's operation was recognized as having great quality, but was miniscule in size at only a few thousand cases per year. He produced some excellent wines – he had been an assistant winemaker to Andre at BV ten years earlier, and everyone knew he would make fine wines after he started his own winery. Technically, Joe had his feet on the ground as a winemaker. He knew what he was doing, but his company wasn't yet established as a solid business in the minds of many consumers. The same thing was said about Freemark Abbey at the time.

BV, Louis Martini and Charles Krug were the names to know in Napa Valley in 1968. There were a few smaller producers known for other varietals, such as Fred McCray's 'Chardonnay winery' Stony Hill and Warren Winiarski's Stag Leap Wine Cellars. Fred had developed an unsurpassed reputation for Stony Hill's Chardonnay, but his was not a Cabernet winery. Robert Mondavi had a split within his family at Charles Krug and started his own winery in 1966, but didn't yet produce enough volume to be noticed. That is to say, his wines were not yet noticed, but he certainly was.

---

[11] Heublein Corporation was a large food and drink conglomerate, headquartered in Hartford, Connecticut. Their main brands were Smirnoff Vodka, Hamm's Beer, A-1 Steak Sauce and, later, Kentucky Fried Chicken.

Bob was out there beating every drum he could find, telling the world all about the excellence of his wines whenever possible. I thought at the time that the smartest decision Bob made was to drop the former pronunciation of his last name (Mon-dáy-vi) and to begin introducing his new pronunciation (Mon-dáh-vi). His brother, Peter, kept the American pronunciation, and both Bob and Peter openly continued their personal disagreements. More than once, visitors to Napa Valley noticed the two pronunciations, and asked which was correct. The answer was always, "depends on whose side you're on." Among the residents of Napa Valley at that time, I know of no one who chose sides. It was generally agreed that both men were better off without the other one. Everyone remained friends with both sides, and their personal disagreements were not discussed by outsiders. Of today's quality Cabernet producers – including Chateau Montelena, Dalla Valle, Diamond Creek, Freemark Abbey, Groth, La Sirena, Phelps, Shafer, Stags Leap, Silver Oak and Turnbull – not one was in full operation in 1968.

The situation in 1968 and 1969 was that Beaulieu Vineyard had the field all to itself. If you went to a fine restaurant, and looked for domestic wines on the wine list (if there were any domestic wines at all), you would find Beaulieu Vineyard, Louis M. Martini and Charles Krug. There might have been Almaden or Masson on the wine list as well, but no one in Napa Valley paid much attention to those two brands. Their prices were mid-range, and their wine quality was not considered more than mediocre, although I always thought both produced some nice wines on occasion. Wente and Concannon were already well-known as two of the best white wine producers in the 1960s, and there were a couple of other 'comers,' but that is essentially all California had to offer in 1968.

One of the older Napa Valley wineries, Beringer, did not have a quality operation in those days. Their wines were universally spoiled, with bacterial and spoilage yeast (Brettanomyces, or 'Brett') off-flavors. Beringer was completely out of sync with the rest of Napa Valley in 1968. The first sniff or taste of the wines betrayed Brett spoilage and bad barrels, but the Beringer family did not seem to notice (all they knew was their wine sales were slowing). I did not understand how one winery could have become so blind to their competition and remain in business.

I found the probable answer in the summer of 1968 at the Bohemian Grove in San Francisco. There was a live public presentation of *The Most Happy Fella* stage play in the outdoor theater. There were only twelve winery members in the Napa Valley Vintners organization in 1968. One representative from each of the twelve saw the show; we were there to pour samples of our wines for the public and actors at intermission. I represented Beaulieu, and the winery tables were arranged alphabetically in a large semicircle. The Beaulieu table was right beside the Beringer table. The Beaulieu table was jammed with tasters, and I was extremely busy pouring wine into the phalanx of glasses thrust out in front of me. Out of the corner of my eye, I could see Otto Beringer standing quietly behind his table, bottle in hand but not pouring much wine.

I was embarrassed for him, as his friend, but was so busy pouring BV wine that I had no time to do anything else. I was plenty tired just twenty minutes later, when the announcer warned the audience to begin moving back to their seats. As I was cleaning up, Otto came over to my table and remarked that I had poured a lot of wine. I nodded and he asked whether I had ever tasted his wine. I answered, "Oh yes, I make it a point to taste all the competitors' wines I can. Have you tasted Beaulieu wines?" "Hell no!" he blurted out, a little too loudly, I thought. "I drink Beringer, Beringer is what's good and that's all I drink."

I was stunned, because his answer seemed too aggressive for the situation. Otto was a very big man, taller than my 6' 3", and he must have weighed three hundred pounds. He was known by his nickname, Tiny. I didn't know what else to say, and answered only, "Well Tiny, everybody's different. I just like to try what I see others drinking." Fortunately, we had to rush to get back into the theater, and the conversation ended. I now believe it was a classic case of 'house blindness.' If Beringer winemakers tasted only their own wines, and avoided the wines of BV, Martini, Charles Krug and others, they would not know how different their own wines had become. By drinking only their own wines, they became blind to the competition as well as to the consumer. The microbial spoilage that existed at their winery was not noticed because they got used to the taste of their own wines, and did not compare their wines with others. The rest of us felt sorry for them, but it was none of our business, so we butted out.

Beringer was sold to the Nestlé Company in 1971, and the new owner-ship hired Myron Nightingale from the Central Valley as winemaker. Myron was well known to everyone who attended American Society of Enology meetings and had a great reputation. One day he stopped by to see me at Beaulieu shortly after his name was announced as the new winemaker for Beringer. He wanted to ask a serious question: "What would you do in my position at Beringer?" I answered without hesitation, "I'd dump the wines, burn every one of the barrels and wooden tanks, sterilize the winery and start over with new barrels, hoses and stainless tanks." I said it too fast, and was afraid Myron might think I was being a little harsh, but he laughed out loud! Between laughs he told me, "You're the fifth guy I've asked that question, and every one of you gave me the same answer. Joe Heitz told me that, Andre told me that, Louis Martini told me that, even Jack Davies said the same thing." "Well," I said, "if the big guns at Nestlé give you the OK, I'd stay and do it for them, but if they fight you, start your own winery." Myron did what all of us had told him, and the result is that today Beringer is known as one of the best of the large wineries in Napa Valley. Beringer wine quality is now first rate, and I am happy that the ownership kept the same name, perhaps to honor Tiny's memory.

Madame's Legacy

It was late 1968 when the stainless steel question first got Madame de Pins' undivided attention. I wasn't able to get stainless steel installed at BV until 1969 – more than 30 years after Andre Tchelistcheff first started producing America's very best Napa Valley wines in the same buildings. Andre had tried many times before then to install stainless steel in the winery. He had made several studies of the numbers and sizes of tanks that were needed, and had even chosen an area in back of the main fermentation building where the tanks could be located. He had made a plan, including a tentative tank layout, and had gotten price estimates for their construction. Every time he had approached Madame de Pins for approval and permission, she had thrown him out. The exact conversation might have differed each time, but her refusal always amounted to two reasons: stainless costs too much, and it was not traditional in France. Nevertheless, Andre knew the real reason – she expected money to flow freely from the winery to her, but never from her to the winery.

The Andre/Madame relationship was an example of what can happen when a manager, however competent, gets too close to the boss and becomes 'family.' Andre's word was no longer given the weight that it deserved. Andre had been close to Madame de Pins and her family for three decades, years of close, personal and everyday contact. His voice was not listened to as intently as that of a newcomer from the outside. In 1968, I was the newcomer from outside the family, so my input was heard. When I discussed the needed stainless steel, Madame said to me, "Oh, it seems to me Andre may have mentioned that to me once or twice before. I'm sure you are right."

We did not get the $125,000 approval for buying stainless tanks on that day; that came a few months later, after a good deal more prodding, pleading and pushing. I had finally made it clear that this was not a question to be postponed much longer. We dusted off Andre's earlier plan, updated price quotes, and I made a formal proposal to the board of directors (Madame de Pins, attorney Ted Kolb, and Madame's family) in May, 1969. "Beaulieu will have to install these stainless tanks now or expect to lose its position of quality prominence in Napa Valley. Further, additional refrigeration will be just as mandatory," I warned. Andre and Otto Gramlow (Beaulieu business manager) supported my proposal. There was family discussion for the next hour or two over a grand lunch. The next day, Madame called me to her sitting room. She came in, looking very solemn. "Okay, Dick Peterson," she said as she shook her pointed finger at me, "you can install your damn stainless steel tanks, but I don't want anyone calling attention to them. I do not want any of the winery visitors to see them. I want those stainless tanks painted earth color!" I said, "yes Madame," without smiling.

It was a strong statement; I hadn't heard her use the word "damn" very often before. Whether a stronger word ever crossed her lips, I don't know, but I noticed later that most of the time when she did use that word to me, it was connected with the word 'winery.' I knew she had accepted what I had been telling her. Andre had been telling her the same things for years, but she had successfully ignored him. She now saw that these things could no longer be postponed, and she had to take it seriously.

Madame de Pins had made another monumental decision – far more monumental than any of us realized at the time. She had not just decided to spend $125,000 for the first stainless tanks in Beaulieu history; she had decided to divorce that damned winery once and for all. The winery had betrayed her and her family, after all. It was derelict in its duty to her, despite the promises made by her father, Georges de Latour. She would leave the wine business entirely! Two weeks later, we were astonished to hear her quietly tell us all, gathered together in her living room, that she had decided to sell the company, her father's beloved Beaulieu, to Heublein, a large vodka, spirits and food corporation. Even Legh Knowles, VP of sales and unofficial business chief, was completely surprised by her decision.

I had a strong impression that Madame's decision to sell the winery to Heublein in 1969 was based on one simple conclusion. On the one hand, she had a chance to take several million dollars out of the winery; on the other hand, if she didn't sell, she would have the obligation to pony up the money for the stainless steel tanks (plus even more for refrigeration and God knows what else). It must have finally occurred to her that the winery was actually wearing out. Andre had been telling her the truth all those years. In fact, Andre had been doing a magnificent job of holding things together with baling wire for a decade. She'd heard the same story from both of us: if Beaulieu Vineyard was to retain its image of superiority over the other wineries of California, she would have to undergo a program of putting money into modernization and new equipment. That must have scared her, and I had the strong impression that fear of this worn-out winery becoming a cash drain was a major factor in her decision to sell the business. She postponed it for as long a time as possible. In the end, family members pushed her into making the decision when the offer was there, rather than later when she might have difficulty in finding a suitable one. Wineries were not being sold everyday, and it was not easy to decide how to evaluate the value of a long-established image.

Immediately upon purchasing Beaulieu, Heublein elevated Legh

Knowles from sales manager to an additional new position: general manager. Later, Legh reminded me that Madame had not spent any money for the stainless tanks; rather, it was Heublein money. I suppose that is true; the decision was hers and the bank loan to finance the tanks was made by her in May 1969. She sold the company a month later, and the new owner picked up the loan obligation as part of the purchase.

I remember being a bystander at an argument between Andre and Madame de Pins in June 1969. Just after the sale of the winery to Heublein, Andre had suggested that Beaulieu might have been a better legacy to leave to her grandchildren than the stocks and bonds she would actually leave them. I remember her stating vehemently, "Listen Andre, what you don't understand is that I have an obligation to my grandchildren. My father promised me that this winery would always take care of us. Dagmar has four children, my grandchildren, and I have an obligation to them. I need to see that they have the good life that they deserve. The money will give them that."

My own point of view, spoken only meekly to Andre but never to Madame, was "Gee, what better lifestyle could you give them than to be owners of the very finest chateau of California, Beaulieu Vineyard? Owning that winery, financing the business as necessary, continuing its superb leadership in wine quality, and keeping it as a family winery would be a fantastic legacy for those grandchildren." When Madame felt that the winery had reached a point where she'd have to put money into it, then the winery was no good to her anymore. She sold it to Heublein thinking, "Let them put money into it. We'll use money from the sale to continue living in a lifestyle befitting my station." Her selling price for Beaulieu in 1969 was leaked out to be 8.5 million dollars.[12] In 1980, Legh Knowles told me that Heublein was earning 5 million dollars every year from sales of Beaulieu wines. We did not know at the time, but the decision to sell was said to be pushed onto Madame de Pins by Walter Sullivan, husband of Dagmar, Madame's daughter. Apparently, both Madame and Dagmar were distressed for

---

[12] *Napa*, by James Conaway Avon Books.

years after selling, especially when they realized that Heublein had gotten the winery for a rock-bottom price.

I had strong and positive feelings toward Madame de Pins. I loved her in the way the British love their Queen. I never felt taken advantage of; rather, I felt a strong sense of duty to keep up her lifestyle, and all of us tried very hard to serve her while we also served the winery. I think that everybody who worked for her loved her in this way, and thought of her and the family as our royal family. Employees certainly got upset from time to time and found her impossible to deal with, but they thought of her as their queen without reservation. How many people get to know an actual queen in their lifetime? How many get to have lunch with royalty once or twice a month? I can never forget the royal 'feel in the air' as I sat telling her all that was going on around the valley over lunch.

The de Pins' property, vineyard #1, was not included in the sale to Heublein. Madame and Marquis had retained ownership of her country estate and continued to reside there for a few weeks from time to time. I saw them occasionally driving by, but neither Madame nor Marquis ever visited the winery again. I felt a very personal loss and a definite sadness when I read some years later, in November 1982, that Madame de Pins had died. It was a distinct loss even though I hadn't seen her in seven or eight years. Marquis de Pins had died about five or six years earlier, and he, in true French style, had chosen his burial place beforehand. It was in Montbrun, Gascony in the south of France at the original de Pins family property. His burial site was located in a natural crypt of some kind. The size and shape of the space was such that he would have to be placed in the crypt with his legs bent because it was not quite long enough to accept the full length of his body. Even though he was not a tall man, this would be the only way that he could fit into his rightful spot along with the previous members of his family. Marquis had told me in one of our early discussions that he had agreed to this bent-legs arrangement twenty-five years earlier.

Heublein: A Different Language

After the sale of Beaulieu in June 1969, we were visited by a series of Heublein staff, none of whom understood the tiniest bit about the Beaulieu concept of quality and image. Three who stand out in my memory are Andy Beckstoffer, Don Jackson and Chris Carriuolo. I spent a day with Andy in the BV vineyards explaining what we were doing in each vineyard block, what each block needed and how I planned to correct the many deficiencies in each. He was a personable young man, not long out of business school, and was primed to convince me that I should use business school approaches to maximize profits for Heublein. Heublein profits were my goal too, but Andy and I were never to agree on how to go about it. He insisted that wine grapes were merely a commodity, and that we were wasting our time growing grapes at Rutherford. He said grapes could be purchased much more cheaply from large Central Valley growers, and he could connect me with United Vintners whose growers would be happy to sell to Beaulieu. (Heublein had purchased United Vintners four months earlier.) I told him I had spent ten years at Gallo easily beating Italian Swiss Colony, United Vintners wine brand, because Gallo had better grape varieties. Italian Swiss Colony had to make do with the Thompson Seedless grapes of their growers, and I actually felt sorry for my friend, Ed Rossi, who was head of wine production at "Swiss." I stressed to Andy that Gallo had passed Italian Swiss to become the nation's largest wine company in 1967, which I still believed was solely due to the vastly superior Gallo wine grape quality.

I admitted it was inefficient to grow grapes the way we had been forced to grow them at Beaulieu. I informed him that Italian Swiss Colony had none of the varieties that the Beaulieu business had been built on, and emphasized that Thompson grapes had a richly deserved reputation for never producing quality wine under any condition. Then I thought to myself, "I couldn't even make baked sherry out of it." In any case, we could not use non-Napa grapes if we were to continue the high image of Beaulieu. Andy thought image was something we should leave up to the marketing people, and felt they could create any image they wanted through advertising and promotion. I was certain that I had not taught him anything about BV wine that day. If I had taught him anything about vineyards, it was that ours needed to be replanted in stages as soon as possible due to missing vines, diseases, and the need to replace old, outdated varieties. If we replanted all at once, Beaulieu would run out of wine, as new vines have to develop for four years before they begin producing fruit. He was sure we could find replacement grapes for Beaulieu to use in the meantime. I cautioned him to discuss it with Legh Knowles because Legh would have strong opinions about which grape sources could, and which could not, be used for Beaulieu wines. Overall, it was an enjoyable day with Andy, but I could see clearly that Beaulieu and Heublein were speaking different languages.

Don Jackson was a finance man who had come to California to make a complete study of the Beaulieu wine business. I was to give him as much time as he needed and to be very open about where we stood within a reasonable business plan. I was also to give him ideas about what the company needed, and what I thought would be the best way to get there. I gave Don a much shorter tour of the vineyards than Andy because he was interested only in present-day costs. I spent much more time with him describing exactly what treatment each wine received along its path from grapes to bottled wine. I described everything we did for each grape variety in the cellar, and estimated how many hours the grapes, juice, must and wine had spent in each stage of winemaking, bottling, warehousing and aging. Don's goal was only to calculate the actual costs of our current operations; he had no interest in the image or public relations aspect of Beaulieu, nor did he have an opinion about 'winegrowing' vs. 'grape growing.' His goal was "just the costs, Dick, just the actual costs."

Chris Carriuolo, Heublein's national sales manager, had been selling wine for many years and was a long-time friend of Legh Knowles although they had always worked for different companies. As would be expected, Chris was a typical out-going, always smiling, glad-hand extrovert. "He's the best type of wine salesman there is," Legh had told me. Chris buttonholed me on his first visit to the winery, and wanted to know all about the winemaking I had done at Gallo. I told him that none of what I had done at Gallo would apply to Beaulieu, and his answer changed the subject, "How do you feel about travel?" I said I had traveled the U.S. by car and knew every square inch of California because I had flown over it in Army airplanes and helicopters many times. Chris bounced back to the subject of winemaking and Gallo. He told me that an old friend of mine from Gallo days, George McCarthy, now worked for Heublein and George had told him that I had made and improved many new wines for Gallo. (Legh Knowles was also a graduate of 'Gallo University' and had confirmed George's story.) I told him that I knew what went into every Gallo wine, but I was not going to discuss that with non-Gallo people. Chris laughed, and asked me if I could make new wines out of Portuguese grape varieties. My answer was, "Of course. All I'd have to do is experiment with them a little while." I said I had enjoyed experimenting and developing new wine types before, and would enjoy doing more of that. He finally told me what he had in mind.

Heublein, in partnership with a Portuguese company, owned Lancers Rosé. I knew Lancers, having tasted it several times at dinners and tastings. It was a light orange-pink carbonated wine that came in a uniquely shaped glass bottle painted orange-tan to look like a crock bottle. It had been selling well across America for some years, and Chris wanted me to make a new Lancers wine for him. This one had to be a white wine, to partner with the Lancers Rosé. The bottle would be the same shape (maybe a different color), and I would make a carbonated white wine for that package. White wines were outselling reds and pinks in America, and I could see why he wanted to expand the Lancers line in that direction. My only hesitation was that I did not want to move from Beaulieu to Portugal. Chris said I could stay at Beaulieu and go to Portugal from time to time to develop White Lancers. He would get back to me.

Andy Beckstoffer asked me to meet him for breakfast at the Silverado Country Club one morning. After settling in, he asked why I was using Chenin Blanc grapes to make BV champagne. I assumed he was questioning the quality level of the champagne, and I felt pleased that Andy appeared to care about quality, after all – maybe I had misjudged him that first day in the vineyards. I was apologetic, and told him that I had wanted to use Chardonnay, of course, and that Andre had wanted to use better grapes as well. The problem was that we needed all of our Chardonnay grapes for the Beaufort Chardonnay table wine label, and I had to use the next best variety, Chenin Blanc, for champagne. "That's not what I mean," he interrupted, shaking his head slowly, with a slight frown. "Don't you realize that you're paying $900 a ton for Chardonnay when you could get

Thompson Seedless for $60?" [13] I was absolutely stunned. When I caught my breath, I said, "Andy, there isn't anything you could say or do that would cause me to use Thompson in any BV wine. Let's just finish our breakfast and go away friends." With a condescending grin, Andy looked at me and said, "Dick, you'll never make a million dollars." I was so shocked that I could not think of an answer, and the rest of the breakfast was simple talk. Later, when I told Legh, he thought I should have asked, "What will you do with the millions you'll make? Enjoy Italian Swiss Colony raisin wine?" Legh kept that story alive, and Andre Tchelistcheff referred to Andy Beckstoffer as the "Thompson Seedless King" in conversations for months afterward.

Don Jackson did not take long to complete his financial study. After only one month, he called a meeting at Beaulieu to present his 'Preliminary Analysis.' He had made a direct comparison between two varietal wines: Cabernet Sauvignon and Gamay Beaujolais. Cabernet was our most costly red wine to produce; Gamay Beaujolais was our least. Private Reserve Cabernet wines required four years of aging (two years in barrels plus two more years in bottle), while Gamay Beaujolais required only months (four to six months in barrels and virtually no time in bottle) prior to sale to the public. Also, Cabernet required more expensive land since the variety needs a warmer climate, while Gamay Beaujolais can grow in cheaper soil, closer to the cold California coast.

Don Jackson presented his findings to an astonished group of the Beaulieu managers in a meeting at the winery and made the following comparison between the two varietals.

We agreed that his estimated costs sounded correct, but Gamay Beaujolais would sell at a considerably lower price than Cabernet. Don's

---

[13] At Beaulieu in 1968, we crushed 105 tons of Chardonnay, which was nearly 15% of all the Chardonnay in Napa Valley. Most of the tonage was grown by Charles Krug, Beaulieu, Martini and Beringer, with the rest bought from growers (Andy Pelissa and Laurie Wood). The variety was famous in France – in Champagne, Burgundy and Chablis – but had not yet caught on in California, where it was incorrectly called 'Pinot Chardonnay.'

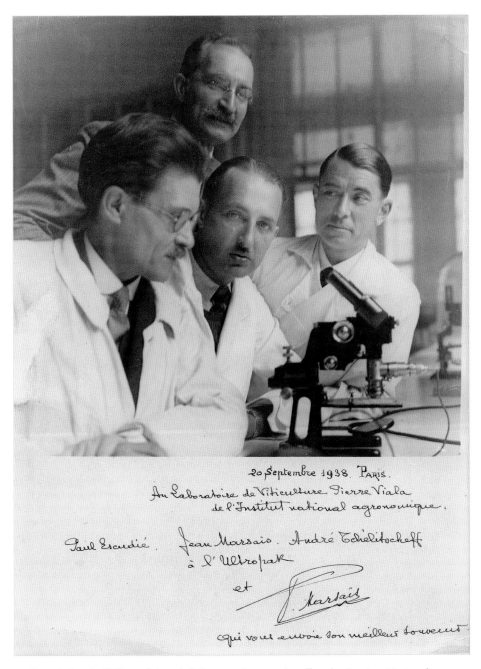

20 Septembre 1938. Paris.
Au Laboratoire de Viticulture Pierre Viala
de l'Institut national agronomique.

Paul Escudié. Jean Marsais. André Tchelitscheff
à l'Ultropak

et

Marsais

Qui vous envoie son meilleur souvenir

Andre Tchelistcheff (*far right*) with fellow students and staff at the Institut National Agronomique (National Agromony Institute) in Paris in 1938. Georges de Latour hired Andre to become the first winemaker at Beaulieu Vineyards in Rutherford, California, shortly after this photo was taken.

The Beaulieu Winery
building in 1938.
The building was already
old at that time, but still
stands today, more than
seventy-five years later.

The Marquis and
Marquise de Pins (*left*)
enjoy a wine tasting
together in the Beaulieu
champagne cellar
in 1957.

Madame Hélène de Pins
and Andre Tchelistcheff
(*opposite*), shortly after
Andre's marriage to
Dorothy Andrew in 1969.
*Photo by Dorothy
Tchelistcheff.*

Beaulieu's first three winemakers *(from left)*: Theo Rosenbrand (3rd winemaker), Andre Tchelistcheff (1st), and Dick Peterson (2nd) at the home of Joe Heitz in St. Helena, 1968. *Photo by Joe Heitz.*

Warming the vineyard air at ground level by burning diesel oil in smudge pots, Beaulieu vineyard #2 at about 5 a.m., late April, 1970. This was the most serious frost season I experienced at Beaulieu and one of the most serious in the Napa Valley. Between mid-April and mid-May, for twenty nights, everyone was out all night protecting the vines. Despite these efforts, Beaulieu lost half its crop in 1970 to severe spring frost damage.

A Cabernet Sauvignon grapevine suffering from Leafroll virus disease in Beaulieu vineyard #3 in 1968. Leaves on infected grapevines curl downward, changing color to yellow, orange or red, depending on the grape variety. Healthy leaves remain green and uncurled.

Two of the Portuguese wines made by the author for Heublein in 1970. The wines were produced and bottled at José Maria Da Fonseca, Internacional, Azeitão, Portugal. The Lancers Vinho Branco (*green bottle*) outsold Heublein's original Lancers Rosé in its second year. All Lancers distinctively shaped bottles were made of glass painted to look like crockery.

Paul Tchelistcheff, Dimitri's son and Andre's grandson is shown riddling bottles in the Beaulieu champagne cellar in 1969.

The author sampling wines from barrels in the wooden Beaulieu barrel racks in 1968. Working with barrels in racks like these was a nightmare of difficult, hand work. There was no better way to handle barrels at that time; it wasn't possible to identify or repair leaky barrels or even fill or empty them easily. *Photo by Ray Brisebois.*

Andre Tchelistcheff in the
Beaulieu cellar in 1968.
Photos by the author.

Andre Tchelistcheff tasting
a barrel sample of wine from
the same (hard to access)
wooden barrel racks at
Beaulieu in 1968.

Barrel aging red wines at the Firestone winery in 1975. Many wineries wasted space in warehouses like these because there was no way to easily stack and handle full wine barrels. The row of barrels standing on their heads (ends) are empty; barrels resting on their bilges are full of wine. *Photos by the author.*

Barrel aging whisky at National Distillers, Memphis in 1962. Standing on end, full barrels could be handled (carefully) by a fork lift. Wine can never be stored in barrels standing on their heads like this, because the wine would spoil.

Stuart Watson, Chairman of Heublein (*left*) with Legh Knowles, General Manager of Beaulieu (*right*) attending a wine tasting at the winery in 1969.

Harry Waugh, a well-known English author of wine books, in discussion with the author and his first wife, Diane, at a competitive wine tasting event.

Barney and Belle Rhodes, working hard at a typical wine judging competition, 1972.
Photo courtesy of Hélène Schwartz.

Most of the Napa Valley Vintners in 1972 (*above*), gathered at the 20th Anniversary of Hanns Kornell Champagne Cellars: (*from left*) Brother Timothy, Louis Stralla (Mayor of St. Helena), Bob Mondavi, Bob Travers, Marylouise Kornell, name unknown, Peter Mondavi, Chuck Carpy, Hanns Kornell, Dick Peterson, John Hoffman, Joe Heitz, Roy Raymond. Missing from this group picture are Jack Davies, Louis Martini, and John Daniel.

Wine tasting at Mondavi Winery for visiting wine book author, Alan Young, from Australia. Attending: (*from left*) the author, Robert Mondavi, Tim Mondavi, and Alan Young.

BV sales tasting session in progress in 1968.
Attending: (*from left*) Andre Tchelistcheff,
Hank Rubin (restaurant owner), and Legh
Knowles (sales manager at Beaulieu).
The author was also participating (seated
at the empty chair in the foreground).
Photo by the author.

A tenth bottle of 1970 BV Beaumont
Pinot Noir, opened for a special dinner
on December 26, 2014. The cork was
stained evenly and only about ¼ inch
from the end (sign of an excellent seal).
The wine was beautiful and fully alive
after forty-four years. This is one example
proving Andre's claim that good Pinots
often out-live good Cabernets. A 1968
bottle of similar wine caused unique
allergy symptoms in the author's nasal
cavity – the only wine to do so in over
sixty years of wine tasting.

Awarding the first Andre Tchelistcheff Scholarship prize ($5,000) to Dan Chellemi in 1988 (*above*) a new graduate student at UC Davis. Various amounts are awarded annually. *Photo by Dorothy Tchelistcheff.*

Andre Tchelistcheff (*left*) at the Coppola property in Rutherford where he was consulting in 1977. *Photo by Scott Clemens.*

Dorothy and Andre Tchelistcheff (*left*) in a Carneros vineyard in the late 1980's. Andre did a great amount of vineyard and winery consulting over a twenty year period after his "retirement."

Grape Varietal	Investment per Case	Return on Investment
Cabernet Sauvignon	$28.79	17%
Gamay Beaujolais	$11.70	49%

numbers for return on investment for Gamay would have to be lowered substantially. He had assumed that both wines would be sold at the same FOB price[14] to distributors, which was his most glaring error in data gathering.

It was too bad that none of us had objected to his numbers. On a roll, Don then dropped his bombshell: He would propose to Heublein management that Beaulieu drop all production of Cabernet Sauvignon in favor of becoming a 'Gamay Beaujolais winery.' There was silence for several seconds, and we thought he was kidding. I could not believe what I had heard. Then Legh, always the gentleman, said quietly, "Stuart Watson, chairman of Heublein, has told us that he intends for Beaulieu to grow from our present 150,000 cases per year to 500,000 cases. What makes you believe that Beaulieu could sell half a million cases of Gamay Beaujolais, *at any price?*" Don shrugged his shoulders and said, "Heublein is a marketing company. There is no point in selling products that do not make money. We need to optimize profits by selling products that *do* make money."

Legh was pissed; he was also very surprised at what he had heard. There was a huge and growing demand for BV Cabernet all over America. It was an easy sell and probably was primed for a price increase.[15] On the other hand, 1968 was our very first vintage of Gamay Beaujolais. It had been released for sale only a few weeks earlier, about the time Stuart Watson was having dinner with Madame de Pins, offering her 8 million dollars for the

---

[14] FOB: Free On Board is the price at which distributors purchase wine from a winery. FOB price of bottled wine is close to half the retail price.

company. Legh had no idea whether Gamay Beaujolais would sell at all, how much of it he could sell, or at what price. He did know it could never approach the price or the level of demand for BV Cabernet. Nowhere in the world had Beaujolais developed a quality or price image anywhere near that of Cabernet Sauvignon.

For the next few months, there was a great deal of back-and-forth debate between each of us at Beaulieu and various people at Heublein on this subject. Legh was a master at explaining how the wine market worked, but his words fell on mostly deaf ears. BV Cabernet was in big demand. It is no exaggeration to say that Beaulieu *owned* the Cabernet market in 1969! How could any intelligent person think for a minute that Gamay Beaujolais could replace Cabernet in the marketplace? If BV had stopped selling Cabernet, it would not have been long before at least twenty other wineries would have begun pushing their own Cabernet wines. None would have been as good as BV in the beginning, but with time, many new wines could become as good or even better. Heublein would have given away a perfectly good market for high-quality Cabernet table wine. The wild dream that Gamay Beaujolais could replace the dollars that would be lost by cancelling Cabernet production was absurd.

Legh did not give up. To his credit, he was at least partially successful in getting both Chris Carriuolo, sales manager and Stuart Watson, chairman to see some folly in caving in to abstract financial calculations. There existed a solid market demand for Cabernet in the U.S., but almost none for Gamay Beaujolais. Indeed, Legh suspected that Gamay Beaujolais might never be able to match Cabernet's dominance in any wine market. With hindsight, it was clearly in Heublein's best interest for Don to lose the battle to Legh, for Heublein would have destroyed BV's high-quality image if they had blindly followed Don Jackson over the cliff. I marveled at the way Legh

---

[15] The current average FOB selling price in 1969 for BV Cabernet in the U.S. was $16.95 per case; retail price would be double that, or about $33.90 per case/$3.00 per bottle). Employees could buy Private Reserve Cabernet for just over the FOB price, $1.90 per bottle. I bought several cases of every vintage at that bargain price and enjoyed them over the years.

remained on friendly terms with his bosses while fighting the uphill battle to save them from their own arrogance. I once asked him whether it was worth it. He answered, "Yes, it was worth it. We saved one of the country's great treasures. The Heublein people own Beaulieu, but they do not yet realize what they have. They are nice guys – but they're vodka guys and think they can remake Beaulieu in Smirnoff's image."

We were surrounded by more and more evidence of that. One example hit both Legh and me squarely at the same instant. Heublein had recently hired Dick Oster to become the new president of United Vintners. Following a corporate social custom, Legh invited all the Beaulieu staff to meet Dick at a dinner party held at Legh's Silverado Country Club home near Napa. My wife and I arrived a few minutes early. She went into the dining room with Legh's wife, Maggie, while I helped Legh open some wine bottles. After a few minutes, the doorbell rang, and Legh opened the door to greet Dick Oster. Legh had glasses of the 1964 BV Private Reserve Cabernet on a tray, and I held a fresh bottle of chilled BV Champagne ready to open and pour, depending on which wine Dick would choose to begin the evening. He started to reach for a glass of Private Reserve from Legh's tray, but quickly jerked his hand back and asked, "Oh ... don't you have Smirnoff?" Legh was visibly taken aback, but recovered in seconds and answered, "Well, uh …. yes I have Smirnoff, but…." "That's what I'm on tonight," Dick said firmly. Later in the evening, Legh took me aside and said quietly, "Wouldn't you think that the president of a large wine organization like United Vintners would, for Chrissake, at least *try* a glass of wine some time during the evening?" I nodded, shrugged my shoulders, and shook my head slowly, looking down at the floor. I couldn't think of anything to say.

In the end, Legh didn't exactly win the Beaujolais battle. It ended up a compromise, but BV Private Reserve Cabernet was saved. A written Beaulieu Vineyards business analysis was officially released to the corporation in January, 1970; it was six months after the study had begun. The analysis reported the same cost and profit projections that Jackson had first calculated, but did not announce any plan to eliminate Cabernet or limit the company to a few items of assumed high profit. It stated that, "A product mix was selected after consultation with Legh Knowles as an initial 'best guess' which subjectively weighed the market need for a balanced line, product growth trends and general product profitability." The words could have been written by a government bureaucrat, and it allowed for the product mix to change in the future. The report included a section in which Legh Knowles made projections of expected future price increases by wine type.

More ominously, the report openly minimized the importance of owning vineyard land and pointed out that farming costs were high and were likely to remain high. The final projections recommended, even assumed, that the company would buy its grapes in the future rather than growing grapes. My heart nearly stopped as I read those words. After all, half my job was farming the company's 750 acres in a way that would produce fine wine. Winegrowing did not exist in that corporate mindset. Neither grape variety nor vineyard location had anything to do with it in their view. They were clearly *proud* of owning United Vintners, with its lock on all those Thompson Seedless grapes that Julio Gallo had so wisely rejected. I felt truly incompetent when I failed completely in my attempts to explain winegrowing to Stuart Watson and Chris Carriuolo. I had watched a nightmare come true: They knew nothing about wine, but believed they knew everything about wine. For the first time, I began to wonder whether it would be wise for me to remain as Beaulieu winemaster.

Now that we had Heublein money, we were able to install the first stainless tanks in 1969 for fermentation and storage of white wines; in addition, we ordered a new crusher, must pump (replacing the old wooden drag conveyor) and press system. Beaulieu was finally able to handle Chardonnay grapes without juice losses, and more importantly, we now handled white grapes and fermentation without bacterial intervention in what needed to be a highly sanitary fermentation operation. With the installation of stainless tanks and equipment, we were able to make white wines in an efficient, sanitary and technologically-sound operation. However, there was one piece of equipment that I was not able to install, due to interesting resistance from Legh Knowles. Legh became super sensitive whenever writers implied that the corporation was ruining Beaulieu by changing winemaking procedures from those Andre had used. He was especially quick to fight against any change that might be seen as something originating with Heublein.

One of the improvements I had wanted to use in making better white wines was a centrifuge, and I had discussed it with Legh many times. German centrifuges had long since proven their worth in improving the delicate flavors of white table wines, and I proposed a new centrifuge to accompany the new stainless tanks we were installing. The Westfalia Centrifuge Company was looking for a winery in which to install one, so they could bring local winemakers to see it in action. I had even given a tentative acceptance to the sales representative who offered to install the centrifuge at Beaulieu for a month's use without charge. If Legh, Andre or I did not like it, there would be no obligation to buy, and they would move it to another winery. Unfortunately, the centrifuge arrived for unpacking on a day when Beaulieu was toured by no fewer than three Greyhound busloads of visitors. Legh hit the roof, and made sure that half of them heard his objection: "No, no, no! This is Beaulieu; we are not going to change this into some ordinary winery. Get that thing out of here." I remembered Andre telling me later, "Because of the public's attitude toward corporations like Heublein, Legh won't ever want modernization. You got to [sic] make improvements at Beaulieu slowly, if at all. In a funny way, Legh is very much like Madame de Pins."

The stainless tanks certainly did make a big improvement in white wine quality. White wine fermentations became reliable and secure because in addition to the stainless, we also installed a big chiller (with more overall refrigeration capacity). We were then able, for the first time, to make white wines in the way Andre had always wanted white wines to be made. I mentioned to Andre that Madame would be very pleased to hear this news, but Andre said simply, "She didn't care in 1952, she doesn't care now."

After installing the stainless tanks, Andre and I were pleased when we got approval from Heublein to replace the small redwood tanks with American white oak tanks from Canton Wood Products. These turned out to be relatively good tanks, and were very useful for red wines. The tanks made proper use of the space in Room B, and I was thrilled to get rid of the old, leaky redwood. Of course when we removed the redwood tanks and cleaned out that area, the first thing we did was to pour new concrete floors over the dirt, sloping the floors down towards the front so that cleaning behind the new tanks would be a snap. We simply used a high pressure hose; a blast of water onto the wall behind would hose down all the dirt and gunk towards the front gutter. From the point of view of cleanliness, Heublein became a lot easier to work with than Madame de Pins. Their engineers understood sanitation and did not care about cellar mystique, but I missed the early days when the Marquis would wander randomly through the winery, turning lights off all the time, and muttering whenever he saw a slab of concrete covering the ground.

Prejudice? Incompetence?

Heublein was a turning point in BV history – on one hand it was a technical turning point; BV began living up to the promise in white wine quality that it had demonstrated for so many years with red wines. In contrast, writers were not going to allow the public to believe that. Although Beaulieu white wine quality improved several notches in 1969 due solely to the equipment modernization provided by Heublein money, I was astounded to see that wine writers, restaurateurs and the wine trade didn't notice. In fact, writers seemed overly anxious to criticize Beaulieu. From the moment Heublein stepped in, I didn't think our wines (or Heublein) got a fair shake. With what seemed like overnight timing, the wines were arbitrarily criticized in the wine press; I do not remember a single writer during 1969 and 1970 who correctly noticed that the white wines were cleaner, fresher and better. Heublein did not deserve to see our greatly improved Beaulieu white wines criticized.

In blind wine competitions, BV did quite well in Chardonnay tastings; however, there are two aspects to wine evaluation – medals won in blind competitions and the stories that writers publish. Beaulieu was winning a great many gold medals, but writers seemed unwilling to write the truth about the wines any longer. It seemed that once a big corporation took over Beaulieu, the winery would probably never again command the old image of 'First Growth' wine producer in the eyes of wine writers.

Oddly, one writer embarrassed us without meaning to. In 1970, due to a disastrous spring frost, we were short on Sauvignon Blanc and Semillon grapes, although we were producing three labels that required those varieties in the blends. We had very little of the best quality 'free run' wines from these varieties, but did have Sauvignon Blanc and Semillon press wine [16] which we blended together, referring to it as 'Dry White.' We ended up using some of that Dry White press wine in the blends for all three of our Sauternes-type wines. Dry White became nearly half of the Sweet Sauternes blend, and the wine was an embarrassment at first. The wine tasted too grassy – it was pressy, stemmy, and not very drinkable. Andre had always made Sweet Sauternes by 'baking' – he heated the wine to 160°F for 48 hours to partially oxidize and soften it. I went ahead and baked ours, knowing the heat treatment would reduce the grassiness and improve the wine. We bottled it because there was demand for the label, though not sophisticated demand, and we thought no one would notice. The one thing in our favor was that all 1970 wines had higher quality than usual because the 1970 crop size was half of normal size. One of the few things a winemaker can expect from Mother Nature is that, when she cuts the crop size in half, she doubles the flavor in the crop she delivers. Consumers who drank Sweet Sauternes wanted the slightly maple-like baked flavor with sweetness, and Legh Knowles said he absolutely had to have a few cases. It was a calculated risk when we went ahead with the blend; I just hoped that no one would notice.

Then the worst thing happened. One of the best-known wine writers at the time, Robert Lawrence Balzer, called attention to our Sweet Sauternes, oohing and aahing in a magazine article. He wrote a glowing report of the new vintage Sweet Sauternes, telling the world they owed it to themselves to try this really good one, just this once. I do not believe he had ever mentioned that wine in any previous article about Beaulieu, and we were surprised, to say the least. I am sure Balzer thought he was doing us a great favor. Other writers had been criticizing BV non-stop since the Heublein purchase. I was never proud of that wine, but his write-up made it sound

---

[16] Press wine comes from pressing drained pomace from a red wine fermentation. It is more tannic than free-run wine, which separates on its own from crushed grapes.

like it was one of the greatest wines we had ever produced. After getting to know Balzer well over the ensuing forty years, I came to realize that his selection of BV Sweet Sauternes for accolades was no accident.

Robert Lawrence Balzer was a unique individual who had done much with his life: He had been a United Press International correspondent, professional photographer, Air Corps pilot, Buddhist monk, you name it. In wine and food, Balzer searched for uniqueness. He much preferred to write about the 'newest' winery, the newcomer to the industry and one-of-a-kind wine. He had known the wines of Beaulieu very well, and often praised their superiority over all others. I am sure he was surprised at the change in the relatively unknown 'Sweet Sauternes' from BV. Whether he thought it was good or bad was not important to him. It was different – and he just could not wait to tell the world about it!

The relationship between wineries and wine writers is often like that. My experience with many writers is that, often, they are not particularly good tasters. Robert Balzer was an excellent taster, but sometimes was too anxious to accept badly spoiled wines as 'brilliant winemaking feats' on the strength of a unique flavor he had not tasted before. He could separate one taste sensation from another fairly well (that's good), but he sometimes did not recognize desirable and clean from spoiled and bacterial (that's bad). I have seen many examples in which a writer heaped high praise onto a wine that was clearly flawed. Vinegar content is an index of bacterial spoilage in table wines. The chemical term is V.A. or volatile acidity, but V.A. is vinegar, period. As if to guarantee confusion, sometimes a minute trace of vinegar in a certain wine can add a fruity acidic taste that is not unpleasant; in that case, the small amount of V.A. is not considered a flaw. More than once, I have seen writers praise wines with V.A. levels that were much too high (near the legal limit)! This whole subject usually ends with a statement to the effect that, "Taste is subjective. Some people like lots of garlic on foods, I do not. Neither of us is wrong because taste is subjective."

I always thought Balzer made an error when he judged that Sweet Sauternes as being something special. He was certainly right – we had not made one like that before! I never complained to him, never mentioned it at all, because he meant well and wrote in a positive vein. Looking back,

I am doubly embarrassed; we never received one letter of complaint from any consumer about that vintage of Sweet Sauternes! Balzer was in fact, completely correct. It shows how little the winemaker knows sometimes.

Conversely, when a writer tells his readership that a wine is awful (but it may be the winemaker's own personal favorite), the writer's statement is difficult to reconcile. Balzer was never guilty of that, but some winemakers have received similar treatment from a few, usually new, writers. It is truly astonishing to read bad press about perfectly good, sound, even excellent wines – but it has happened from time to time in American wine writing. The public is probably leery of writers who write very bad reviews about specific wines, because it implies something that is not out in the open. To be honest, it may simply be a difference of taste – some writers allow their personal bias to affect their evaluations. Some love the taste of oak, or acidity, or sweetness or alcohol, while others have views opposing those taste sensations. It sometimes happens that a competent writer has an honest dislike for one style of wine that is highly prized by the winemaker. Some winemakers have told me that a few writers have deliberately panned good wines to settle some kind of score with the winery, but I never noticed that kind of attack. Frankly, I didn't think those complaints were correct.

It does seem that writers are sometimes too willing to accept whatever PR statement a winery puts out. Wineries generally issue press releases hoping that wine writers will be lazy and print them verbatim, and it is amazing how often this happens. The good writers question everything, but have no preconceived notions. They will call the winery to dig further into a subject, rather than accepting a press release as the whole truth; too often, however, press releases are printed verbatim (even under a writer's by-line). Writers, like winemakers and winery owners, often have oversize egos – they like to see their names in print, and to be seen as authorities higher than their actual knowledge justifies. It is not surprising to see many writers take the next logical step of printing anything that sounds important, new and 'in' as fast as it comes to them from the winery public relations department.

I know wine writers who, recognizing the above, make a special effort to bend the winery's public relations announcement a little, just enough to make the article sound like the writer is not a flack of the winery, but an independent thinker. Their knack is to be critical of the news release, while printing it nevertheless. Here is where the reader (and the winery) can most easily judge whether the writer is competent. If the writer criticizes points that are not important while printing the fluff language that already was written by a wine salesman, you can forget that writer. But, if the writer cuts out the fluff and prints only known facts (with or without his impressions) then you can believe that he or she might be trying to be objective.

It was distressing to see writers suddenly become critical of perfectly good Beaulieu wines immediately after the winery was purchased by a large corporation. They started criticizing our wines long before the corporation had any influence at all on the wine quality. The writer had obviously written something that the public wanted to believe, and I think that kind of writing was lazy. Winemakers sometimes overrate deliberate malice, and underrate the simple incompetence of some writers. Few writers seemed fair to Beaulieu Vineyard's wine evaluations for the first few years after Heublein bought the winery in June, 1969. God knows I believe that Heublein ownership was bad for Beaulieu, but they were 100% innocent of the charge that they 'made bad wine' for us.

The best examples of unfairness and wine writer incompetence were found among the articles criticizing BV 1968 Private Reserve Cabernet Sauvignon. We released the wine to distributors for sale to the public in early 1972, at just about the peak of the anti-Heublein bandwagon. Being highly critical of big corporations that bought in to the California wine industry was very much in vogue. Writers assumed (or at least wrote) that BV wine was now being made from the Heublein head office in Hartford, Connecticut, as if neither Andre nor I had any say in the matter. I am the first to agree that Heublein deserves criticism for much of their conduct in the wine business, but they were never guilty of making the wine from Hartford. Andre made the wine, I made the wine, Theo Rosenbrand made the wine, but Heublein did not make the wine while I was at Beaulieu. Not one drop.

Vintage 1968, in retrospect, was one of the highest-quality vintages in BV history. Many collectors still say it was the best vintage in the whole history of the company, but we got soundly trounced in the press, at least temporarily, by several wine writers. (I notice that new writers are doing that to some wineries today.) The BV 1968 Private Reserve Cabernet Sauvignon was already very soft and extremely pleasing at the time it was bottled. Almost anyone would say it was ready to drink immediately, but I knew it also held a great deal of tannin, giving it longevity in the bottle. Tannin in wine is often recognized by its bitterness or astringency, but not all tannins have those characteristics. Too many wine writers think that a wine has to be rough and harsh when young to guarantee a long life; that view is simplistic and often very wrong. They may criticize that it is rough and harsh (they don't like the wine), or praise that it's rough and harsh (it's a great wine that will live a long time). In either case, they can be glaringly incorrect. Sometimes a wine can fool the winemaker. A big, tannic wine that he thought would live for thirty years can simply fall apart and become old before its time. As my old Cleveland Indians pitching pal, Bob Feller, said, "sometimes an excellent pitcher just can't go nine innings."

The 1968 BV had plenty of tannin, but it was soft tannin that some writers didn't recognize. The wine was pleasing and smooth, and while it was ready to drink shortly after bottling, the wine ended up living forty years or more when stored in cool cellars. Oddly, the '68 had none of the mouth-drying powdery tannin that some of our other vintages had. Even so, it would, in fact, end up as one of the best vintages in Beaulieu Vineyard history, ranking with the '51, '58, and '70. I was astonished at the number of admonitions we'd gotten from some writers telling about how BV had died since Heublein took over ownership, and how the winemaking had fallen apart. We read, "the '68 sure isn't like the BV of old"; "It isn't going to hold up"; "It doesn't have any guts to it"; 'It doesn't have any body"; and "It isn't going to live." The reviews bothered me especially because Heublein didn't buy Beaulieu until 1969. We were being unfairly treated, not because of bad wines, but because we'd been purchased by Heublein

Vinho Branco/Rubio

My Gallo friend, George McCarthy, now a Heublein wine salesman, alerted me in February 1970 to get my passport ready. I was to start on Lancers white wine in Portugal by early spring. Chris Carriuolo would go along, mostly to introduce me to the people in Lancers' ownership. We made the trip in March, and I tasted and evaluated each of the white varietal wines and blends that the Portuguese winemakers had on hand. Some were quite nice, and I could see that we'd have a choice of several possible directions in making the product – it would not be difficult because the Portuguese were good winemakers. I knew the personality of White Lancers had to be similar to the existing Lancers Rosé, and that became my underlying theme. I had a good idea from previous tastings and competitions in California what the Lancers Rosé consumer might like in a white wine. After several possible new blends were tried and tasted blind by my panel composed of everyone in the Portuguese lab and half the office, I had whittled the choices down to three. I took some samples back to California for a modest consumer test with some colleagues whose tasting abilities I trusted. One of them was Darrell Corti of Corti Brothers Delicatessen in Sacramento, a good friend and one of the best food and wine tasters I have ever met. I did not tell him what I was doing, just asked his blind opinion of three different wines. He liked all of them, but had a slight preference for the one that I had already decided was my first choice. He may or may not remember now, but I'll never forget his comment after the tasting. He said, "Dick, those wines taste Portuguese." I knew White Lancers would be a commercial success.

I returned to Portugal to complete the white wine (now named Vinho Branco 'white wine'). The winery, J.M. da Fonseca Sucesores, Internacional, was located in the small town of Azeitaõ, about thirty miles south of Lisbon. Chris liked my Vinho Branco blend, and it would be easy to expand production as necessary because the varieties used were widely planted there. It was bottled in the same shape glass as Lancers Rosé, but Vinho Branco had a dark green bottle in contrast to the tan color of the Rosé bottle. It became an instant success in American cities over the next few months, easily out selling the long-established Lancers Rosé. I needed to return to Portugal again because Chris now wanted me to make another new wine – Lancers Red. The name they used was 'Rubio,' a clever take-off on Americans' lack of knowledge of languages. Americans would assume that Rubio probably meant 'ruby,' or maybe 'red' in Portuguese; actually Rubio means 'blond' in both Portuguese and Spanish, but nobody cared.

High Theater

Cesar Chavez had begun trying to organize farm workers in California in the 1950s. By 1972, he was head of the United Farm Workers, and in 1968 he organized a boycott of table grapes in an effort to unionize agricultural workers in the table grape industry. He had enough success that boycotts would become his primary weapon against some big companies in the wine industry. Very soon that would include Heublein.

When I first joined Beaulieu, I learned that Andre had been hiring the same workers for the previous twenty-five years. Most lived in Mexico during the winter, came to Beaulieu each spring to work all summer, and returned to Mexico in December after the harvest. Andre was a very good manager, the farm workers liked him, and I continued Andre's practices, expecting no problem in the vineyards.

In the summer of 1969, just after Heublein purchased Beaulieu, an organizing attempt was made by Cesar Chavez's UFW in our vineyards. Beaulieu had seen organizing attempts before, and Andre had simply agreed that the agriculture workers could go ahead and have an election to see whether they wanted to unionize. In past years, all or most of the workers had voted not to unionize. We agreed to the election this time as well, because both Andre and I believed that the Mexican workers would not want to unionize. They had heard about horrible experiences among the unionized vineyard workers from neighboring wineries. The UFW required them to donate their Saturdays to picket Central Valley farms where the UFW was trying to unionize. I could understand why the workers would not want to give up their weekends for no pay to try to unionize someone they didn't know. Apparently, the organizers wanted their picketers to be unknown to the companies they were picketing, as it would eliminate later repercussions. In any case, our workers voted in the election, and every one of them voted against unionizing; I believe the actual vote was twenty five to zero. We relaxed and forgot about the union, but only for a short week or two.

We promptly received an order from Heublein to unionize all our vineyard workers and to "Do it now!" I think the order went from Heublein to Legh Knowles as general manager; in any case, the decision certainly came from above all of us. Both Andre and I objected on the basis of the election outcome among our workers. That made no difference at all to Heublein, and we were told to unionize despite the election! I was not sure we could override a legal election, but Legh was given no option. Evidently, the UFW had organized a major 'Boycott Smirnoff Vodka' campaign in big eastern cities, especially Hartford, Connecticut. It was killing sales of Smirnoff, which was one of Heublein's primary profit producers – maybe its biggest single profit producer. As soon as the BV contract with UFW was signed, the vodka boycott did stop, but it was an uneasy truce from our point of view.

After unionization, every time I talked to Andre, it involved increasingly worse news about the vineyards. We had lost nearly all of the workers who had worked for him as far back as Andre could remember, some for as long as twenty-five years or more. All had simply quit and gone to other farms, where they could work in the same way they had always worked at Beaulieu. One day a crying Jimmie Garcia came to see me at the winery. Jimmie was the son of Ed Garcia, the best vineyard superintendent we had.[17] Jimmie was a good worker, but had been told by the union that he (and all the other Beaulieu workers) had to drive nearly thirty miles to the union office in Vallejo every morning to be assigned a ranch where he was to work for the day. It was usually the same Beaulieu ranch where he lived and had always worked, but the union reserved the right to send him someplace else. After the assignment, he then had to drive back to Beaulieu vineyard #3 to begin work – at six in the morning! It cost him an hour and a half of sleep to drive to Vallejo and back, at his own expense, before starting work each day. A daily check-in was the union rule, and Jimmie could not live with it. He wanted me to change that rule somehow, or give him a job in the winery where he could work instead. I did not have the power to change the rule, and unfortunately, I had no new job available at the winery. Our signing

---

[17] Ed Garcia and his family were living in the house on vineyard #3 and both Andre and I had considered Ed to be Beaulieu's best and most reliable vineyard manager.

the union contract had cost Beaulieu every one of its time-tested workers.

The UFW could not supply replacement workers of Mexican descent for Beaulieu, and when we complained, they sent us a mob of ragged hippies instead. We had trouble getting the hippies to do any work; worse, if they did anything, it was not done correctly. They had no intention of learning the job, because they had no intention of working. One day, Andre drove into one vineyard to see twenty of his thirty-five hippie 'farm workers' (both sexes) sitting, lying down and standing in line for one of the outdoor field toilets. They were laughing and joking; playing "grab-ass" was what Andre called it. He told them to get to work, and the identical answer he got from ten or more at once was, "It's nature, Man. You cannot tell me when to go to the toilet. It's my right, Man." They would work if and when they felt like it, and Andre could go to hell. Andre Tchelistccheff was one of 'them fucking bosses' that Chavez hated. Their pruning was atrocious, and that became a serious problem for the winery. How carefully a vine is pruned determines how much fruit the vine will produce in the coming year. Too much fruit reduces quality and delays the harvest date into rainy weather. Too little fruit, and the vineyard would neither pay for itself, nor produce quality wine. We came to believe that the Chavez union was not really a labor union; rather, it was high theater in which Chavez used his hunger strikes to gain support from national level politicians for what amounted to a social revolution. Newspapers and TVs blared that a great martyr named Cesar Chavez was doing wonderful things for the agricultural workers in California. That was certainly not true at Beaulieu in 1969, as all of our Mexican workers lost their jobs because of the Chavez Union.

A Wooden Stake

As the months progressed, Andre became more and more anxious to retire and did so in March, 1970. Legh Knowles organized a 'retirement dinner party' for Andre and his wife, Dorothy, at the El Real restaurant, which was located almost directly across Rutherford Road from the Beaulieu Winery. Every Beaulieu employee attended with their spouses. We had a grand time, but Andre obviously had mixed emotions. In a private conversation with

Legh and I, as we sat beside the dining table, Andre blurted out, "Legh, I predict that under Heublein's influence you will strangle this little baby Beaulieu with your own two hands." Legh was perplexed and did not know what Andre meant. At the time, neither did I.

Only a few weeks after the dinner, Legh started having second thoughts about making Andre's retirement public. He too, had noticed how blatantly anti-BV some wine writers had become in their criticisms of our wines from the instant of Heublein's purchase. When Heublein bosses Stuart Watson and Chris Carriuolo heard that Andre had retired from the company, they decided to ask him to return. Andre refused to return as an employee of Heublein as he suspected they only wanted to use his name as their defense against bad publicity – his hunch was correct, but we did not learn the whole truth for another few months. Andre asked my opinion, and I suggested that he use the opportunity to collect as much additional retirement income as possible; after all, Madame had not been generous with him, considering his outstanding service for 32 years. Andre was uneasy because of the difficulty we had encountered in stopping Don Jackson's steamroller from eliminating Cabernet Sauvignon from BV's stable of fine wines. Legh finally surrendered to Stuart Watson, and pressured Andre into a consulting contract for three more years, until 1973. They had not done him any favor. Later, I witnessed Andre having terrible arguments with Legh after he had heard an ad or seen a Heublein PR announcement telling how he was still in charge when, at the same time, they ignored his advice. To make matters worse, only months after signing the consulting contract, Andre was banished from entering any of the Beaulieu vineyards. As a practical matter, so was I, because Heublein would soon give away their vineyards.

Andy Beckstoffer seemed to be directly involved in more and more of Heublein's vineyard decisions. The company organized Vinifera Development Corporation to buy Napa land, in order to produce grapes for Beaulieu and Inglenook. Andy was put in charge, and apparently thought that any piece of land would be as good as any other. He bought the Keig Ranch on Rutherford Road without asking our opinions on whether it would be suitable; it was not, but neither Andy nor Heublein appeared to care. Andre had told me many times: "When you see an open piece of bare land in Napa Valley at a time when vineyard land is in short supply, be very cautious. There is a reason why that land is not planted. It would be better to build a structure on that land instead of trying to grow quality grapes."

As Jim Conaway wrote in his excellent book, *Napa*, Andy Beckstoffer found himself in the right place at the right time. When the UFW organized the 'Boycott Smirnoff Vodka' campaign in eastern cities, and we were told to unionize our vineyard workers, Andy recognized a golden opportunity for himself. As Andy rationalized to me, "If Heublein didn't own any vineyards, then it wouldn't be legal for Chavez to attack non-grape Heublein products like Smirnoff Vodka as a tactic to unionize the BV vineyard workers." Andy's remedy was for Heublein to transfer ownership of Vinifera Development Corporation to him (he would no longer be employed by Heublein) and Heublein would thus assure its future protection from Chavez.

Andy told me he was doing Heublein a favor, and it appeared that Heublein upper management believed him. Not one person at Beaulieu agreed, but then we were all 'too lacking in business acumen' to have a vote. At the time, no details of the deal were shown to any of us at Beaulieu. According to Conaway, the price was set at just $625 per acre for existing vineyards, although the going price for vineyards in Napa Valley was between $3,000 and $4,000. Heublein even loaned the money to Beckstoffer to buy the vineyards, agreed to fund him an additional $500,000 for replanting, and signed a contract to buy all future grapes from him for Inglenook and Beaulieu at market price. Heublein was giving Andy the prime assets of Beaulieu: Georges de Latour's precious vineyards! With this move, Heublein had single-handedly changed Beaulieu from the pinnacle wine property of America into just another Napa Valley winery. It guaranteed that Beaulieu would die the strangulation death that Andre Tchelistcheff had predicted to Legh and myself at Andre's retirement dinner. In that very same move, the corporation had made Andy Beckstoffer an instant multi-millionaire.

I saw Andre Tchelistcheff upset, really mad, only about five times in my life. In each one of those instances, his anger was directed at Heublein or their managers. The worst time was shortly after the vineyard ownership was transferred to Beckstoffer. Andre came to the winery and told me, tearfully, that Beckstoffer's manager had asked him to leave Beaulieu vineyard #3, saying that his presence in any of the vineyards was no longer desired! He told me it felt like a wooden stake had been driven through his heart. "Dhose God Demm Bastids," he said, over and over again. Andre had long since become a second father to me, and I felt his pain as if it had happened to me. In truth it had, since I, too, was no longer allowed to farm the famous vineyards of Beaulieu. Both Andre Tchelistcheff and I had lost our winegrowing jobs. Heublein did not recognize it, but there were two even bigger losers: Beaulieu had lost its winegrowing image and Heublein had destroyed the public perception of its famous Beaulieu Vineyard wines.

A Greatly Enhanced Position

Stuart Watson's secretary called in late 1971 asking me to meet him at the Oakland airport – he would be between flights and wanted to see me for an hour or so. When I did, to my surprise, he was accompanied by Dick Oster, the recently appointed president of United Vintners who I remembered as the wine executive who preferred Smirnoff Vodka to BV Private Reserve Cabernet. Stuart offered me a "greatly enhanced position in the wine industry: Vice President of United Vintners and Technical Director for Heublein Wines." From my office in Hartford, Connecticut, I would be in charge of Beaulieu, Lancers, Inglenook and Italian Swiss Colony winemaking. I was surprised that they would place all those brands under the United Vintners umbrella. United Vintners was owned 82% by Heublein and 18% by Allied Growers. I told him Heublein would risk losing the high images of BV and Inglenook if they were positioned under Italian Swiss Colony, a giant, low-price brand that had little positive image of its own. Stuart seemed shocked, and told me that United Vintners was already their major wine division; all other wineries (including Beaulieu) were positioned within United Vintners. I had not even suspected as much.

I told them my success in winemaking depended on smelling and tasting wine tanks regularly and correcting any problems immediately. If my job held me in an office a continent away, then I would fail in that job. Stuart said, "Don't worry about that, you'll have an unlimited travel budget so you can spend all the time you need at the wineries." I told him that I had never thought Italian Swiss had anything close to the level of wine quality as Gallo, let alone Beaulieu. Beaulieu was the crown jewel of wineries, and it had taken a crown jewel like that to drag me away from Gallo. I believed my current position as winemaster of Beaulieu was already a more important position than United Vintners VP.

Dick Oster remained more or less quiet, but Stuart Watson was animated. Stuart said I failed to understand what they were doing for me. He was talking 40 million cases, not the miniscule 150,000 cases that were then produced by Beaulieu. He said, "We have great plans for Italian Swiss. We plan to increase sales to the level of Gallo." I answered, "With all due respect, unless United Vintners makes a major change in the grape varieties they use, they have no chance at all of catching Gallo." The problem I saw with Italian Swiss Colony was in their contracts with Allied Grape Growers, whose members grew mostly Thompson Seedless grapes (many were harvesting as much as 16 tons of garbage grapes per acre per year). I told Stuart that if I were in charge of United Vintners winemaking, I would stop using that variety for most of the wines; only then did I see the possibility of competing effectively against Gallo. He was a nice guy, and I knew he did not want to hear that, but I was not about to salute and charge forward with what I (alone) knew to be an impossible task.

I liked making high-quality wines from varietal grapes, but couldn't imagine making anything drinkable out of the Allied Growers' table and raisin grapes. I could handle Beaulieu, Lancers and Inglenook very easily, but simply did not know how to use Thompson, except in very small amounts. I thanked Stuart for the compliment, but said that I did not think it could possibly work the way he wanted it to. I knew I had pissed off the chairman of a large corporation, but I told him the truth as I knew it. A few days later Legh Knowles told me that Stuart had told him, "Peterson was overconfident." Legh told me he had answered, *Of course!* He's winemaker at Beaulieu. He has Private Reserve Cabernet in his veins."

Immediately on returning to Beaulieu I asked Legh Knowles, "Did you know that both Inglenook and Beaulieu are positioned under the Italian Swiss umbrella in the Heublein hierarchy?" Legh answered quickly, "Not for sales purposes, that's just for accounting. We're going to continue selling and promoting Beaulieu as an independent winery." I told him he would have to come up with a new definition for personal honesty to do that. Legh and I were starting to say things to each other that were better left unsaid. We were both hoping we could eventually educate Heublein about fine wines. Andre had given up on them, and left for the second time. Legh had been trying desperately to preserve Beaulieu's image by putting up a good front, but it seemed to me he was clutching at straws; he had to watch BV's image disintegrate as writers attacked Heublein in print.

Legh told me Stuart would catch on, but I became less and less convinced as they continued to pressure me never to say 'No' to the big corporation. Saying 'No' to a big corporation is something Legh told me, "just isn't done." I told him, "I'd rather get fired than tell them I can do something that I know cannot be done." He said simply, "Don't give up, Dick. Heublein has intelligent managers, Stuart Watson is a successful guy, and they'll get it right soon." Legh was extremely persuasive, but the only future I could see was producing flavored wines from Thompson Seedless concentrate for Heublein PR people to brag about in the press. That kind of lip service for shoddy winemaking was not in me. I knew Legh well enough to tell him that Mom hadn't named me Jesus, because there were some things I just couldn't do with wine; that ended the conversation.

Even though I was no longer allowed to farm the vineyards at Beaulieu, the winemaking, equipment repairs and reconstruction kept me very busy. With constant support from Legh, I managed to sidestep most of the corporate pressure to move to Hartford. Legh also knew the importance of disconnecting Beaulieu from United Vintners in all public statements. We both knew that connecting my name to United Vintners would mean that I would have to resign as Beaulieu winemaster; otherwise, Legh's ongoing story of BV's independence would be exposed as an ungainly corporate lie. Legh told me he intended to do whatever it took to avoid any reference in the press connecting the two companies; that included keeping United Vintners personnel away from the Beaulieu Winery.

One day, the chief engineer of United Vintners called Legh telling him he was coming to Beaulieu for a visit. Legh answered with only one word,

"Why?" The engineer hesitated and said, "Uhh, I'm looking at all our properties to see where I can best help you." Legh shifted instantly into his 'Mr Knowles, General Manager' booming baritone voice to reply, "I want to make something perfectly clear to you. Beaulieu has successfully operated this winery since the early 1900s without any help, and we don't need your help now." The engineer never came to visit Beaulieu.

Legh Knowles' position at Beaulieu was hardening his personality, and he saw his job increasingly as one of protecting Beaulieu from all outside interests. I became aware of a building conflict between Legh's public relations statements, Heublein's organizational structure, and my attempts to bring Beaulieu winery equipment into the present century. As time went by, he became more and more negative about our installing any new equipment. He believed that anything new would be seen by the wine press as having been done by Heublein and therefore bad; he was probably correct with that thinking. He never gave up trying to convince the public that Beaulieu continued to excel by making wine with its own superior and unchanging methods. When visitors asked him about Heublein's influence, I heard Legh's answer many times: "Heublein's smart investment in Beaulieu didn't change Beaulieu. There is no question that Beaulieu held a position of superiority between 1938 and 1970. It retains that position today by making wines in exactly the same way as Andre did in 1940." Eventually, Legh's responses to my requests for new equipment became, "Did Georges de Latour use that equipment in 1937? Did Andre have it in 1940 when he established Beaulieu's preeminent quality position? The answer is no." In a nutshell, he was saying publicly: Beaulieu was best; Beaulieu doesn't change; therefore, Beaulieu remains best.

I continued visiting Portugal three or four times a year to monitor Lancers' wines and to produce more new Portuguese products for Heublein. Chris Carriuolo usually arranged his visits to correspond with my trips, and there was always pressure from him about my moving to Connecticut. He was a fun guy to be with, but he never let me forget that he intended to move me to Hartford sooner or later. The red Lancers (Rubio) sold okay, but not as spectacularly as the Vinho Branco. I chalked that up to the current boom of white wines, but it is also true that when a winemaker carbonates a red wine, he has to deal with a special problem: the tannins in red wines taste bitter when the wine is carbonated. To counter the bitterness, most winemakers sweeten the wine a little to cover the bitter taste. That works more or less, but carbonated reds never sell as well, often seeming too sweet. I also made Portuguese 'flavored wines' for Heublein, one called Faísca, but the American market for flavored wines had dwindled a decade earlier. I enjoyed the Portuguese people and their country, and especially enjoyed working with Portuguese table wines. Most varieties were very different from what we had in California. The work was exciting, with some eye-opening contrasts between the wine types that were selling in Portugal and those that would sell in America. It was a wonderful experience and Portugal remains my favorite European country to this day.

The Big Discovery

In the spring of 1973, I'd been working at Beaulieu for five years when a Central Valley farmer, Myron McFarland, called and wanted to stop by and talk. We hit it off immediately; the flies on the wall must have thought it was just two old farm boys 'talkin' and kickin' turds.' The McFarland family was comprised of long-time farmers. The town of McFarland (twenty-three miles north of Bakersfield in the Central Valley) was named decades ago for their great grandfather. This visit, however, had nothing to do with the Central Valley. His family was now farming fine wine grapes on coastal land in Monterey County. Myron, his brother Gerry, and their partner, Tom Stratton, had been gathering groups of investors together into 'Limited Partnerships' (LPs). Each LP bought several hundred acres of farm land in Salinas Valley on which McFarland Management Co. had been planting wine grapes since 1970. By the end of 1974, they expected to have planted an unbelievable 9,600 acres of fine wine grapes in Salinas Valley! This is an area of Monterey County where grapes had never been planted before, and I was more than a little amazed that growers could undertake such a huge farming venture in a new area without alerting California's (normally jealous) big wineries.

All I could say was, "Wow! The whole Napa Valley is only a little larger than that. I'll bet the price of varietal grapes in the North Coast will drop in half when all that fruit starts coming in." Myron wasn't worried. He told me they had spent their whole lives growing commodities and were used to seeing prices fluctuate from year to year. I was astonished that they could have done enough research on soils and climate to convince big money people to risk the vast capital needed for such a venture. I had not heard of significant vineyards in Salinas Valley, except for the small plantings made by Paul Masson, Mirassou and Almaden over the past few years. Myron told me they had taken great pains to study the area while keeping it quiet because they believed they had made a big and valuable discovery, and he related their findings to me.

He said current textbooks showed Salinas Valley to have nearly identical climatic and soil conditions as other coastal valleys in California. This was especially true when the climate researchers compared Salinas Valley with Napa and Sonoma Valleys. Each valley was shown as containing Region I (cold climate) nearest the ocean, Region II (moderate) in the middle areas and Region III (warmer climate) inland. Every textbook they looked at seemed to agree. Soils were deep in Monterey County (a good sign) and more uniform than either Napa or Sonoma (a very good sign). Neither Myron nor his partners worried that soil could become a problem for vineyards. He pointed out that, since no grapes had lived in the Salinas Valley soil before, there would be no Phylloxera (fill-óx-er-uh) insects to be protected against. That meant they were free to plant the best wine grapes without grafting onto American vine roots, saving huge amounts of money.

He continued, "That was by no means the only way we saved money in this project; the size alone saved us money by simple economies of scale." I knew that doing almost anything on a vast scale would be cheaper than if done on a more modest scale. He gave a single example, "A farmer growing grapes on ten acres of land finds that his tractor spends considerable time in just turning around at the end of each vine row – contrast that with a bigger farmer who plants a single 500-acre vineyard. His tractor cultivates nearly full time because each row goes almost to the horizon; he wastes very little time turning around." Myron went on and on, about planting, irrigation, cultivation, harvesting, etc. He was no spring chicken, but he was clearly excited about what his group was doing and his excitement was infectious.

The group was planning to build a winery and go into the wine business as soon as their vineyards matured. Their winery would be a classic estate, albeit a large estate, in which the winery would use grapes from their large vineyards. All the vineyards were being planted exclusively to high-image wine grapes (at least 20 different varieties), and all varieties were planted where climates were similar to those of Napa Valley. Myron asked me directly if I was I interested in designing and building that winery and then running it for the investors. Obviously I was unable to make such a decision on short notice. I would have to see the vineyards and winery site and think it through before committing to anything like what he had in mind.

After Myron left that day I thought only of my situation at Beaulieu. If Beaulieu Vineyards had remained what it was at the time I moved there in 1968, I would never have given Myron or Monterey a second thought. At that time, Beaulieu was at the absolute pinnacle of quality for the wine industry, and I loved 'winegrowing' our vineyards with the specific goal of making the best table wines in the Western Hemisphere. It was exactly what I both enjoyed doing and was good at. Unfortunately, I had to admit to myself that the Beaulieu of 1968 no longer existed. Throughout the summer of 1973, I continued to weigh the pros and cons of my situation.

One thought kept jumping into my mind: I'd been looking at vineyard land to buy in Napa Valley for the past year, and had located an eighty-acre block on Bella Oaks Lane with a 'for sale' sign. I had talked to the owner who told me he was hoping to get $300,000 for it. When I told Andre what I was thinking, he almost came apart. "Good God, man! That is $4,000 an acre! Napa Valley land was only $3,000 the last time I checked. My dear sir, I know that particular vineyard very well. It is old and needs replanting, which will cost you plenty. You'd better be careful; don't do it, my dear sir," he said with the authority of my father. Andre had lived there since 1938 and certainly knew the land; he might be right. When Myron McFarland's 9,600 acres of coastal grapes came into production, it would drop the price of grapes everywhere, so I figured I'd be better off to wait a couple of years to buy land. I postponed the decision.

The Trigger

I was preparing for my sixth vintage at Beaulieu in August, 1973, when I was visited by one of the technical people from Hartford. He was on an inspection tour of sorts, and did not have any reason to stop at Beaulieu except as a friendly visit. As he was leaving, he took me aside and asked me when I was planning to move to Connecticut. I told him I was not planning to move. He then said that Chris Carriuolo had announced at the most recent Heublein board of directors meeting that he was moving Dr. Peterson to Hartford to become technical director of the Heublein wine properties. I told him that we had talked, but no decision had been reached. He said simply, "Well, Chris certainly thinks a decision has been reached." I thanked him, and we said goodbye in our usual friendly manner. That discussion became the trigger that forced me to make a decision.

About a week later, I gave Legh Knowles a letter of resignation. I told him that I would stay through the upcoming harvest season, because there would not be time to break in a new winemaker before the grapes would be harvested by Beckstoffer's workers. I did not want to harm Beaulieu by walking out just before harvest for obvious reasons, and I knew my being there would be critical. I recommended that Theo Rosenbrand be elevated from cellar supervisor to winemaker and promised to call Theo periodically over the next year to help him with any problems. Theo did not have a degree in winemaking, but he had been in charge of the cellar under Andre for nearly twenty seasons as well as under me for the previous five. We had hired Tom Selfridge, a graduate of UC Davis, two years earlier, planning to move Tom up to assistant winemaker, but he was not mature enough and was still working in the cellar as an hourly union member until he could become the leader that Beaulieu would need. I thought it would be better for Beaulieu to move Theo up until Tom was ready, and Legh agreed.

So it was that I left Heublein after six seasons at Beaulieu. Never at any time could it be said that I wanted to leave Beaulieu, but I had definitely decided to leave Heublein. I became employed by McFarland on the first of November 1973, but remained in Napa Valley until the following summer since my primary job at that time was to design and start construction of the new winery building near Gonzales in Salinas Valley.

I have continued drinking Beaulieu wines at dinners from time to time since then. In discussions about the BV Private Reserve Cabernet wines of the 1980s, I'm often asked, "What happened to BV? It used to be the finest Chateau, but not anymore. Did Heublein ruin it? We knew they would all along and it appears that they did." The answer, I think, is not so simple. Heublein certainly made some catastrophic mistakes. As a liquor company trying to handle high-image wines, it was almost axiomatic that they would have a "tough row to hoe," as we said in Iowa. I have never heard of a liquor company that succeeded in the fine wine business. Liquor sellers deal in products that people drink for only one reason – alcohol. They can't imagine people drinking fine wines for an aesthetic experience to enhance the enjoyment of food. Of course alcohol is a part of the character of table wine, but alcohol is not usually the primary reason people drink fine wine with meals. Why would someone pay $100 (or more) for a bottle of wine that contains only 13% alcohol if alcohol was all he was after? A $7 bottle of Bourbon the same size contains 50% alcohol!

The Heublein liquor and business school mentality totally destroyed the image of Beaulieu as a Chateau, but what about the wine quality? Corporate bureaucracy probably garbled the quality of BV wines somewhat, especially during the 1980s. Friends at BV during that time told me that winemaking decisions were made almost entirely by committee. I tasted most of those vintages, and was astonished at how high the acidities in Beaulieu Cabernet wines had become. I could only guess the reasons: winemaker committees probably could not distinguish between the tastes of tannin and acid. Were the grapes not quite ripe? Were the committees forced to use lesser grapes, such as those from Beckstoffer's Keig Ranch? Were acidity decisions compromises? Excessive acidity in some red wines was the only real flaw I could detect, but it was definite, and it stuck out. I'm reminded of the old saying that "camels are horses that were designed by a committee."

I mentioned the high acidities in BV Cabernets to Andre when he had resumed consulting for Beaulieu in the late 1980s, and his answer was quite revealing: "My dear sir, you got (sic) to realize that I am a consultant. They are not required to do exactly as the consultant says." Some of the other BV wines' qualities changed, but I believe most of them did not. I thought Beaulieu wines got better in the 1990s after Joel Aiken became winemaker; the red wines produced between 1990 and 2000 at BV seemed (to my taste) very similar to the same quality level of those produced in the 1940s and 50s at the same facility. They were very nice wines. The problem for Beaulieu was that 'the wine racetrack had gotten faster.' New wineries came along, new technologies came along – the other wineries got better and better, while Beaulieu stood still.

I now understood what Andre meant when he predicted 'BV strangulation' to Legh Knowles at his first retirement dinner in Rutherford in April 1970. Legh, in his infinite rigidity, probably saw to it that Beaulieu winery equipment did not change much. Right up until the day he retired in 1988, Legh insisted that BV should continue to use the same methodology it used in the 1940s. By 1990, Beaulieu was no longer among the top twenty Cabernet Sauvignons. A sweepstakes judging by the *Wine Spectator* that year listed sixteen of what they thought were the best Cabernet Sauvignon wines in California, and Beaulieu was not listed among them. That is a judgment call: BV might have had a chance of being one of the sixteen with better luck. In any case, Beaulieu is not 'Number One' any more, but it used to occupy first place by a wide margin. Over time, the competitive wines became a little better year after year, while BV remained motionless. The rest of the wine industry simply overtook it, and Legh could not have it both ways. He fought to retain the old standards and defend the ability to say, "BV hasn't changed a bit. We're still BV. The more Napa Valley changes, the more BV remains the same." In the end, the wine world passed it by, and the Beaulieu of Madame de Pins was buried by time.

Big Business Farming

I left Heublein after completing the 1973 harvest season for Beaulieu and spent a month visiting wineries, winemakers and equipment manufacturers to study winery layouts and equipment. McFarland Management Co. had already chosen Keith & Associates near Santa Rosa as their architect, and I met with Dick Keith frequently during November and December. Dick had designed a dozen new wineries in the previous few years as the California wine industry was entering a major expansion phase. A winery construction boom of sorts had happened immediately after repeal, but most had been add-on expansions of very old and dilapidated buildings that had lain fallow during Prohibition. Few, if any, truly new designs appeared until the late 1960s when Robert Mondavi's Oakville winery construction began. His was the first large winery to be built in California since Prohibition, nearly four decades earlier. I wanted to evaluate the new facilities before deciding on the building design and equipment I would use in the new Monterey winery. Dick Keith had calculated overall winery size and capacity using estimated tonnages and harvest dates he'd received from Gerry McFarland. That made my job easier, once I had completed my inspections and evaluations of the newest winery equipment in California.

Choosing which types of winery equipment I would use was not an easy decision. Many new methods for handling grapes, must, stems, juice, wine, and pomace[1] were already in use by 1973, and several types of presses, pumps, conveyors, filters, tanks and valves were available for the choosing. Any design that I had not used before had to be checked out by weighing the pros and cons through discussions with winemaker friends who had used them. By mid-December, I had chosen most of the equipment and had only to work with Keith & Associates to place the tanks and equipment in a most logical and compact design. After that, Keith would be free to offer several possible building designs with aesthetics in mind. If I heard Keith say it once, I heard it a hundred times: "Form follows function. First, decide which tanks and equipment you want. Second, we'll design the correct size buildings to be pleasing to visitors."

The McFarlands had purchased a building site central to the vineyards at the edge of the small valley town of Gonzales, twenty miles south of Salinas in Monterey County. When I first saw the town, the nicest compliment I could think of was, "This part of old Mexico certainly isn't much." Gonzales, population 600, had a single long street with no stop lights at any of the few cross streets. The town was squeezed between Hwy 101 on the east and railroad tracks connecting San Francisco to Los Angeles on the west. There was one dusty bank, one dusty restaurant, one dusty grocery store, one dusty medical clinic, a few small bars ... I'd seen identical towns in old class B Westerns. The odds favoring any fool building a modern commercial building with an assessed valuation higher than all the rest of the town combined would have been infinitesimal; nevertheless, that is precisely what would happen when Gonzales was chosen as the site of the new winery.

I would remain in Napa Valley during the Monterey design and construction phase since Keith & Associates was close by, and I could commute by air between Napa Valley and Gonzales as needed. Since 1970, I had shared ownership of a Cessna 182 aircraft with Ed Beard, a friend who

---

[1] 'Must' is the name given to a mass of freshly crushed grapes, including pulp, juice, seeds and stems. 'Pomace' is the name for the waste solids left over after the juice and wine are removed from must by the press.

lived near Yountville. Only three miles away, John Trefethen's vineyard on Oak Knoll Avenue had a straight, thousand-foot long, blacktopped driveway with vineyards on either side. John gave us permission to land our airplane on his driveway and park it at the north end, out of sight of the avenue. During the first year after leaving Heublein, I used our airplane to commute between Trefethen's driveway and a vineyard strip near Gonzales. It would have been a three hour drive, but I could fly it in one hour.[2] Our first crush at Gonzales would be in September, 1974. My family and I would move from Napa Valley to Monterey just in time.

Although wine industry magazines screamed the news about new plantings in Monterey County totaling 10,000 acres, Myron and Gerry McFarland and Tom Stratton, their partner, rarely confirmed this and never bragged about it. Total Napa County plantings were only 13,000 acres, with Sonoma County having about the same number. The McFarland group would increase the total tonnage of coastal varietal grapes available for crushing by nearly 40%! They shied away from the press, knowing that conversation about huge size would make them juicy targets for government bureaucracies, labor unions, competitors, and taxing agencies; however, they were more than ready to discuss individual vineyard limited partnerships (LPs) as they were constantly looking for new limited partner investors.

Each vineyard LP was a separate company, ranging in size from 140 to over 500 acres with McFarland Management Co. as the general partner. Percentage ownership was proportional to the investment made by each investor-partner. Under a new law, each partner gained huge tax benefits for having invested money in agricultural projects; investing in the agricultural partnership allowed investor-partners to deduct their entire investment from taxable income for the current year!

Each limited partnership vineyard had its own appealing Hispanic

---

[2] Trefethen planted trees along both sides of his vineyard drive some time after I moved away, eliminating our old landing field. I sold my half of the plane to John when we moved to Monterey in 1974.

name and list of investors: Carmel, Cypress, Del Mar, El Camino, El Dorado, El Segundo, Hacienda, Mantes, Monterey Vineyards, Puente del Monte, Rincon and Santa Lucia. More were planned for future years, although it was uncertain whether the favorable investment law would be extended past 1974. I wanted the McFarland group to avoid marrying all their vineyard partnerships to a single large winery. Instead, I suggested building several small wineries here and there, each to make wines for one to three individual LPs. I was certain the partnerships would have an easier time selling their wines separately rather than all selling a single label through a single, very large winery. I did my best to explain to them that operating out of a single, huge winery would give them a terrible public relations disadvantage. I said, "Wine writers flock to promote wines from small wineries in competition with each other, whereas they often turn up their noses at very large wineries." It was a fact of wine industry life, but nothing I could have said would change the company structure they had already built.

They had tied the vineyard partnerships together, expecting to gain economic advantages by capitalizing on large size. Their concept was built on using 'economies of scale,' a notion Tom Stratton was especially proud of. He, Myron and Gerry had sold the LPs as great investments served up on a silver platter for investors by the legislators. First, the government would pay for most of their investment up front. Second, they could produce their wines cheaper than competitors because their vineyards were huge, the winery would be large, and marketing would be on a grand scale. Every step of production, storage, shipping and marketing would save money because of economies of scale. I was uneasy with the marketing part, but could not argue with their financial reasoning. I had told Myron on my first visit to Monterey County that making the wine would be easy; the hard part would be selling it. His answer was immediate: "Oh, we know that. We also know you have to collect the money after you sell the wine. We have a deal with Foremost-McKesson to handle all the wine sales for our new company. They are the largest wine and liquor sales organization in the country. They pay their bills." I knew zero about Foremost-McKesson, but Tom, Myron and Gerry had, indeed, been busy.

I was relieved to hear that they had spent time on the wine sales question, but could not forget what Justin Meyer had told me years earlier. As part of his planning for creation of the Silver Oak Winery in Napa Valley, he made a major study to answer the question. "Why do some new wineries succeed and some fail?" His studies found that some succeeded despite producing poor-quality wine; some failed despite making great-quality wine. Some succeeded with high-price wines, but some failed. Some operated in great wine areas like Napa and Sonoma Counties, but many failed in those same areas; some succeeded in unlikely wine areas, while others failed in the same areas. Justin concluded that the single, most important reason for success or failure was how inexpensively the owner had gotten into the wine business! Those who built expensive winery properties before crushing any grapes usually failed. Those who started in a garage or other building 'on a shoestring' and did not build an expensive winery building (or offices) had a much greater chance of success. The secret was to avoid spending money until your success at selling wine was assured. Justin found that even if a new winery produced great wine at fabulous prices, they had trouble selling it at first. He convinced me that there is a natural law that "no new wine brand catches on in public acceptance until it has been in production and sales for at least five, and often ten, years."

I made a suggestion to Myron, Gerry and Tom. "Maybe we should build a small winery at first and then make additions to it after we have gained experience selling the wines we'll produce." All three were adamant. "Look, Dick," Tom said firmly. "We've committed all this acreage to vineyards where the university tells us we can create another Napa Valley. We already have the money to move forward according to our plan. John Hancock Life Insurance has committed 29 million dollars to building this modern winery; a quarter of their money is equity, so we don't pay interest on that. We have great vineyard managers who have spared no expense in planting and irrigation. You've seen the miles of overhead sprinkler systems we have installed. We aren't relying on simple drip systems for irrigation because we want to be prepared for spring frost. You know how damaging frost can be to a vineyard; your own experience at BV in 1970 proves that. We know there will be variations in crop yields from year to year; we are farmers, after all. Our grape vines are already in the ground; now we have to build the winery to handle those grapes. We have the biggest and best wine marketing company in the country setting up to sell the wines."

"Okay, okay," I said. I admitted I had never been a wine marketer and never thought of myself as a salesman. I dropped the subject, but did have one more thing to discuss. From experience, I knew that there would be differences in wine quality and style from vineyard to vineyard. I suggested we might discover, for example, that Rincon vineyard might produce a better quality Chardonnay than El Segundo. Their wines might differ in value from each other, and the grape prices would be different. "Oh no," all three interrupted at once, almost in unison. "Dick, we can't do that," Tom injected. "But, that's the nature of wine," I said. "You always find variations in quality and style of wine from vineyard to vineyard. Sometimes the differences are small, but some..." He interrupted, "We never promised one investor anything different from what we told all the others in selling these limited partnerships. We simply have to treat all partnerships equally."

I thought about that for a while and said, "I hope I'm wrong in this case, but if there are serious differences in wine quality between vineyards, it will be difficult to hide them. Land owners always discover the quality differences between their fruit and that of their neighbors. I may have to do some blending that will upgrade some grapes and downgrade others. I just don't want any secrets." "That's why we chose you," Tom ended the conversation. I liked working with Tom, Myron and Gerry very much. They had gotten in pretty deep without fully understanding grapes or wine, but all were honest and straightforward, with no beating around the bush. I always knew where I stood, and there were no giant egos to endure. I was impressed that they had gathered together all the money in the world to engineer this major project. At the same time, I felt a little out of place inside the cloud of big business farming, which I had never seen up close before. On the one hand it would be a definite challenge; on the other, I always enjoyed challenges. I found myself hoping that the quality differences from vineyard to vineyard wouldn't be great, but if I'd been thinking realistically, I would have known better than that.

Winery Design

I went back to work with Dick Keith and his assistant architects on winery design. By December, I had placed orders to Valley Foundry and other suppliers for fermentation tanks, piping, presses, a centrifuge and other equipment to ensure installation would be complete by the following September in time for the first crush. It would not be possible to build the whole winery in a few months, but I wanted to be sure we had the minimum equipment necessary for the 1974 crushing season. Gerry McFarland was predicting nearly 2,000 tons of grapes for our first crush. I knew that first season predictions are usually exaggerated and guessed it might be closer to 1,500 tons. I would watch crop levels closely as the oldest vines matured their fruit, adding tanks as necessary in the late summer. We would build two separate fermentation buildings, each containing about 65,000 square feet of space. One would produce red wines and the other would handle whites. The crushers and hoppers were placed outside between the fermenting buildings, providing a smooth traffic flow regardless of the type and quantity of grapes to be delivered on a given day. For that first crush, we would use only one building, crushing red grapes on certain days and white ones on other days as the tonnages would be relatively small.

Keith & Associates was quite progressive, trying to modernize and streamline in the interest of appearance. For example, Dick Keith felt that the large must lines and other piping of most wineries were an eyesore. Most wine pipes and hoses in small wineries were an inch in diameter; medium wineries used two-inch sizes, and very large wineries used between three- and six-inch pipelines. Must lines were always larger than wine lines because they had to convey freshly crushed grapes, solids and juice together. Those big pipe lines convey fresh must and grapes from the crusher to the fermentation tanks (for red wines) or to settling tanks or de-juicing screens (for white wines). Keith wanted to hide the must lines from view by placing them underground, but I threw up my hands immediately.

"What are you thinking?" I asked. "We have to clean must lines after use every day, then rinse and let them drain dry overnight. I can't drain them if they're underground." "Sure you can," Keith answered. "Pump the last of the must through the lines, flush with a little water and then blow air through the empty lines until they are dry." "C'mon, Keith, be serious," I said. "I'd be the laughing stock of the industry if I installed underground must lines. Put them above ground where I can ensure that our workers will keep them clean." "Dick, we've buried must lines underground successfully for new wineries several times," he said. "I was trying to make you proud of the facility's appearance." Shaking my head, I insisted that all wine and must lines be installed out in the open where they would be easily visible; I knew this would eliminate future worker errors. However, Keith was just as adamant, quoting from a design textbook that I'd never heard of, "Once a water line is installed, there's no need to ever see it again." He said, quoting with authority, "Water lines can be safely hidden underground." Neither of us could afford the time to argue, so we made a compromise that neither was happy with; he would design the wine and must lines above ground and the water piping underground.

The large fermentation buildings were to be essentially square. To break up the large wall monotony, Keith designed large pilasters at the corners that allowed daylight into the buildings through evenly spaced vertical windows extending from ten feet above ground nearly to the roof, almost thirty-five feet high. On seeing the window spaces, my wife offered to draw designs of grapes and wine that could be installed as stained-glass windows instead of ordinary glass. The cost was not high, and her idea ended up making the red wine building a more artistic and pleasant place in which to work.

Since we didn't need the capacity of both buildings in year one, we decided to complete the red wine building first and then add the white wine building in either year two or three; however, a barrel warehouse would be necessary from the start. We'd need to age red wines in oak barrels, even though I had not yet designed a suitable pallet on which to clean, store and handle the barrels. None existed in the industry. I knew I couldn't live with antiquated methods of handling wine barrels by 'hand stacking,' as we had done at Beaulieu; nor was I going to build one of those clumsy, oversize, 'framework' wood beam racks that a few Napa Valley wineries were installing (including the one that Bill Amaral built for Andre Tchelistcheff at

Beaulieu). I told Keith & Associates to design the barrel building with two floors connected by a single, large elevator. I would plan to take barrels of wine up to the second floor by forklift in the elevator as soon as we could come up with a suitable barrel pallet design.

I didn't dare forget that the clock was running; I would have to complete the design of a new barrel pallet very soon. Storing wine barrels standing upright on their heads on a flat wooden pallet was not an option. The upper head would dry out, crack and leak air into the barrels, spoiling the wine. That system worked well for whiskey and sometimes for dessert wines, since the flavor of dessert wines like port and sherry is partly oxidation anyway. The more I thought about it, the more certain I was that a simple steel pallet on which to handle barrels full of wine by forklift could be designed. I had better get on with it.

I considered handling four barrels at once on a single pallet, but realized it would take too big a fork lift to hold that much weight cantilevered out in front. Each barrel full of wine would weigh 500 pounds, even if it was only a 50-gallon American oak whiskey barrel. French oak barrels would be even heavier. Handling two barrels at a time per pallet would make it possible to use a smaller forklift, and if I wanted to lift four full barrels at a time, I could simply stack the barrels in twos. I decided to stick with a simple pallet design to handle only two barrels at a time and got to work.

Farmers Marketing Wine

Myron, Gerry and Tom had named the winery company 'Monterey Vintners,' and hired Charles H. (Chip) Plomteaux III to head up winery marketing efforts in 1973, a full year before I was hired. Chip was young and not terribly experienced, but Tom wanted him because he had been in the sales department at Gallo Winery for the previous two years. Tom told his partners, "If you want somebody good, hire him away from Gallo. The best employees are always Gallo grads."

Even though the winery would not have its own wines to sell for another two years, Chip began introducing the Monterey Vintners brand name to wine consumers. He bought a small inventory of Sonoma County Zinfandel bulk wine, had it bottled by a custom bottler, and tried to sell it directly to consumers. The sales effort failed miserably. When I finally saw what he had done and tasted the Zinfandel, I was seriously taken aback at the lack of professionalism in that early attempt. The label was not classy, the wine was so-so, and there was nothing to connect the Monterey Vintners brand with either Monterey grapes or the winery to be built in Gonzales. There was even a legal problem with using the Monterey place name to sell a non-Monterey wine. Nothing about the experiment was well thought out, and I thought it had killed the value of the Monterey Vintners brand name. Myron, Gerry and Tom would never agree to dump it and take the loss – Chip had told them it was superb wine and, not being astute wine drinkers, they agreed. However, to sell it off at a low price meant that we could not expect the public to later accept new wines at higher prices under that label. I decided to hold back my criticism until the sales partners had developed a real wine program. I hadn't claimed to know anything about selling wine and the board had just proven to me that none of them did either.

The McFarland Group finished their negotiations with Foremost-McKesson later in 1973 and finalized their earlier handshake agreement to use McKesson as their exclusive wine marketer. McKesson would not handle the wines directly, but through a new joint venture company, Monterey Bay Co. (called Bayco), owned half by Foremost-McKesson and half by the winery, with McKesson naming four board members and the winery naming three. This was intended to allow McKesson to break any tie. McKesson was assumed to have the marketing experience, and McFarland felt comfortable yielding to McKesson on any question about marketing. Fine tuning the marketing organization could wait until they had grapes to crush and further meetings with McKesson were put on hold.

In June 1974, McKesson brought in an Englishman, Gerald Asher, as the man they wanted to hire as president of Bayco. He was a well-known writer, very wine-knowledgeable, though primarily Europe oriented. Gerald and I were given the job of working together to establish a brand name, label and marketing plan, with him assuming a leadership position on all marketing questions. I found Gerald to be knowledgeable, a logical thinker and easy to work with. He was an excellent and well established public relations expert, but he admitted up front that he had never before managed the total sales effort for a large winery. When Gerald saw details of Chip's early experimentation with bulk Zinfandel, he looked at me and we both rolled our eyes. Without saying a word, we had agreed to distance ourselves from the Monterey Vintners brand name. Chip Plomteaux had already recognized that he wouldn't fit into the Foremost-McKesson sales operation and resigned, moving to a sales position at San Martin, another Monterey County winery. Gerald and I had no difficulty in agreeing that our brand name should be 'The Monterey Vineyard,' to accurately tell the public what our winery was about. The board agreed to drop the old Monterey Vintners mark, renaming the winery The Monterey Vineyard (TMV) to match the brand and avoid confusion. Gerald and I then worked together to design a basic wine label that would tie our wine directly to the history of Monterey. He chose a design of a classic sailing ship that I liked very much, and the rest of the label design fell into place.

Neither Gerald nor I recognized it at first, but when sales began in 1975, an obvious conflict became apparent between the McFarland Partners and Foremost-McKesson regarding the asking prices for wines. The vineyard partnerships wanted as high a price as they could get for their wine grapes. McKesson, on the other hand, was used to selling both wines and liquors as ordinary commodities; most of what they sold was on the basis of price. If the price was low, McKesson salesmen could sell whole pallet loads; if not, there would not be many sales. I noticed that their selling approach had many things in common with Heublein, and I shared my Beaulieu experiences with Gerald in some detail. We knew that Monterey wines cost more to produce than Central Valley wines and agreed that we'd work together to put extra effort into positioning Monterey as an 'up scale' wine line.

Gerald's approach was realistic: "We want to sell our wines at optimal prices, but the prices have to be acceptable to the consumer." Gerald would sell wine in the manner of a European negociant – show the line to distributors, assume they will love it, and step out of the way. I was comfortable with that approach, since it was similar to the way Legh Knowles had been selling BV wines. To me, it was the time-tested professional method for selling high-quality table wines.

Gerald told me his next step would be to study the sales results of leading California wineries prior to deciding which varietal wines would be the easiest, and which would be the most difficult for us to market. Obviously no winery made its sales records public, but a writer, Lou Gomberg, had developed a successful business by using the wineries' own private records to perform a genuine service for most California wineries. Lou was well-known to leaders in the wine business, and his method was as clever as it was widely read. He collected the alcohol tax records of all significant wineries from public filings of federal and state agencies throughout the country, and published a monthly report, to which every large winery and many of the smaller ones subscribed. *The Gomberg Report* was the only genuine, reliable source for watching which wines were selling where, which were growing and which were not. Readers could see which wineries and wines, and at what prices, were most successful in various regions of the country. *The Gomberg Report* was the industry source for historical records of wine sales by wine type and by winery. Gerald was looking in the right places.

The original retail prices proposed at Gerald's first meetings with the Bayco board were beginning to look a little high. Coastal varietal grape prices had reached a moderate high in 1973, but had already dropped precipitously by mid-1974, as word got out that Monterey County would begin harvesting exaggerated tonnages by fall. Lower grape prices would eventually lead to lower wine prices, and the huge McFarland plantings in Monterey County threatened to upend both grape and wine prices.

In January 1975, he made his final decisions for projected pricing of the upcoming wines from TMV. He listed Del Mar Ranch (a blend of three white varieties) at $2.50, Grüner Sylvaner at $2.65, Chenin Blanc at $2.75, Johannisberg Riesling at $4.00 and Chardonnay at $4.25. He was handicapped by not having any red wine to sell in year one, since all the reds required barrel aging before being released for sale. He also pointed out that, according to *The Gomberg Report*, Chardonnay and Chenin Blanc were the white varieties in highest demand, while Cabernet, Pinot Noir and Zinfandel led the red varieties.

I was impressed with Gerald's initial public relations effort. In the library, he discovered that the town of Gonzales had been named for an early land grantee, Theodoro Gonzales. He wrote, "Dating back to the 1800s, the early land grant happens to correspond surprisingly well with today's McFarland properties." I did not see a close resemblance between those properties, but that didn't matter; suddenly, we had a story to tell, and one which gave us a link to the past hundred years. No longer were we a raw newcomer; TMV now had a rich legacy spanning a century of California history!

Peterson Barrel Pallets

I hired Todd Cameron[3] in June to help me ride herd on the suppliers, and he put me in touch with Luigi Fortino as possible cellar foreman, Pete Bachman as assistant winemaker and Mark Middleton as maintenance manager and bottling foreman. All were good choices, with the right kinds of experience; all left their previous employment to accept the jobs we offered, and all showed up on time to begin work in early September. It was almost October before we would receive our first ripe grapes at the crusher, so each had time to become well acquainted with our facility. It was the perfect time to finish the barrel pallet design.

None of them had used barrels in a winery before, but Mark was a welder, and I asked all of them for help in building some test design pallets to use for storing and handling oak wine barrels. Luigi showed me an existing design used for steel drums, but it could not be used because of the curvature of wine barrel staves. I wanted to build some test designs, using square steel tubing to make them light, strong and easy to handle. Mark could not do it, but Luigi had friends who owned a small company near the town of Gilroy who could "weld anything." I gave him my ideas for the first trial designs. I wanted to heat, bend and twist small pieces of flat steel stock, welding them to square tubing so that oak barrels could fit exactly into the pallet.

---

[3] Todd Cameron had been a salesman for Scott Labs, selling supplies to the whole wine industry. He was a perfect choice to find the correct department managers to hire, since he knew all the production people in the industry.

The pallet bottom and top would be identical to allow a pallet to sit securely on top of barrels while allowing more barrels to nestle down into the pallet. If we did it right, pallets would look the same upside down or right side up. My goal was to make each stack earthquake proof by snugging each barrel down into the pallet rather than just sitting on top of it. With this design, any earthquake would have to lift the barrels up at exactly the same instant it shook them sideways in order to break a stack, and I knew that most earthquakes would not exhibit that kind of complex timing. To guarantee against barrel stave warping and leakage, I specified that the pallet length had to be within an inch of the barrel head-to-head distance; each barrel head would fit directly over the flat stock 'feet' of each pallet to ensure that it would be barrel heads (and not the staves), that would support the barrel weight. It was simple, but very effective. I was proud of the final design, especially after struggling to perfect it for so many years. Winemakers would no longer have to empty barrels in order to move them by hand; a forklift would do the job, moving full barrels as easily as empty ones.

Luigi Fortino took my design to his friends and we started a trial-and-error experimentation to get the barrel pallet design finished. Luigi caught on quickly and brought new samples of welded steel back to me every week. It only took about three weeks before we had our steel barrel pallet design finalized. Luigi got a quote for building fifty pallets with the exact dimensions I had given him; the price was just over thirty dollars each. That sounded fine to me, and I ordered them. We would need to palletize new barrels shortly after the fermenting season ended; most red wines would be ready to go into barrels by December or January.

After the design was completed, I did something that provoked many friends to ask, "Are you crazy?" Instead of patenting the design, I decided to give it to the wine industry as a token of my gratitude. The industry had been very good to me, and I wanted to pay something back. Others thought I should license out the design or start a company to build pallets, but I never seriously considered doing either. I was a winemaker and would focus my life on making and improving wines. I made an engineering drawing of the pallet and showed a slide of it as I presented the design to the industry at the annual Wine Industry Technical Seminar (WITS) in

Fresno on November 14, 1975. I don't deny that it was a terrific ego builder when the audience (about 300 wine professionals) gave me a standing ovation at the end of my speech that morning. Julio Gallo found me after the presentation and asked me to confirm what I had told the group. I told him, "Absolutely. You are free to use my design under the condition I gave the group: If you improve the design, you will let me use your improvement for nothing." He said, "Pete, you've got a deal," and thanked me again. My text and drawing were published in the official WITS transcript a month later. Remembering that a gift isn't a gift if you want something in return, I gave Luigi Fortino full credit in the text as my primary helper with the final construction. Today my pallets are used in most American wineries and many around the world; I am certain that they have saved a huge amount of effort and prevented worker injuries.

Vineyard Surprises

The McFarland vineyards had been planted in stages between 1970 and 1974. The 1970 plantings, the first and smallest, would produce The Monterey Vineyard's first crop in 1974. I drove my car between vine rows in those blocks every week all summer. I was in a race against those same grapevines; they kept working, sitting there in the fog, wind and sun, growing and ripening their grapes, while I pushed and pleaded with equipment makers to get our machinery installed at the winery in time to win the race.

By late June I began to notice mysterious symptoms on vine leaves in certain vineyards. There were burned areas around the perimeters of leaves on vines planted through the middle of the valley; vines growing along the edges of the valley did not seem to have the problem. The symptoms did not match any vine disease I had ever seen, and I asked the vineyard managers, Don Johnson, Gary Robinson and Dave Little what it was. They had seen the symptoms as well, but none could recognize what they meant. Dave thought it looked like salt burn, but their irrigation water analyses showed the water to be almost salt-free. His next step would be to collect some of the burned leaves for analyses, and he would let us know what he found.

The other thing I noticed was that all the vineyards remained 'socked in' by heavy ocean fog until late in the morning every day. The summer Monterey fog didn't hug the ground, as it often does in central California during winter; rather, the fog base remained several hundred feet above the ground, but the air between the fog layer and the land was very cold. Sometimes I didn't see the sun's disc until noon. That was very different from Napa Valley, where the sun normally burned through a delicate, hazy fog by 9 a.m. Also, I was surprised at how strongly the wind blew every afternoon in Salinas Valley. I first experienced that in landing my airplane on a small strip in the vineyards; the fact that the strip was lined up almost exactly in the direction of the prevailing wind is the only reason the strip was usable. You could count on at least ten knots of wind by 2 p.m. every afternoon (an hour later, it was often twenty knots or more). The wind always came from the same direction, bringing fog directly in off the ocean and blew right down the valley towards King City, sixty miles inland. The strong wind finally stopped late at night, after delivering the thick fog ceiling that would remain in place until late the next morning. For the first time, I realized why no house in the Salinas Valley is equipped with an air conditioner.

Driving through the McFarland vineyards in July, I stopped the car and got out to pick some of the burned grape leaves I'd been observing. Dave Little showed me the results of his analyses, which indicated that the leaf burning was, indeed, caused by salt on the leaves – even though the irrigation water was salt-free! I picked a few leaves and licked the burned areas with my tongue. There was no fear of licking pesticides off the leaves since wine grapevines were never sprayed. There wasn't any question about it; the taste was definitely salty, and I could even feel the roughness from tiny salt crystals on the surfaces of the dry leaves.

Suddenly, as I stood there confirming the taste of salt and contemplating what it meant, all hell broke loose. I found myself caught in the middle of a water deluge. The giant irrigation system had kicked in, and I ran at top speed through a veritable rainstorm to get back to my car, muddy and soaking wet. I sat there shivering a moment in the driver's seat and wondered whether anyone had seen me (they hadn't). As I drove out from under the artificial rainstorm, I noticed an odd but telling sight: The sprinkler system shot huge amounts of water up into the air, but none of it was falling close to the sprinklers directly below. Once in the air, the water was being blown at least twenty feet downwind before it finally fell to the ground. Every sprinkler was irrigating an area centered about twenty feet downwind of the sprinkler itself. No water fell on the vines upwind, or even near the sprinkler head. I knew immediately that Dave's guess was right when he concluded that the irrigation system was mining salt out of the 'salty ocean wind' and depositing it onto the vine leaves. As the wet leaves dried quickly in the wind, a coating of microscopic salt crystals remained and burned the leaves to death. I caught a slight cold collecting that information.

The vineyard planners should have used a drip system instead of sprinklers in the first place. Protected by fog, Salinas Valley turned out to be nearly 100% frost free, so the sprinklers had not been needed after all. Sprinklers wasted water, and drippers would have been much more effective in irrigating the vine roots. Drippers would have irrigated only the vine roots directly below, but none of the weeds in between the vines. The main downside to sprinkler systems was their cost, which was probably triple that of drip systems. I forced myself to halt that line of thought because it wasn't constructive. It did no good to criticize the past; the proper question was what could we do now to correct the problem for the future?

The vineyard managers, Gary Robinson and Dave Little, found a good solution almost immediately. They changed timer settings so that irrigation was no longer done during the day when it was windy. By irrigating at night, when high winds were rare, Gary and Dave had earned their salaries; the leaf burning stopped almost completely, and the sprinkle pattern centered around the vines near each sprinkler instead of only downwind. Most important to me, I never again almost drowned in a deluge of water from that huge sprinkler system in broad daylight.

I found one other vineyard with badly burned leaves, but it was immediately clear that this leaf burn had nothing to do with salt from the ocean air. One of the smaller vineyards had been planted immediately downwind from the large cattle feed lot named 'Fat City,' just east of the town of Chular. From a distance, viewers noticed that there was little or no growth among those vines; indeed, there were few green leaves to be seen on any of the vines. Close inspection showed a surprisingly heavy coating of steer manure dust on every grape leaf – the leaves were dying from organic nitrogen and salt burn. The vines at that location had little chance of producing grapes at all, and there was no chance I would use those grapes for making wine. On hearing this, Gerry McFarland abandoned that vineyard block without ever producing a single grape from it.

Keith & Associates people were easy to work with, as were the suppliers. Getting the crusher and grape hopper installed with enough tanks for our first crush would be a snap. The wine tanks were coming along nicely, but a question arose between labor unions, with me hanging helplessly in the middle. I had ordered sloping bottom tanks, including installation onto our sloping concrete foundations, from Valley Foundry in Fresno. Out of nowhere, I got a phone call from someone claiming to represent a labor union called the Millwrights in the San Francisco Bay Area. He told me I had to use his union to install my tanks or there would be big trouble. I had never heard of any such union doing winery work and told him I did not think his workers were experienced at installing specialty wine tanks. In any case, Gonzales was not close to the Bay Area, and it would make no sense for his workers to commute more than two hours each way to work on the few tanks we had to install. He blustered that his people could do any job that he told them to do. He kept pestering me and various others by phone until I finally called Pete Peters at Valley Foundry and told him what had happened. Pete told me that recent newspaper stories about my move to Monterey to help the McFarlands build a 'New Napa Valley' were to blame. I remembered discussing with McFarland partner Tom Stratton the fear that publicizing such a large winery would make us a target, but I had not realized it would stir the interest of a union that seemed so out of place in Gonzales. The only thing I could do was to leave it up to Pete.

My only worry was getting all the pumps, valves, piping and other minor equipment together with enough extra parts to be sure we could handle any emergency during the harvest. Delays always happen; as we fell behind on receiving certain items, I increased my vineyard visits so as to revise the estimates of exactly when I could expect the grapes to ripen. McFarland's vineyard managers had made estimates assuming similar ripening dates as the same varieties in Napa Valley. I had an advantage because I still lived in Napa Valley. Flying between Trefethen's Yountville strip and McFarland's airstrip in Monterey County, I monitored the same grape varieties in both regions all summer, and estimated their 1974 harvest dates. Wow! The Monterey grapes were not ripening at the same rate as Napa grapes at all. I estimated that Monterey grapes would not be harvested until a full month later than the same varieties in Napa Valley; the Gonzales climate was that much cooler. I was astonished. None of us had expected such a dramatic difference between these two vineyard areas, but there it was! The good news was that we would have an extra month in which to get our winery equipment ready. I considered that great luck, because there was already at least one office pool circulating around the McFarland organizations as to just how many days late the winery would be once the grapes were ready for harvest. I never bought any squares in the pool; instead I smiled and said quietly, "We'll be ready when your grapes are ready."

The 1974 Harvest

The harvest had been going on in Napa Valley since late August and would be finished by November first. Gerry McFarland called me in mid-September to ask about scheduling our harvest; I told him I'd been checking the grapes, and they didn't taste ripe even though some of the white varieties were above 23 Brix.[4] Linda O'Brien, lab technician, had noticed the acid analysis of the grapes was very high even though the Brix was getting high as well. During normal ripening, Brix readings (sugar content) rise as the acidity in the juice diminishes. The only way both sugar and acid could go up would be if the grapes had somehow dried out, concentrating both sugar and acid. The grapes tasted 'green' to her, and we became certain that those high afternoon winds were dehydrating the grapes instead of allowing them to ripen fully. We didn't yet recognize it, but that dehydration was

---

[4] Brix, pronounced 'bricks,' is an analysis of sugar content used for checking grape ripeness in the field. A reading of 23 Brix means the grape juice contains 23% sugar.

also a virtue. It was concentrating natural flavors inside the grape berries! I decided to hold off another few weeks to harvest, explaining the reasons to Gerry, Tom and Myron. They agreed that our primary goal was quality, not tonnage, and had no objection to my delaying the harvest.

We harvested a few loads of the earliest ripening grapes (Riesling, Pinot Blanc and Pinot Noir) in late September, but our main harvest took place in October and November. I'd asked Father Denis O'Hara, priest at the Catholic Church in Gonzales, to come to the winery to bless our first grapes. That was a tradition at many of the wineries in Napa Valley, and it was always an excuse for a luncheon in which local politicos and news people were invited. We did that as well, and it was a happy day for everyone.

Unexpectedly, Zinfandel was the last variety to ripen, even later than Cabernet Sauvignon, which really surprised me. I delayed harvesting some Zinfandel vineyards until December, which was unheard of throughout the history of California. The Zinfandel wine we produced was quite nice and Gerald Asher would highlight "December Harvest" on the label very effectively when the wine was released a year later. It certainly called attention to the unusual climate of Monterey.

Almost as unusual as the late ripening, Gerry McFarland noticed that some vineyards near the river had mold forming on some grape clusters. He called to ask me whether wineries in Napa ever had to treat their vines with a fungicide to get rid of mold. "Never," I said, and then asked him, "What color is the mold?" "Oh, just grey, I guess," he answered. "Do you see any green or black?" I pressed for information. "I don't think so," he said. "It looks like light grey mold to me." I was excited by then. "Gerry, this could be great news," I said. "Where exactly is the mold? I want to see it ASAP." He met me at the site in Santa Lucia Vineyard, and I could not believe my eyes. Right in front of us, nearly half of the Johannisberg Riesling and Sauvignon Blanc grape clusters had beautiful coverings of Botrytis cinerea 'noble rot' mold. Unbelievably, I found some noble rot on a few of the Pinot Noir clusters in Santa Lucia as well. "That would be a blockbuster if it holds up," I thought to myself. It was almost unheard of to find Noble Rot in black grape varieties anywhere in the world.

I couldn't wait to call Gerald Asher and tell him the news, but first took the time to tell Gerry not to spray anything at all on those vines. I made sure he understood, "This is a very rare and special mold,[5] and is highly prized in the few places in the world where it exists. We can make a magnificent dessert wine from these grapes, so please don't let anyone disturb them, okay?" "Sure," he said and hurried off to tell his brother, Myron. I called Gerald and told him it looked exactly like the Botrytis Semillon grapes I had seen at Chateau d' Yquem in Sauternes on an earlier visit to France. He answered my first question before I had time to ask, "Yesss! I want you to make a Botrytis dessert wine from whichever grapes have the noble rot mold."

First Monterey Wines

The 1974 harvest was finally completed in mid-December with a total crop of just less than 800 tons. The winery equipment was ready two weeks ahead of the grapes, and the 'pool' of bets against the winery being ready to receive ripe grapes was quickly forgotten. I felt a little smug because the few other wineries using Monterey grapes were complaining loudly about the vegetal character in most of their wines. I was certain we would not have that problem because our winemaking was above reproach; plus, I had delayed the harvest to allow as much full ripening as possible to reduce vegetal character in the wines. We fermented all the wines using the same procedures (including identical Pasteur yeast) we had used at Beaulieu in Napa Valley. After fermentation and stabilization of the new white wines, I began to taste lab samples of every tank with our lab technician, Linda O'Brien. We were both stunned to recognize that many of our 1974 wines had a vegetal character to some degree. Dang it!

---

[5] Books have been written about the famous 'noble rot' mold. Pronounced 'Bo-trý-tus,' it produces France's finest sweet Sauternes dessert wines, as well as superb German TBA 'Trockenbeerenauslese' Riesling wines. It grows on the ripening fruit of certain grapes only under specific climatic conditions, which is why it is so rare and highly prized.

I knew the winemaking was not to blame. It had to be the very cold summertime climate and not the soil; I had made excellent wines before from grapes grown on soils similar to the decomposed granite of Salinas Valley. Since the vegetal character was caused by the cold Salinas Valley climate, then the UC authors had erred terribly in their published evaluations of the various coastal valley climates. College textbooks are universally thought to be inviolate, well thought out and always correct. I had been confused by the apparent dichotomy between textbook statements and the actual coolness I had experienced all summer in the McFarland vineyards. Now, suddenly, it was starting to look as if the university was very wrong in the favorable comparisons of the Salinas Valley climate with those of Napa and Sonoma.

Weather people compare climates by totaling up heat received from the sun in each region. Prior to 1974, it was common practice to calculate the number of 'degree days' of heat at each location by averaging the high and low temperatures for the same day. Subtracting a standard base line of 50°F gave the number of 'degree days' for that day, and adding all days together gave the total heat units in a growing season for that site. The method is precise only when the temperature holds at the daily high for twelve hours and at the daily low for twelve hours of each 24 hour day, which never happens. As an easy estimate for comparing climates at two locations, it was assumed to be close enough for most purposes.

No one noticed, but this method fails dramatically at the northwest end of Salinas Valley because of cold ocean wind and fog in summer. At Salinas California, it is not unusual in June and July to experience a full *eighteen* hours near the low temperature of a day, with only *six* hours near the daily high! As a result, the historical method of calculating heat summations tells a big fat lie to anyone wondering how the area compares with 'normal' regions, 'normal' being loosely defined as experiencing around twelve hours of warming from daytime sun and about twelve hours of cooling at night.

Those who live near the ocean in Monterey County are accustomed to their very cool climate, but farmers from a warmer region (like central California) could easily make the mistake of trusting climatic reports that were built on the standard estimation method. Averaging the daily highs and lows makes no sense in a windy ocean area like Salinas. Taking the readings on an hourly basis rather than once a day would be more accurate. Better yet, measuring the area under the temperature curve gives the true answer, since that is exactly what each grapevine experiences every day.

We were to produce and bottle five wines immediately from the first 1974 vintage: Chenin Blanc, Chardonnay, Johannisberg Riesling, Del Mar Ranch (a blend of white varieties) and Sylvaner (for which Gerald used the Germanic name Grüner Sylvaner on the label). Red wines requiring extended aging and Botrytis Sauvignon Blanc would come later. The good news was that the Johannisberg Riesling and Gewurztraminer were beautiful wines, fruity and perfumey, with no trace of vegetal character. The Gewurztraminer was intensely fruity, with a Germanic, spice-like flavor, but we didn't have enough in 1974 to bottle on its own. I was pleased with the Pinot Blanc and Pinot Noir as well, noticing that the Pinot Noir gave my nose no allergy symptoms at all, unlike the '68 BV in Napa Valley.

All other varieties, even the Chardonnay, had a tendency to smell and taste a little 'green.' The Chenin Blanc had a particularly strong Chenin flavor – fruity, and reminiscent of newly-mown hay. It reminded me of Iowa summer and autumn days in the oat and alfalfa fields. The flavor was pleasant, but it seemed too strong. Obviously we would have to do something to fix these wines before they could be bottled.

Linda made lab trials to see whether we could remove or temper the vegetal character by judicious 'fining', without upsetting the fruitiness.[6] A fining agent, for example egg white, can be added to a wine in small quantities if the winemaker wants to remove excess natural tannin. The egg white reacts with tannins, forming a precipitate that settles to the bottom of the tank. The precipitate contains the added egg white attached to some of

---

[6] Fining is an important part of winemaking. Federal regulations list a series of food compatible 'fining agents,' approved for use in wine under certain, specific conditions. Fining produces better-tasting wines by removing excessive amounts of various components without changing the rest of the wine.

the tannin. The precipitate can easily be removed by filtration, leaving the wine softer and less harsh to the taste. After such fining, the wine contains less tannin than was present originally, and the excess tannin was removed without affecting other components. [7] Winemakers do this by trial and error to make decisions as to whether or not to use a specific fining agent to improve the flavor and mouthfeel of a wine. The fining agent is not an ingredient of the wine since it doesn't remain in the wine.

Linda tried various fining agents on wine samples in the lab, evaluating by taste; she and I agreed on using two ounces of an insoluble fining agent nicknamed 'PVPP' per thousand gallons of Chenin Blanc wine prior to bottling. It made the wine cleaner, reducing the vegetal character, and we thought the wine was improved by that very small treatment. PVPP absorbs undesirable components and removes them from the wine.

I selected a group of tasters to help us make the final decisions on wine quality. The group included Todd Cameron, Luigi Fortino, Pete Bachman, Linda O'Brien and Heidi, my oldest daughter. I included her in as many late-afternoon tastings as her high school schedule would permit. Linda prepared tenth-size (375 ml.) bottles of lab-fined Chenin Blanc for each of the tasters to take home that night. They were to drink the wine with dinner, criticizing every aspect of its taste for me the next day. I had learned over the years not to make a firm decision about fining agents only in the lab. It's a little like coming home in early evening to the smell of onions cooking in a stew. The smell seems strong at first. After half an hour, one of the kids arrives and remarks that the house smells like onions, but neither you nor your spouse are still aware of the strong smell. One gets used to smells quickly and becomes less sensitive over time.

---

[7] Tannin in wines comes from the skins or seeds of grapes and, if a wine has been barrel aged, from oak barrels. The taste of tannin is astringent and mouth-drying, but tannin also adds body and 'bigness.' With too much tannin the wine may taste too harsh or even bitter. Fining with common proteins such as egg white, gelatin or casein from milk, removes excess tannin, making the wine taste softer and more pleasing.

I opened my bottle of treated Chenin Blanc at dinner and was amazed at how strongly 'green' and hay-like it smelled and tasted, unlike my earlier impressions in the lab. I didn't like it at all and was glad that we had made this take-home test before bottling the wine. Other tasters reported the same impression the next morning. We went back to the lab and continued to make fining tests and blends with other wines. In the end, we gave the wine a much heavier fining and sweetened it slightly.[8] The finished Chenin Blanc later won gold medals because we took care in fining, as well as blending with a small percentage of excellent Pinot Blanc prior to bottling.

A similar thing happened with Chardonnay. It tasted like fruity green peas at first, but after aging in French oak barrels a few months, followed by fining and blending with 15% Pinot Blanc, it became a nice example of the kind of Chardonnay I was hoping to produce. By mid-1975, I was beginning to understand that the very cold summertime climate of Salinas Valley, although different from Napa in the extreme, could be forced to produce some beautiful table wines. The primary difference I noticed was that Salinas Valley wines had a much more intense varietal flavor than the same grapes grown elsewhere in coastal California. I had never read that cold summertime climate is a major cause of intense varietal flavor in wines, but the evidence was there! I began saying that in PR statements and ads.

The Del Mar Ranch label was Gerald Asher's idea. I liked it; it reminded me of the approach I had tried to inject into Tom Stratton's thinking back in 1973. Bottling a special wine that was grown on just one of the Limited Partnership properties had sales appeal because both the wine and the label were unique. No other winery could copy it, since no one else could use grapes from that particular property. Del Mar Ranch wine was a blend of Chenin Blanc, Pinot Blanc and Sylvaner, with a very small percentage of Gewurztraminer. It was nearly bone dry, which made it an instant success.

---

[8] In California, wine is never sweetened by adding sugar. Instead, grape juice or concentrate is used. The California regulation was enacted "to insure absolute purity of California wine (made from grapes, with nothing added)." It also, ahem, satisfied the grape grower politicos since wineries have to buy more grapes to use as sweeteners when they aren't allowed to add sugar.

Dr. Barney Rhodes and his wife Belle visited The Monterey Vineyard (TMV) with his First Growth wine appreciation group in the spring of 1975, shortly after Gerald had announced the release of TMV wines for sale. The group fell in love with Del Mar Ranch wine and bought several cases immediately. Later, Belle Rhodes sent me a menu from the 110th Dinner of the Society of Medical Friends of Wine held on June 4, 1975. TMV Del Mar Ranch and Johannisberg Riesling wines were highlights, along with Cabernet Sauvignons from two other new wineries, Sterling Vineyards and Robert Mondavi in Napa Valley.

Two other 1974 wines were released to the market a year after the first group of whites. Zinfandel hadn't been harvested until December 1974, and after aging in American oak barrels, it became a standout when released in late 1975; its flavor was an interesting combination of the raspberry fruitiness often found in coastal Zins with the delicate black pepper of warmer-area Zin. It was not a huge wine, but a very pleasing one; a nice example of full-flavored Zin which went beautifully with food. Looking back, it appears that we made a mistake in naming it December Harvest, even though that was a true statement. In some consumer's minds there was already a firm belief that late harvest meant bigness, with lots of alcohol, tannin, etc., and that may be what the term "December Harvest" said to them.[9]

The other late arrival became one of Monterey's unique and unexpected dessert wines: the 1974 Botrytis Sauvignon Blanc. No one else in California had produced a Botrytis Sauvignon Blanc until TMV did in 1974. This was made using the time-tested procedures for making Sauternes: allow the heavily Botrytis-covered grapes (picked mostly as natural raisins) to

---

[9] U.S. Tax and Trade Bureau regulations specify that table wines must contain 14.0 % or less alcohol, while dessert wines may contain more than 14.0% alcohol. Consequently, dessert wines pay a higher tax. The hot taste of 14+% alcohol in dessert wines is more acceptable in 'cocktail wines' (wines drunk as cocktails at parties) than as food wines (served with food). Wines containing more than 14% alcohol often contain residues of sugar to counter the strong, hot taste of the higher percentage of alcohol. The alcohol content is stated on the front or back wine label, although in tiny print. Many consumers never notice the alcohol statement on the label.

ferment slowly for about a year, then bottle and expect it to continue aging for decades. The wine did exactly that. When released in early 1976, it was syrupy sweet with an intense Sauvignon Blanc flavor that changed from 'grassy fruity' to 'grassy pineapple' in the bottle over the first few years. I continued tasting that wine periodically over the next forty years, and it became more and more unusual, moving in the direction of a fine Sauternes. Other wineries have copied TMV since then, but there are almost no other regions in California that match the extent of Botrytis found in Santa Lucia, along the Salinas River near the upper end of Salinas Valley.

The Cabernet Sauvignon wine we'd fermented was clearly going to be a problem. It smelled and tasted like asparagus and green bell peppers. I knew I could not bottle this wine unless it changed drastically during barrel aging. It had the expected berry and currant-like fruitiness, but both were covered by a flavor caricature of 'unripeness.' "OK smartass, you like challenges, how's this?" I asked myself. At least I would have a year or two to figure it out; nobody expects Cabernet to be bottled for at least two years after fermentation. We filled various types of barrels with new red wines, as we wanted to see whether barrel age would help clean up the vegetal problem. Among the experiments we tried, only three things significantly minimized the veggie taste: ion exchange in the cellar,[10] judicious fining, and blending with warmer climate non-vegetal wines.

With less than one year's experience, we understood very little about the climate of the upper end of Monterey County's vineyard area. When the

---

[10] First used at Gallo to stabilize white wines, but later by many wineries, 'ion exchange' uses an insoluble resin to remove excess potassium from white wines, making the wine 'cold stable.' If not minimized, the excess potassium can form unsightly crystals of 'crème of tartar' in the wine whenever a bottle of wine is chilled for too long or at too low of a temperature. After ion exchange treatment, the wine is said to be 'cold stable' because no amount of chilling will cause new crystals to form. By chance, the ion exchange resin also happens to remove some of the noxious vegetal character from certain cold climate varietal wines (primarily Cabernet Sauvignon). 'Sodium' ion exchange can add sodium ions to wine. Its use is minimized by winemakers to preserve the natural high potassium content and 'low sodium' wholesomeness of table wines.

crushing season ended in December 1974, the flavor and general quality of the wines told us we were operating in one of the world's coolest summertime climates. This was not expected when I first accepted the job of making the best wines we could in this, California's newest wine region.

The vineyards were influenced primarily by the Pacific's cold Alaska current, which moves south along the full length of North America's west coast and keeps all but the biggest show-offs from swimming in the ocean off Washington, Oregon, or California at any time of year. Scuba divers have to wear their heaviest wet suits if they expect to stay in the water for more than a few minutes. 3-D maps highlight the mountains and easily identify the one place along California's coast where a large opening in the coastal mountain range exists; that place is Monterey Bay, and only there can the cold ocean winds blow in unabated onto flat, agricultural land. The exceptionally cool summertime climate is particularly good for growing salad greens and vegetables. Salinas ain't called the "Salad Bowl" of America for nothin'.

My winemaking challenge was to reduce the vegetal character in these Monterey County wines. Of the methods I had been trying, I had a distinct taste impression that blending did a better job of diminishing the vegetal character than either fining or ion exchange. To my taste, it seemed that the cool climate was doing more than simply retarding the ripening process within the grapevines. It was also producing a 'caricature' of the varietal flavors – some flavor characteristics in Cabernet and Chardonnay seemed exaggerated while other parts of the varietal flavor were retarded.

I developed a tentative theory to partially explain what the tasting seemed to tell us: Since all fruits taste green until they ripen, plants first produce vegetal characters in the green fruit. Only after metabolic ripening begins do we see the green characteristics start to diminish, while fruitiness becomes stronger and stronger. Fruit flavors are complex, often a mixture of many different organic compounds. A strawberry, for example, has countless numbers of different compounds that, when smelled and tasted together, make it taste like a strawberry. It is unlikely that all these compounds could be produced in the plant at identical rates. More likely, some are produced rapidly, while others are slower to appear. Most are at their optimum when we say, "the berry is perfectly ripe." If something has interrupted the ripening (such as too cold a climate, too much wind, too dry, too wet) the plant is likely to produce a 'caricature' of the perfectly ripe flavor. That seemed especially true after wind dehydration had concentrated sugars, acids and flavors (both green and ripe) inside the grapes.

Flavor caricatures, I think, are what we saw in some of the new 1974 wines at The Monterey Vineyard. Logically, the best way to correct a flavor caricature in an unripe wine would be to add a mature wine which contains all of the flavor components missing from the unripe wine. Simple fining could remove flavors that 'stuck out,' but fining could not add flavors that were never produced by the vine in the first place. One thing was certain: over and over again, we always noticed that judicious blending fixed the vegetal problem in wines more successfully than any other method.

Oh, Pioneer

The New Year began on an excellent note: TMV received the first of its new steel barrel pallets in January. I was thrilled that the pallets worked exactly as I had hoped and envisioned for so many years. It was the first successful barrel pallet design in the wine industry, and within two years, most of the wineries in coastal California were using them. It was disappointing that the company which made them for us gave no credit to either me or TMV for the design. But I realized that didn't matter, and I soon got over it; most winemakers have long since forgotten where the design came from anyway, even many who had given me that standing ovation in Fresno when I first presented it to the industry. Today's winemaker has become so accustomed to handling barrel pallets by forklift that few would believe how difficult it used to be for Theo Rosenbrand and other cellar workers at Beaulieu to fill, empty, stack, wash, move and repair barrels by hand prior to 1975. The welding company sold so many pallets in their first three years, they couldn't keep up with demand and were unable to continue. They sold their company to Western Square, which still produces Peterson pallets decades later. I never begrudged Western Square's profits; it seemed to me they kept their price low enough to be useful to the wine industry, which was my real goal. The pallet made winemakers' jobs much easier, and I smile with pride when I see them all over the industry forty years later.

Gerald Asher kicked his selling plan into high gear in spring by holding a series of events to introduce the newly released TMV wines to the public. There were several events in California, both in the south and north. I went with him to New York City where his friend Diana Kennedy, a well-known author of cookbooks on authentic Mexican cuisine gave a large party at her apartment to introduce TMV wines to the public in that area. We were moving forward as promised, and the PR plan was beautifully executed. The only negative I heard came from McFarland murmurings about the salesmen for Foremost-McKesson.

Gerald arranged a whole day tour of the Gonzales winery for Foremost-McKesson salespeople in April, shortly after the wines were released for sale. Two large buses brought dozens of sales people to the winery where I gave them a tour, telling about how unique the area was and showing where and how the wines were made. For the first time, I began saying publicly that this was the "coldest summertime winegrowing climate in the whole U.S." Gerald later told me that "coldest" has negative connotations, and he would prefer that I use the nicer word "coolest," which I quickly agreed to do. We offered all our wines for sipping on the tour, but many in the group didn't seem very happy about being there. I walked around talking to various salesmen here and there, but did not have a good feeling about what I overheard them saying to each other.

The luncheon was ordinary Mexican food – tortillas, enchiladas, and burritos, with rice and refried beans. Nothing special to begin with, the meal suffered from having been prepared ahead of time; much of it was not hot by the time it was served. The barrel building was cold, the day was grey and there was no way to heat such a large building. Some of the salespeople had come without coats and most were shivering by the time they were served a cold lunch. Gerald and I kept up a positive tone in our remarks to the group, but we knew the day wasn't our best.

This group didn't look like other wine groups I'd seen. Jim Gibbons, winery financial VP, told me too loudly, "They look like a bunch of liquor salesmen to me." He screwed up his face and scowled, "D'ya need any scotch? D'ya need cheap bourbon for the well? Want some wine? Whadd'ya want, red or white?" "Shhhh, Jim, not so loud, for Chrissake," I cautioned. "We need them to sell wine." Later, he showed me his records of McKesson orders. "McKesson hasn't ordered nearly enough wine to match the amounts they are contracted to sell this year," he said. I answered, "It's early, Jim. They're just getting started. It will take time to establish the brand." I liked the way Gerald was promoting our wines, and didn't want anyone to nit-pick the first results so early in his sales and promotion activity.

Shipments from the winery during 1975 seemed to go well, but Gerald quickly cautioned me not to read too much into what I'd seen. He told me, "The first shipments only fill the pipelines. Don't confuse shipments to regional McKesson distributors with actual sales. Actual sales are shown only by inventory depletions from the wine shops and restaurants. That takes time, and you'll see shipments to Bayco slow down until we see retailer depletions." He described the situation as "the normal difficulties" that lie in wait for start-up pioneers: "A pioneer wine label starts out totally unknown to the public, which doesn't know whether it is a good buy until they pay money to try it. That is not easy for us or for the consumer. Some of the first wines from Monterey County (Mirassou, Paul Masson and Almaden) had vegetal tastes, which got Monterey's reputation off to a bad start. We are slowly working our way through that." I nodded, "I understand, Gerald. It does not stop with labels, even the wines are different. In a new region with a new climate, you can't always bottle the first wine you get out of a fermenter. You have to fine, blend and age carefully to make the wine good if it doesn't come to you that way."

Competition was ugly. I received a letter from a consumer complaining about a bottle of Monastery Vineyard Heritage Rosé wine. The fine print on the label said "Produced and bottled by Mirassou," but the customer hadn't noticed. With great expectations, he and his wife had served it to guests for dinner at their home and gotten the shock of their lives. The wine was spoiled; he poured it down the sink and wrote to complain that he thought the wine had been stored too warm. I called Gerald and asked,

"How should I complain to my friend, Dan Mirassou?" He suggested, "Don't complain. Competition is fierce in wine. I would be subtle in explaining the brand name to customers. I'd then replace the bottle with a bottle of our wine." I wrote back to them, enclosing two bottles. I told them that I was sorry they'd had a bad experience with the wine and explained that their bottle had not come from The Monterey Vineyard. Their original bottle had been produced by Mirassou Winery and their brand name 'Monastery' was easy for a busy person to misread as 'Monterey.' I said that the wine they had tried was undrinkable to my taste as well, as I had bought one to check. I asked them to accept the enclosed bottles of our Del Mar Ranch and Zinfandel, with my compliments. I assured them that Mirassou had done nothing illegal; it was just a shoddy choice of brand name on Mirassou's part. I explained that we were extremely proud of our wines and invited the couple to visit us at their first opportunity. He wrote back, thanking me and said my samples had made them fans for life. They did visit the winery tasting room later although I was traveling at the time and missed meeting them.

From time to time other wineries tried to use the Monterey name on wines from appellations other than Monterey. We simply wrote each winery, asking them to stop because what they were doing was illegal. In every case, they wrote back apologizing and notifying me that they had stopped. No legal action had been necessary.

3,000 Miles Away

Unknown to any person in Gonzales in 1975, the Coca-Cola Company in Atlanta Georgia was thinking 'outside the box.' Albert E. Killeen, vice-chairman, executive VP and corporate marketing director, had a challenge to broaden the base of the company's business beyond the field of soft drinks. He put together The Business Development Group, a research department staffed by bright, young MBAs who were asked to review and identify new profit opportunities in food and beverages.

Since its inception in 1886, the Coca-Cola Company had never been involved in marketing alcoholic beverages. Indeed, rumors abounded to the effect that a dichotomy existed within the company. It was said that half the officers and directors followed the Southern Baptist credo that alcohol was an invention of the devil, while the other half apparently followed the Catholic credo – wine was used by Jesus and his followers and was even a necessary part of the sacrament, Holy Communion. Killeen asked the opinion of his boss, Chairman and CEO Paul Austin. Was there in fact a taboo carved in granite stating that the company would never engage in the beer or wine business? Austin felt they would be derelict in their duty to the company's shareholders if the group did not at least take a hard, bold look at those new and seemingly exciting industries.

Their studies eliminated beer. No suitable candidate was available for acquisition, and the wine industry was much more appealing. The probable scenario for table wine growth in the eighties was projected to be far more promising than beer, and acquisitions were possible. More importantly, the wine industry in America appeared to be evolving from its historic production orientation to a more outward focus on the consumer. That meant there would be an opening for mass merchandising of consumer packaged wine goods. In short, there was some excitement, but the following facts needed to be considered: Wine is agro-based, with viticulture largely confined to two areas, California and New York State. Alcoholic beverages are highly regulated at both the federal and state levels. The wine industry is highly capital and planning intensive (requiring long lead times). Wine industry functions are far more complex, diverse, and sophisticated than similar functions in the soft drink industry. Wine is both an art and a science. The wine sales cycle is far more seasonal than that of soft drinks.

Despite these challenges, wine represented a unique business opportunity in a growth industry not far removed from the soft drinks, coffee, juices and tea spectrum already occupied by the Coca-Cola Company. Managed effectively, the wine industry might just give Coca-Cola an opportunity to broaden its base of business in the United States and, over time, significantly increase its earnings. Al told Paul Austin that development of a tentative master plan would be forthcoming.

Uh Oh!

In mid-summer, 1975, Jim Gibbons notified the TMV board of directors in a memo that the winery was running short on cash because shipments of wine to Foremost-McKesson had been well below estimates. He was asking for more borrowing in order to pay the company's bills. He pointed out that most of the vineyard partnerships had been paid for their 1974 grape deliveries, but there would not be enough money in the TMV coffers to pay for the expected arrival of the company's 1975 vintage grapes. I spoke up, asking why he had paid the vineyards 'North Coast' prices for their grapes, as they were considerably higher than recently established 'Central Coast' prices. He told me that board members Tom Stratton and Gerry McFarland had insisted that there hadn't been enough history to consider the recently announced 'Central Coast' prices as firmly established. The contracts between TMV and the vineyard LPs stated that, "If no local pricing for grapes was established, then TMV would pay the vineyards for grapes on the basis of North Coast (Napa and Sonoma) prices." That was just one of the major conflicts of interest our wine company would encounter.

I was absolutely flabbergasted by Jim's memo to the board. How could the company that 'had all the money in the world' when they hired me a year ago suddenly be out of money? I knew our winery construction was not running over budget, so I went to Jim's office and asked him to explain to me how the company was organized financially. He was astonished to sense my confusion. I was president of the company, but I had never been told anything about the financial structure of TMV! I explained that Myron, as chairman, retained financial control; I was hired not for my financial acumen, but for my ability to build and operate a winery and make quality wine. I concentrated on the winery and winemaking and was now shocked to learn that the winery was not financed sufficiently to withstand the first few years of establishing its label in the market. Jim carefully explained to me that all the McFarland properties had the same basic structure. This included the vineyard limited partnerships, the winery and the marketing company. All had been organized around a basic block of shareholders, who owned each company. Shareholders hadn't contributed large amounts of money, but had instead counted on borrowing most of the money (the operating capital) from banks and insurance companies. He couldn't confirm that John Hancock Life Insurance had promised a total of 29 million dollars for the winery building, but told me it might be true. Hancock's investment was complex because part of it was equity and part was a series of loans. In addition to the Hancock involvement, banks were the source of day-to-day funds with which to run the winery.

I told Jim about my ancient discussions with Justin Meyer and his finding that the most successful wineries were the ones that got into the business 'on the cheap,' without borrowing much money. Even those rare wineries that produced excellent wines in 'year one' found it difficult to grow their wine sales for the first eight or ten years. It is a natural law of wine that the public needs time to get comfortable with a new brand name before that name can become established. All new wineries need enough starting capital to withstand several years of low income, because of low sales, until their labels finally catch on. After that, the winery can look forward to long years of success, provided they make good wine. Jim Gibbons was telling me that TMV would have to borrow money to pay interest on the money they borrowed each year (and the year before, and the year before that) and keep it up for ten years. I was not a financial man, but I knew a recipe for bankruptcy in the wine business when I saw it.

I told Jim I was quite happy with Gerald Asher's successful start in selling the Monterey Vineyard wines. He asked, "How much wine do you expect him to sell during this first sales year, 1975?" I shrugged and said, "I hadn't expected him to sell as much as he already has, given the sales people he has to work with. However, even with great salesmen, I wouldn't expect him to sell more than maybe twelve to fifteen thousand cases in year one." When he told me they were contracted to sell a hundred and six thousand cases, I almost laughed out loud. "Jim," I said, "this is a start-up winery. We won't have anything but a few white wines to sell this year. Next year we will release one or two of our first red wines, and possibly the Botrytis Sauvignon Blanc sweet wine; only then will the public begin to see the complete personality of our winery and its wines. I think we might sell a total of 12 to 15 thousand cases next year, same as this year. We can't expect the numbers to pick up for at least another three or four years. Only after this winery is ten years old will we see numbers approaching your hundred thousand cases."

Jim walked over and looked out the window, deep in thought for a few minutes. Finally, he looked back and said, "You know, these guys are farmers; they're used to growing crops that sell for cash. They receive cash for the crop shortly after delivery. They wrongly assumed that wineries would operate in a similar manner. Here's the problem: they expect the winery to sell all the wine they make and receive cash for it within a few months, or maybe up to a year, after buying the grapes. Dick, you are telling me that the winery won't start selling as much wine as it makes each year until ten years after entering the wine business. So the winery will need several years' worth of capital just to avoid bankruptcy for the first ten years. Can that be true?" I blurted out, "Jim, that is exactly what I'm telling you. Everybody in the wine business knows that. Haven't you heard that stupid, worn-out recipe for making a million dollars in the wine business? You start with four million dollars and after a few years, sure enough, you'll have your one million, plus some inventory."

Jim had been a bank executive before joining the McFarland vineyard and winery project. He said, "I'm amazed that Myron, Gerry and Tom, three very intelligent guys, jumped into this without understanding how capital intensive the wine business is. They expected the winery to buy all their grapes every year and sell all its wine every year and continue buying all their grapes every year, on and on to the millennium. They planned to borrow money as needed and pay it back every year like they were running a supermarket." I nodded, "Yeah, I don't think they realized how different the wine business is." Our conversation ended with my decision to ask for a board meeting to discuss this with Tom, Gerry and Myron as soon as possible. I didn't get one restful night's sleep for the next month.

Another reason to toss and turn occurred a week later. Cellar supervisor, Luigi Fortino, asked that I meet him in the red wine building to feel the concrete floor with my hands. The concrete was more than lukewarm; it was hot to the touch! Together we felt the floor in all directions around us and found that a circular area of concrete floor about thirty feet in diameter was hot. The rest of the concrete floor was normal. I asked Luigi whether the water boiler was running and he nodded. "The boiler has been running night and day for the last week, but I didn't know why until I found this hot spot on the floor." All I could say was, "I knew it! Sonofabitch, I knew it! Sonofabitch!" I kicked the air. He was surprised to hear me use such language, but we both knew that 'Dang' wouldn't cut it. Both of us knew exactly what the problem was. At least one hot water pipe had sprung a leak somewhere under the tons and tons of eight-inch thick reinforced concrete flooring. "That goddamned know-it-all architect," I said out loud, but inside I knew it was not the architect's fault. The fault was mine – and mine, alone. The architect thought he knew, but was mistaken. I was the one who did know better, but had allowed him to push me into burying the hot and cold water piping under the concrete floors of the building. I remembered him telling me, "Once a water line is installed, there's no need to ever see it again. Water lines can be safely hidden underground." I felt beyond stupid. Where on earth had my common sense been on that day?

I waited another whole day before calling Dick Keith because I was afraid of what I might say. When we did speak, he was all over himself assuring me that this was a single 'bad luck' occurrence and, after repairing it, we'd be happy forever. I did not let him finish his defense, "Dick, that's bullshit," I said. "This is not going to happen again because that f---ing plumbing contractor is going to fix the damage and compact the dirt before we re-pour that part of the concrete floor. I'm abandoning all the underground water pipes, and we will duplicate all those water lines above ground where I should have put them in the first place. I want to see dry pipes every time I walk into the cellar. I won't discuss this again." My voice had become more and more shrill as I spoke, and the conversation was over. My next call was to Frank Farella, our company attorney, and board member of TMV. His firm, Farella, Braun and Martel, would handle both the plumber and general contractor a lot more effectively than I would.

Pioneers in Peril

The mood was somber at the TMV board meeting in July. Myron, Gerry and Tom had been scrambling to find new money for buying the grapes over the next several years. Jim Gibbons had been correct. These guys were commodity farmers who grew a crop, delivered it, and then collected their money. They hadn't noticed that winery companies did not sell all their wines immediately after producing them. Even after I told them, they couldn't imagine that TMV would need eight or ten years to develop its label. Gerry said, "Selling wine was supposed to be Gerald Asher's job. Why was Foremost-McKesson so poorly motivated? They're supposed to be the largest wine and spirits distributors in the country, maybe the world. They're not showing us much." I tried to explain how wineries worked, and how long it took for the public to warm up to new wine labels. Understanding this was going to take more than a single discussion.

Gerry told me that they didn't expect the winery to bottle and sell all the wine it made immediately. He said, "Obviously some wines have to be aged before bottling, we know that. We also know there is a thriving business in the bulk market, where wineries sell their excess wines in bulk to other wineries. Where is your bulk wine department? Why wasn't the winery sales manger Chip Plomteaux, out there calling on Gallo and other wineries to get rid of your excess?" I answered, "Gerry, this is the first time I've heard from anyone that you expected that. All our discussions to date have assumed that Foremost-McKesson would be the total marketing arm for TMV." "Sure we did," he agreed. "But, no vineyard/winery combination comes out even every year. It was understood that you would use the bulk market to keep your inventories under control." I told the group, "Well, I expect to do that, of course. But, combining McKesson's sales ability, your vineyard projections and the realities of starting up a new label in the marketplace, what I see is this: bulk sales 95% – bottled goods 5%. There's a problem with that ratio. Your LP Vineyard contracts call for high grape prices for vintage-dated varietal wines. You should understand that the bulk market is basically a commodity market and that means lower prices. No winery can continue paying high prices for grapes when it has to sell most of its wine at the low prices of bulk wines."

Every day or two I got phone questions from Gerry or Tom asking how Gallo did this and how Beaulieu did that. Only after hearing similar answers from others did both understand that all wineries live with a basic truth; they need to be well capitalized to succeed, and they need to restrict their grape buying in the early years.

Over the next several weeks, Myron, Gerry and Tom began planning a new secondary offering of common (and preferred) stock for TMV. They hoped to sell another two million dollars worth of stock to partners who were already invested, either in the winery or the vineyard limited partnerships. "After all," Tom reasoned, "it's in their best interest to invest further. It adds strength to their existing investments." Recognizing that TMV was not organized with enough capital, they asked Frank Farella to write up new proposals for one or more secondary offerings. If successful, the winery could do a better job of buying grapes while avoiding the cost of excess borrowing in the early years. I cautioned the group that two million dollars wouldn't do it. In the next few weeks, Myron began trying to find an older, well-established winery that could buy some of their crop for the next ten years. He would do his part to lighten the load on our fledgling winery, and I for one appreciated his effort.

That October, I was in Myron's office when he called Ray Herrmann, VP of Foremost-McKesson. He asked why they were having a problem fulfilling their commitment to sell a hundred-thousand cases of TMV wines in 1975. It didn't look like Bayco would come close to the contract commitment. Ray answered, "I'm glad you called, Myron. I've been meaning to discuss this with you ahead of the upcoming board meeting. I've been hearing from our sales team that they're getting resistance to the prices we ask for TMV wines. I think we may have made a mistake in the contract. You know the board didn't set specific prices when we created Bayco. Gerald set those prices after talking with Dick. Now we're seeing that at current prices, big sales won't be there. The market takes time to develop." Both were upset, but each tried to placate the other.

Myron asked, "Does anyone complain about the wine quality?" "Oh no, we're happy with overall quality, it's just that the market isn't there for so many cases at these prices," Ray answered. "One problem is that we have only the five white wines for sale. We can't sell to some retailers because they won't consider the brand until we offer them red, white and rosé wines

266

as a complete line. Sales people need a full line of wine types to get the attention of every retailer." He asked, "Can you look at cost and send me a price proposal? Our people will review it and determine what is and isn't doable." Myron answered, "I'll check with the winery and see when they expect to release a more complete line of wines." Ray said, "Yes, Myron. I think that's where we have to start. We want this joint venture to work." I was not calmed by their friendly discussion, and wasn't sure they had really heard what each other was saying. I didn't believe either of them had convinced the other to knuckle under on price.

The 1975 crushing season started in late September, closely paralleling the 1974 season except that we received a more complete line of grape varieties to crush and more overall tonnage. As in 1974, I was pleased with the Pinot Noir, Pinot Blanc, Johannisberg Riesling and Gewurztraminer wines, but again stumbled over the Cabernet, Zinfandel and much of the Chardonnay. The cool climate Burgundian and Germanic wines were clearly better than Napa Valley wines made from the same varieties, but the warm-loving French and Italian varieties had flavors that we called 'in your face' and were much too vegetal in character. By 1975, I had started to recognize that those heat-loving grape varieties would have to be grafted over to cool-climate grapes before the Monterey area could blossom. I reported specific grape varieties in certain vineyard blocks to Gerry, telling him that I doubted that those varieties would ever produce usable fruit. There was far too much cold wind, and I didn't think some of those locations were suitable for any grape variety. I recommended abandoning some vineyard blocks altogether and moving farther inland for certain varieties. It was not at all clear that the McFarland management would agree to my suggestions. They did not like me saying that vineyards in the windy center of the Salinas Valley were in trouble, but vineyards along the valley edges, like Santa Lucia and Paloma, were doing well.

I remembered a conversation I once had with Tom Stratton on an early vineyard tour. I had asked, "How did you decide which varieties to plant in your limited partnerships?" Tom said, "It was easy. We asked the investors what kinds of wine they liked to drink. We agreed to plant varieties that would make the kinds of wine they wanted. They are the ones putting up the money, so we thought that would be appropriate." I paused before giving him the unwelcome news that I thought everyone had known, "Some grape varieties require warm climates, while others require cooler climates. You were lucky in some locations, but unlucky in others. I don't know which varieties will be best in each vineyard as yet, but I can tell you that Pinot Noir insists on having a cool summer to grow good wine, while Cabernet Sauvignon won't ripen unless it receives a whole lot more heat. Different varieties have different requirements. They can't all be planted in the same place."

I told him even more that he didn't want to hear. "I now know that vineyards growing in strong wind near the center of the valley will not produce usable grapes at all, but vines along the edges of the valley are producing terrific quality fruit. I never find vegetal character in Pinot Noir, Pinot Blanc, Riesling, Gewurztraminer or Sylvaner, but Cabernet is terrible." Tom asked whether I was certain and I said, "Yes, I'm afraid it's pretty definite." Tom had told me when I was first hired that they had been careful to treat all investors alike; they had intended to keep grape prices on all the partnerships equal, but he now knew that wouldn't be possible. Words could not express how sorry I was to be the one who gave him that bad news. Tom, Myron and Gerry were among the very nicest people I'd ever met.

In November, Gerald Asher sent another report to the board of Bayco, in which he presented and discussed his sales results to date, giving reasons for falling short of forecasts. It's unfair to paraphrase his three pages of superb English prose, but my translation into Iowan said, "The wines are good. For greater sales volume we will need to add a new label – a blend of medium-quality wine to be sold in half-gallon decanters rather than fifth-size bottles. Sales are below forecast because the forecast was made two years ago. The market has changed. To sell more wine, we must adjust our thinking." His report ended the thought with, "It makes no sense to continue using old, outdated market projections for today's market planning. It is not possible to achieve brand recognition, projected volume and high profit all at once within such a short period. Without brand building, the operation becomes a pointless exercise, so establishing the brand has first priority. Case sales objectives must be revised accordingly for both the current year and the next to better coincide with reality." He then reduced predicted sales for 1976 to 65,900 cases. Sales to date were 18,000 cases and were projected through the end of year to be 24,900 cases. He had clearly put a lot of effort into this plan and I would try to help him sell it. I thought Gerald had done an excellent job in our first year of sales.

Myron, on the other hand, was incensed after reading his recommendations. McKesson had agreed to sell the product and their failure was difficult for him to forgive. Only a day or two after Gerald's report arrived, Myron called a board meeting. Myron and Gerry held the floor for the first fifteen minutes, extremely upset that Gerald and Foremost-McKesson had failed so badly in their responsibility to live up to their commitments. Myron reported that Ray Herrmann had been trying to get him to make large reductions in the prices the winery charged Bayco for wines. Jim Gibbons agreed that McKesson had missed their numbers by a long shot, but told the board, "Dick doesn't think Gerald has done such a bad job, and he may be right. Given the kind of sales people at McKesson, maybe Gerald did as well as he could have." I could feel all the frowning eyes in the room turn to focus on me.

Trying to appear relaxed, or at least not defensive, I said, "Well, it isn't simply that McKesson has mostly liquor salesmen and very few wine salesmen. That is true, but it's also true of most other big sales companies; they make their real money selling spirits. This board already knows that I felt it was unrealistic to expect a single company to make huge sales right out of the gate with only one brand new winery and only one brand new label. Even now, it doesn't seem possible that one sales effort could keep up with 9,600 acres of vineyard land by selling only a single label from a single winery. That isn't how the wine industry works." Gerry interrupted, "But why weren't they honest with us? Why did they say they could sell that number of cases when they had no intention of doing so? Why didn't they tell us the truth when we formed Bayco?"

I hesitated only a second before answering, "I don't know, Gerry, but my guess is they think like liquor people and not wine people. Liquor salesmen sell only one thing – alcohol. The cheaper it is, the more of it they can sell. They're not comfortable with high prices and probably thought they could sell any amount you had by lowering the price until it would sell. I believe McKesson is surprised to learn that you expect all your grapes to sell at North Coast prices every year. All of us in this room have the same desire – to sell quality wines at higher prices. Gerald wants that, too. He knows how to sell high-quality wines, but he knows that those sales don't come easily, especially in the early years of a new winery. If Gerald lowers prices on these wines, the quality image will collapse, so he proposes to come out with a mid-quality brand of blended wines to sell in large-size bottles, like half-gallons and gallons. Most successful wine companies have done exactly that, and I agree with that approach. We have to be prepared to outlast the slow start we are seeing, because this kind of slow start is the norm."

I suspected that the board knew I was correct, but it distressed them to think that McKesson had misled them. They were going to lose a lot of money. McFarland had made their deal with McKesson before either Gerald or I was hired. We couldn't know who had misled whom – or if anyone had misled anyone. Wine sales had been suffering at the hands of liquor mentalities since the repeal of Prohibition; wine was best sold as an accompaniment to food, while liquor was sold only for its alcohol. How could we expect the two approaches to be compatible?

The board agreed to seek an infusion of more capital, if possible, from existing shareholders. Tom would begin writing up a private placement memorandum to offer 2,000 shares of 7% Convertible Preferred Stock in The Monterey Vineyard, Inc. The shares would be convertible into common shares at any time in the future at $1.50 per share, the current established price for common shares. The price per share for the new convertible preferred would be $1,000 for total projected proceeds of $2,000,000.

Atlanta, Georgia

Coca-Cola's business development group nearly had their proposed master plan completed. Director Al Killeen knew that if Coca-Cola was to enter the wine business, it would not be done by making investments in an existing winery, especially one with a questionable financial structure. It was not their style to become a partner with any other company, even a financially strong one. It was decided that any entry into the wine business would need to follow four primary objectives: Establish a strong production and distribution base on both U.S. coasts. Develop a balanced industry position, with quality products from both coasts. Create an opportunity for growth, with objective, imaginative and innovative marketing, and promotional and advertising programs targeting the consumer. Be driven by exceeding the existing industry growth.

Killeen's team had no knowledge of TMV and would not have given TMV a second look even if it had. Instead, they focused on the Taylor Wine Company of New York which had recently purchased a neighboring winery, Great Western. Taylor had the best-known trademark (next to Gallo) in the U.S. It was respected for premium wines of high quality, but Taylor's long-range planning and marketing was considered parochial, conservative and unprofessional. In California, Coca-Cola looked at wineries in Napa and Sonoma Valleys; there was no Central Valley winery for sale that had anything valuable to sell. Virtually all the larger wineries were relics of Prohibition Era structures, ready to fall down in a wind storm, and none had an established high-quality label that was widely respected. The group liked Sterling Vineyards because it was becoming known for quality in the Napa Valley. It was the type of winery which could give Coca-Cola access to fine restaurants, clubs, hotels and wine merchants, but could not be considered as a possible strong production and distribution base on the West Coast. It had neither the capacity nor the technical competence that Coca-Cola required.

The Giant Awakens

The McFarland's final straw occurred on January 14, when John Boyce-Smith, McKesson VP, wrote Myron a letter to reiterate the McKesson point of view. He wrote that the philosophy of Bayco had been accepted by both sides, as stated in the contract: Bayco would receive wines from the winery at prices that would allow them to be competitive. In 1973, when the agreement was finalized, there was a shortage of good varietal grapes and wines. Since then, two factors had changed. First, the market had not developed as predicted so that demand for table wines had not increased, while jug wines had grown much faster than projected. Second, severe price competition had become a fact of life. These two changes had made the launching of Bayco's wines more difficult than projected. The prices proposed by Myron would limit Bayco's flexibility to adjust prices to meet changing conditions in the marketplace.

John Boyce-Smith's letter also said that McKesson would investigate the fair market price of 'bottled unbranded wines of similar quality, quantity, variety, age and condition' to determine what they believed Bayco should be paying for each variety. Bayco needed assurance that the winery was not selling similar wines in bulk to other purchasers at prices lower than Bayco was paying. He stated that McKesson's purpose was not to reap a windfall for itself, but to put Bayco in a competitive position so as to compete successfully with other wine companies. He felt this could not be done unless Bayco owned its wines at reasonable cost.

It took no imagination to visualize that his report went over like gasoline in a fire extinguisher at the McFarland Management Co. They still believed that McKesson had promised to sell all the wines the McFarlands could produce. Reading between the lines, I came to believe that, most likely, neither side had discussed the market prices of the wines to be produced when they had made their agreement back in 1973. It seemed obvious to me that both sides had trusted that the other would be the 'perfect partner' without understanding exactly what each other really needed. I felt betrayed as well, but I also knew that the fault was partially mine since I had reservations about some of the vineyard developers' plans from the beginning. I was overwhelmed by the size of the McFarland and Stratton plans and assumed that any organization with such gigantic plans and financing must know more than I did about what they were doing. I had no one to blame but myself, and I knew it.

In February, John Hancock Life Insurance Co, the chief lender and mortgage holder of the winery property, woke up. The winery, with much less income than projected, not only couldn't make the mortgage payments on the huge winery building, but also couldn't pay the contracted prices for the increasing tonnages of grapes coming in from the vineyard limited partnerships. The winery was in default on both payments by early 1976, and I wondered what alternate plan the founders had for contingencies. It turned out they didn't have a contingency plan. They expected the vineyards to produce grapes and sell them to TMV winery. They also expected TMV winery to make wine, bottle it and promptly sell it to Bayco. Finally, they expected Bayco to sell the wine to consumers and promptly pay TMV, so the winery could pay the vineyards.

When none of the above happened – due to an unexpectedly drastic weakening of the varietal wine market, failure of vineyards to produce expected tonnages, and a drastic drop in grape prices – the pioneers were in deep doo-doo. Hancock asserted their security interest in the winery building and equipment. The preferred shareholders of TMV hired a consultant to study what went wrong with the system established by the general partners. They also asserted their security interest in our wine inventory, meaning that, from now on, we would have to get approval to bottle or ship any more wine. To minimize their losses, these powers assumed the option to sell our wine out from under us and take the cash.

The Financial Troubleshooter

With no fanfare in February, the board hired trouble shooter Ed Borchert to replace Myron McFarland as chairman of TMV, leaving me as president and Jim Gibbons as VP, secretary and treasurer. Myron, Gerry and Tom Stratton continued as directors of TMV, but no longer had positions of authority. Ed Borcherdt was a financial man with experience as a company manager, but had no experience in or knowledge of the wine business. At his request, Jim Gibbons and I made concerted efforts to educate him about the winery's history, goals and problems as an upstart saddled with far too much debt. His initial effort was to get control of the business on behalf of shareholders, formulate a plan to save the company and resume making and selling wines as if nothing had happened. It was in John Hancock's best interest to go along, as bankruptcy would be a difficult thing from which to recover.

Ed canceled the company credit cards and injected round after round of cost cutting, including staff reductions. Jim Gibbons had hired Dan Lucas as winery controller in late 1975, but the following March, Borcherdt eliminated the title of VP finance by firing Jim and keeping Dan Lucas as controller. I knew nothing about these terminations ahead of time as Ed never discussed his plans with anyone. His staff-cutting savings seemed like peanuts compared to the real problem, which was the winery's obligation to buy increasing tonnages of grapes that we didn't need and hence had to dispose of through bulk sales to other wineries at huge losses.

Over the next several months, Ed brought in various tire-kicking entrepreneurs, all of whom presented nearly identical plans: each proposed setting himself up as chairman, bringing in outside investors for capital, and continuing to run the company as before. Every one of them assumed that I would stay on as winemaker, but I would not have agreed to do that under any of the proposals I saw. My reason was simple: not one of the proposed new CEOs knew anything about the wine business. I might have been stupid to take the original job in Gonzales, but I was not going to repeat the exercise with a new non-wine CEO and expect different results.

Gerald Asher continued selling and promoting the Monterey Vineyard wines with generally good results. I supposed that Bayco continued operating in hopes that, if Hancock took a more active role in winery operations, the winery might be released from most vineyard obligations. Bayco just might work out after all despite the hard feelings between the two major partners. TMV remained in default to vineyard limited partnerships by more than $500,000, but there was enough control of both entities by the McFarlands that most of us assumed it would eventually sort itself out. The fact that McFarland Management held all the authority in the vineyards and many shares of TMV – while seemingly a conflict of interest – might be a plus if they were able to continue refinancing as they had so often in the past.

It Hit the Fan

Unknown to Gerald Asher, Dan Lucas, Ed Borchert or me, Myron wrote a letter to each of the shareholders in the vineyard limited partnership named 'Monterey Vineyards.' Unfortunately, that name was confusingly similar to the name of the winery, The Monterey Vineyard. More unfortunately, Mon-

terey Vineyards LP was a very large public partnership (the largest Mc-
Farland vineyard partnership by a wide margin). Myron was chairman of
Monterey Vineyards LP and his letter to the multitude of shareholders was
devastating. It stated, without emotion, that TMV winery was in default of
payments to the partnership totaling over $500,000 for grapes delivered to
the winery during 1975. It was unclear whether the winery would ever be
able to pay its debt to the vineyard partnership; therefore, the partnership
would not be able to pay the expected normal dividend. Myron hadn't realized it when he wrote the letter, but in that single mailing he had killed all
hope of Gerald's success in selling TMV wines.

Telephones rang off the wall. Managers were screaming and wringing
their hands. Good friends yelled at each other with bloody murder in their
eyes. I wrote a nasty letter to my good friend, Myron, demanding to know
why he had deliberately killed the very winery he had hired me to operate.
It paralleled the reasoning in Gerald's letter to Myron, which he must have
received in the same truckload. Myron was truly amazed at all the commotion. He called me to ask what the furor was all about. I told him his letter
was public and soon would appear in all the wine magazines since it was
big, big news. It meant that none of the retail outlets or restaurants cur-
rently buying our wines would buy any more. Gerald's job was thwarted
because he would no longer be taken seriously. Already both Gerald and I
had received calls from retailers asking us why they should continue buying
our wines if they would be stuck with it when the winery went out of business. With the winery out of business, retailers would cut prices to get rid
of inventory, and they asked if the winery would cover their losses.

Myron was not apologetic. He claimed he had not told anyone that the
winery was going out of business. Rather, as chairman, he had a legal obligation to keep all the vineyard shareholders informed of the condition of
their investments in the Monterey Vineyards LP. His hands were tied and it
wasn't his fault that Bayco hadn't sold enough wine to allow the winery to
pay for the grapes it was obligated to buy. Myron could not see why we were
so upset. He saw no reason for retailers or restaurants to stop buying the
wines. "If Bayco was thought to be running out of wine, the retailers would
want to buy more," he told me. "There should be a run on the wine, increasing

your sales, not reducing them." It was frustrating because I knew that Myron had the most to lose. He had the most invested and I felt deeply sorry that we had encountered these problems over the past two years.

Within a few days, John Boyce-Smith wrote to all the board members of Bayco to begin the process of dissolving the Bayco partnership between TMV and Foremost-McKesson. It would not be finalized until August, but most Bayco sales of our wines had stopped for practical purposes. It was left to Ed Borchert to work out details of returning Bayco's inventory of unsold wine for credit and to determine who'd own the trademarks and labels.

The summer of 1976 went by slowly for everyone but me. Myron was quietly trying to sell grapes to outside wineries. I tried to get him to hold back certain varieties and sell them to TMV for our existing labels, but he disagreed. He thought his responsibility was to sell all the grapes from each partnership to a single buyer and felt that would assure that he was impartial to each investor in the partnership. The directors of TMV were jockeying back and forth, choosing sides against each other to a large degree; preferred shareholders were unwilling to put in more money themselves, but wanted new investors to come in with big money to save their investments. They preferred continuing to run the winery in the same way it had been envisioned by the McFarland interests, but with more capital. John Hancock was hoping to get out with minimal losses, but would not have minded continuing to be the major lender for the vineyard partnerships. Ed Borcherdt clearly worked for TMV and against the vineyard LPs, and Myron and Ed were firing salvos at each other at every opportunity. Tom was trying to protect the preferred and common stock investors, most of whom had invested at his suggestion. Gerry had his hands full struggling to get the vineyards to produce grape tonnages as if this cool climate were a warm climate. It was 'every man for himself' and there was a lot of shit flying in the air.

Traveling Man

I was asked by the board of TMV winery to visit the various distributors around the country who had been buying our wines from Bayco. The board felt that if anyone could convince distributors to continue buying, it might be me, although it was not certain that any would even talk to me. Bayco managers had no objection and provided a complete list of distributors and their cities, with names and phone numbers of the managers. Gerald Asher had been hired by Foremost-McKesson after the Bayco dissolution; they needed him and I was sure he would help them learn to sell other fine wines. But I no longer had his help and direction. As a one-man sales department, I was certainly in over my head.

Todd Cameron, Luigi Fortino, Pete Bachman, Dan Lucas and others operated the winery day by day, while I traveled to many of the distribution houses to which Gerald had been selling TMV wines. The wines had been sold in eighteen states, including the most populous ones in the east, but only California, Nevada and Hawaii in the west. Gerald had recently added five more and had planned to introduce the wines into another thirteen during the next year. I concentrated on the twenty-two states that already had our wines, ignoring Hawaii for the time being. I started by calling the managers in clusters of states that were close enough together to make each trip worthwhile. It was inefficient because not every manager was available when I wanted to visit him. I traveled for about two weeks, then returned to the winery for a week to taste wines and plan work for the staff during my next absence of a week or two. It worked well for two reasons: Todd, Luigi, Pete and Dan were good at their jobs, and communication with them by telephone went smoothly. Looking back at my sales trips, it was clear that tenacity made up for the fact that I didn't know what the hell I was doing.

Many of the earliest wineries of Monterey County, most notably Mirassou, marketed wines that had strong vegetal flavors. By 1974, the whole region of Monterey was accused by simplistic writers of producing only vegetal wines. I noticed an arrogant-sounding letter to the editor from some guy in one newspaper stating, "Everybody knows that the grapes in Monterey County are grown on land where only vegetables were grown for decades. That's why all Monterey wines taste like vegetables." The statement, of course, was stupid and totally false. Plant biochemistry does not work that way; plants rarely, if ever, take flavors directly out of the soil to keep for themselves. Once I was invited as a guest speaker to talk about the Monterey area to Robert Lawrence Balzer's wine appreciation class in L.A. At one point, Robert asked a question that he thought might be on the minds of some of his students. "Is it because vegetables have been grown there for a hundred years that Monterey wines have a vegetal character?" I told him at once, "First, not all Monterey wines are vegetal; second, much of today's vineyard land in Monterey County has never grown vegetables, but was grazing land; third, plants never take flavors directly out of the soil. Fourth, I want to tell you a true story. I grew up in Iowa on a very small farm. We raised strawberries on our property. Every spring we took manure (we raised hogs and had our own milk cow) and spread it on the ground around the strawberry plants. Spring rains soaked the manure into the soil and those strawberries grew like everything. And you know something? In the twenty years that I picked and ate strawberries from that patch, those strawberries always tasted exactly like strawberries – they never tasted like manure. Not once!" Balzer, and half the class, roared with laughter, and the point had been made. Balzer reprinted my answer in his regular wine column several times over the next few months, as Monterey wines became better known. Robert was a great friend. He reminded me of my quip repeatedly over the years, until his death at age 99 in 2011.

In talking to the managers of wine distribution houses, I was no salesman and didn't try to be one. I simply met each manager in his office and told the same story to everyone. Monterey was a unique wine region, with the coolest summertime climate in the U.S. and one of the coolest in the whole world. Cool growing seasons gave the wines intense natural flavor, and I expected that we would provide them with some of the very best Pinots, Chardonnays and Riesling wines in the country. I was unsure of Cabernet and Syrah and told them that unless those varieties were excellent, I simply would not bottle them. I was excited about the occurrence of Botrytis in the vineyards along the river near Gonzales and thought it was certain to produce some nice, and unusual, dessert wines.

One thing stood out in every wine distribution house I visited. Most businesses made more money on spirits than wine, but every place had one, two or three people who specialized in quality wine. These few individuals had a deeper interest in the nuances of wine appreciation than others. It often seemed snobbish to spirits salesmen, but the wine people didn't care. The spirits guys sold whatever wine their company offered, and immediately left. Wine guys sold the same wine, but then hung around to discuss controversies about the origin of Zinfandel in the world, or the reason 1968 was such a great year for Cabernet in Napa but a total flop in Bordeaux – and yet 1945 had been a great year for Cabernet in both regions! True wine connoisseurs weren't satisfied to just sell wine and go away; rather, they wanted to hang around to discuss the finer points of wine ad nauseum.

I found that sales people who talked about wine nuances were the ones most interested in what I told them about the Monterey area. They found it fascinating to learn that, after growing up with the fantasy that California had the same climate year after year, Monterey was a new region that didn't follow any of the previous rules. I generally allotted an hour to each visit, but soon noticed that there was so much interest in serious wines that I sometimes spent two hours or even more. I got questions about the wines of Beaulieu, questions about Gallo and still more about one type of wine or another throughout the world. Occasionally, I was invited to speak to their whole sales group when their sales meeting coincided with my visit. I left most of those businesses with the feeling that there was much more interest in Monterey than we had believed from sales figures. People I'd just met were anxious to help us provide their customers with some unique and delicious table wines to enjoy.

My question to them was always the same: would they continue to sell our wines in their areas if I kept them apprised of our progress to find a nationwide distributor replacement for Foremost-McKesson? I told them wine grapes were always going to grow in Monterey County regardless of who owned the winery, and distributors would be needed in their area to sell our wines. They'd already made a good start, and I wanted them to continue selling with new vigor. The John Hancock Insurance Company had so much money invested in the vineyards and winery that I couldn't imagine them not finding a suitable partner to own and operate the business. I assured each of the distributors that I would not leave TMV in its present state. I was in it for the long haul, and I hoped they would remain as well. I invited each of them to call me at any time if they had questions about any of our Monterey wines and many did over the next few years.

Yet Another 'Uh Oh'

One day that summer, Ed Borchert asked me to go with him to see one of the vineyard blocks in the Monterey Vineyards LP. There were some sick grapevines with odd symptoms that he thought I might recognize. What I saw was surprising: there stood two dead vines, side by side, completely surrounded by strong and healthy vines. The dead vines had been growing well, as shown by their full canopy of lush leaves on strong canes, but the leaves were now brown and dead. What could cause a few healthy vines to abruptly turn brown and die? Gophers maybe, but I saw no evidence of gophers on the ground near those vines. I'd read about the great wine blight from Phylloxera aphids [11] in the 1870s and 1880s with those exact symptoms, but all vines in California were grafted onto native vine roots from the Midwest, which were immune to Phylloxera. I couldn't help the vineyard with any suggestions except that they ought to dig down to the roots of the vines and look for other symptoms. As we drove away I couldn't help but think, "That's all the McFarlands need – yet another problem, a new disease in the vineyards."

About a week later, Gerry McFarland hired Professor Bill Hewitt to come to the vineyard to identify the problem. Bill was an outstanding viticulture expert and he spotted the cause almost immediately. He suspected it when Gerry told him they had planted all their vines on their own roots. They had saved money by not using phylloxera-resistant rootstock, but

---

[11] Pronounced fill-óx-er-uh, these microscopic insects had nearly wiped out all the wine grapes in Europe when the great blight entered France in the late 1800s. They had come from America, clinging to the roots of American hybrid potted vines that were introduced as an experiment to France. Once there, they killed all the European vines they touched by sucking the juice out of vine roots. The insect could live on American roots without killing the vines, but they decimated any European vines that were growing on their own roots.

The tasting room terrace for visitors at The Monterey Vineyard (TMV).

The long straight driveway to John Trefethen's winery was home base for our Cessna 182 from 1971 to 1974. Using this strip, I could inspect vineyards in both the Napa Valley and Monterey's Salinas Valley on the same day. This direct comparison proved that the Monterey grapes were ripening considerably more slowly than the same variety in Napa, unknown information to nearly all winemakers in the early 1970s. Monterey, 150 miles to the south, is noticeably cooler in summertime than Napa; text book heat summation assumptions were just plain wrong. The winery is at top of photo and Oak Knoll Avenue is along the bottom.

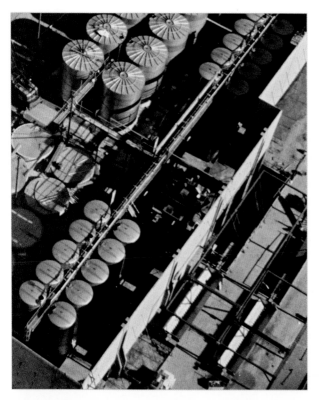

Air view of The Monterey Vineyard winery building under construction in August 1974. The roof was not installed for another year. The crushers (bottom right in photo) outside the building were in use three weeks later, when selected white wine varieties were harvested to begin TMV's first wine crush.

The first crush and Blessing of the Grapes at The Monterey Vineyard in September 1974. The winery was only partially complete, but operational.

The author and his daughter Heidi (*right*) in The Monterey Vineyard laboratory in 1978. *Photo ©Helen Marcus.*

Heidi Peterson's first job in the wine industry (*middle*) working in the cellar at The Monterey Vineyard, age 18.

Del Mar Ranch wine (*below*) and Grüner Sylvaner labels from The Monterey Vineyard. Both sold well and received excellent reviews.

MONTEREY COUNTY
Grüner Sylvaner
DRY WHITE MONTEREY WINE
Produced and Bottled by The Monterey Vineyard Gonzales, California USA
ALCOHOL 11½% BY VOLUME

The Monterey Vineyard nestles between the Gabilan heights and the Santa Lucia mountains. It covers some of the choicest acres in upper Monterey, originally granted to Teodoro Gonzalez in 1836.

The emphatic character, that sets Monterey wines apart, is captured by the vines reaching deep into the crumbled granite of our hillsides. Warm sunshine tempered by cool breezes from Monterey Bay does the rest.

Grüner Sylvaner

is the name given to Sylvaner in South Germany, where it is picked in early season to give an unusually fresh and flavory wine. Cool summers enable us, too, to pick Sylvaner before its delicacy is lost.

`0  7 0728 43604`

Luigi Fortino (*left*), cellar supervisor for The Monterey Vineyard, explains the workings of a centrifuge to Bruce Macumber, sales manager of Coca-Cola's Wine Spectrum. Luigi was my primary helper in getting getting the first steel barrel pallets built.

The author and Linda O'Brien in the laboratory trailer at The Monterey Vineyard. The lab was divided into a large tasting area and a smaller area for wine analysis and blending trials in producing the highly successful Taylor California Cellars wines.

Barrel warehouse at The Monterey Vineyard in 1976. The ceiling heights were designed specifically for storing wine on the new Peterson barrel pallets. The building's vertical stained glass windows were designed by artist Diane Brisebois Peterson.

Explaining how to use new Bavarian oak horizontal casks from Germany to a cellar worker. These large vessels were shipped in pieces for assembly in situ. Bavarian oak tanks were used for lighter, more delicate red wines such as Pinot Noir, while heavier reds were aged in smaller American oak barrels.

Greeting Andre Tchelistcheff at The Monterey Wine Festival Scholarship Auction in 1984. An oversize bottle of The Monterey Vineyard wine is on display in the background.

Talking wine with actor Burgess Meredith. He was a frequent visitor to The Monterey Vineyard. Burgess gave me his tape recorder with the order, "Make frequent notes of what's going on in wine with this recorder and promise me that you will publish the story in book form." Here's the book my friend, I think you would have liked it.

A promotional picture taken in 1981 in the barrel warehouse, demonstrating the winery's new stacking system using Peterson steel pallets. The steel pallets were an instant success, and became widely adopted throughout the wine industry.

The author's original drawing of the steel barrel pallet design. The drawing was shown in a presentation given to the WITS (Wine Industry Technical Seminar) meeting in Fresno on November 14, 1975, and published in the WITS Official Transcript.

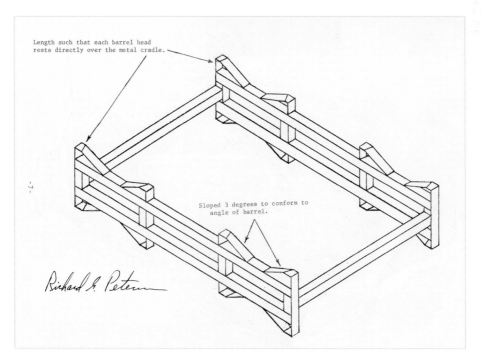

Length such that each barrel head rests directly over the metal cradle.

Sloped 3 degrees to conform to angle of barrel.

Richard G. Peterson

A classic cluster of Botrytis Semillion from Château d'Yquem. We found almost identical clusters of Sauvignon Blanc and (unbelievably) Pinot Noir in the Santa Lucia Highlands Vineyard in 1974, 1975 and 1976.

The initial discovery of 'sick vines' in Monterey Vineyard's main block in late 1975 (*below*). In the midst of healthy vines, two became sick and suddenly collapsed. Close microscopic examination of the roots showed hordes of Phylloxera, a root louse, feeding on the roots and destroying them. McFarland Vineyard Management had included some potted plants along with their bare root vines when planted in the early 1970s. The potted plants contained soil from central California nurseries that carried the Phylloxera insects. These quickly destroyed many acres of the original plantings. Today's plantings in Monterey are grafted onto American vine roots which are resistant to Phylloxera.

thought they were safe because there had never been grapevines growing in that part of Salinas Valley throughout history. Since phylloxera had to have some type of grapevine on which to survive, they assumed there wouldn't be any phylloxera living in Salinas Valley. They were told that the soil was tested and phylloxera free. Now that Professor Hewitt had found the insects on these vine roots, Gerry knew the infestation would spread; it was only a matter of time before all his vines would collapse and die without warning.

Professor Hewitt wondered how such a thing could have happened. How was it possible to get a phylloxera infestation when there were no phylloxera living nearby? Phylloxera insects lived many miles away, up-wind in central California, but they could not fly – they could only crawl. The insects are microscopic, too small to be seen by the naked eye. They would require hundreds of years to crawl a mile even if they could walk a straight line and knew which way to go. They would also have to bring their lunch, since there were no vines on which to feed enroute.

Gerry looked up sheepishly and said, "Uh oh." He told Prof. Hewitt that they had always planted bare root vines, which would have no living phylloxera insects on them. However, the nursery had run short of bare root vines in one shipment and had finished the shipment with small, pot-ted vines without asking whether it would be OK. The soil in the pots was ordinary nursery rooting soil from a central California nursery, and that was obviously how the phylloxera arrived. Dammit! Dammit! Dammit!

Gerry later told me, "When they're on your side, they use BB guns. When they're against you, they shoot artillery!" I answered him with a riddle that I first heard from my Pop when I was a teenager in Iowa: "How do you iden-tify the pioneer in a room full of people? He's the guy with arrows sticking out of his ass." Gerry smiled, shook his head and said, "Well, you're looking directly at a dyed-in-the-wool, bona-fide, genuine, 100%, hard-headed pioneer." We both laughed because we were hurting too much to cry.

Two things of note happened on August 13, 1976: First, John Boyce-Smith, McKesson VP, sent a final memo to the board members of Bayco asking them to sign, giving approval to dissolve Bayco. At the same time, McFar-land Management Co. released an offering circular for selling 4,000 new shares of Monterey Vineyards LP, which would add another $4,000,000 to the existing 8,301 shares (or $8,301,000) in equity ownership. Regardless of Bayco not working out, the wine business was growing, and the Monterey area would, in time, succeed as one of the fine regions for growing wine grapes in coastal California. It was also clear that there would be many wineries besides TMV to which the LP could sell its grapes in future years. The money from this offering would allow the company to replant as necessary and continue to farm their considerable acreages.

Finally! A White Knight

At almost the same time, John Hancock hired an independent contractor, Paul Toeppen, to look at the TMV winery project with his experienced and imaginative eye. Paul was exactly the right man for the impossible job of sorting out how best to correct the financial mess. He was invited to explain the position of Hancock, the primary lender, to the investor group at a board meeting. The directors knew that the company would need $500,000 to continue operating for another year, until August, 1977. Paul Toeppen told them that Hancock would go along with the company's proposal if they came up with a sincere pledge for new money to avoid bankruptcy. He was willing to sit down with them and write off some of Hancock's equity to make it easier for shareholders to continue running the company. The pros and cons of bankruptcy were discussed, and it was determined that bankruptcy had to be avoided to preserve certain benefits for the company's creditors, employees and investors.

Toeppen told the group that they had had more than enough time in which to save their investments by adding capital. He noted that the board had many factions within it, and Hancock was displeased with the dissension. He felt that it was a waste of time to look again at the figures, since no one was willing to offer a way out. He said John Hancock would foreclose and take over TMV if the group offered no additional money by December.

As no additional money surfaced, on December 3, Paul wrote the board asking for a meeting to finalize John Hancock's plan for foreclosure. At the board meeting, all directors executed releases of claims against everyone else involved with the winery, so that no one could later claim that someone else had caused the winery's difficulties. Dan Lucas was made a director, and all other directors resigned except for Dan and me. In accordance with Hancock's request, the company then had just two officers and directors: I remained president and Dan was made secretary/treasurer. Dan and I would continue operating the winery for Hancock with the current employees, and I would continue working with our various distributors around the country who were selling TMV wines.

The shareholders had lost all their equity in TMV. That included myself, since Tom Stratton had arranged a large bank loan for me to pay for the TMV stock I was issued at the time I was hired. Paul Toeppen carefully planned a strategy for Hancock to recover as much of their losses as possible. There might even be a profit; it depended on keeping our staff operating the winery well and finding the right new buyer. A new buyer would gain a great opportunity to own a producing winery without having its hands tied by obligations to buy more grapes than the winery could use. TMV also provided significant goodwill value; we had a reputation for making unique, excellent wines that were gaining consumer acceptance by the day.

Paul's plan was straightforward: All previous board members would sell their TMV shares to me for a nominal price, making me the sole owner of all the shares. Hancock would retain an option to buy the shares back for a total price of $50,000. Paul's intention was that I would continue operating the winery as before, with Dan as treasurer and the operating staff unchanged. If each of us did our jobs well, producing acceptable wines until the winery was transferred to the right buyer, Dan would end up with a bonus of $15,000 and I'd get $50,000. All the employees would gain job security without losing a dime in the deal.

Our end-of-year sales totals, including those of Gerald Asher and McKesson, amounted to 26,000 cases. The winery crushed only 600 tons of grapes for our own use in 1976, but kept our machinery busy by crushing several thousand tons for other wineries. TMV charged a fee for crushing and fermenting the grapes of others, and our company brought in over $200,000 for that service. Myron McFarland jumped in and sold most of that season's grapes from the vineyard LPs to the Gallo Winery in Modesto.

Our wine sales continued at a slow, steady pace and I was kept busy with my unusual combination of travel and winemaking. Dan did a good job of watching over the winery, although he felt out of place in that position. He'd never been inside a winery until a year and a half before, when he was hired by Jim Gibbons. Paul Toeppen was actively seeking a buyer for the TMV Company and often worked from his office in Los Angeles. He came to Gonzales periodically to show the operation to possible buyers or for our discussions when I returned from one place or another.

One Tired Traveler

The Monterey airport (MRY) was remote and well out of the minds of major airlines. There were only a few daily flights in or out, mostly by United Airlines to and from Los Angeles or Denver. Very tired, I was returning from an eastern trip one Friday afternoon for a meeting with Paul at Gonzales; my last leg was from LAX to MRY on a United Airlines flight, and I was looking forward to sleeping during the hour-long flight. Unfortunately, three loudmouth gentlemen were seated in the three seats directly in front of me. The flight was nearly full, and I couldn't easily move to find another seat; besides, I was near the front and wanted to get off the plane as quickly as possible after landing so as to hurry to my meeting. The more I tried to sleep, the louder these guys talked. Their subject was mostly wine, and everyone within several rows of them became aware of their obnoxious conversation. Each man was obviously there to impress the other two with his wine knowledge, but I could easily tell that their knowledge was skimpy at best. They mentioned wineries from time to time, but I tuned them out as well as I could. I was barely awake when one guy mentioned "Monterey Vineyard" a few times. I didn't hear a varietal name, and so I couldn't tell which of our wines he was discussing and whether he liked the wine or not.

When the captain announced that we were on final approach for landing, I awoke and began trying to listen; at least I'd get an idea of how these guys felt about one of our wines. The plane taxied in, and as we stood up to retrieve our carry-on bags from above, I got a gigantic surprise. One of the three gentlemen ahead of me pulled his bag down from the overhead compartment, and I noticed a Schenley Liquor Company logo on his ID tag. I quickly looked down at the floor. Never glancing at any of them, I took my bags from the plane and went straight to my car. I knew I would beat them to Gonzales by nearly an hour because they obviously had a rental car to pick up, and I would take the River Road shortcut to the winery. Only when I saw the ID tag on that carry-on bag did I remember that Paul Toeppen had told me he was expecting visitors from a large wine company this afternoon. Evidently, Schenley still owned winery properties and was interested in buying TMV, but I had a different idea.

When I arrived, I went straight into Paul's office. I told him of my experience on the plane and suggested that Schenley Liquor Co. would not be a good fit for either myself or this winery. I told him when I first joined Gallo as a new PhD from UC, I was aware that Schenley owned the Roma Winery, headquartered near Fresno. In 1958, Roma was the largest winery in America, but it didn't take Schenley long to lose that bragging right. Roma had disappeared from the list of largest wineries by the time I'd been at Gallo four years, allowing Italian Swiss to move into first place, with Gallo second. I was quite surprised to learn that Schenley was out kicking tires on wineries once again. Paul told me I would not have to meet with them, but he'd let me know what they had in mind.

I watched through my office window as they drove in, parked and entered Paul's office. Less than an hour later, they went back to their car and drove away, never to be seen again. Paul came into my office smiling and said, "You were right, Dick. The most favorable impression they gave me was that they had no idea what it would be like to operate a winery. We won't hear from them again." I had done Schenley a favor. I went directly home and was asleep by nine. I didn't wake up until seven the next morning, very refreshed. I had no doubt that Paul Toeppen, our white knight on a gigantic white horse, would eventually find a winner for us.

PART V

Taylor California Cellars

1977-1986

Coca-Cola – It's the Real Thing

In 1977, The Coca-Cola Company made its move. With the purchase of Taylor Wine Company of New York, including Great Western, Coca-Cola now had its East Coast production and distribution anchor. Both wine names were well established and had enjoyed excellent reputations in the industry. More importantly, Taylor had a good chain of well-run distribution houses across the country that could be expanded; in short, these people knew what they were doing. Director Al Killeen's intention was to tie the existing Taylor name to a source of completely new, high-quality wines from California which would be produced and marketed by a new organization within Coca-Cola – The Wine Spectrum. The group had been studying how best to take advantage of the Taylor name, and how to tie it together with California in a classy and effective way. After thorough and pragmatic brand and marketing research, they made the simplest and most straightforward decision. They would combine the Taylor name with California and add another trigger word, 'Cellars.' The brand would be called Taylor California Cellars (TCC), which their research showed would do exactly what they wanted it to do. The final necessary step would be to find a suitable winery in California that had both the size and technical competence to produce totally new wines of high quality to match Al Killeen's specifications – a West Coast production and distribution anchor.

Five months later, the Coca-Cola Company purchased Sterling Winery, near Calistoga at the north end of Napa Valley. Sterling was not courted as a possible West Coast base for Taylor California Cellars; rather, its small size and quality image would provide access to high-end sales outlets and enhance the image of other Wine Spectrum wineries and brands. The search for a West Coast anchor was still ongoing.

It was inevitable that Paul Toeppen and Al Killeen would eventually meet. They began talking, and quickly realized that each offered exactly what the other needed and wanted. Paul and Al were each able and constructive in their own ways. In early June, Paul introduced me to Al, and I showed him our entire operation and answered his exhaustive questions about my wine-making experience and history. When it looked like there might be a good fit between the needs of The Monterey Vineyard and the desires of Coca-Cola, Al told me exactly what he had in mind for The Coca-Cola Company.

It was obvious to me that he had done his homework and equally obvious that he was the most astute mass marketer of consumer goods I had ever met. He had studied the history of Monterey Vineyard backwards and forwards. He knew we had failed, not because of the wines we'd produced or how the winery was operated, but because we were saddled from the start with a huge obligation to buy grapes of uncertain quality that had to be sold at a loss. He asked why I had put myself in such a position. I said, "Al, I didn't know I was doing it at the time. I'm neither an accountant nor a salesman. I am an engineer, a good taster, and I keep up with the chemistry and biochemistry of wine. I was told by the founders that finance and marketing would not be a problem for me because they were financiers; they had agreements with a very large, very experienced company for selling all the wine I could make." Al laughed and said, "And you believed that?" I said simply, "I not only believed that, but the guy who told it to me believed it as well. He lost his ass on the whole project. I only lost momentum. I am embarrassed to have been so stupid when I took the job." I liked Al Killeen a lot and could tell that he would be a guy I could work with very well. I was anxious to meet others from Coca-Cola, and would do so in the next few weeks.

The Fun Begins

Not long afterwards, Al came into my office and asked, "Dick, if I asked you to make four wines that were discernibly better than similar wines from competitors, could you do that?" I answered, "Of course I could, but you already know that. What exactly do you mean by 'discernibly better'?" Al said he wanted me to make wines that he could submit to a panel of judges for tasting, and he wanted to know absolutely that my wines would win in their evaluation. I laughed and said, "It depends on the judges. Many people claim to be good judges, but I've seen quite a few who claimed they were, but weren't." Al said quickly, "Okay, I will guarantee that the judges will be excellent, professional judges. Now can you do it?" I told him, "I absolutely can, *if* I am allowed to taste and analyze the other wines that my wine will be judged against. I have to know the context. If you buy the competitors' wines, and let me taste and analyze them, then I can definitely make blends for you that will most likely win in a professional judging. However, even then I have one caveat: You have to realize that the professional judges might be having an off day. Even the best judge is wrong occasionally. You shouldn't rely on two or three judges – the more judges you have, the more confident I am that they will find our wines to be superior."

Al thought about that and said, "Okay, that's fair. I can accept that. The wines I want you to make will be mid-priced wines that will be sold in 750 mls, 1.5 liter magnums and also 3.0 liter sizes. That's the hot market today, and I envision having a Rosé, a Burgundy, a Chablis and a Rhine wine." I asked one more question, "When do you need them?" He said, "I'll get back to you, but if Coca-Cola buys The Monterey Vineyard, I'll get samples of the competitors' wines to you in plenty of time to crush the grapes you'll need this season. It'll take a few months to complete this purchase with Paul Toeppen, and I want to make a big splash when we release these wines a year from now. Are you with us and can I rely on you?" "One hundred percent," I answered. This was going to be a fun job.

Over the summer, various staff people from Coca-Cola visited us at

Gonzales, and I was not surprised to see that they left no stone unturned. I made sure that Todd, Luigi, Dan and Pete understood that they were to answer all questions from anyone with a Coca-Cola badge on his chest. I wanted them to understand every detail of everything we were doing and why we were doing it. Al Killeen brought dozens of staffers and VPs, as well as the chairman of The Coca-Cola Company, J. Paul Austin. I loved working with smart, vigorous people, and it did not bother me that none had any real experience in the wine business. Above all, they were quick learners and great mass marketers.

One of the pluses of working with Coca-Cola was the contrast I saw between the spirits producers I had known (Schenley, Heublein and McKesson) and the employees I met that summer. The spirits group knew very little about fine wine, but thought they knew everything. The Coke people knew nothing about fine wine, but were already studying and said, "Please teach us everything you're doing." Even a busy and important man like J. Paul Austin took the time to understand much of how we handled grapes and wine.

By late August, it was clear to all of us that The Coca-Cola Company would purchase Monterey Vineyard. We had exactly the right assets and would soon become Al Killeen's necessary West Coast anchor. The final papers were signed in November 1979, and I became an employee of The Coca-Cola Company, along with all the other staff of the Monterey Vineyard. The ensuing experiences became a major, positive highlight of my professional life as a winemaker.

I had been busy all summer tasting and evaluating the tank inventory of our accumulated Monterey County wines. I had to be sure I had told Al the complete truth: I wanted one more proof that we could use our existing inventory to produce wine blends that would be discernibly better than the competitors (Almaden, Masson, Inglenook, Charles Krug, Sebastiani and Gallo). Our inventory included red varietal wines from 1974, '75 and '76 and white varietal wines from 1975 and '76. When classified by taste alone, the Monterey wines clustered themselves into two groups: good wines, ready for bottling without much treatment, and wines with such strong flavors that I still wasn't sure how to make them palatable.

The first group had only to be preserved in cold tanks, with normal precautions to protect the wines from oxidation. The second group was another matter. Some were quite vegetal in character, even though they dated back a full three vintages; others were less vegetal, but with such strong varietal flavors that I wasn't sure what other treatments and blending would be needed to make them acceptable. I called my friend, Joe Ciatti, whose brokerage business connected wineries selling generic bulk wines to other, usually smaller wineries for fining, blending and bottling. I asked for 750 ml samples from several Central Valley wineries that I knew would have good blending wines available for sale in the price ranges Coca-Cola required. Bronco, Franzia, Gallo and Giumarra were usually best, but we occasionally got nice samples from others as well. I wanted only Central Valley wines because their prices would be OK and their natural flavors would be subtle; just the thing to temper the overly strong 'nose and taste' of some of the Monterey wines that made up our inventory.

Lab manager Linda O'Brien dedicated one whole counter (half the length of the lab) to categorizing and tasting by our panel: Linda, Pete, Luigi, Todd, myself and my daughter, Heidi. Working first on white varietals, each of the tasters ranked the wines, placing them left to right from best to worst. Eliminating the obvious losers, I made the final decision after considering every judge's comments on each of the wines. After we had selected the top few white wines for possible use in Chablis blends, we moved on to Rosé and then to the Rhine and Burgundy-style wine varieties.

After two or three weeks, we had reduced the number of samples to manageable numbers, and I began suggesting trial blends to Linda for blind tasting by our panel. We concentrated on Chablis blends first, then the others, one at a time. Linda made 750 ml sample blends in the lab, combining measured amounts from each tank of the selected base wines; the tasters then smelled and tasted the blends against wines poured from bottles of the competitive wines we wanted to beat. It took a week to taste and evaluate each of the blends for Chablis, then another week for Rosé, and so on. Eventually, we had a good idea of the direction in which we would need to go, and I had a good estimate of the varieties and the tonnages we would need to crush at Gonzales in 1977. I notified the Central

Valley source wineries of our preliminary results, so they would be ready to supply what we would need the following spring.

The Wine Spectrum

Al Killeen's staff was busy during the last half of 1977 and early 1978 developing the new division of Coca-Cola that would be responsible for production, label design, advertising, marketing, sales and all other phases of what was destined to become the most successful new wine product introduction of the past decade: Taylor California Cellars (TCC). Al had named his wine organization The Wine Spectrum, which included TCC, Taylor New York, Sterling Vineyards and Monterey Vineyard. He brought together people from all backgrounds with various areas of expertise. The sales manager was Mike Cheek, a Gallo graduate who I instantly recognized as a magnificent choice. Mike's assistant sales managers included Lloyd McGee and Bill Culhane of Taylor New York, both equally astute choices. Lloyd was about to retire, but Al convinced him to stay and help get The Wine Spectrum off to the right start. Al Killeen proved his brilliance to me many times, but nowhere was his excellence shown more clearly than in his choice of the managers installed at every level in The Wine Spectrum.

I marveled at Al's energy; he was not young, but it was obvious how much he enjoyed working. Al had me traveling by December, just after Coca-Cola's purchase of our winery was completed and the crushing season ended. I went with him and Mike Cheek to sales group meetings, and it was clear that I would be even busier than before, with both winemaking at Gonzales and speaking to various groups to introduce the wines. Early in our discussions, I told him we needed a professional manager to control all phases of the winery, and I wanted to hire someone as soon as possible. I had neither the ability nor the inclination to manage multiple departments and could not do as good a job as would be needed. With the requirement to travel, it was a no-brainer decision. He told me he had someone in mind, but this person would not be available until after the New Year. The man turned out to be Harry Teasley, an excellent manager, who had headed Al's business development group that had made all the right decisions in getting

The Wine Spectrum established. I could not have imagined a better choice. Harry was to make every facet of my life at The Wine Spectrum easier; he removed any obstacle I needed removing, which allowed me the freedom to produce the best wines we could. It was a bonus that, after only a few months of tasting instruction and practice, Harry became as good a taste panel member as we had in the group.

Between June 1977 and June 1978, I heard Al Killeen answer the same pointed question many times: "What if all this fails? What if the TCC wines are not as good as you think? What if you throw this party and nobody comes? You will certainly piss off the rest of the industry with this approach to marketing. How will you handle them if you fail?" The question came in different forms, but it was basically the same question. It underlined the fact that nobody in the wine industry wanted Coca-Cola to succeed; everyone expected and wanted them to fail – and fail miserably. Everyone but me, that is. Al's answer did not surprise me.

Typically, he would look at the questioner and say, "OK I will give you some advice: Do your research very carefully and thoroughly – then, look at where you are going, not what could happen if you fail. Self esteem is everything, and it is clear to me that both winning and losing are habits – the winner knows he will win. In The Wine Spectrum, I have put together a group of smart people who are winners, not losers; each one raises the high jump bar to a new record. We do not fight each other, we encourage each other, and there isn't one individual who will let the others down." Al then turned and walked away. It reinforced my knowledge that any group waiting to see Albert Killeen fail would have a long wait on their hands. I'd tell them, "Bring your sleeping bags, boys. Your vigil to watch Al Killeen stub his toe will take some time. You might want to bring some big books and maybe a chess set and some decks of cards."

Creating the Winning Wines

The grape crush of 1977 went smoothly. We contracted to buy the grapes I wanted to use for Taylor California Cellars (TCC) wines from two of the

McFarland's Vineyard LPs. The same variety of grapes grown as little as one mile apart in Salinas Valley showed vast differences in the quality of wines they would produce! Myron, Gerry and Tom had made a devastating mistake in thinking that each of the grapevines in the various LPs would be equivalent to each other, and that "wine grapes are a commodity." Nowhere is that less true than in coastal Monterey County.

I began searching for red wine grapes from inland vineyards (as far as 100 miles downwind from the icy ocean gales of Gonzales), and found good Cabernet and Zinfandel between King City and Paso Robles. The summer climate there was more similar to that of Napa Valley. The wines would be more agreeable than any grown closer to the ocean. I had already decided the only red variety we should accept from the windy valley area would be Pinot Noir. Santa Lucia and other LPs along the western, less windy edge of the valley continued to produce superb Pinot Noir, Pinot Blanc, Riesling, Sylvaner and Gewurztraminer wines. I became less and less interested in using grapes from the central part of Salinas Valley. Even those tiny phylloxera insects are smart enough to live underground, sheltered from the winter winds of June and July. Most importantly, I continued to find that judicious blending of Monterey wines with warmer-climate wines would correct just about any problem we might encounter with vegetal off-flavors.

By February 1978, we were moving ahead at flank speed[1] in creating the final TCC blends. Harry Teasley delivered a few cases of several target wines, including Inglenook, Gallo, Charles Krug, Almaden, Masson and Sebastiani in 750 mls, magnums and 3.0 liter bottle sizes. We compared all sizes in case any of the target wineries used different wine blends for different size bottles. White wines (and the rosé) were easy to blend because we had many wine tanks of excellent quality varietals that had accumulated since 1975. Blending several varieties of young wines together with small amounts of older wines often added a degree of elegance to the winning

---

[1] Flank speed is a Navy term, meaning the absolute top speed of any boat. Military pilots said, "Balls out," a fighter pilot term that was never misunderstood.

blend. It would not be easy for competitors to figure out what we had done. By taste and analysis, one could not easily detect age components in our wines – they had excellent mouthfeel and an elegance that the competitive wines lacked. To make the Burgundy blend, we tried several approaches, all of which were more complex and difficult than making the Chablis and Rosé blends.

I remembered what one of the flavor company salesmen had told me twenty years earlier when I was working with flavored wines at Gallo. I had assumed the flavor companies would carefully remove all rotten (or abused) fruit from the loads of strawberries as they were dumped from trucks into receiving hoppers for extracting natural flavor. I was wrong. Questioning their procedure, I was told in no uncertain terms that a few overripe (or even rotten) strawberries in the mass made the overall flavor 'more complex, more satisfying, more natural and, ahem, more valuable.'

Translating that into the problem at hand, I tried using small amounts of the 'unusable, too-vegetal Cabernet' wines from Gonzales in blends of central California generic red wines we bought from Bronco, Franzia, Giumarra and others. The first trial blends did not work, but with perseverance... Bingo! We found winners. More importantly, we now had an effective method for depleting our inventory of too-vegetal wines in future blends. In a year or two, we would work our way out from under the old inventory that had been hanging over our heads since 1974.

Bottling the new blends would not be a problem for 750 ml bottles, but we were not set up to handle larger sizes.[2] It would be possible to add change parts to the bottling line equipment, but if sales were as successful as Harry Teasley expected, we would need to find another winery to bottle some of our blends. Hauling our wine to another winery for bottling would present no problem, as the industry had long since developed fool-proof

---

[2] U.S. bottle size regulations were changed in 1977. Up until that year, fifths, half-gallons and gallons were correct legal sizes for wines; afterwards, only metric sizes (375 ml, 500 ml, 750 ml, 1.5 liter and larger multiple liters) replaced the old English system for bottle sizes. Airlines could use containers as small as 187 ml.

hauling techniques for moving wines between wineries without so much as a microscopic blemish. Harry put on his engineer's hat and made arrangements to bottle many of our blends at the Franzia Winery near Ripon (later named The Wine Group). One of Harry's strong points was an uncompromising insistence on maintaining good control of the process, so our wines would not suffer any loss of quality due to additional handling. The result was that we were in full swing with bottling by June 1978, right on schedule for Al Killeen's expected launch in September.

The Nose Knows

The Wine Spectrum was developing nicely under Al Killeen's stewardship. He had created a complete, integrated marketing plan for the introduction of TCC Chablis, Rosé, Rhine and Burgundy wines in three bottle sizes. They would be available in most states immediately, as distributor contracts were nearly complete in all but a few areas of the country. Al had asked the advertising agency, Kenyon & Eckhardt, to commission the nationwide Consumer Testing Institute, Inc. to design and implement a wine-tasting test. It was to be scientifically structured and carefully monitored – a study that relied on the objective ratings of a panel of 27 knowledgeable wine tasters to determine the rankings of wine selections when tasted without prior knowledge of any wine's identity. Kenyon & Eckhardt would film many phases of the San Francisco judging, since Al intended to use film clips in TV advertising as part of his promotion effort. He would accept whatever results the wine judges found; such was his belief that his TCC brand would be proven superior. He intended to establish that this new brand of premium generic wine was discernibly superior to the wines of the leading national competitors in the same wine category. I knew nothing of the people, time, place or procedures used in the event, and only learned the final tasting results when Al called me in July. TCC had won first place with three of the wines and came within a single vote of tying for first with the fourth. The Burgundy had ended up a close second to Charles Krug Burgundy, a Napa Valley blend. Al was pleased as punch.

Laboratory blending tests had been an eye-opening exercise for all

the tasters. The Gallo and Charles Krug blends had been the most difficult to beat, and I was sure we knew why. Unlike other coastal wineries,
Charles Krug had always maintained their wine quality. They used Napa
Valley wines even in their Central Valley blends to improve them. The Paul
Masson, Almaden and Inglenook wines were similar to each other in that
all were 100% Central Valley (cheaper) wines. Gallo, on the other hand,
had probably added about 10% coastal (higher-quality) varietals into their
blends, and it showed up in their wines as better balance and complexity.
Julio Gallo still knew what he was doing.

For years, I had noticed a practice among coastal wineries that I called
the 'Winery Profit Scheme.' Robert Mondavi created an image of high quality in Napa Valley – that allowed him to open a winery in the Central Valley
(Woodbridge) where he could make cheaper wines and sell them at high
prices for profit. He used the company's high image in Napa Valley to get
higher prices for his Central Valley wines. Beringer, Sutter Home and other
coastal wineries did the same thing. Now, in 1978, coastal (high-image) wineries (Inglenook, Paul Masson and Almaden) used cheaper Central Valley
wines to cut their costs and increase profits. However, they weren't meticulous winemakers; their wines were only average in quality. That made them
vulnerable to Coca-Cola type marketing.

Ernest Gallo realized he had an 'ordinary' image, because Gallo was located in the Central Valley. Therefore, Julio blended a little coastal wine into
his bulk wines to improve Gallo quality, knowing that consumers would
recognize that they had better wines despite the geography. He knew that,
sooner or later, their sales would climb. Coca-Cola followed that tried-
and-true Gallo marketing approach, but with a 'kicker' added: TCC wines
were better because they were not simply Central Valley (low-flavor) wines.
Rather, they contained various amounts of Monterey County (high-flavor)
varietals in the blends, improving the quality to well above that of the competitors' wines. That was my secret in creating the TCC wine blends. A
booster that Coca-Cola added was to call on recognized expert tasters to
evaluate the wines in an objective competition. The results became a news
event which told the public that the TCC wine quality was better.

After the results were made public, producers of the losing wines complained to the Bureau of Alcohol, Tobacco, Firearms and Explosives (BATF), the taxing and 'watchdog' agency of the federal government. That group monitored and controlled many of the actions in the wine industry as well as the other alcoholic beverage industries. The results of these tests, the methodology used in the tests, and the storyboards of the TV commercials on the tests were shown to BATF at an early stage, with the proviso that The Wine Spectrum would be happy to supply whatever further information they might require to enable them to approve the Taylor introductory advertising campaign. BATF apparently didn't know what to do with the information, and simply stalled (Al said they had "stonewalled"). He also said, "Although they could find nothing misleading or deceptive about our ads, they [BATF] went through all the convolutions and indecisiveness of any regulatory agency when faced with a precedent-making decision." Killeen knew that the advertising meter was running – and running fast. Initial production costs for the ad campaign were $300,000, and he was committed to a TV expenditure of nearly $2 million. He asked the court to declare that the Bureau's policies regarding comparative taste-test advertising violated TCC's first amendment rights, and that their refusal to preclear the ads was arbitrary and capricious.

Although the district court dismissed the action as premature for judicial review, the government's attorneys admitted in open court that, at the time, they could see nothing in the ads that would cause the Bureau to commence an enforcement proceeding. Since Al knew the taste-test procedures met the most rigorous standards, and standing firm in the belief that the wines were indeed better, he ordered the comparative taste-test commercials to go on the air. The commercials ran for five continuous weeks. In obvious response to pressures from the competitive wine companies, BATF raised eight specific questions regarding the advertising and advised that, if TCC did not respond by October 20, its license would be at risk. Al Killeen pointed out publicly that the pressure on BATF had not come from consumers, wholesalers, growers or the Federal Trade Commission, but only from producers of the losing wines. I certainly knew that. Within days, I received registered letters or telegrams (addressed to me, personally) from each of the companies that owned the competing wineries, telling me to stop those ads immediately. I never answered any of the correspondence, since I had played no part in the design or placement of any of the offending ads. I don't deny that a smile crossed my face when I saw the envelope from the legal department of Heublein, Inc., owner of Inglenook, as I had tasted the tell-tale hollowness of Thompson Seedless grapes in their white wines during my lab comparisons.

Within hours of hearing that BATF had specific questions about the advertising, Coca-Cola voluntarily suspended the advertising 'to demonstrate their good faith and willingness to cooperate in every way with the BATF inquiry.' In a further gesture of good faith, Al informed the agency of their willingness to continue the suspension of these advertisements if the Bureau would promptly initiate rulemaking to set standards and guidelines for wine taste-test advertising. Coca-Cola said further, "We believed then, as we believe now, that such advertising stimulates competition and is beneficial to consumers." Killeen listed the complete history of their experience with Taylor California Cellars in a speech to the legal Division of Coca-Cola in San Diego on December 10, 1979. The complete text, as later copied to many wine journals, read, "Our response to the eight questions raised by BATF was factual, hard hitting, meticulously documented and explosive as a hand grenade. I'm sure the BATF realized that if they played around with our response, the package could blow up in their faces. Furthermore, we saw to it that every responsible newspaper and wine journal had a copy of our response in their possession. The rest is history."

Al told us, "If you were to ask me: Would I do it all over again? The answer is: Yes, I would. It was the cutting, competitive edge that allowed us to gain instant consumer recognition." The thing that impressed me most was that companies usually have to pay for advertising to educate the consumer. But in Al's case, the test results became news on their own – they were widely published and convinced consumers of the excellence of TCC wines without Al having to buy much advertising. Radio, TV, newspapers and magazines told (and retold) the story to consumers, allowing Coca-Cola to spend less for advertising than would have been necessary without the controversy. It was a fortunate add-on that the losing wineries raised so much hell. It caused a public uproar which repeated over and over again in news reports that TCC wines were superior. Al Killeen was brilliant.

The four TCC generic wines were released to the public in early September. By year end, they had sold 500,000 cases to a well-satisfied public. I was kept busy speaking to sales groups for the next several months, as well as to Taylor distributors around the country. I always described each of the wines in words that anyone could understand. I reasoned that, if salespeople were educated to confidently describe the wines and tell why they were better, the word would get back to the consumer – and sales would climb. Shortly after the introduction of these wines to the public, I began getting requests from salespeople as well as consumers: "The blends are nice, but I like to drink Chardonnay on its own, or pure Cabernet, or Zinfandel. When are you going to produce more wine types, especially pure varietals?" I jumped in with both feet and, within a few months, we had expanded the TCC line to more than ten different wines – and sales kept on climbing. During calendar 1979, they sold 1.5 million cases.

In calendar 1980, sales totaled 3.8 million cases, climbing to 5.4 million in 1981. By that time, I had produced about twenty different new wine types for TCC and a dozen or so for the more expensive Monterey Vineyard label. Al Killeen retired as chairman of The Wine Spectrum in mid-1980, and was replaced by Harry Teasley. Harry was a solid manager and knew the operation well enough that employees of The Wine Spectrum hardly noticed any difference, except that all of us missed seeing Al at our various meetings. I loved everything about Al Killeen. His knowledge of the wine trade was as deep, accurate and professional as any other leader in the wine industry, and he had acquired all that knowledge by concentrated study in the short window between 1977 and 1980.

Excitement in the country about this new wine brand, Taylor California Cellars, continued building to a fever pitch. The best way to describe it came from a news announcement I saw in a Los Angeles newspaper: 'Mr. & Mrs. Cellars have named their newborn baby daughter California. They intend to call their daughter by her nickname 'Callie.'

Growing Pains

With increasing sales, we found that some consumers were confused about the distinction between the Monterey Vineyard and TCC wines. No matter how many times they were told that Monterey Vineyard produced vintage dated varietal wines as opposed to TCC's non-vintage generic blends, consumers had the two brands merged together in their minds. Many did not see why varietal wines should cost more than blends, and it appeared that some consumers thought both brands were made from identical grapes. Probably my name had been thrown about too often as winemaker and spokesman for both labels, or maybe The Wine Spectrum had put too much on the consumer's plate at one time. Peter Sealy, another superb manager within The Wine Spectrum, made the suggestion to separate TCC from Monterey Vineyard brands in the consumer's mind by appointing a president of TCC (parallel to my position as president of Monterey Vineyard). I agreed immediately for more pressing reasons; I was not able to spend the time on winemaking that I wanted, I was beginning to tire of the constant travel, and my wife, Diane, was unhappy since all of her friends lived in Napa Valley, not in Monterey County. Our kids were away in college, making us realize that we didn't have much in common any more. We separated in 1979; she moved to St. Helena and we were divorced.

In the cellar, manager Pete Bachman was completing some blends by following our recipes, and I got to taste some only after the blends were ready for bottling. Pete was completely competent; never once did I conclude he had made a mistake in any blend, but I knew we were being unfair to him and wanted to cut my travel to make both of us more comfortable. We discussed it with Harry Teasley and shortly afterward, Harry hired Ed Hamler to become TCC president. It was an excellent move, and we followed up by promoting Pete Bachman to assistant winemaker for TCC wines.

Based on Harry's projections for sales and my projections for production, we began planning to expand the size of the Monterey Vineyard winery. I had made no contingency with the architect, Dick Keith, to expand beyond building an additional white wine cellar (a duplicate of the existing red wine cellar we had built back in 1974). However, a glance at the sales growth graphs made it clear that simply doubling the main wine cellar would not be enough. Both the total cooperage and bottling lines had to be expanded, and we would need a much larger building to do both. We also had another goal: to keep Monterey Vineyard as The Wine Spectrum's highest-quality brand in Monterey County separated from TCC, which was The Wine Spectrum's mid-quality brand. The original winery had a single line for bottling wines into 750 ml glass, and would not need to expand soon; TCC, on the other hand, had to bottle 750 ml, 1.5 liter and 3.0 liter sizes, as well as smaller packs for airline sales. Harry began to design an all-new facility for TCC, keeping facilities for the two brands separate. Visitors could be shown either facility, depending on their interest.

Wearing his engineering hat once more and with input from Luigi Fortino, Pete Bachman and Tom Peterson, Harry designed a new TCC winery nearly triple the size of the original Monterey Vineyard winery, and began the construction as soon as we'd all agreed to the plans. For me, it was just another Coca-Cola example of how quickly and easily a large facility can be constructed when competent people work together without internal strife. Even the approvals for construction funds from financial managers in Atlanta were obtained promptly and we were fermenting, processing, blending and bottling wines only a little longer than a year after construction began. Throughout the new construction, TCC sales in the marketplace continued to climb, and we were careful never to shortchange the consumer by shortcutting any of the blends we prepared and bottled. Validation of our procedures came in the form of strong and growing sales without significant customer complaints. We handled the few complaints or inquiries we received by writing personal letters, explaining to the best of our knowledge how the defect happened and replacing the wine in question.

Several managers from The Wine Spectrum attended a wedding reception for Art Ciocca and his bride in Ripon, California. Art had been chairman and chief operating officer at Franzia Wine Co. since its purchase by the Coca-Cola Bottling Co. of New York, and was instrumental in bottling our TCC wines into most of the large-bottle sizes during the first two years. I noticed Ernest Gallo in the crowd, and went over to talk with him; I hadn't seen him for nearly twelve years, since leaving Gallo in 1968. I told him that I had driven over with Harry Teasley, that Al Killeen had retired, and asked whether he wanted to meet Harry. He said, "Sure," so I found Harry and brought him back to make the introduction.[3] Ernest was very complimentary to Harry, and I wondered whether he would have been so if Al Killeen's 1978 competition between TCC and the other wineries had included Gallo products. It reminded me that I had asked Al shortly after the big win why no Gallo wines had been included in the competition. Al's answer made it clear that he had, indeed, thought it over before choosing the competitive wineries: "Gallo didn't have as high an image as the other wines in the taste competition. Sure, Gallo wines were often better than Almaden, Inglenook and Paul Masson – but there was no real glory in beating Gallo because they weren't thought of as among the best of the mid-priced generic wines. I didn't want TCC to be seen as merely better than Gallo. I wanted TCC to be seen as better than Almaden, Paul Masson and Inglenook. There was no reason to include Gallo because beating them wasn't worth the trouble." He did not tell me the other part of the answer, but I had no trouble in guessing. Suppose in the off chance of random tastings that Gallo had won? That unlikely event would have been a calamity for TCC.

The Wine Spectrum continued to push for expansion of its wine business by researching new avenues. Harry and I took a trip to Argentina for two weeks to learn about the possibility of importing a new line of table wines from another country. The Wine Spectrum had recently been appointed exclusive importer of Cinzano from Italy and was already in the process of creating a new line of imported table wines under the Cinzano label. Some were being test marketed in certain cities, but it would take time to properly judge the progress. A deal with Argentina didn't work out as we had hoped, and we dropped the idea. Although we found some excellent Argentinian red wines, there would be no possibility of producing the

---

[3] 'Coke of New York' is a totally different company from The Coca-Cola Co. (based in Atlanta), which owned TCC. The Coca-Cola Co. sells its flavored syrups to bottling companies around the world along with the rights to use the Coca-Cola brand name and sales literature in making and selling soft drinks to the public. 'Coke of New York' has been the largest 'Coke' bottling company in the northeastern U.S. for many decades.

white wines we were hoping for. Nevertheless, I appreciated the sense of humor of our hosts. To show us that our trip wasn't a complete bust, Harry and I, as foreign dignitaries, were appointed judges in the Miss Argentina Beauty Contest for 1981. Both of us voted for the eventual winner.

Six months later, I married my second wife, Sandra Henry, a teacher. Sandra brought a wonderful bonus to the union; her two daughters, Lisa and Gayle, were in grade school, which gave me the pleasure of raising another set of two daughters all over again. That was especially nice for me, as it made me see the folly of previously 'having been married to the winery,' and I wisely adjusted my personal priorities.

Amid the uproar that followed the introduction of TCC wines, it was perhaps inevitable that competitors would start rumors to the effect that the current TCC wines were no longer as good as those first ones had been. It was a back-handed way of whispering that we had produced a set of very nice wines to get the consumer's attention; then having done that, we showed our true colors by dumping ordinary Central Valley wines onto the unwary public. They didn't know me very well. At no time did I reduce the quality levels of any of the wines. We continued to produce the same high-quality blends that had put TCC on the tasting map in the first place. Fortunately, several chapters of Les Amis du Vin conducted their own independent repetitions of the original taste-tests in the first few years after the TCC introduction. Each tasting compared all four generic wines with those of Almaden, Paul Masson, Inglenook and Sebastiani or Gallo. The Les Amis du Vin groups always found the same result: TCC wines were preferred when tasted blind by the panels. The net effect of these 'ad hoc taste tests' reinforced the original result and TCC sales continued their steady climb. Projections called for over 8 million cases in 1982, and the company was suggesting 20 to 25 million by 1985.

I was expecting to see both Almaden and Italian Swiss sell off their wine businesses, since they had both lost big time sales numbers to TCC over the past few years. While waiting for the final FCC court decision, Wine Spectrum reduced our advertising budget from the $15 million of 1982 to $5 million for 1983. Coca-Cola was obviously saving money which, I supposed, would show up again in 1984, when it would have the greatest effect in the market.

Wine Spectrum profits were up again in 1982, but a price war of sorts developed in early 1983; most wine companies had to lower prices to match competition from each other, and everybody's profits diminished. Since Wine Spectrum shipments were still increasing, it seemed like a good time for Coca-Cola to keep up the pressure on competitors. Mike Cheek, VP of sales for The Wine Spectrum, announced a rebate campaign for TCC wines. Coupons were issued allowing buyers to receive rebates of nearly a dollar for each purchase. It was successful in larger markets, but California ABC filed suit to halt the practice. ABC won, but the decision was reversed on appeal when the FCC could find nothing wrong with the rebate program.

Seagram: New York, New York

Edgar Bronfman was chairman and a major owner of The Joseph E. Seagram Company, which owned Paul Masson Winery in California. Paul Masson was not their only winery, but it was the only one in direct competition with TCC, and had suffered the most from that competition. Edgar looked out the window of his office in mid-town Manhattan, as he spoke on the phone to his brother at the Seagram head office in Montreal. "No, Charles," he said. "We don't see any possibility of increasing liquor sales in the next year or two. It's a lifestyle change, I think. We still see the spirits side of beverage alcohol in a serious decline. The area that seems most likely to improve next will be wines, especially table wines." Charles answered quickly, "Wine sales have been flat to down for two years. Why do you think wine sales will improve before spirits do?" "That wine downturn was mostly recession-related, Charles. We think the 5 to 6% growth we saw in wine three years ago will start to go up again very soon. We've already seen an increase so far this year. Our consultant has confirmed that we need a long-term strategy for the wine business. We are told that we have to get a lot bigger or get out of wine altogether. Since wine is more likely than spirits to show future growth, I say we need to get bigger in wine."

Charles had one further question, "So how does Taylor fit into your plan? They've been a real pain in Paul Masson's side." Edgar thought out loud, "I don't have any business plan that includes Taylor as yet – we could develop one as we go along. I heard rumors that Coca-Cola might want to sell Taylor, so I asked David Sacks to check it out with their chairman. He did, and it's true, so I asked our CFO to meet with Coca-Cola's CFO to give us a proposal. It appears we could get The Wine Spectrum at book value, which I know you'll agree is always a good deal for a growing company." "You're right," said Charles.

One afternoon in September 1983, Harry entered my office and sat down. He had just gotten back from attending Coca-Cola's regular board of directors meeting in Atlanta and appeared to be in an uncharacteristically serious mood. He said simply, "The Coca-Cola board of directors isn't happy with the long-term profit picture of The Wine Spectrum. They have decided to sell the whole division and have found a possible buyer in The Joseph E. Seagram Company." I stared at him wide-eyed. Eventually finding my voice, I protested, "But Wine Spectrum *is* profitable – very profitable, in fact. I've seen the numbers." Harry looked at me, then down at the floor, and finally back up at me with a slight smile, betraying that he was now going to let me in on a great secret. "Dick," he said slowly, "I will express this to you in your language, not mine: Coca-Cola makes obscene profits selling soft drinks. The wine business cannot match those obscene profits, so they are moving their money back into the soft drinks business." It was a blockbuster shock, and no other questions came into my mind. Obviously, my job would be to continue all operations at the wineries in Gonzales to assure that the new buyer would retain full value of the property they were buying. Until told otherwise, we would continue under the new ownership as we had under the old.

Harry loved the wine business as much as I did, but had long since dedicated his working life to making Coca-Cola succeed. He was torn by the company's decision, but it was not a surprise to him; he could not argue against the reasoning, because it made sense. Since 1977, he and Al Killeen had discussed the relative profits of soft drinks vs. wine several times while on fishing trips to Iceland, Scotland and elsewhere. They had agreed that after the Coca-Cola board of directors had thoroughly digested the financial results of Wine Spectrum, they could not 'look their shareholders in the eye' and argue that they should remain in the wine business. The wine business was profitable, and Wine Spectrum was successful and made more money than most other wineries. However, the board would look at it from their own narrow perspective: How do wine profits compare with soft drink profits? Most of the Coca-Cola board would answer, "You can't make real money in wine." Harry had suspected this would happen eventually – and 'eventually' had finally arrived.

He would move back to Atlanta and begin work on whatever new facet of the soft drinks business required his expertise. He told me it would take at least a month working with the Seagram people to inventory the Gonzales and Napa Valley assets and establish values for inventory and equipment; the final sale price would depend on book value of all the assets. He was the primary person within Coca-Cola to determine the details, and he would necessarily remain in Gonzales throughout the closure. It was not an easy job to explain to the financial people in Atlanta just what they owned in Gonzales, and Harry was having difficulty explaining it.

The Seagram investigator working with Harry was having the same difficulty. After weeks of phone calls back and forth between Gonzales and New York, the guy turned to Harry in desperation and said, "My God, Harry, Seagram doesn't know what they are buying!" Harry laughed loudly and openly, answering, "Well, Coca-Cola doesn't know what they're selling, either." Somehow the two of them reached suitable compromises on the difficult items and the job concluded with mutual respect.

I felt blindsided, yet it was nobody's fault. I had never felt blindsided before. When I left grad school, I was headed for Gallo. When I left Gallo, I was headed for Beaulieu. When I left Beaulieu, I was headed for Monterey. When Monterey collapsed, I was headed for Coca-Cola. Now suddenly without warning, my employer was leaving me, but I had no pre-conceived notion about their replacement. I knew nothing about Seagram except that they were a Canadian Liquor company that owned Paul Masson Winery and a few other wine operations. I wondered whether they would be another Heublein, Schenley or maybe, hopefully, another Coca-Cola.

As a condition of sale, all employees of The Wine Spectrum were asked to resign their jobs to give Seagram the option of keeping them or letting them go. Common sense told me that Seagram was buying the wine company because we were successful, and I reasoned that they would want us to continue our crushing season as planned. I told everyone at the winery to continue marching, as if no sale was happening.

My first Seagram letter (from President Phil Beekman) gave me a more thorough picture of the company. I had not realized that Seagram was 'The world's largest producer and marketer of distilled spirits and wines, with subsidiaries or affiliates in 29 countries – last year's sales approximated $3 billion.' Seagram brands were sold in an unbelievable 175 markets, in addition to North America. The company occupied an important position in the wine trade, with about 300 wines, champagnes, brandies, sherries and ports. The brands included Paul Masson and Gold Seal in the U.S., Mumm and Perrier-Jouët champagnes, Partager and B & G French wines, Black Tower and Julius Kayser German wines, Brolio, Ricasoli and Bersano Italian wines and Sandeman ports and sherries. Wow! I had underestimated the scope of my new employer.

On November 1, a week before the sale would close, I received a letter from Edgar Bronfman, CEO and primary owner of Seagram, asking me to stay with the company. My resignation was not being accepted, and he promised to keep me informed as details of the sale worked out. The letter said that Seagram expected to move The Wine Spectrum's headquarters out of Atlanta, but no plans beyond that could be projected for the time being. A follow-up welcome letter came the same day from the Human Resources Director, promising to contact me within two weeks to answer any questions I might have. The good news was that I had a good friend at Paul Masson (Morris Katz), and another good friend from the old Gallo days (Dick Maher) had just been hired as president of the Seagram Wine Company. The bad news was that Seagram didn't appear to have a definite plan for The Wine Spectrum. Spectrum had smaller, higher-image brands (Monterey Vineyard, Sterling, Taylor, Great Western and Gold Seal), but the prime focus for the purchase was a single wine: TCC.

There was a vivid and obvious contrast between the attitudes of Coca-Cola and Seagram when each company came into my life. Coca-Cola arrived with a serious and well-thought out plan, including a detailed outline as to how the plan would be implemented. Al Killeen brought a truckload of momentum with him. By contrast, Seagram's top management had not yet considered what should be done with TCC, or for that matter, our other labels. No one knew Seagram's intentions, most of all Seagram itself.

I visualized Coca-Cola and Seagram as horse stables, each with a prize race horse: Coca-Cola's TCC horse was like a young Seabiscuit – spirited, smooth functioning, already a huge winner, eager and ready for bigger races – dreaming of winning the Triple Crown, anticipating the next race, going for it. Seagram's Masson horse was older, but had won big races in its youth. Despite recent losses, he was still capable of winning, but was yearning for days gone by and jealous of newcomers. His internal conflicts would need to be controlled. Now that Seagram owned both horses, it would be interesting to see how they developed each one. Time would tell.

Changing of the Guard

We were in the midst of the 1983 harvest and crushing season when the sale concluded and Harry Teasley said goodbye. Although U.S. wine sales had begun to slow in the current year, Wine Spectrum sales continued to climb, but with a greatly reduced rate of increase. With no input from Seagram on sales projections, I had no idea whether we were crushing appropriate tonnages of grapes. Our new owner remained quietly at the far-away eastern edge of the continent. The only information we were able to glean came not from the corporate office at 375 Park Avenue, New York, but from industry news sources. *Wines and Vines* magazine reported in December that Marc Henrion, former president of Seagram's Barton & Guestier French wine subsidiary, had been promoted to chairman of The Seagram Wine Group. Both Seagram Wine Co. and Coca-Cola's Wine Spectrum were being placed inside the Seagram Wine Group, whatever that meant. Several more new titles appeared, and we were confused by most of them.

Sam Bronfman, Edgar's oldest son, walked into my office one day to introduce himself and discuss our just-completed crush season, quality level of the wines in inventory and his sales plans. I liked Sam instantly because of his open, friendly and constructive attitude. Dick Maher, president of Seagram Wine Company, reported to Sam, and I reported to Dick. He and I knew each other well, we were both ex-Marines, and there was a built-in trust that made our relationship positive, productive and pleasant. I would continue to be in charge of winemaking for both TCC and Monterey Vineyard, and also travel to help sales staff around the country by speaking to retailers, distributors and the public whenever it was requested through the chain of command.

Edgar Bronfman visited the Monterey Vineyard and TCC facilities at Gonzales a few weeks after the sale closed in November 1984. His entourage included Phil Beekman, Seagram's president, Marc Henrion, chairman of The Wine Group, and Dick Maher. We walked through our whole facility, and I explained how it worked and answered questions about capacities, limitations and our abilities to produce various types of wine. Edgar was very interested and asked questions that told me he had done a good job of reading up on the past history of the Gonzales facilities. It was a very pleasant day, and I was happy to explain how we operated the winery in some detail.

The Teacher's Teacher

Marc Henrion took me aside and said he wanted me to spend a week with him in France visiting wineries in different regions that were producing wines to be sold by Seagram. We would be accompanied by Professor Emile Peynaud, a name I knew well by reputation, although I had never met him personally. I was thrilled to hear Marc's plan; I had visited many wineries in all parts of France over the years and had many friends there, but I'd never been accompanied on a wine tour by anyone so reputable as Emile Peynaud. American winemakers referred to Professor Peynaud as 'The Maynard Amerine of France.' French winemakers called Maynard Amerine 'The Emile Peynaud of America.' Both references were compliments to both men.

We agreed on a schedule, and I arrived in Paris on a Sunday night. Marc Henrion, Emile Peynaud and I were driven around by an American woman who lived in France and was employed by Seagram to serve as driver and interpreter for various visitors. We drove to Beaune the next morning to visit several classic Burgundy wineries, tasting and discussing every wine detail that came to mind. On the highway, Emile Peynaud would interrupt whatever conversation was going on with a single, loud word, "Stop." The driver would pull over, and we would get out looking at some vineyard or winery detail he wanted to show us. From the first village, we quickly became accustomed to Professor Peynaud's "stops" and each one was more worthwhile than the last. He knew I was experienced in vineyards and winemaking, but had a desire to learn more, so he took full advantage of every opportunity to stop and show me something. If I were asked to describe him in few words, I would call Emile Peynaud 'the teacher's teacher' in the most complimentary terms. He loved to explain things in his chosen field – grapes and wine – and his vast knowledge of the subject was expressed in a manner that made it easy to understand.

By noon the first day, our driver noticed that she really didn't have much translating to do. Although I did not speak French, I could read scientific French well enough especially on subjects like grapes and wine. French and German were the two 'reading ability' languages I mastered as a requirement for receiving my PhD from The University of California. Likewise, Peynaud did not speak English, but could read scientific English and therefore knew a great many English words. We found early on that, as he described the subject in French (spoken slowly), I usually understood what he said; likewise, when I spoke to him in English, I spoke slowly and he, too, could understand what I said. We found ourselves working together on language effectively, because it was in both our interests to do so. Peynaud had known Professor Maynard Joslyn (my PhD professor at Berkeley) and Professor Maynard Amerine at UC Davis. They had visited each other on sabbaticals and communicated on vineyard and wine subjects during their teaching careers. All had used the same method for communication because all were good at reading the foreign language, but not fluent in speaking it.

Emile Peynaud was the author of a particularly well-written book on the technology of wine and winemaking, titled *Knowing and Making Wine*. He gave me a signed copy in French that I referred to during our trip that week. Later, I bought a newly printed English translation in California, which I continue to use. From Burgundy, we made one stop in Beaujolais and then continued on to the Rhone. I had to confess that I liked a great deal about the subtlety and finesse of red Burgundies, but was not as enamored about the flavor roughness of Rhone red wines. Winemaking was first class in both regions, of course, but there was something special about the Pinot Noir wines of Burgundy that simply couldn't be matched by the best Syrah blends grown in the Rhone River Valley. Over the years, I have come to believe that it is simply a personal bias that I cannot explain. I love Pinot Noir when it's at its best, but I can take or leave Syrah, even a good Syrah.

I admit that many of the Pinots of Burgundy have suffered from Brettanomyces ('Brett') yeast spoilage from time to time, and I have never liked the 'animal skin' barnyard-like aftertaste that Brett imparts to the wines it affects. I remembered when Bob Mondavi was especially proud of having bought some used oak barrels from a winery in Burgundy in 1972. Within two years, tasters of his 1972 and 1973 Pinot Noir wines complained about 'barnyard spoilage' in his wines. It was traced to those used barrels, and it didn't take long for the whole wine world to begin gossiping that Bob Mondavi's winery had 'caught the clap' from intimate relations with dirty French wine barrels. I told the story to Emile Peynaud, but he already knew about it. The group even told me the French term for 'catching the clap,' which I've long since forgotten. Nothing travels faster than bad news gossip, and language is never a barrier. Professor Peynaud has long been a proponent of sanitation for wine barrels and has cautioned many wineries and offered methods to keep Brett under control while aging red wines in oak barrels. Tasting the wines from several wineries, I could tell that some winemakers in France listen to the great professors, while others don't pay attention – just as is true in America.

Marc Henrion had previously arranged for overnight stays at selected stops along our way, as well as lunch stops. The whole trip was perfectly planned, I learned a great deal, and enjoyed that week as much as any other wine trip in memory. We went on to the south of France from the Rhone, and I was not surprised to taste some of the beautiful Muscat and other dessert wines grown there. The flavors were rich, and I detected a slightly higher acidity level in many wines; it gave them a nice crispness not often seen in California dessert wines. I had seen these wines before, when I accompanied Gerald Asher on winery visits in the south of France back in 1974. The area gets overlooked because of the brilliance of Burgundy and Bordeaux, but I recommend the south to anyone who wants a pleasant wine surprise in 'out of the way' France.

Our car then turned west along the Mediterranean towards the walled city of Carcassonne and then north, to end up in Bordeaux for the final two days of our trip. On the way, I asked Emile about the levels of acidity in those dessert wines we'd just tasted. He told me that, despite the taste sensation, the acidities were rarely higher than about six grams per liter. All the table wines we had tasted while in central France had higher acidities; certainly higher than similar table wines in coastal California. We continued discussing the influence of acidity on the mouthfeel and taste sensation of those wines. I was listening intently to his technical explanation in French, concentrating on translating every word to myself. He was saying, "Avec six gramme ..." (in spoken French, 'six gramme' sounds like 'see ... grahhm'). He stopped, his eyes and face suddenly perked up, and he announced in English, "Seagram." We all burst out laughing at the unintended double meaning translation, and the driver had to pull the car over to the shoulder to regain her composure. That coincidence of language may not be funny to the reader, but in that car, on that day and at that time, it was a scream. We laughed many times about Emile Peynaud's sudden jump from dry, boring French wine chemistry to a fun 'double meaning word game.'

Shortly after returning to California, I was pleasantly surprised to hear that Marc was bringing Professor Peynaud to Gonzales to see the facilities (Monterey Vineyard and TCC) as well as the Paul Masson winery. I was especially happy to discuss with him my experience in the exceptionally cool upper end of Salinas Valley. On our vineyard tour, I noticed that many of the earlier vineyards planted by McFarland Management Company were no longer in existence. We could see evidence that they had, indeed, been there, but all the residual vines were now dead – killed by Phylloxera. After returning to the winery, Emile asked for a map of France. He spread it out on a table and showed me that the same very cold summertime winds occur along the Atlantic coast of France for many of the same reasons that

"A unique thing happens to Johannisberg Riesling in Monterey that does not happen in Napa, Sonoma or other coastal areas."

Dr. Richard G. Peterson,
President and Winemaster, The Monterey Vineyard

The Monterey Vineyard barrel room in a newspaper advertisement for the wines in 1981. Beginning wineries, especially in new wine regions, need prominent advertising to get the public to try their wines.

Coca-Cola's Harry Teasley (*right*) evaluating a Monterey wine in 1978. Harry became chairman of the Wine Spectrum when Al Killeen retired in 1979.

"Wines from Monterey County generally have more intense varietal flavor and aroma than wines from other coastal areas such as Napa or Sonoma."

Dr. Richard G. Peterson, President and Winemaster, The Monterey Vineyard

"And for good reason.

"Upper Monterey County is blessed with California's coolest, longest grape growing season. Due to the influence of Monterey Bay, with its morning fog and chilly evening breezes, our grapes mature more slowly and develop more flavor and complexity than grapes grown in other coastal areas of California.

"You'll notice our unique quality the moment you taste The Monterey Vineyard Classic California Dry White. It combines a rich fruitiness with a crisp dryness. And one thing about it is unmistakable: it has a bigger, more complex flavor and aroma than comparable wines from other California regions.

"I've made wines in other parts of this state — Napa, for instance — and each region offers something different. If a crisp, complex wine is what you like, taste The Monterey Vineyard Classic California Dry White."

© 1979 The Monterey Vineyard, Gonzales, California 93926

Introducing Classic California Dry White.

1978

The Monterey Vineyard

CLASSIC CALIFORNIA
DRY WHITE
Monterey County
Vintage Table Wine

The Monterey Vineyard

Big flavor, big bouquet.

A full-page magazine advertisement published in 1979, highlighting the importance of viticulture on wine quality and the special characteristics of the cooler climate found in 'Upper Monterey County.' The Monterey Vineyard 'Classic California Dry White' became very popular.

Sandra and Dick Peterson at home in their wine cellar near Carmel Valley in Monterey County, 1983.

Three of the most unique vintage wines produced by The Monterey Vineyard (*from left*): Botrytis Sauvignon Blanc, Thanksgiving Harvest Johannisberg Reisling and December Harvest Zinfandel.

On a winery tour of France inspecting vineyards and wineries accompanied by Professor Emile Peynaud, famous French wine expert (*above left*). These photos are from a tour of Châteaux Lafite Rothschild, in 1985.

Dinner among the barrels at The Monterey Vineyard with Professor Emile Peynaud (*above, second from left*) in early 1986. Pictured below (*from left*): Tom Peterson, Dick Peterson, Professor Emile Peynaud, Marc Henrion and Gary Ibsen.

Edgar Bronfman (*above right*) got a thorough tour of The Monterey Vineyard and Taylor California Cellars facilities in 1985. He wanted to see how the operation and brands would fit in with Seagram's other properties. Marc Henrion (*below left*) and Len Cairney join in the discussions.

Gary Ibsen (*left*) listens to a barrel aging discussion between the author and Edgar Bronfman (*center*); Dick Maher and Phil Beekman are standing to the right.

Phil Beekman (*far right*) and Edgar Bronfman taste fresh samples from nearby tanks.

The author with Marc Henrion (*right*), visiting Sterling Vineyards in 1985. Marc and Emile Peynaud were genuine bright spots in the Seagram organization. Both were productive, knowledgeable and very enjoyable to work with.

A promotional photo of the Seagram original wine cooler bottle superimposed onto a wall mirror containing a room thermometer. The wine cooler was quite successful, but was not followed up with additional wine products.

they occur along the California coast. Even as far south as Bordeaux, the Atlantic water is so cold that no quality wine grapes are grown on the coast near the mouth of the Gironde River. The French had known long ago what we learned about Monterey County only recently: The coldest coastal areas of France and the coldest of California (Salinas) are not suitable for grapevines! I thought to myself, "If only the McFarlands and Tom Stratton had done more research before planting those 9,600 acres in an unsuitable climate..."

Flavors for Spirits, but Wine? Oh My!

My first contact from non-wine staff at Seagram was from a manager of new flavored products in New York. He came to Gonzales to see the winery and to discuss his newest project – flavored wine coolers. Wine coolers (a mixture of wine, water, sugar, acid and flavor) were beginning to attract serious public attention in America. He asked whether I had worked with coolers before, and I said, "No." "But, I understand you've done a lot of work with flavored wines in the past?" I said, "Of course, I'm very familiar with using natural flavors in wines. Do you want me to make a cooler for Seagram?" He answered quickly, "No, no, no, that's my department. I need you to tell me how to make a cooler." "I don't understand," I objected. "Didn't you tell me that is your area of expertise?" "Yes, that's my department, but we haven't made a cooler as yet. I'm here to learn how to do that."

Hiding my disbelief, I took the time to give him a short course on the steps he should take in making a cooler – it would depend on what, exactly, he wanted. A light, bubbly, carbonated cooler would be one thing; a heavier drink would require different flavors and base wines, possibly even red wine blends, and no carbonation. I said he should use only natural flavoring materials because of wine labeling regulations, and he needed to add the flavors to various wines by 'trial and error' until he found the combination of flavor and wine that he wanted. Then he should adjust the sugar and natural acidity of the wine for a balanced taste, and check the finished product for flavor stability over time at elevated temperatures. I stressed that many natural flavor materials are unstable in wine; they decompose af-

313

ter a week or two, making them impossible to use. I suggested testing each flavor by adding it to wine, storing the mixture at 110°F for a week or two, then tasting to see whether the flavor would keep.

Apparently, his department had occasionally worked with flavors in higher alcohol mixed drinks, but never in wines. He was completely confused by the sulfur dioxide in white wines; the chemistry was mysterious, and it bothered him to learn that many natural flavors are ruined by the SO_2 content in wine. It seemed odd to me that Seagram would make wine coolers near the head office in New York, rather than in a winery staffed with people experienced in both winemaking and flavor use. I did my best to give him example recipes to use as a start, and agreed that he could call me for further advice after getting some experience with wine in his New York laboratory. He seemed as confused on leaving as he had been on arrival.

I forgot all about wine coolers for a month or two; I don't recall whether it was Sam Bronfman, Dick Maher, or perhaps Jim Bareuther, wine sales manager, who renewed the subject. Whoever it was asked me to make a proposed wine cooler and send a few bottles to him in New York. They hadn't gotten a usable wine cooler from the New York Seagram lab and wanted to do a blind tasting of competitive coolers at the head office before deciding on an entry for the market. I called a friend at Fritsche Flavor Company, from whom I had purchased flavors twenty years earlier for wine products at Gallo. I told him I wanted samples of lemon, orange and lime flavors for use in wine for a Seagram project, and I would get back to him if the project amounted to anything. The samples arrived in three days, and I found a nice combination of stable lemon flavors to use in a delicate, sweetened Chenin Blanc wine diluted with carbonated water. I sent several bottles of the sample and got a call only a few days later. My sample had been chosen over all the others, and I was to forward my recipe to the head of new flavored products in New York immediately. I did, and notified Fritsche to expect to sell my flavor choices directly to Seagram.

Two months later, the same new products guy called, saying, "Our wine cooler is a big success in the market" – I had seen that in the news media, but nobody at Seagram had mentioned it to me. He said, "I need you to make several more new wine coolers for me." His tone of voice had a tentative, somewhat guilty ring to it, and I asked, "What do you mean when you say: Make new coolers *for you?*" He answered, "My department has to produce more wine coolers and get them on the market as soon as possible." I thought a few seconds and said, "I want to ask you a question. Do the head people at Seagram know that I was the one who made that first wine cooler?" He hesitated, then gave a wavering explanation: "We … we follow company procedures to the letter. All new flavored products for Seagram have to come out of the new products department in New York. That's our function, and management requires us to do that. The Bronfman family has a strong hand in controlling new products. If it's made at 375 Park Avenue, they know it's done right." I was speechless.

The blatant dishonesty of his last sentence surprised me. I did not raise my voice; I simply told him, "I'm busy now, and will speak to you later." He was still dancing around the subject as I hung up. Two weeks later, he called and left a message, which I didn't return. One week after that, he called to ask how I was coming along with the newest wine coolers. "I haven't made any new wine coolers," I replied calmly. "But you were going to make more coolers for the Seagram wine cooler program; remember the last time we talked?" I waited a few seconds, and then spoke slowly and deliberately, "You … must be mistaken. I made the first Seagram wine cooler as a favor to someone in the Seagram Wine Company. I'm happy it's very successful in the market, but – I don't work in the New York lab. I can't make wine coolers in California because they wouldn't be 'done right.' You told me that yourself." The word cooler was never again mentioned to me by anyone in the Seagram organization. I noticed that Seagram did market several new 'spirits' coolers in the next two years, but I'm not aware that they ever marketed another wine cooler.

Musical Chairs

In the ensuing months, I had increasing difficulty trying to understand the constantly changing structure of the wine organizations within Seagram. I received many memos announcing staff promotions, but none clarified the company structure or intentions. Most announcements spawned more questions than they answered. The memos' authors seemed to be more interested in to whom the person reported, rather than what his job was. At first, we were told that Marc Henrion was president of The Seagram Wine Group (which contained both The Wine Spectrum and Seagram Wine Company). However, a later announcement stated that Dick Maher, President of Seagram Wine Company, would report to Phil Beekman, President of Joseph E. Seagram & Sons (the main corporation). What?

Seagram quietly clamped a total ban on any further use of the names 'Coca-Cola' or 'The Wine Spectrum,' either in print or in any speeches. A speech given to the Advertising Research Foundation by a VP of Kenyon & Eckhardt Advertising reminisced about their setting up the original expert blind tasting of Taylor California Cellars, which led to what he called, "One of the half dozen really major new product successes of the last decade." He sent me a copy and I asked why neither Coca-Cola nor Wine Spectrum was mentioned. The speaker told me privately that he was forbidden to mention those words; further it was implied to him that it would please Seagram if listeners credited Seagram instead of Coca-Cola for the highly successful introduction of TCC back in 1978! I would never make it on Madison Avenue in New York.

Ed Hamler was let go as president of TCC in May 1984 as part of transferring Monterey Vineyard, Masson and TCC into a new 'West Coast Operations' division of Seagram Wine Co. Wine production for Masson and TCC was to be managed by Masson's Morris Katz, president, and Frank Jerant, executive VP. I would no longer have anything to do with TCC and was to limit my scope to Monterey Vineyard. It was confusing, because my responsibility was to continue dictating wine specifications for Monterey Vineyard but the cellar production of Monterey wines – the cellar production of all wines – was to be controlled by Frank Jerant. Under Wine Spectrum, Monterey Vineyard and Sterling, the highest price and quality wine brands, were produced independently and sold by a separate sales group. Now, responsibilities for production of all three brands were lumped together under Masson managers, all the sub-managers who previously had reported to Ed or myself would now report to Frank Jerant. Seagram hoped to save money by transferring production, aging and bottling of Masson wines to the newer winery at Gonzales, and closed the nearby Masson winery.

I was given an additional title, Technical Director of The Seagram Wine Company. The added title implied a promotion, but left me with a problem; it would be difficult to keep up the quality of Monterey Vineyard wines, when all the winery foremen who had reported to either Ed Hamler or me would now report directly to former Masson managers (who carried giant-sized 'anti-TCC' chips on their shoulders). I would think that Seagram, in buying a new, successful winery, would take advantage of its experience by promoting the best TCC managers and cutting the weaker ones, while making similar promotions and cuts to Masson managers. That is not what Seagram did. They promoted Masson management personnel, en masse, to posts previously held by TCC managers. Both brands were now owned by Seagram, and I wondered why Seagram top management did not include precautions to avoid in-fighting among employees.

Eventually, I realized that Seagram top management had a 'hands off' management style, and many Masson managers had probably stepped in as managers of the Gonzales facility by default – not hearing otherwise from top management. Because Seagram had owned Masson for a long time, it was natural for Masson managers to consider themselves more senior to personnel of any company Seagram might buy. Former Masson employees were injected into the Gonzales winery without a plan for integrating and teaching all cellar workers to work together with the joint goal of helping each other produce the proper wines for both Masson and TCC. It was an unstable blend of workers, especially considering the well-established attitude for 'guarding my space' that was so very visible among long-time managers within Seagram. I was surprised to see in-fighting everywhere; employee squabbling had not been condoned under Coca-Cola.

Frank Jerant had a running battle with Dan Lucas almost from the day Frank had arrived on the Gonzales premises. Dan had run the winery al-most single-handedly while I was out pleading with distributors around the country to keep sales moving. Dan was aggressive to be sure, but he had a good deal of knowledge and experience under his belt, and a constructive attitude. Frank lacked experience (and often common sense), but was dom-ineering and hell-bent on beating down others, especially Dan Lucas, in the hierarchy of the company. It was reminiscent of Jack Fields at Gallo in the 1960s. If it had been only Frank, the problems could have been contained, but his automatic support for Masson subordinates over TCC personnel created inflexibility. Many of the Masson workers thought they didn't have to learn Gonzales procedures, as they outranked the 'non-Masson' guys (including myself) and didn't have to follow my rules for handling Monterey Vineyard wines. Frank's open and personal fight with Dan lasted more than a year, culminating when Dan gave notice and moved to Christian Brothers in Napa Valley. I was not surprised when Dan later told me, "At Christian Brothers, the bosses are intelligent."

In discussions with home office representatives, I discovered a similar attitude – that an employee at any level from the head office in New York outranked the boss of any new company bought by Seagram. The ineptitude I'd experienced with the flavored cooler was only one example, i.e. it doesn't count if we didn't do it in New York. The tendency for in-fighting really hurt Seagram – some employees spent months fighting each other. This was in direct, polar contrast to the attitude at Coca-Cola, where the approach was: "We fight our battles outside the company; inside, we help each other meet company goals."

Musical Chairs, Round Two

With Masson people heading all the cellar production of wines, I saw no major change in recipes for wine blends, but I did see a huge increase in the bureaucracy of operations at Gonzales. Masson had a manual of standard recipes for all phases of wine production: all white wines were treated this way, all red wines were treated that way – as if every vintage had identical weather and all varieties were identical in their cellar requirements. I criticized that standard recipe approach many times, both verbally and in writing, referring to it as 'lowest common denominator' winemaking. One of the stipulations in the manual was to add far too much SO_2, and far too often, to wines during processing at the winery. Many wines did not need additional SO_2, and each decision should have been made by a competent winemaker instead of cellar workers following a recipe book. My guess was that adding extra SO₂ automatically as 'insurance' had been written into the Masson manual as a CYA ('cover your ass') practice by some long-forgotten cellar manager. The result was that many wines ended up with 'too much chemical,' causing the wine quality to suffer. It was interesting that no one fought back openly against my criticisms – rather, they quietly ignored my specifications and continued following their outdated standard manual. Since I hadn't come to Gonzales from Masson, I didn't need to be heard.

I was happy to no longer be involved in TCC wines. My goal had always been to make wine for the higher image Monterey Vineyard, and I monitored all operations to make sure wine quality was maintained. I found it frustrating to witness so much jockeying for position among Gonzales winery workers, whose point of view depended on who used to sign their check. Too often, 'getting the job done correctly' was not as important as the reporting hierarchy among workers. From the time we built the winery, long before Seagram's involvement, I had taught experienced workers not to allow inexperienced workers to run a piece of equipment in a dangerous (or sloppy) manner. Under Seagram, workers ignored that in favor of following the Masson manual, and were usually supported (I thought, stupidly) by Frank Jerant. That made the problem of protecting wine quality difficult in the cellar.

Within three months, another memo announced that Marc Henrion was now president of Worldwide Wine Operations, and I was given yet another title: International Enology within Worldwide Wine Operations. Marc continued with his former title, President of Barton & Guestier Wine Company in France, but I never heard the Seagram Wine Group mentioned again. It seemed likely that decisions about personnel reporting hierarchies were changing from week to week at the whims of individuals at much higher levels in the company. I wondered whether anyone was really managing.

I was pleased to continue reporting to Dick Maher; he was as competent as any wine sales and marketing manager I knew. He helped me understand that there were multitudes of inconsistencies within Seagram that he and I had no ability to repair. The company had its reasons for doing things, even if we didn't understand. "If we don't have the power to fix it, then let it go. Maybe we'll be able to fix it for them later. For now, all we can do is continue trying." He had one of the best attitudes I encountered in the various corporations I worked for.

I was in New York and stopped in to see Dick at his office in the Seagram building one afternoon. It was a hot day, and noticing that Dick had removed his suit coat, I took mine off and looked around to see where I should hang it. Dick noticed my confusion and said, "Oh, just throw your coat there on the couch; that's where I put mine. In this building, nothing attaches to any wall without the personal approval of Edgar's wife; they're designing me an upscale coat hanger. It'll probably cost a couple thousand dollars and take three years, but I'm not allowed to put up my own hanger." I dropped my coat on his couch without comment, but I had noticed during my walk towards Dick's office that there were a great many scars and blotches on the walls, missing paint, plaster patches, etc. in the building. I thought to myself, "What would it have hurt if an employee had simply driven a sixteen penny nail into the wall on which to hang his coat?" I learned much about the company's management on that trip just by listening to the many things people said between the lines.

SPIRITS & Wine

Seagram was not finished announcing major company changes. In early 1985, the company began the promotion of a new (and major) campaign called Alcohol Equivalency. Apparently, as a last attempt to reposition spirits above wine as the leading income producer for the company, Seagram unrolled a major effort that was obviously intended to raise the alcohol taxes on wine and beer without changing taxes on spirits. It didn't mention taxes; rather, it stated, "the campaign is a public service – to correct the misconception that distilled spirits are 'stronger' than beer or wine." The wine industry was uniformly irate, since this would seriously erode wine sales, and certainly cut into wine profitability. Seagram insisted that it was in the public interest to know that 12 ounces of beer, 5 ounces of wine and 1¼ ounces of spirits all contained about the same amount of alcohol. Seagram wanted people to believe that it was wrong to think that wine was a beverage of moderation to serve with food.

Wineries rebuffed the Seagram campaign by pointing out that the drinkers of spirits drank only for its alcohol impact. Wine drinkers, by contrast, often used wine as an accompaniment to food at mealtime and did not necessarily consume wine only for its alcohol content. They agreed with many in the medical profession who showed evidence that the alcohol in wine, taken with food at mealtime, was absorbed into the body much more slowly than the alcohol from spirits. They added that table wines were increasingly used in hospitals and nursing homes for therapeutic value because they added to the patients' feelings of well-being. Therefore, stating only the quantity of alcohol ingested did not tell the whole story, and the Seagram equivalence message was misleading to the public.

The campaign created a huge problem for wine managers within Seagram since it was a direct attack on their product line and would certainly reduce the sales of wine (including Seagram brands). Wine Institute asked member wineries to develop spokesmen against the Seagram ads. At the same time, I was asked to attend an executive TV workshop that Seagram's Bill Carr was planning at 375 Park Ave. in New York. I asked him for an outline of what would be covered, as I had a busy schedule and wasn't sure I could make the trip. The packet he sent made it very clear that his goal was to develop speakers to travel around their individual regions – speaking in favor of the Seagram equivalency campaign! I wrote back saying that he had misunderstood my job responsibilities in inviting me; my job was to work with vineyards and wineries to produce high-quality wines and not in any way to become a spokesman for the corporation on other subjects. I would not attend, as joining would present a conflict of interest. I never heard from anyone about it again, and was a little surprised that I didn't get fired or receive a picture of the chairman frowning. Where would my loyalty find a resting place?

To further strengthen spirits sales at the expense of wine, the company reorganized yet again. Seagram Wine Company was split into two separate divisions: production (in California) and sales (in New York). Historically, the Seagram liquor organization had been divided simply between production of all brands and sales of all brands. That split had worked because communication between a spirits producer and its seller was not necessary. Spirits are bought solely for their alcohol content. Consumers do not expect big differences between flavors of different spirits, as they rely on the 'mixer' for the drink's flavor profile. Part-full bottles of spirits can be shelved for long periods without spoilage; no precautions are necessary. Sales can be increased by cutting prices without affecting the product image.

It is a different situation with wines. Consumers of wines like to know the person who made whatever wine they are drinking. If they don't know the winemaker, they like to have visited the winery, or know someone there, or heard stories about it, or have some other connection. Unlike selling spirits, it is easier to sell wine if that wine (or winery) has a story to tell. Consumers treat their wines like old friends; as a unique accompaniment to food, from a special grape variety, or clone, or country of origin. Table wine flavor is spoiled by exposure to air or heat; care must be taken in storage. In selling table wines, a small discount can improve sales, but if the salesman cuts the price too much, consumers reject the wine, believing there must be something wrong with it. I suspected the Seagram equivalency program might be a forerunner to their getting out of wine altogether.

Musical Chairs, Round Three
Are we having fun yet?

Here we go again: Dick Maher was moved from sales (where I thought he was badly needed) to Gonzales to head production, replacing Morris Katz, who had retired. Dick reported to Mel Griffin, executive VP of manufacturing in New York, while wine sales would now be headed up by Jerome Mann, a spirits manager who had no prior wine experience. Seagram was subordinating the wine division to spirits in the apparent belief that alcohol equivalence would increase the importance of spirits over wine. It had never been a secret that the company made much more money from spirits than wine, and someone had decided that spirits should once again become the fastest growing profit producer for Seagram. As if to confirm that outcome, sales of Seagram wines were tanking badly by 1986. As Edgar Bronfman stated shortly after purchasing Wine Spectrum, Seagram had formulated no specific plan for selling both TCC and Masson wines after the purchase. The apparent goal was their unfocused desire to 'get bigger' in the wine business. Their lack of a logical plan for handling sales of any wine caused an overall sales collapse of all their brands.

During Coca-Cola's great expansion of TCC from 1978 to 1983, there was a huge amount of jealousy, even hatred, aimed at the company and its wine brands from competing wineries. Such resentment came from Masson sales people as well, and I witnessed it on many occasions. After buying TCC, I expected Seagram would capitalize by continuing to sell TCC wines through the existing, and very successful, Taylor distributors, but they did not. Sales observers told me a chaotic situation had been brewing almost from day one; it didn't happen en masse, just a few markets at a time. In cities where there had been a distributor for Masson wines and a competing distributor for TCC wines, Seagram terminated the TCC distributor outright. Suddenly, the former TCC distributor had lost the right to handle and sell TCC wines. Since that was a big loss, that distributor looked around to find new brands with which to compete against Seagram's brands. As often as not, the best brand waiting in the wings was a new competitor from Sonoma County called 'Glen Ellen.' Sales of Glen Ellen wines exploded upwards, as distributor after distributor around the country replaced their former stock of TCC wines with Glen Ellen wines. Former TCC people complained loudly, "My God, Seagram bought TCC just to kill it," which seems absurd, but the evidence looked that way to them. It was weird.

Worse, when Seagram took TCC away from its former distributor, they gave the brand to the Seagram's Masson distributor in the same city. This thoughtless decision became horrible news for the Masson distributor – and for Seagram wine sales. The Masson distributors had to divide their sales efforts to accommodate the newly acquired TCC brand. That meant half their time, money and effort was taken away from Masson sales to try to keep TCC sales going – and TCC never received half the sales effort it had enjoyed under Coca-Cola. The result was easy to predict, even to a non-salesman. The Masson distributor had been fighting against TCC wines in the market for five years, and distributor attitude was not going to change overnight. How could the distributor's Masson salespeople suddenly begin selling TCC wines with the same zeal? The hard feelings increased when all salespeople realized they were expected to divide their Masson shelf space in stores to accommodate both brands.

I never again spoke for TCC, as my job involved only Monterey Vineyard; however, in sales divisions, I was remembered as a TCC man. More and more often, Masson labels occupied enviable 'eye level' shelves, while TCC labels were relegated to bottom shelves and out-of-the-way places. This bias was pointed out to me when I went into the market to meet a store owner, check on Monterey Vineyard sales or speak to a group.

Unbelievably, it got worse. Management for Seagram wanted Masson to regain its lost positioning as a quality label among mid-price wines in the mind of the consumer. Perhaps to convince consumers that Masson was the superior wine, they reduced prices for TCC and raised prices for Masson on store shelves; consumers were expected to assume Masson wines were better simply because of the higher asking prices. Unfortunately, the production people at Gonzales made no quality improvement to the Masson formulas. Those wines were still 100% made from cheaper Central Valley base wines, while the TCC blends contained a good percentage of higher-quality Monterey varietal wines. Consumers comparing the two could taste that TCC wines were richer, more flavorful and had better quality, even though Masson wines were priced higher. The result was that sales for both plummeted, and consumer confusion raged.

It was a sales disaster for Seagram and a wonderful windfall for Glen Ellen. In their attempt to punish Coca-Cola's original TCC distributors, Seagram had pissed away much of their wine business to Glen Ellen, and Glen Ellen's wine quality and sales people were fully up to the task of growing their brand. Within a year, the Seagram sales results for all wines were in sad shape. Asked about it later by the press, Edgar Bronfman was quoted as saying, "The wine market hasn't developed as we expected," and "Seagram is disappointed in the market for modestly-priced wines." Over the same time period, Gallo, Bronco, Franzia and Glen Ellen sales were booming.

I had my hands full preserving the high quality levels of Monterey Vineyard wines. The fact that I no longer was involved in TCC winemaking helped me concentrate on my first goal – improving quality and preserving the image of Monterey wines. As president of the newly created Seagram Classics Wine Company, Sam Bronfman asked me to write a detailed 'Product Profile' report listing parameters for all Monterey Vineyard wines. It wasn't easy because premium wines aren't made by recipe; we'd get the best out of our grapes in each vintage year, and wines would vary between vintages. He said, "I understand that, but at the same time I have to have generalities to tell the sales people so they have a good idea of the personalities of each wine." He was right, of course, and I wrote the report 'as if each wine was produced from a recipe' with explanations of how the winemaker should bend the recipe wherever nature allowed him to improve it in any given year. I listed optimum microclimates by variety and gave examples of locations in Monterey County where I believed each variety should be grown for optimum wine quality. I detailed winemaking methods, including when to ferment in barrels and when in stainless, optimal pH and alcohol levels, barrel aging and whether to age in bottle for a time before releasing wines for public sale.

I copied Seagram managers, Jim Bareuther, Ken Onish and Dick Maher as well as Masson's Frank Jerant, Armond Rist and Glenn Salva, assistant winemaker. Sam and I had hoped to get general acceptance (down to each sub-foreman in the winery) on how to manage the better vintage, varietal wines we were making at the Gonzales winery. Sam's newly formed company included only the best of Seagram's wines (Mumm Champagne, Monterey Vineyard, Sterling, Brolio, Bersano and Ricasoli Italian wines, as well as wines of seven privately owned boutique wineries in California) and he intended to make it the best of the best. Sam knew I was uneasy about getting Frank Jerant to take wine quality control seriously; Frank was already allowing Randy Chodola, subforeman, to go around me and ship TMV wines immediately after bottling – without waiting for my stipulated bottle aging period to correct bottle sickness and allow time to develop 'bottle bouquet.' I had insisted on a hold period of up to six months after bottling, depending on the wine type and variety, but did not always get it. Many fine wines don't taste exactly right if consumed immediately after bottling, and are said to be 'bottle sick.' These same wines become okay again if allowed to stand for a month or two before shipping. For that reason, most fine wines of the world are not shipped directly from bottling lines. 'Everyday' wines, however, rarely suffer from bottle sickness and can be shipped directly from bottling lines to outlets for sale.

Rampant Bureaucracy

At the winery, rampant bureaucracy was progressing nicely. A Quality Improvement Plan (QIP) was instituted throughout the company in accordance with a plan developed by the 'Joseph E. Seagram Quality Improvement Team' (QIT). Randy Chodola sent out an eight-page memo containing minutes of the first QIT meeting chaired by Larry Brink, production manager. The charter took up another three pages, and made it a firm responsibility of all team members to "Make recommendations to the steering committee concerning the acquisition of resources required from outside to implement the QIP plan, and develop a budget for QIT." I read it many times, but never understood what it was intending to say. Copies of the eleven pages went to a total of thirty-one people (8 team members, 7 steering committee members and 16 unsuspecting other named employees). The steering committee comprised officers at the highest levels of the parent corporation including chairman Edgar Bronfman Jr, Phil Beekman, Mel Griffin, Steve Herbits, Russ McLauchlan, David Sacks and Ron Watkins.

The group's charter had a statement for every QIT member to sign; it set up a budget for travel, posters and other expenses. The heart of the statement was to follow a 'Fourteen-Step' Program, which included education, quality awareness, recognition, cost of quality, goal setting, measurement, error cause removal, corrective action, management commitment, zero defects planning, a zero defects day, and a final step titled 'do it all over again.' The implication was that reference to these steps, sent to the PR department and printed on posters around the winery (but never on office walls), would create a commensurate improvement of quality – although I never saw a description or definition of 'quality' or the question 'quality of what?' being contemplated. The QIT team members would continue meeting every Wednesday morning at 8:30 for one hour; afterwards, complete minutes would be sent out to the large mailing list. I felt warm and fuzzy all over to realize that our company was going to have its quality improved, and that it would be confirmed in writing and promoted by the PR boys and girls.

Jim Bareuther, sales manager, sent me a copy of his sales projections for Monterey Vineyard wines for the ten year period 1985 to 1995; I found the numbers to be completely unrealistic, as if pulled out of a hat. Starting with actual sales for 1985, his projections were to increase nearly fivefold, from 84,000 cases to 387,000 cases. In addition, his projections for the Monterey Vineyard Classic Red, White and Rosé wines (to be sold through the Sheraton Hotel chain) were expected to jump, by 1986, from the current 17,000 cases almost sixfold to 100,000 cases – in one year! Overall total for the same Classic Wines was projected to jump to 897,000 cases in ten years. Because Monterey Vineyard produced our highest-quality wines, priced well above those of TCC or Masson, I couldn't see how they could possibly increase sales by those huge numbers. Their projections had never been reliable in the past, so I decided to take them with a grain of salt, retaining my wait-and-see attitude.

In Memphis six weeks later, I made several sales calls in between presentations to sales and consumer groups for Monterey Vineyard wines. I got a similar impression from all of them, but one visit made the point most clearly. One retail outlet had our White Zinfandel priced at $3.99. Other White Zins were 'on sale' at $4.99. Most were priced at $5.29, and Beringer was selling well at $5.49. Monterey White Zin (the overall sweepstakes winner at the 1985 California State Fair) had never lost a tasting to Beringer as far as I knew, but in that Memphis store, no other White Zinfandel sold below $4.99 – only Monterey Vineyard was a full dollar below all the others. The wine was deliberately priced as if it wasn't any good!

I asked the proprietor the obvious questions: "Why $3.99? Why no point-of-purchase cards telling consumers that Monterey Vineyard had won the 'Best of State' award in Sacramento? Why the 'jug wine' positioning?" His answer was very enlightening: "But Monterey Vineyard IS a jug wine!" he said. "Look, we position all wines the way the distributor tells us to.

The Monterey Vineyard has always been positioned as a jug wine from the time Seagram first brought the wine to us." I explained, perhaps a little too pointedly, "Monterey Vineyard has produced only vintage-dated varietal wines and never produced any jug wine in the history of the company." He was surprised at first, thought for a minute and then said, "To tell you the truth, your wines always won our jug wine tastings, but I had no idea we were comparing coastal Monterey varietal wines with Central Valley jugs. Just this month the distributor told me we have to start moving a whole lot of Monterey wine. I told him it wouldn't move very fast at $4.99, and he told me to drop it to $3.99."

I couldn't believe what I was hearing. The Monterey Vineyard wines had been subjected to the same games the Masson distributors and salespeople had been playing against TCC wines. It appeared that a great many sales people, both at the company and in distribution houses, would never forgive us for those glory days under Coca-Cola when TCC ate their lunch; now they were killing both TCC and Monterey Vineyard. Far worse, their owner, Joseph E. Seagram & Sons, Inc., was paying for it! I never learned why Jim Bareuther had spearheaded the plan to greatly increase the sales of Monterey Vineyard wines at drastically lower prices. The net effect, certainly, was devastating to the image of the Monterey Vineyard brand, which would never recover. Now I understood why former TCC salesmen were openly complaining that, "Seagram bought Coca-Cola's Wine Spectrum just to destroy the TCC brand." I did not add to the ongoing verbal gossip, but I knew it would be easy to include the Monterey Vineyard brand in their statement. The Monterey Vineyard that I had so carefully nurtured with Gerald Asher and many others from Wine Spectrum had been assassinated.

I had reached my limit; I could not stay and continue trying to fix unfixable problems. I decided to accept the next realistic job offer I received. As chance would have it, I attended a fortuitous meeting with John Andersen, Chairman and CEO of Whitbread North America, a week later. I'd been turning down job offers routinely since 1983, but John would make me an offer I couldn't refuse. I was especially sorry to leave Sam Bronfman, as I genuinely enjoyed his company. He called, asking me to stay, but I had to say, "No, Sam, I've committed myself to taking this new job and I will not change my mind. On a personal level, I'm very sorry to leave you."

I left Seagram in April, 1986, without knowing that Dick Maher would depart one month later, and Phil Beekman (president of Seagram) would leave only a month after that. One year to the day after I left the company, Seagram sold the majority of its U.S. wine properties, including both Masson and TCC, all the wineries and equipment involved with those brands, and the Taylor, Gold Seal, and Great Western wineries of New York State. I was happy to hear that Sam had retained the higher quality brands.

Three years earlier, I had fanaticized about two mythical racehorse stables named Coca-Cola and Seagram. Coca-Cola's horse was named 'TCC' and Seagram's horse was named 'Paul Masson.' Coca-Cola sold its horse to the Seagram stable and I wondered how that stable would accommodate its two fine racehorses. Now I know: Seagram's horse-training staff was busy developing a promotional campaign to enhance their image. They postponed training and developing the horses, leaving them to run free in one of the large barns. In a fit of rage, Paul Masson started kicking TCC and didn't stop until TCC lay dying on the ground. The extreme exertion totally exhausted Paul Masson, and his heart gave out. He died at the still-warm feet of the other horse. The Seagram stable sold off the remains of the ranch, and the owner was widely quoted as saying, "I just don't understand what got into those horses. We are the best and largest animal training facility in the whole Western Hemisphere. We gave our horses the very best of care."

PART VI

Atlas Peak & the Valley Beyond
1986...

Atlas Peak Chairman's Plan

John Andersen had a varied business background, but had been involved with consumer package goods for most of his career. "I've managed every consumer package goods item you can identify; from automobiles to cosmetics, distilled spirits, magazines, food and wines," he said proudly. He started in advertising, working for ad agencies and handling consumer products accounts for Proctor & Gamble and Union Carbide. He then worked for two major companies, Armstrong Cork and Norton Simon, after which he served as president of Sonoma Vineyards, and later as executive VP of Marriott. In 1983, John joined Whitbread (English Beer PLC) as chairman and CEO of Whitbread North America, which included two divisions: Buckingham/Wile (wine sales) and Fleischmann Distilling Co. (spirits sales). John was personable, but in any conversation with him one never lost sight of the fact that he was 'all business.' He seemed to be constantly planning, thinking, scheming, developing, soliciting and asking a multitude of 'what if' questions to anyone and everyone with whom he worked. He was proud of past accomplishments and rather domineering, but not in an unpleasant way, whether dealing with subordinates or those above him in the Whitbread organization.

Whitbread, Inc. had begun expanding outside their brewing business in 1982, and by 1984 had collected a sizeable group of beer and spirits brands which offered great opportunities to grow the size of the company. The smallest division was wine, with important entries from only Italy and France. They wanted to expand their wine division considerably, and chose to build a new wine segment of premium and super-premium brands to be produced in Napa Valley; this job fell to John Andersen.

As CEO, John purchased an 1,100-acre property in Napa Valley from William Hill, who had planted some vineyards for show, and then put the whole property up for sale. Hill had planted 170 acres of what he said would eventually become 650 acres of vineyard on the property, a large plateau (nearly two square miles) surrounded by higher hills near Napa's Atlas Peak. The plateau, named Foss Valley, was located about four miles from Silverado Trail at the eastern end of Soda Canyon Road at 1,400 feet elevation. Hill had obviously gotten in over his head; he'd tried to develop the large, rocky 'moonscape' into something that only began to look like a vineyard 'in uteri' years later. John recognized that Hill was a good salesman and suspected that some of his statements wouldn't hold up to bright lights, but had purchased the land in the belief that, "They're not making Napa Valley land anymore. You have to take what's available and build it into something yourself." He knew of my experience at Monterey Vineyard and asked for a meeting to discuss the project.

John had formulated a plan for his Napa Valley project (officially named 'The Chairman's Plan') that was surprisingly comprehensive even though some assumptions leading up to the plan were not yet confirmed as true. When we discussed his plan in detail, he told me that Whitbread North America had recently signed an agreement with Piero Antinori (Tuscany, Italy) and Christian Bizot (Bollinger Champagne, France) to partner in the Foss Valley project. The three partners were planning to build a winery estate, and wanted me to consider completing their 650-acre vineyard development by designing and building a winery and making wines for the Buckingham/Wile sales company to sell in the U.S. and Europe.

John asked me, "Are you interested?" I replied, "Can I own a small piece?" He didn't bat an eye, "Of course. We value the property when completed at over $30 million, and we would like you to earn 2% of it by agreeing to stay for a full ten years." I was 55 years old and wanted to work for at least ten more years before slowing down. "John, you may have just become my new best friend," I answered. "I want to inspect this property as soon as possible." John told me he had a young financial man, James Barnes, in Napa who would assist me in whatever I needed.

Good News / Bad News

After returning to Gonzales, I flew to Napa in a borrowed Cessna and was met by James at the Napa airport for the drive to Foss Valley. The first thing I saw was a huge earth moving project already underway, with many large D-8 cats and even larger 'scalper' earthmovers in action. They were building an earthen dam across a gully near the higher elevation southern edge of the property. All the reservoir work was being done by an earth moving contractor, and it was obvious that he knew what he was doing. No wells would be necessary, and there wouldn't be a long term problem with irrigation water for this vineyard. The final reservoir, after completion, would measure 960 acre-feet of water holding capacity, and the water source would be 100% rainwater run-off. Annual rainfall in the area would provide an average of more than 300 acre-feet of water per year, so that the reservoir would normally contain a three year supply of irrigation and frost control water. It would preserve more than enough water to farm all of Foss Valley in wine grapes. If Whitbread did nothing else, the company already had given Napa County a precious gift of stored rainwater to use in fighting nearby wild fires. The reservoir and vineyard irrigation would raise the underground water table – great news for nearby property owners with wells.

John Andersen told me that James had obtained preliminary verbal approval of the building permit for a generic winery plan. They had rushed the plans through approval at the Napa County Planning Department as a condition for the property sale. After studying the property and projecting the expected grape tonnage, I calculated that the planned winery was about triple what was needed; we could easily reduce that winery size, making it a better marriage for the eventual vineyard. We would simply re-apply to Napa County for permission to replace the planned giant winery at the property center with a smaller one tied to a cave near the property entrance.

That was the good news; the bad news was that I discovered what had stopped William Hill in his tracks – several strips of hard, volcanic rock were visible along the surface of the ground, running across the property. Those rock veins would stop any vineyard cultivator cold, probably leaving it as a broken mass of steel pieces. The vineyard blocks would have to be planted in between those rocky strips, even though they occurred at odd angles. We might have to locate the vineyard avenues on top of those volcanic veins, which might be a special problem; it was a safe bet that even more unseen rock strips would be found just below the surface. I thought to myself, "Dang! William Hill might have been smarter than John Andersen after all – at least Hill knew when to give up and get out."

I told John what I'd seen. He wasn't worried about the soil and told me he knew I could plant that vineyard better than anyone else he knew – not the first time someone had gotten me to do a better job by applying a generous amount of verbal butter. I told him we might find that there were not 650 plantable acres in Foss Valley; suppose we did our best, but couldn't plant more than, say, 450 acres. Would the project still be worthwhile? "Absolutely," John said. "I expect to have a little talk with that guy Hill if you find he was bullshitting me about the 650 acres." I told him, "I'd like to try using dynamite to remove some of those rock veins on the surface. I'm not certain it will work, but I would like to try." "Do it," he ordered.

In New York, I met with Corny Marx, president, Gary Nordmann, VP finance and Steve Greenberg, VP legal counsel, in addition to John Andersen, at the Buckingham/Wile sales office. Within a couple of days, we had a contract drawn up and signed. I went on to France for a joint meeting with Piero Antinori (10% partner) and Christian Bizot (5% partner) at the famous Bollinger Winery at Ay, across the Marne River from Épernay in Champagne. Both represented leading families in wine, and both families had been in wine for hundreds of years.

A year earlier, the Antinori Winery had celebrated six hundred continuous years in the wine business under Antinori family ownership. Piero Antinori was chosen *Decanter* magazine's 'Man of the Year' for 1986 in honor of recorded references that a member of the Antinori family (Giovanni di Piero) was registered as a member of the Vintners Guild in 1385. The article stated, "No doubt there were Antinoris trading in wine before that, but this record is proof that the family was correct in celebrating six continuous centuries in the wine trade." The Bizot family had owned Bollinger for nearly two centuries, which made Bollinger the partner with the least amount of history to celebrate. The largest partner at 85%, Whitbread (famous around the world for English beer and ale) was older than the United States, having been established in 1742. I was working with solid partners – salt of the earth, conservative people who knew their businesses. Each had his own reasons for wanting to expand into the highest-quality portion of California's wine industry. Each wanted no shortcuts taken, but fully intended to become accepted and respected members of the Napa Valley wine industry.

I returned to California in July and noticed that Napa Valley 1986 was very different from the place I had left in 1974. The Napa Valley Vintners group had grown to nearly 100 members, up from 20 members in 1974, not to mention the miniscule 12 members in 1968, when I first moved to Beaulieu.[1] Most of the old wine industry names were still there, but they were completely overshadowed by dozens of wide-eyed newcomers to the Napa area. It was equally refreshing and disturbing to see all the new faces and names. On the one hand, new, intelligent entrepreneurs brought big ideas and excitement to the valley; on the other hand, most were not trained in winemaking or experienced in handling wine, and a great many mistakes had to be corrected before some of the new wine labels would become reliable bets for consumer dollars. The net effect was that the overall personality of the Napa Valley had completely changed. Gone was the sleepy hollow feel in the air of the 1960s. In its place was a modern, Hollywood-like aura of newness that was more exciting, more 'tourist destination' and infinitely busier than before. The entire Napa Valley wine scene was continuing to

---

[1] Later, the continuing rapid growth would resemble an explosion – from over 400 members in 2013 to over 500 members by 2014.

change. I would be too busy to pay much attention at first, but many differences would become apparent as time unfolded.

Vineyard Manager's Nightmare

After the transition from Monterey to Napa, I set about the serious job of vineyard development in Foss Valley. William Hill had used a sparse, 'frame house' office building near a shallow well that provided enough water for a typical office staff of four or five people. The rectangular building had four small offices, a coffee room and restroom, which was all the office space we would need until we built the winery in a couple of years. James Barnes had chosen one of the offices and I took another. None of the William Hill vines would produce fruit for another two years. We would not harvest more than a few pounds of grapes for awhile, and would not need to install significant amounts of winery equipment or tanks until then. We would concentrate on earthwork and vineyard layout for the time being.

I will never forget my first day on the job at that office in Foss Valley. On my initial inspection, I noticed a hand written sign taped to the upper part of the toilet fixture: "Do Not Sh-- in Toilet." I asked James to explain the meaning of that sign. "Well," he answered, shrugging his shoulders, "It seems that your friend, William Hill, has been operating this office for the past few years illegally, without a septic tank connected to the toilet!" I had never met William Hill, but had trouble believing that any modern vineyard developer could be that sleazy. "James, are you telling me that he built this building and installed the toilet inside, but the outside sewage pipe from the toilet fixture just stops at ground level without connecting to - - anything?" "That is exactly what he did," he answered. "Well, James, here's your first assignment: Get on the phone and get a septic tank installer here – tomorrow, if possible – and get a standard size septic tank installed outside and connected to this toilet fixture. Don't wait another minute, and, by all means, report what we discovered to the Napa County authorities. I want to be sure they watch William Hill carefully in case he does any more construction in Napa County."

Next, I called Glenn Salva in Gonzales to offer him the job of vineyard manager. I had hired Glenn away from the Taylor Wine Company in New York to become vineyard relations manager for the Monterey Vineyard after the purchase of those wineries by Coca-Cola. Now that the Gonzales facilities were being mismanaged so badly, I knew Glenn would be looking for a new job. More importantly, Glenn was a first-rate vineyard manager, and I needed him in Napa County. After Glenn arrived, we began studying the various vineyard blocks in order to begin a logical vineyard layout for optimum use of the Foss Valley property.

Early on, James had discovered that the original vineyard manager had been unable to break through some of the volcanic rock formations that criss-crossed the surface of the property. The whole of Foss Valley was quite rocky, but that wasn't the only problem. Because the land was nearly flat, it was necessary to install large perforated plastic drain tubing several inches below ground level at intervals through each vineyard – and along the edges of each vineyard block. The drain tubing would channel excess rainfall away from the vine rows and into the main reservoir during heavy winter rains. Without proper drainage, heavy rainfall would sit in puddles until vine roots rotted, killing major groupings of grapevines.

Contrary to what Hill had told John Andersen, we found only small areas where the drain tubing had been installed correctly. In most locations, the tubing was actually lying on the surface or only partially buried. Later, when disc cultivators passed through, the discs cut through the drainage piping, destroying the drainage system. I asked "Why did they bother to partially bury the drain tubing in the first place, when the net result was the same as if no drainage had been installed at all?" John told me, "The answer is obvious: The owner was trying to sell the property, and needed to convince prospective buyers that vineyard drain tubing had been installed. It was left to the buyer to determine whether the installer had been competent. I am not surprised at what you found."

In other areas the veins of rock acted as dams, causing water to stand in elongated puddles along the veins where it was certain to kill grapevines by rotting the roots. In some places drain tubing had been installed only where the ground could be dug easily – up to the location of a volcanic rock vein. Then, when unable to continue the drain system past the rock vein, they had cut the drain tubing off and started the drain line again on the downhill side of the rock vein. Rain water would collect along every level of rock vein, later washing out whatever soft soil the water could find. It was a vineyard manager's nightmare, and Glenn and I agreed that we had to find a method to cut channels through those rock veins in many places. Only then could we turn this moonscape into a vineyard.

Glenn's first job was to make a layout of the property in order to identify spots where drainage was a serious problem. We had to abandon the sophomoric effort Hill's workers had attempted in what was sold to John Andersen as "a well-drained vineyard property, already more than 25% planted." I told Glenn that John may have been 100% correct in his belief that "if we want Napa Valley vineyard, we have to swallow hard and pay the going price; later, we will correct whatever difficulties we find on the property." My job, and soon to be Glenn's as well, was to erase those errors and give the Whitbread group the pristine and workable property they wanted.

To Drill or Not to Drill

Early in my evaluations, I noticed the Whitbread property included a hillside overlooking the vineyards that might be a perfect site for caves. It would be a huge plus, if the winery building could be constructed just outside the cave entrances, further reducing the building size by storing much of the wine inside caves instead of inside a building. Cave drilling was much less expensive than building construction, but that was only part of the picture: No heating or air conditioning would be necessary for whatever caves we might dig, as earth caves tend to hold a stable temperature year round. The exact temperature inside a cave is close to the average outside air temperature at that location for a complete year. In most caves of Napa Valley, the natural temperature is between about 57°F and 61°F – perfect for storage of table wine, whether in tanks, barrels or bottles. Since Foss Valley was located 1,400 feet above Napa's valley floor, the temperature in our caves would be as much as five degrees cooler than caves near sea level in Napa. That was perfect from our 'wine aging' point of view.

The Whitbread reservoir construction required a consulting geological engineer to be on-site periodically, and I asked him to determine whether the geology of the hill would allow a cave to be located in the hillside. His preliminary study indicated that caves would be easy to dig; his only unknown was whether the interior of the hill would require concrete support material (shotcrete) to support the cave walls and ceilings. He told me the only way to answer that would be to start drilling the cave and let him inspect the rock structure on a continuous basis, as there was no way to know what was underground except to "dig and inspect." I called my brother-in-law, Gene Miller (Miller the Driller) in Iowa, as he had been drilling and installing underground pipelines, culverts and conduits for nearly four decades all over the country. On many occasions, Gene had installed concrete piping and conduit as large as six or eight feet in diameter under railroads and busy highways without disturbing whatever was going on above him. There was no doubt in my mind; I knew Miller the Driller would be the expert of choice to do this drilling job.

When I made the proposal to Whitbread North America, they agreed, but I was forbidden to make any direct deal with Miller the Driller for fear of a conflict of interest. John insisted that James Barnes do all the negotiating with Gene, and I had to keep quiet altogether. James, a former banker, thought his job was to strip all of Miller the Driller's operating profit out of the deal, something no contractor could accept. Every time Gene gave in on one negotiation, James came up with another demand. Finally, after several days, Gene threw up his hands and told James he would not become an 'unpaid employee' of Whitbread for the duration of that or any other job. He would operate his jobs as a separate contractor or he would not take the job at all. No matter how much I wanted Gene to do the job, it was impossible to reach an agreement between James Barnes and Miller the Driller. I would either have to get rid of James (who had the backing of my bosses) or not use Miller the Driller to do the job, and I knew the answer. I learned a hard and unpleasant lesson from that experience: We could not use Gene, the right man for the job – not because of any real conflict of interest, but because it was possible for someone in the company (whether in England, France, Italy or New York) to perceive a conflict of interest. It was no one's fault, just an ordinary no-win situation that all of us had to eschew.

Alf Burtleson was the only experienced cave drilling contractor operating in Napa Valley at that time, and he was busy. Whitbread would have to wait in line and pay whatever price Alf asked; his best current asking price was $60 per square foot of cave space, and that price would certainly increase by the time our turn came around on Alf's waiting list. Several others were trying to enter the business to compete with Alf, but none had any experience and I couldn't trust them. Gene Miller told me he would quietly find the right drilling machine deal for me and that I should consider drilling the caves with our own employees. He searched several of his business catalogues, made a few phone calls, and told me that the best deal I could make would be to buy a used 'Dosco' drilling machine that was just completing a mining job in New Mexico. The cost would be $250,000, and it might be possible that we could sell the Dosco machine for a decent price after using it. John Andersen accepted my belief that we could do it. (Why not? He knew Gene Miller would quietly give me whatever advice I needed as the job progressed.) On Gene's advice, I told John that I expected to do the cave drilling job for half of Alf Burtleson's price, and received his approval.

To convince me that we could do this, the Dosco Company arranged for my visiting a deep underground coal mine in England, located near the Nottingham Forest of Robin Hood fame. Watching the machine work was impressive, and I sensed immediately that we could drill our own caves in Napa with little effort – Dosco made it look so easy. The seams of coal near Nottingham are several times thicker than those in Iowa, giving the large Dosco machine a generous twelve feet of head space in which to operate. No one in England believed my story that Pop had worked on his hands and knees in the shallow coal mines of Iowa during the Depression in America. Many times on that trip I caught myself wishing for a single miracle: I wished that Pop could somehow come back to life and watch that Dosco harvesting coal out of its resting place. I no longer had any doubts that we could dig through the rock of Napa Valley just as easily as they were digging coal a thousand feet under England.

When we purchased the used Dosco machine in New Mexico, the seller agreed to send an experienced operator, who would drill our caves for three months and teach our operators how to run the machine. We agreed to pay his wages and expenses according to the scale they suggested. The only Dosco machine parts that were expected to wear out were the hardened alloy 'teeth' on the drilling head, and we could buy new teeth directly from Dosco as needed. It would also be possible to buy any other part for the machine, even though most other parts were not expected to wear out routinely. The machine we received was old, and I understood that they couldn't guarantee how long any single part would last, but I knew it was in Dosco's own interest to treat us fairly. They wanted us to be successful, as they could see many winery opportunities in Napa Valley for cave drilling in future years. There was something about making the handshake deal with Dosco that reminded me of dealing with Paul Toeppen, Al Killeen or any Iowa farmer. To this day I consider it one of life's great pleasures to work with people whose word is good – and Dosco's word was good.

Bargain of the Century

The Dosco operator's first job was to teach me and two of our men, Jim Crowley and Richard Fike, how to operate the Dosco. Jim overheard us talking about volcanic rock throughout the vineyard, and interjected that he had lots of experience with dynamite, clearing road obstructions on highway projects. He answered my next question before I finished asking it, "Hell yes, I can do it. I've spent most of my life shooting rock." I turned immediately to Richard (Dosco operator #2) and promoted him to temporary Dosco operator #1 for a few months, as I suddenly had a more pressing job for Jim – using dynamite to correct our surface drainage problem.

Jim filed the necessary forms for buying and using dynamite. I was surprised that so few permits were necessary, but Jim was well known to the county people as a reliable blaster, and whatever permits we needed were quickly issued. In the next three years of using dynamite intermittently on our property, I never received a single complaint from neighbors about either noise or safety. Later, I estimated that Jim Crowley had single handedly created nearly fifty acres of new vineyard land that we could not have planted without fracturing and removing those strips of rock from the surface. After each dynamite sequence, our vineyard crewmen drove through the area on a tractor, dragging our 'rock rake' to pick up loose rocks (some as large as two feet in diameter).We stored them in random piles for later use in filling road gulleys, or building rock walls where we decided to 'hide the rock out in the open.'

The Dosco was the meanest looking machine we had ever seen; creatures looking like Dosco relatives decapitated each other in sci-fi movies. Hanging from the heavy Caterpillar frame were three protrusions in front and one in back. The main boom protruded about twelve feet in front, ending in a twenty-inch diameter ball with more than two dozen hardened metal 'teeth' pointing outwards from the ball at odd angles. The ball would spin slowly, allowing its teeth to chew away at whatever it touched, as the driver inched the whole machine forward. As the boom pushed into a hillside, the teeth ripped bits and chunks of rock and dirt away, to fall on the ground in front of the machine. Two matching star wheels at ground level channeled loose rock and spoils onto a steel conveyor running along Dosco's keel all the way back – angling upwards behind the machine. The conveyor dropped spoils into a loader truck behind the Dosco; the truck driver hesitated under the boom until his bin was full of spoil, then drove away to dump his load while another truck took its place collecting refuse. The Dosco caterpillar tracks along each side were almost hidden from view by the heavy metal pieces of the drilling machine.

Operating the Dosco was reminiscent of instrument flying. The driver moved the machine forward slowly, guided only by a single red laser dot projected onto the wall ahead by a surveyor's instrument. He inched forward, turning the Dosco left or right to keep the laser dot a foot below the cave top and directly in front, while swinging the rotating boom in an arc from the front to each side, cutting its way forward to create a beautiful 'half circle' cave 13 feet wide and 13 feet high at the center. With its flat floor, the resulting cave looked like you were inside the upper half of a giant rock tube. The cave was as beautiful as the Dosco was ugly.

Since the work was underground, Dosco used electricity from a diesel generator outside the cave. A large suction blower provided cave ventilation, pulling out dust and occasional smoke. Heavy cables conducted power to the Dosco, and we made everyone memorize safety rules for protecting employees, visitors, cables and equipment. Small trucks made steady trips back and forth to haul the crushed rock out, as the Dosco chewed its way forward, extending the tunnel. The operation went smoothly and we had no accidents in the two years we spent digging 40,000 square feet of cave. I worked a single weekend as the sole Dosco operator, digging a thirty foot long section of tunnel 'just to brag about.' The only thing I really had to brag about was the fact that neither of the regular operators ever razzed me about how sloppy my walls looked in comparison to theirs.

Nature sometimes averages out bad luck with good luck. We had horribly bad luck in finding volcanic rock throughout the vineyard, but the needle swung our way when we saw what the cave hillside was made of. Deeper into the hill, the geologist found boundaries on the walls, with different rock types that exposed the ancient history of that mountain. We saw evidence of two separate volcanic eruptions, eons apart, which piled rocks of all sizes among a matrix of clay and dirt to create the mountain. The rock and clay mixture had set up like concrete over time, becoming very strong, yet easy for the Dosco machine to grind its way through. The resulting 'spoils' mixture was easy to haul out of the cave, where it was spread to produce a level area on which to build the future winery. Our best luck was in finding that the cave walls and ceiling were naturally quite strong. We needed no shotcrete for support except at intersections where the 'straight in' caves met the 'cross caves' at acute angles. I designed the cave with four 'straight in' entrances (A, B, C and D), which were intersected by more than ten numbered 'cross caves.' Cross cave number 1 was located thirty feet in from the outside; each succeeding cross cave was located fifteen feet deeper than the previous cross cave. The final result looked on the drawings like an expanded tic-tac-toe pattern; the four alphabet caves intersected numerical cross caves at right angles. The geologist required keeping fifteen feet of undisturbed rock between the thirteen foot wide caves to produce a strong structure which would last as long as California. I had 'street signs' placed at each cave intersection so that anyone could easily find his way out. We installed light fixtures throughout, with three-way switches to allow anyone at either end to turn a section of lights on or off. As digging in each section was completed, the floor area was leveled and concrete was pumped in, one 13 foot square block at a time. Each of the straight-in caves was sloped slightly upwards into the hillside so that interior water seeping into the cave would automatically drain to the outside at the front. Eventually, the whole cave had lights, smooth concrete floors with rounded unfinished rock walls and ceilings.

As drilling progressed, we collected large amounts of loose rock and clay outside the caves. The geologist tested it and told me it would be ideal as a road base throughout the vineyard property. How lucky could we get? Glenn Salva made a plan for square roadways and avenues through the vineyard, and it was easy to build our own roads by using a Caterpillar to level and spread the material in nicely arranged roadways. It became compacted by driving cars and trucks over it when wet. We needed no budget for roadways, since we used the cave vehicles to build our roadways as we got rid of the cave spoils.

This will look like a misprint, but it is not: The total cost of creating the finished caves at Atlas Peak (including 5-inch thick concrete floors and lighting) was less than $20 per square foot of usable floor space. Subtract from that the potential cost of heating and air conditioning that would be saved (because neither would be needed inside caves), and it is clear that Whitbread got the bargain of the century in building most of the winery underground. At the time of completion in 1989, there were probably fewer than twelve caves in Napa County, even counting the very old hand-dug caves of Schramsberg, Beringer and others. Against the high cost of large winery buildings, it is no wonder that the era of digging wine caves in Napa Valley was just beginning. I don't know the number of wine caves in Napa County today, but it may exceed fifty.

Aside from caves, the most intelligent thing we did for Whitbread was the early decision to plant an experimental block containing one acre each of twenty-five or thirty different wine varieties. The climate of Atlas Peak was unknown to viticulturists; there were no existing vineyards within miles of the Whitbread project. No one could have known which grape varieties, if any, would excel on that land. If summers were often cold, Gewurztraminer and Rieslings should flourish; at the opposite extreme, if summers were very warm, then Cabernet or Zinfandel would be better bets. Vineyard development is expensive. Farmers can't afford to plant the wrong variety in a vineyard, since it costs four years and cash aplenty to graft the wrong variety over to a more suitable variety. My thought was to make laboratory amounts of wine from each of the possible thirty grape varieties we tested at Atlas Peak – that would tell us which ones would produce the best wines on the property. As soon as we learned which varieties would make the best wines, we could easily graft the losers over to winning varieties in that small experimental block without much expense. My goal was to have the entire 600 acres producing optimum amounts of the very best five or six grape varieties for the area within six years.

A Prince Arriveth

When the caves were about half finished, I returned from a trip one afternoon and was met by Glenn Salva, who told me a neighbor had driven in to see our progress. Glenn showed him what we were doing and the guy erupted into uncontrolled anger. He told Glenn he didn't want any winery near his property. He was a self-styled artist living in San Francisco with a weekend retreat in Napa Valley near the entrance to Atlas Peak Vineyards. He didn't want to look at a winery from his weekend cottage and had what seemed like unlimited wealth with which to fight anyone in the wine business. As arrogant and pompous as anyone I'd ever met, this guy was irate at the thought that somebody he didn't know had the nerve to build a winery within sight of his property. His name is not worth remembering, and it was natural for us to refer to him as 'the Prince.' It especially grated him to learn that the encroaching Whitbread people were foreigners. With puffed-out chest, he swaggered up to houses along upper Soda Canyon Road, organizing residents by telling them, "We have to stop these f---ing foreigners from destroying our lives, using up all our water, causing forest fires, poisoning our air, killing our pets and ruining all that we have here in Napa Valley!"

He was powerless to stop the cave construction, but intended to fight tooth and nail to stop Whitbread from building a winery of any size on its Foss Valley property. It made no difference that Whitbread already had a perfected building permit[2] and half-built caves, allowing us to greatly reduce the size of the approved winery project. He apparently didn't know whether Whitbread would have public events at the winery, since it didn't lessen his hatred to learn later that neither tours nor tastings were part of the project. Nor had the Prince discovered that we had been using dynamite mid-week to clear land obstructions. His was truly a weekend retreat, and he was never around when Jim Crowley was shooting rock between Mondays and Fridays. We had been careful to avoid blasting on weekends as a common courtesy to neighbors, and Glenn suggested facetiously that our good-neighbor policy may have backfired by saving the Prince from having a heart attack. We were surprised that the Prince had resorted to such great lengths in his war against Whitbread. Neighbors told us that Whitbread was accused of secretly planning all kinds of illegal events, holding loud parties and would quadruple the traffic on Soda Canyon Road.

I drove around the valley re-connecting with old friends in the wine industry and asked most of them the same question: "I've been away from Napa Valley for twelve years and am astonished to see some of the changes during my absence. What happened here?" When told about our project being attacked so viciously by the Prince, the common response was, "Well, Dick, welcome to today's Napa Valley." They confirmed that Napa Valley had taken on a much different and more selfish air than what I'd known a decade earlier. In the 1970s, Napa communities were either farm oriented (grapes, walnuts or cattle) or bedroom communities for workers in the greater San

---

[2] After a building permit is issued, the builder has a period of time (usually a year) in which to begin the work. After significant work has been done, the work is considered to be in progress 'perfected,' and the county can no longer rescind the permit. A permit could be rescinded under certain conditions prior to the permit becoming perfected.

Francisco Bay Area. The low-key farm community of the 1970s now had a business community existing alongside. Both communities stemmed from and supported wine, so random newcomers to Napa Valley were not to blame; most had arrived specifically to work in the greatly expanded wine industry. The yesterday I remembered was primarily farming and winemaking, with most wine promotion and sales taking place somewhere far away from Napa Valley. Legh Knowles, the Beaulieu sales manager, for example, worked in San Francisco in 1968, as did the sales and advertising teams of most other Napa Valley wineries. By 1986, the sales and other business functions of most wineries were physically located at the wineries.

Direct sales of wine to consumers were miniscule a few decades ago; suddenly, tasting room sales to winery visitors had become a big business. Tour guides were hired by the dozen in recent years by most wineries, but many of these new employees did not live in the valley. This unanticipated influx of winery employees had blossomed since the 1970s, which greatly increased highway traffic as well as the harsher attitude of county officials towards new wineries. It was relatively easy to get county approval for a new winery back in 1968. By 1986, there was a large and growing anti-winery sentiment among county employees, as well as county residents. Those not connected to grapes or wine, such as the Prince, had no reason to support the growth of new wineries in the valley. If anything, they tended to be anti-winery even if they drank and served wine at home. Those already connected to a winery wanted to keep other wineries out for purely competitive reasons. It was easy to see why the combination of both groups had generated big changes at the county level in Napa Valley.

Surprisingly, the Prince collected two dozen property owners to follow him into the Napa County courthouse and demand that Whitbread be stopped. He went to great lengths to convince county supervisors to vote against our request to relocate and redesign the approved winery. My defense for reducing our winery size was ignored by many, as two county supervisors surprisingly spoke out in favor of those with the loudest voices. It was obvious that legally, Whitbread could not be forced to relinquish its right to build a winery on the property, and it surprised me that two members of the planning commission and another two of the county supervisors actually voted against allowing Whitbread to move forward. The net result was only to increase the project cost to Whitbread, and it called attention to the fact that today's new wineries would have to fight absurd battles just to operate normally in the valley. I paid for a full-page "Letter to my fellow Napa citizens" as an advertisement in the *Napa Valley Register* explaining the Whitbread position. My letter gave the public and any supervisor who read it complete details about Whitbread's right to continue their goals in Napa County. I called attention to the half-truths and outright lies promulgated by the Prince, but it was by no means certain that our right would prevail in the vote of the county supervisors. We might have to go to court to prove to a judge and jury what was clearly a restatement of the law.

In the end, Supervisor Mel Varrelman stood out as a thoughtful voice of common sense in casting the winning vote in favor of Whitbread. His short speech was superb, but I never thought the two dissenting supervisors heard what he was trying to tell them. They knew Whitbread was correct in the eyes of the law; nevertheless, they voted against the law and in favor of the Prince! The only explanation I received from onlookers was that the dissenting supervisors thought they stood a better chance for re-election in a few months if they appeared to support 'the people,' which is to say they voted with the loudest voices in the crowd instead of considering the question at hand. Neither was re-elected in the ensuing election, and I don't mind admitting that I donated considerable sums of money to support the candidacies of the two new supervisors who defeated them. I never liked it, but that is politics in the U.S.

Whitbread Stirs, Then Rolls Over

John Andersen asked me to produce a line of new varietal wines for sale by the marketing arm of Whitbread under the J. Wile brand. I worked with a new winemaker, Jeff Runquist, who was making wines in the old Napa Valley Co-Op Winery on Highway 29 south of St Helena. I knew those premises well – it was the ancient winery facility that had been making wines for Gallo during the time I was employed there, twenty years earlier. Jeff's wines were superb given the price restrictions we had, and the bottled wines were shipped to Buckingham Wile in New York.

Illustrating the astonishing speed of positive changes in Napa Valley, both Jeff Runquist and the Napa Valley Co-Op Winery made huge advancements in the following decade. Jeff now produces some of the finest quality wines in all of California under his own label, Jeff Runquist. He is a good bet to produce sweepstakes winners in at least one competition nearly every year; I know of no other active winemaker with that award record. The Napa Valley Co-Op Winery was later purchased by Ambassador Hall, who completely revamped the property; the Hall Winery is now one of the prominent, if glitzy, 'destination wineries' for tourists along Highway 29.

Surprisingly, we were not asked to continue producing the J. Wile line of Napa Valley varietal wines. John Andersen liked the wines, but told me he was disappointed in his marketing organization and expected to reorganize the Buckingham Wile marketing division. That sounded ominously identical to the problem encountered by wineries in many states in 1975. Without sales, no winery can survive. Yet many new wineries had sprung up all over America in the apparent belief that all they had to do was build a winery and ferment grapes. If they did that, the world of wine drinkers would automatically beat a path to their door. Of course, that rarely happened. As new wineries learned the awful truth, namely that they would have to work harder selling their wine than they ever had in making it, they quickly shifted into 'sales mode.' Most hired new sales people and started consumer wine clubs to promote and plan winery sales events. Wineries entered wines into competitions hoping to win medals that would increase consumer demand.

Promotional wine activity happened in Napa as much as anywhere else, and the combined effect increased highway traffic even more throughout Napa Valley. Traffic was the most obvious change I noticed when my wife, Sandra, and I moved back to the area from Monterey in 1986. The 'sleepy hollow' appeal of the valley in 1970 had become a loud and boisterous "Rah, Rah, Rah – Sis Boom Bah – Buy Our Wine – Yah, Yah, Yah!" Napa residents openly complained about the "Disneyland atmosphere" and rolled their eyes to underscore the lament, but were powerless to stop it.

Whitbread delivered a surprise that was equally devastating. Shortly after

John Andersen announced staff reductions at Buckingham Wile, he abruptly resigned as chairman of Whitbread North America. The parent company notified me that I was the new chairman over my astonishment and objections. I knew nothing about reorganizing a wine sales company and had no intention of moving away from Napa Valley. I was a winemaker, and my value to the company was as such, not as a business manager. I probably sounded like a broken record as I insisted that Whitbread would need to hire someone with solid experience in marketing and selling wine. I saw a long and promising future for the Atlas Peak label if they did that, but couldn't offer any speculation if they did not. Inside, my stomach was churning. I had no way of guessing what must have taken place in New York or London while I was fighting the Prince and busy developing Napa's newest vineyard estate.

My primary contact had become Martin Findlay of Whitbread in London, and he and I were regularly on the phone or in face-to-face meetings after the sudden departure of Andersen. Martin was very personable and quite convincing; he openly spoke for the Whitbread company on every question. His answer to my arguments against their attempts to turn me into a wine marketer was an even greater shock: "You need not worry any longer about marketing Atlas Peak wines. Whitbread has decided to sell their interest in the wine and spirits businesses to another English company, Allied-Lyons. Allied is well-experienced in selling both wine and spirits. They will expand their marketing of wine and spirits, while Whitbread will restrict its business to beer and ale alone." He didn't know whether Antinori or Bollinger would accept Allied-Lyons as a partner, but he hoped I would help convince them if possible. "Martin, you're just full of surprises," I told him. I didn't know that he wasn't yet finished and the biggest surprise was still to come.

A day or two later, Martin told me that it would be a serious impediment to Whitbread if I did not agree to a modification of my employment contract. The ten year length of employment would not change, and I could certainly continue my plans not to retire until age sixty-five or later. The problem was simply that Allied-Lyons was uncomfortable with me (or any other individual) owning 2% of their wine company. I believe he said, "If they were buying a company, they would buy all of it and not just 98%." I asked, "Are you telling me that Allied-Lyons doesn't have partnership investments in companies, and everything is owned outright?" "Well, sure, they have partnerships," he answered, "but those are partnerships with other companies, not with individuals. They don't want partnerships with individuals because those partnerships become difficult to handle over time as shares transfer between family members. You understand, I'm sure." Martin told me his job was to facilitate the sale for Whitbread by convincing me to accept payment in cash for the value of the 2% ownership instead of company stock – at whatever time I decided to retire.

I could see the point that individual partners might be difficult for corporations to handle, and told Martin I would help Whitbread as long as it did not affect my plan to work until age sixty-five. He assured me repeatedly that Whitbread's intentions were in complete alignment with my own. I told him I had no personal attorney to represent me, and he answered that the company would take care of all those details. My hiring an attorney would turn this simple amendment into something complex and difficult to understand. He assured me this would not be a negotiation between two adversaries, but a modest change in an employment agreement between an employee and the employer. He asked, "Did you hire an attorney when John Andersen wrote your original employment agreement?" "Certainly not," I answered. "It was simple and straightforward." Whitbread and I had enjoyed an excellent working relationship since my employment began four years ago, and I agreed that it should continue as such.

I began receiving copies of changes to the contract from the Whitbread attorney and noticed that quite a bit of the text had been edited. I told Martin the contract should simply refer to the minor change we agreed to, and he took it back to the attorney. The contract came back written with further legalese that didn't seem necessary, and again I returned it. This was taking much more time than we had anticipated, and Martin continued to tell me that the Whitbread attorneys wrote contracts a little differently than Americans do, but that the verbal agreement between us was what counted. He reiterated that our agreement was unchanged, but that all Whitbread contracts had to adhere to standard language that was the same for all employees. I continued withholding my signature, and he was beginning to get more aggressive in his pleas for it. Martin was my boss and his promises had always been sound, but it bothered me that the attorney's text didn't read precisely the way Martin and I had agreed. I didn't know the exact relationship between Whitbread and Allied-Lyons; sometimes it seemed that Martin Findlay was working for Allied-Lyons as well as for Whitbread, and that added to my growing discomfort.

Finally the attorney wrote that if I were to leave within the first five years of employment, the company would pay me a specified amount (about 1% of the value of the stock), and the full 2% if I remained a company employee for the full ten years, which was what I had agreed to with Andersen. The only part I was uncomfortable with was all the boiler plate legalese that Martin said I had to accept. It appeared to say that the company could fire any employee at any time, without cause, which definitely had not been my agreement with either Andersen or Findlay. Martin told me over and over again that I was a highly valued employee and there was no way that the company intended to fire me. He even said, "Look, Dick, you have my personal guarantee that what I'm telling you is true. You will stay employed at Atlas Peak as long as you continue the impressive work you've been doing, regardless of the wording of the Whitbread contract."

It was a direct challenge: Did I believe him or not? How could I continue my good working relationship, and tell my boss that I didn't believe him at the same time? Finally, I told him that I trusted his word and signed the agreement. It had taken several months and Martin made it clear that my foot dragging had held up the transaction between Whitbread and Allied-Lyons. I was uneasy with what had transpired, but didn't know what else to do except to trust the word of my employer. Neither Piero Antinori nor Christian Bizot, Whitbread's partners in the Atlas Peak joint venture, were involved in my contract with Whitbread and neither had made a decision whether they would remain with Allied-Lyons as far as I could determine. In the end, whether they would stay depended on Allied-Lyons' intentions with marketing, and none of us really knew what to expect.

Very Good Advice

My first communication with Allied-Lyons came while I was attending a seminar on wine chemistry at UC Davis. John Murphy, VP of production, showed up unannounced at the Atlas Peak vineyard, apparently expecting me to be there to give him a personal tour of the premises. He hadn't felt it necessary to contact me ahead of his visit, which surprised everyone on the property. Next, I received a call from a man I remembered at Gallo thirty years earlier, Terry Clancy. Terry had been in sales at Gallo, but we didn't work directly together since he had no involvement in new products. He was pleasant, but all of us thought of him as something of a free spirit; he left Gallo abruptly to spend time in the Peace Corps working on a South Seas island with the stated goal of 'modernizing primitive cultures.' Some years later he turned up selling Paul Masson wine for Seagram, then Callaway Winery in southern California. Callaway was later purchased by Hiram Walker, a liquor company looking for an entry into the wine business. When Hiram Walker was acquired by Allied-Lyons, they appointed Clancy to head their wine interests. I never figured out why, but then I knew nothing about selling spirits; presumably Terry was good at that. He visited me at Atlas Peak about a month after the transfer from Whitbread to Allied-Lyons. Atlas Peak was being placed under Clos du Bois (also owned by Hiram Walker), which made Terry Clancy my immediate supervisor.

Since I hadn't seen him in twenty years, I didn't know what to expect, but was looking forward to renewing our old acquaintanceship. I had sent him copies of the weekly and monthly photo reports that I had been addressing to John Andersen from the beginning. It had been an effective way to keep John (and Whitbread) up to date on our progress in vineyard development, and I thought it would bring Terry up to speed. On his arrival, Terry returned all my reports with faint praise, saying simply, "Very nice." I asked whether he had questions about our progress and he simply said, "Not at this time." He seemed remarkably unimpressed with the property and made it clear that Allied-Lyons would rather be in the "beverage alcohol sales" business than in grape and wine production. "Buying low and selling high, that's what we're about. We don't like investments in large vineyards and wineries," he said. It shocked me to be reminded so brusquely of the spirits mentality that I first heard from Heublein, which couldn't wait to shed itself of the vineyards owned by Beaulieu back in 1969. By the end of our meeting, I was absolutely certain that Terry Clancy thought we had wasted our time developing all those varietal vineyards – when Thompson Seedless would have done just fine. If I was correct, he hadn't paid attention during his time at Gallo, which might explain why he left for the Peace Corps. My next thought was, "Well, maybe I'm wrong. He might surprise us. Maybe he understands fine wine after all. I should give him a chance."

I didn't hear from Terry again for another month, but Martin Findlay had been calling me with an upbeat voice, hoping I was enjoying working with the Allied-Lyons people. I told him we hadn't had much contact as yet, and Martin thought they were probably in an adjustment phase for the time being. I told him that I had prepared the first two vintages of several wines from Cabernet, Sangiovese and Chardonnay grapes grown on Atlas Peak property and expected to bottle them as soon as we had direction from the Allied-Lyons sales people. We agreed to stay in contact, as Whitbread would remain in close communication with Allied. I tried not to let it show, but I was becoming apprehensive because of the lack of communication with our new owners. Then a secretary called and asked me to meet with 'Mr. Clancy' at a local motel in Yountville the next morning.

I walked in five minutes early and sat down, as Terry Clancy was already seated with Jon Moramarco Jr., his assistant manager. Terry seemed cold and unfriendly. In a curt voice he said simply, "We are buying out your Whitbread contract. In accordance with the contract, we will send you a check; we expect you to collect your personal effects and leave the premises immediately." I was being fired without cause! I said that I had a contract for ten years of employment as long as the company was satisfied with my work, which I knew they were. Terry's voice took on a belligerent tone, as if we were mortal enemies, "See a lawyer." I started to walk out, then turned back and asked, "Can you give me a reason for doing this?" Terry answered immediately. "Yes, we've studied your chairman's plan, which we don't like, and we have decided not to market any Atlas Peak wines. Since we won't make or bottle any wines, we don't need a winemaker, so you're out of a job." I turned and walked out, thinking to myself, "This son of a bitch has given me some very good advice, which I intend to follow."

Glenn Salva remained as Atlas Peak vineyard manager and told me that Clancy had ordered him to pull out all the experimental one-acre blocks of varietal grapes. Clancy was putting an end to what he called my 'tinkering' with other varieties, having decided to plant a full one-third of the property to Cabernet Sauvignon, another third to Chardonnay and a final third to Sangiovese. Those were the three varieties of wine that he liked and wanted to sell, so those were his orders to Glenn. By that time, Glenn had already realized that the area was probably too cold in summer to fully ripen Sangiovese and, possibly, Cabernet Sauvignon, although Chardonnay would undoubtedly produce high-quality fruit. I told Glenn, "One correct guess out of three." It was a repeat of Tom Stratton's error at Monterey, where they planted the varieties the investors liked to drink rather than grapes that would ripen properly and produce the best wines in the climate at hand. Over the next few weeks, I learned that Whitbread's French partner Bollinger had decided not to remain with Allied-Lyons, but the Italian partner Antinori had a 'wait and see' attitude. Depending on how successful Allied would be with Atlas Peak wines, he would make a decision later.

Following Clancy's 'advice,' I did some research on legal firms that were experienced in the type of lawsuit I needed to file, and finally selected Berliner, Cohen & Biagini in San Jose. Sam Cohen, general partner, had won a comparable 'theft and fraud' case for a friend of mine who had been a pilot with me in the California Army National Guard. He introduced me to Chris Scott Graham, a litigator who turned out to be the perfect choice. My wife, Sandra, first spotted his primary virtues. Chris recognized that a good litigator has to be a good teacher. His job is to explain fine details to judges and juries in a clear, effective and unemotional way. Sandra's background as a teacher made her an excellent judge of Chris as a litigator, and her intuition was right on. Neither Antinori nor Bollinger was involved in my lawsuit, as neither was part of the Whitbread sale to Allied-Lyons.

To make a long story short, the case went to trial in March 1992, and Chris won the case for me, hands down. The jury of twelve was unanimous in my favor, listing four counts of intentional fraud, negligent misrepresentation, intentional and willful violation of the labor code and breach of my contract. It was a high point during the trial that our daughter, Holly, had found case amounts of bottled Atlas Peak wines for sale in various wine shops. She bought several cases of the wine for me, and we presented one in court as evidence of Terry Clancy's double dealing. He had told me that I was out of a job because Allied-Lyons would not make or sell any Atlas Peak wine, and therefore had no use for a winemaker. Chris pointed out to the jury that, contrary to Clancy's statements, the wine was not only bottled, but Terrence Clancy's name and signature appeared on the back labels of the bottles – as if he had been the winemaker for that wine.

The jury awarded me generous damages for each of the findings and added extra money for punitive damages due to Allied-Lyons' easily proven fraud. I think they knew I did not sue for the money; rather, I wanted the job of turning the Atlas Peak property into a superb vineyard that would produce wines to make the owner proud. Although the Allied-Lyons' attorneys screamed that I would never collect a dime because they would appeal forever, they called my attorney within two weeks to offer a large cash settlement. Even though I told them I would rather have the job than the money, Allied-Lyons had no interest in my returning to work. So, back to the negotiating table we went, only this time I wasn't so nice. I thought they needed to pay a significant sum; otherwise, they would not have learned from the lawsuit. The attorneys drew up an agreement, which I signed, they sent me checks totaling the agreed settlement, and the case was closed.

That is, it was closed, except for one thing: a primary clause in the agreement stated that the details and amount of the settlement were sworn to secrecy by both parties and neither one was allowed to make the settlement details public. I was not surprised to read in the paper the very next day that the ink was hardly dry from my signature when my old friend, Terry Clancy, had gone directly to the *Napa Valley Register* and made all the details public. The amounts Allied-Lyons had to pay appeared on page one under newspaper headlines, not in fine print on some obscure back page. I never figured out why he did that; it certainly didn't make him or anyone at Allied-Lyons look good. I just never understood the guy.

No active manager from Whitbread or Allied-Lyons had shown up to testify at the trial. Clancy claimed that he wasn't healthy enough to testify. Only Jon Moramarco Jr. was left to speak for Allied-Lyons, but he didn't know the reasons for some of their actions and certainly wasn't one of the guilty parties. Jon's testimony was polished, professional and honest. I continue to appreciate his high standards, and we exchanged cordial greetings every time we met in later years. I never learned whether Martin Findlay had lied to me on his own or was used shamelessly by Allied-Lyons/Whitbread. It doesn't seem important to know; he never returned my phone calls after I left him a message that I had been fired. I never knew why Allied had purchased Atlas Peak from Whitbread in the first place, since they apparently had no plan for it at the time of the deal. Mike Fitzsimons, a close friend of John Andersen, told me later that Allied had wanted "only one of the Whitbread spirits businesses: Beefeaters Gin." He said that the Beefeaters brand alone was worth all the money Allied paid to Whitbread, and the Atlas Peak property was simply 'thrown into the deal.' Knowing how profitable some spirits brands are, it's possible that Mike was correct.

Robert Mondavi testified on my behalf and did a wonderful job on the stand. Jurors told me after the trial that they were very impressed that Bob had taken the time to come and tell them about my background, experience and value to the industry. Of course, it was only one man's opinion, but I couldn't have asked for a better man's opinion. Chris Scott Graham was promoted to partner in his firm; he and his assistants, Gayle Mozee and Ross Kay, richly deserved the high praise they received from fellow attorneys for winning what was believed to be one of the highest awards in a jury trial to date in Napa County.

After two or three years Atlas Peak wines disappeared from wine store shelves, and I never saw evidence that Allied continued to use the label afterwards. Piero Antinori completed his purchase of the vineyard and built a small winery in front of the caves and a personal residence on the property. I am certain that it didn't take Piero long to determine which varieties belonged, and which did not, in his vineyard; I'm equally certain that the property has become very valuable under his tutelage. I continue to count Piero among my best professional friends, along with Glenn Salva.

Unexpected Mini 'Career'

During the four years I was employed at Atlas Peak I had periodically turned down requests from various Napa winery owners to consult for them. However, now that the trial was over and *Napa Valley Register* headlines had let my friends know I was out of a job, I had no reason to be idle. First, I agreed to help Al Brounstein find a new winemaker for Diamond Creek Winery near Calistoga. Jerry Luper was Al's winemaker, but Jerry had decided to move to Portugal to continue his winemaking career overseas. Jerry knew that I had made the Lancers Vinho Branco wine there decades earlier, and I told him that I would be jealous if I were twenty years younger, because Portugal is such a beautiful and fun country. I first met Jerry at Gallo where he was a young lab technician doing wine analyses. He was always personable and smart, and I was glad to see how well he had developed as a winemaker. Jerry was particularly well suited to the job. All the best winemakers I have known have had some common personality traits: Each was meticulous in 'getting it right' before any wine was bottled. Each was a good taster, and each understood the chemistry of what he/she was tasting. None of them took shortcuts and none had anything 'better to do' when it came time to prepare a wine for bottling. Each one gave the wine careful cellar treatment until it was pronounced "ready" for bottling.

I tasted Diamond Creek wines with Jerry over the next several months and was impressed with all of them. I was partial to Red Rock Terrace, but some vintages of Volcanic Hill were also superb, and I could see why Jerry often preferred them. Gravelly Meadow was my third choice in many tastings, but it, too, had a large following. Al Brounstein knew time was running short, and finally hired Phil Steinschreiber as winemaker. It was a fortunate choice, indeed. Phil got to spend significant time with Jerry, and when Jerry went on to Portugal, all of us thought that Phil picked up the job beautifully. The Diamond Creek wines continued receiving top awards and, to his credit, Phil was always up to the job. He never failed to get the highest quality out of each vintage, which is all you can ask of any wine-maker.

Fred Franzia called and wanted to discuss a current problem involving the Bronco Winery in Ceres. I had known Fred as one of the most competent leaders in the wine industry since my days at Gallo. Bronco had been a primary source of bulk wine for us during those heady days of exploding Taylor California Cellars wine sales under Coca-Cola in Monterey. We bought many hundreds of thousands of gallons of table wines from Fred over a five-year period between 1978 and 1983. The thing that stood out about him was that, in all that time, I never had a deal go bad. His word was good, and the wines we received always matched the pre-sale samples exactly. His prices were reasonable, and the wine quality was fully as high as I expected. I felt secure when Fred promised to ship a specific wine from a specific tank; dealing with other wineries was sometimes iffy, and more than once we chose Bronco over other suppliers because I could always rely on Fred. Oddly, we heard derogatory rumors about Fred from other wine people here and there. The rumors didn't jibe with our favorable Bronco experience, and we wrote them off merely as a 'Jealous of Fred Franzia Club' somewhere in the industry. He never sugar-coated anything, and just said what he thought at the moment. Sometimes what he said may have sounded overly aggressive, since he didn't mind using the f-word as a routine adjective regardless of who was present. In my experience, Fred's fairness and great sense of humor overrode any misunderstandings, and I thought those club members were snubbing a perfectly good friendship.

Now, Fred wanted to hire me as an outsider to inspect his Bronco Winery whenever I chose, looking for anything that appeared to be suspicious or incorrect. Bronco had been accused of mismarking some grape loads during the harvest season the previous year and, in the legal settlement, Fred offered to hire a suitable expert to keep a close watch on operations at the winery over the next five years. He asked me to meet with the judge and assistants at the court in Stockton; after our discussions, the court was satisfied that I was qualified to inspect the winery operations and would be objective in my evaluations. I was to spend as much time as needed at the winery looking at anything and everything. Whatever I found was to be reported to the Stockton court, copying Fred. In effect, I was hired by Bronco to more or less become 'Big Brother,' watching to see whether Bronco was operating as a good citizen within the wine industry.

Since I lived more than two hours away in Napa Valley, my visits were at weekly intervals, but not on the same day each week. I made periodic reports to the court after setting up a committee that covered all the important sections of the winery. The other four members of the committee were employed by Bronco: Rick Irwin in the vineyards, Warren Stefl in government compliance, Jim Rodrigues in the cellar and Ed Moody in winemaking. At our meetings, we discussed the operations that had taken place since my previous visit and winemaking plans for the following week. I spent considerable time during the first months with Jim Rodrigues and Ed Moody, who showed me every detail of the equipment and machinery in the cellar. I enjoyed the job; it was fun to snoop around someone else's winery and question workers if I didn't understand what they were doing.

My overall impressions of Bronco were quite positive, and I was sometimes amazed to see the degree of modernization, with significant improvements over everyone else in the industry. "My God," I thought. "These guys are doing things better than Gallo." That was a blockbuster revelation, because Gallo had always been the absolute leader of the industry, in my personal view, between 1956 and about 1975. The rigid Bronco cellar routine was under positive control, from both safety and sanitation standpoints. It was clear to me that this large winery was operating efficiently, with constant reminders to the workers that they were handling table wine, a product intended for human consumption. I was impressed, and it was easy to understand why I had found Bronco to be such a reliable supplier back in the late 1970s and early 1980s when I had used their wines in blends for Taylor California Cellars. After the five-year period expired, Fred asked me to continue inspecting Bronco winery operations as before, reporting to John, Joseph or himself whenever I felt there might be something incorrect or not in accordance with regulations. I continue to be impressed with their attitude of "We have nothing to hide on these premises."

An outstanding example of understated excellence happened right in front of my eyes: Charles Shaw 2005 Chardonnay won "Best Chardonnay of California" at the 2008 California State Fair Wine Competition. To competing winemakers, this was absolutely unthinkable. The problem was that Charles Shaw Chardonnay sold at a retail price of only $25 – *not $25 per bottle, rather $25 per case of twelve bottles!* That's barely above $2 per 750, and Charles Shaw was lovingly (and derogatorily) referred to as "Two-Buck Chuck." How could that happen given that the tastings were done blind by experienced and competent wine judges? G.M. Pucilowski (Pooch) had been head judge at the State Fair wine judging for decades. He felt an obligation to check records to see whether the judging had been fair and square. After investigating thoroughly, he found it was true; the judges were fully competent, and the win by Charles Shaw was 100% above board.

Within days, I bought a case of Charles Shaw Chardonnay from the Trader Joe's store in Napa. In comparison with other wines, I found the Shaw to be quite nice, and was not surprised that it had won. I gave out bottles to other winemakers when I heard them speak derisively about the Charles Shaw win. About half complained about the judges, while the other half claimed that Bronco, the producer of Charles Shaw, "must have made a special batch specifically to enter and win the competition." The implication was that a special batch would be far superior to the ordinary 'run of the mill' Shaw. I explained just how impossible a job that would be, and asked them, as winemakers, whether they could make a special wine that they knew would win the State Fair, or any other competition. Even though all agreed it would be unlikely, the mumbling and vocal criticisms of Fred Franzia continued for weeks. I asked them to compare the Charles Shaw in blind tastings with other Chardonnays and to let me know later what they thought. I neither believed nor expected Charles Shaw to be acclaimed as 'the best Chardonnay ever produced in the world' – however, I was disappointed that not a single one called me to report that the Charles Shaw I had given them was a good bottle of wine, and well worth the money.

Why did the higher-priced Chardonnays lose out at the State Fair Competition? I believe I know the answer, which might surprise some readers. Most losing entries in the Chardonnay competition had what individual judges considered to be 'obvious minor faults.' One wine was beautiful except that it was too oaky; another had too much of the characteristic called 'sur lie' flavor; [3] yet another had been a great wine at one time, but was getting old and tasted 'tired' and less interesting than others. A large number of high-priced Chardonnays had too much alcohol for easy drinkability; some were as high as 15%, enough to ruin virtually any white table wine. Another had too much color, indicating a problem with the barrel aging procedure. Right down the line, each of the high-priced Chardonnay entries had one characteristic or another that 'stuck out' and took away from that wine's score. The Charles Shaw wine, on the other hand, was perfectly balanced. It did not have the single best sur lie character, nor did it have the best degree of oakiness or even the best Chardonnay flavor of all the other wines. But it did have a pleasant sur lie, a pleasant oak barrel age, and a nice and complex varietal flavor combined with an alcohol delicacy that complemented the other attributes. More importantly, all the virtues were married together into a well-balanced and perfectly enjoyable Chardonnay dinner wine. Nothing stood out for any judge to dislike; there was simply nothing for them to criticize. The wine with no criticisms won the judging, and I have often found that to be true in the hundreds of professional competitions I've done around the world over many years.

Wine judges notice excessive 'hotness' of alcohol in some highly touted and expensive wines entered into competitions. The winemaker obviously thought that if his wine had some feature that was more prominent than others, it would win the taste competition. Some inexperienced judges vote that way, but experienced judges do not. Knowledgeable judges look for and appreciate exquisite balance and class in a wine. Is there a flaw in the American character that makes people think 'bigger, stronger and more obnoxious' is better than softer, smoother and more elegantly refined?

---

[3] Sur lie flavor arises when winemakers leave Chardonnay wine sitting on its yeast lees in tanks or barrels for an extended period of time. Periodic stirring enhances yeast autolysis and flavor extraction. This adds a buttery, popcorn or sherry-like flavor to the wine, which is highly prized in many Chardonnays. However, if sur lie is too strong, the wine might be thought of as 'over the hill.' Sur lie is usually not done with red wines.

I have also found that low to medium priced wines win top awards over some high priced wines surprisingly often. When that happens, I usually can smell or taste some odd character sticking out in the pricey, but imperfect wine. Some consumers love the feature that sticks out, but most judges recognize it as an imperfection when it overwhelms other nice features. Truly superb highly priced wines are every bit as good as the customer expects and, in the end, it is the consumer's own taste that should make the decision. The astute taster does not automatically accept what someone else writes or says about the quality of a given wine. The consumer should trust his or her own taste without caring what a paid writer might say. If John and Mary Smith liked a certain wine on a certain day with a certain meal, that wine was their perfect choice. At another meal on another day, they might choose a different wine, which they may or may not think was more memorable than the previous wine. That's the fun of enjoying fine table wines with meals. Perfectly grown and made wines are magnificent choices, well worth their higher prices. However, it is also true that some lower-priced wines are shockingly great values.

I also began working for Patrick O'Dell, who had recently purchased Turnbull Cellars. (It was formerly Johnson-Turnbull, when Reverdy Johnson was part owner). I worked directly with the winemakers at Turnbull, and from the start they were producing outstanding wines, especially the Cabernet blends from various individual vineyards. Turnbull prices tended to be a little below those of other high-end wines, but I knew that was not because of quality. More than once I looked around at other, more well-known, wines that were selling at higher prices and asked myself, "Why doesn't Turnbull catch on better with the public? The wines certainly rank in Napa Valley's top tier when tasted blind, but they sell for lower prices. Consumers ought to choose these wines over some of the others they're buying." Then, for whatever reason, things turned around. I don't know what became the trigger, but for some reason, consumers caught on. Suddenly Turnbull wines became big news; prices rose and the wines sold briskly, as they do today. The wine industry is sometimes like that; better quality wines sell a little below the top prices until they get recognized by the public. It takes time for the public to catch on to the name, logo, font, appearance of the label or what someone wrote about any given wine.

Memorable Jobs

One of the most enjoyable consulting jobs I received came via a phone call from my daughter, Heidi. She had been hired as winemaker for Dalla Valle Vineyards by the owner, Gustav Dalla Valle, to solve a unique problem. The previous winemaker had mistakenly added far too much tartaric acid to what had been Gustav's very best 1986 Cabernet Sauvignon blend.

The hapless winemaker couldn't have chosen a more devastating wine with which to make a mistake. Having blundered badly, he had no idea whether it could be fixed and resigned, leaving the premises. When Gustav tasted his wine and discovered what happened, he hired Heidi to fix the problem. She called me to find out whether I had encountered that before and might know what to do. I told her the chemistry is simple: Excessive acidity makes the wine taste sharp and sour, but the acid hasn't hurt the wine if it can be removed promptly. It is similar to using an antacid to correct stomach indigestion. It happens that there is a legal antacid that works well in wine – provided the winemaker does it in a specific way. The antacid is pure potassium carbonate, which is similar to baking soda, except that it contains potassium instead of sodium.[4] All Heidi would have to do is dissolve a precisely calculated amount of the carbonate crystals into a small amount of pure water, then add that liquid slowly (a drop or two at a time) to the tank of wine while the tank was being mixed rapidly. Upon addition, the added potassium carbonate would quickly remove excess acid, and the taste and mouthfeel of the wine would return to normal. It would

---

[4] Wine is a high-potassium food, which is one of its great health features. Winemakers avoid adding sodium and can add potassium salts whenever a metal ion is needed. Potassium carbonate dissolves into potassium and carbonate ions; the carbonate bubbles up and out of the wine as CO_2 gas. The potassium locks onto excess acid and crystallizes out of the wine as harmless crème of tartar, which is then filtered off. Nothing is added to the wine that is not removed immediately.

reduce Gustav's excess acid instantly, and I doubted whether anyone could tell by taste or analyses that there had ever been a problem in the wine. Heidi had only to figure out the best way to handle the antacid solution using Gustav's pumps and hoses.

She warned Gustav, "Even if the excess acidity is corrected, we don't know for sure if that is the only thing wrong with the wine, but the acid correction must be done immediately." In fact, the wine was far more tannic than it should have been, so she had an additional repair job to do. Heidi set up a pH meter on top of the tank to give her a continuous record of the wine's acidity. As she added carbonate solution, the pH level increased slowly until the tank of wine was brought back to its original acidity of pH 3.55. Then, after skillfully correcting the tannin content... Presto! Gustav Dalla Valle's wine was as good as new.

During the de-acidification, she took wine samples from the tank at intervals of ten minutes, and was quite pleased with the results. She lined up the samples with wine glasses so that Gustav could taste and compare the acidic wine with the treated samples to see how the acidity was being reduced. Gustav sat down and sniffed each glass, then tasted each one, spitting out each taste without comment. Finally, he looked up at her and said simply, "Hmmm . . . hmmm, acid is going down – price is going up." Heidi burst out laughing, and Gustav poured himself a full glass of the wine he had been afraid was lost forever. Next day, he called and hired me as his consultant to work with Heidi Peterson Barrett, the new Dalla Valle winemaker. He was proud as punch, and so was I.[5]

I had liked everything about Gustav since meeting him at Napa Valley Vintners meetings shortly after moving back from Monterey in 1986. He had a magnificent sense of humor and a fine gusto for life. It was wonderful to discuss his early experiences in Italy, especially when Gustav was a

---

[5] Heidi later blended a new (and exceptional) wine for Gustav. The blend was 55% Cabernet Sauvignon with 45% Cabernet Franc, and Gustav used a 'proprietary name' on the bottle; it was called Maya, to match the name of his beautiful young daughter.

scuba diver and inventor. He had designed several major advancements in pressure helmets for underwater diving while working in the Mediterranean. Heidi and I enjoyed collaborating (both at Dalla Valle and Diamond Creek) over the next two years, but I quickly noticed something important: I simply was not needed. It made Gustav and Al Brounstein feel comfortable to have me adding my opinions to Heidi's, but both Heidi and I knew the truth. She was a professional, competent winemaker in every respect. It was time for me to step back and enjoy watching her natural abilities shine.

At about that time, I was diagnosed with prostate cancer. Hearing a doctor explain that to me was devastating at first, until I realized that mine had been identified early in its progression. There were several possible treatments with good odds for success. I was explaining the options to Heidi at the Dalla Valle Winery, when Gustav walked in. On overhearing me, he interrupted to say, "Ask me anything you want about prostate cancer. I am an expert and have been fighting it for years." Gustav and I had a lot in common before; now we shared the experience of this devastating cancer. His treatments were continuing, but it was clear that he had only several more months of life. In late 1995, about two weeks before he died, Gustav asked me to come to the winery for a personal talk. I knew what he wanted to say, but dreaded hearing it. He told me he had done all he could to fight the awful disease, but now knew he was losing the fight. He asked me for just one favor. He felt that his wife, Naoko, might not be able to run the winery after he was gone. He asked me to check on her and do whatever I could to make the vineyard and winery easier for her. With tears in my eyes, I told him I would help her in whatever way she asked, and that I knew Heidi would honor her wishes as well. One of the saddest days of my life was in December of that year when I was told he had passed away. Gustav Dalla Valle was a true friend. Both Heidi and I loved him like a brother.

Some good news came several weeks later. Naoko called and wanted to meet. She told me that Gustav hadn't noticed, but she had been paying close attention to how he managed the winery and sold wine. She felt completely competent to move ahead on her own and wanted to do so. I told her I was delighted with her obvious strength and would notify Heidi. We would be available as needed, but would stay away unless she called.

While I was consulting for Gustav, Diamond Creek, Newlan, Turnbull, Paradigm and Bronco, Oakville realtor, Jean Phillips, called me for some help in a potential winery project. I stopped to see her and Tony Bowden at their home on Silverado Trail, not far from Dalla Valle's home, vineyard and winery. It was only in recent years that Napa Valley winemakers had come to realize that this area along Silverado Trail was destined to become one of the valley's very best microclimates for the Cabernet Sauvignon grape. Tony was studying winemaking and had produced small amounts of Cabernet on a home winemaking basis. In 1991, he wanted to ferment significantly more wine, and was beginning to collect a few French oak barrels. They planned to dig a small cave near the house and tie it together with a small building in front which would become the winery.

Tony had realized that he needed tutoring in the art and science of fermentation and aging wine in barrels. With little experience, he was uncertain in deciding which kinds of oak barrels to use, how long to leave the wine in barrels and how to determine when to remove it for bottling. Further, he had no idea whether to 'fine the wines' and when to do it. He'd heard that some Cabernets need protein fining and others do not. Tony wanted to produce the finest wine possible and needed help. I evaluated each of his actions, giving him specific instructions for aging and fining, and returned a day or two later to taste the treated wines. I made sure he knew what to look for in the taste, smell and mouthfeel of each lot of wine after each treatment. We worked together through 1991 and until the end of September, 1992, when the new vintage was nearly ready for harvest.

Jean Phillips asked me several times whether her vineyard and the wines Tony had been fermenting were good enough to sell at high prices in the marketplace. She was experimenting with a very different label and showed me her first sample. The brand would be called Screaming Eagle, and the label would be very small, simple and artistic. It would be a stylistic scene of an eagle with wings spread, soaring high above a vineyard. Jean was a good friend of Gustav Dalla Valle and Patrick O'Dell, each of whom had given her valid advice about how to introduce her wines to the most influential writers. It was well known that many collectors and consumers of high-priced wines tended to follow certain wine writers, even though all wine writers (like all winemakers and all wine judges) are wrong in their wine evaluations from time to time. The fact that writers were not always correct in personal evaluations of new wines was less important than the fact that they were established in consumers' minds. They were simply the writers that new wineries needed to court in order to gain a position in the high-price wine market. It would be important to get excellent comments from the wine critics who were gathering the most followers.

After our efforts with the 1991 wine, I predicted to Jean that her wines could, indeed, be ranked among the highest quality wines in Napa Valley. However, she would need to hire a younger winemaker because a good deal of time would be needed over the months to monitor the winemaking in every vintage. Jean's grape quality was good enough, but she'd need a full-time, creative winemaker who could be counted on to produce the best wines possible with her Cabernet from every vintage. Jean looked up and asked, "Is Heidi available?" I didn't know, but hoped she might have an open time slot. I answered, "If she is, there is no better winemaker in Napa Valley – in my humble opinion."

Jean laughed, then quickly said, "I expect a father to recommend his daughter as the best choice for any job. However, in this case, I happen to know from good authority that Heidi really is the best." Gustav had told her about the acidity incident in his 1986 Dalla Valle Cabernet Sauvignon wine. She told me what I already knew: "Cabernet was Gustav's best wine, and he was absolutely destroyed when he thought it had been ruined by a winemaking mistake. You can't believe how thrilled he was when Heidi came in and resurrected it from the dead."

Jean called her and the rest is history. Heidi became winemaker for Screaming Eagle and spent the time and effort, both in vineyards and the winery, to make each year as good a vintage as possible. Jean gave me a 750 ml bottle of the 1991 (too small a vintage to be commercial), which has a label unlike the others. Today's Screaming Eagle label first appeared on Heidi's 1992 vintage. Jean also gave me a case of the 1992 tenths and an autographed magnum of the 1992 as well. We consumed all the tenth-size bottles at family and special events, but I still have the 1992 magnum and my rare bottle of the first 'trial' vintage, 1991, locked away as prized possessions. I expect magnums of most vintages of Screaming Eagle to live in bottle 50 years, perhaps longer if stored correctly. The 1992 is a terrific Napa Valley Cabernet wine – especially my magnum, since I received it as a gift from a great friend, Jean Phillips. It is said that Screaming Eagle wines are so rare and expensive that you have to give untold riches and your firstborn child for a bottle. As far as I know, I am the only person in the whole world who has ever actually done that.

Jean Phillips, generous to a fault, was not finished giving me large bottles of Screaming Eagle wines. Beginning in 1988, a group of restaurant and hospitality business owners, led by Ted Balestreri and Bert Cutino,[5] originated a public auction for the purpose of providing scholarship money to help students doing research in enology and viticulture. The event was held annually at a dinner on the Monterey Peninsula, where specialty fine wines and hospitality events at resorts were auctioned off to very high bidders. For the first several years, all net proceeds went to create a scholarship fund in the name of Andre Tchelistcheff, first winemaker at Beaulieu Vineyards. After the Andre fund collected enough money to become perpetual, the next scholarships went to students in the names of Balestreri and Cutino. The fourth name in which scholarships were given was my own, and new funds have continued in additional names as decided by the scholarship board. I was chairman of the Andre Scholarship fund from the beginning, and Andre and I together decided which students would get the awards for the first few years. Andre's wife, Dorothy, and I continued to choose candidates after his death and have added committee members to continue in the future. The money is invested by the National Restaurant Association and distributed through the American Vineyard Society.

Jean Phillips was one of the first winery owners to make a high value wine donation for the Andre fund, and later to my fund. Each year between 1992 and 2008, she gave me a magnum of the current vintage Screaming

---

[5] Ted and Bert have been co-owners of the famous Sardine Factory Restaurant on Cannery Row in Monterey, California for many decades.

Eagle wine as her donation. I delivered the donated bottles to the auctions, where the Screaming Eagle auction lot always commanded the highest prices of any of the wine lots. The owners of Paradigm Winery, Diamond Creek, Turnbull, Shafer, Silver Oak and others donated wines to support the auctions as well, and together we have given many scholarships to deserving students over the years. It is satisfying to notice that many of the early scholarship winners are now professors in universities teaching viticulture and enology courses to new students.

Giving Back

The Napa Valley Vintners organization promotes the local wine industry by holding a magnificent public wine auction to support local healthcare, youth education and affordable housing. In 1981, its first year, the auction yielded $140,000; that amount has grown each year since, with the most recent auction, 2014, totaling an astonishing 18.7 million dollars of receipts. Member wineries and their owners donate ever larger auction lots, and the event has grown to become a four day celebration of wine, food and fundraising every June. Auction Napa Valley is now billed as the most successful charity wine auction in the world. Since the beginning, it has provided over 100 million dollars to non-profit recipients.

At the auction on June 10, 1995, the lot bringing the highest price was a single 15-liter bottle of Dalla Valle 'Maya' Cabernet, cradled in a hand-made wooden case. The lot included six 750 ml bottles of the same wine to allow the buyer to try smaller bottles from time to time in order to assess the wine's development over years of aging in the cellar. Undoubtedly, the large bottle will be opened at its precise peak of perfection, and the crowd of lucky friends of the buyer, Patrick O'Dell, will enjoy the treat of a lifetime. The name of the winemaker: Heidi Peterson Barrett.

In the year 2000, at the Millennium Napa Vintners Auction, a 6-liter bottle of Screaming Eagle 1992 Cabernet Sauvignon set a world record that still stands. The reader might well sit down to read the rest of this sentence: the price was $500,000 for the single large bottle! Everyone in the wine world knows the name of the winemaker.

They also know the name of the head chef who planned and prepared a superb banquet for the 2,200 hungry attendees. That was Heidi's sister, Holly Peterson. Holly realized that the problem with such a large gala banquet would be getting perfectly prepared food to the guests all at once (even though freshly prepared by competent hands). Since the 1980s, Napa Valley Vintners had used two serving lines to deliver food courses to the guests at the banquet. However, the millennium 2000 auction dinner would be the biggest auction event in the history of Napa Valley Vintners and would need a unique plan. Holly was booked to chair the dinner event a full five years ahead of time. Who else could they choose? She had been the first woman chef in a Michelin three-star restaurant (Tantris, in Munich, Germany) only a few years earlier. Her final plan for the upcoming Napa Valley millennium banquet specified using an additional twenty serving lines. Holly arranged for 22 excellent chef/maitre d'hôtel combinations, each pair to cook the same recipes for 100 guests; each duo had ten servers to serve ten guests – all perfectly synchronized on a tightly controlled time schedule. Sandra and I attended that dinner and were astonished at how beautifully the event came off. All 2,200 people were served a magnificent meal within five minutes of each other. All the food preparations seemed perfect and the applause was deafening when Chef Holly and her sous chefs were introduced to the whole group at the dinner's end.

I cannot complete the daughter story without bragging about our other two daughters. Gayle Henry has a master's degree in social work and is a licensed clinical social worker. In addition to her private practice, she is a primary therapist at Sharp Mesa Vista Hospital in San Diego. Her specialty is the field of addiction, which includes alcohol dependency as well as various opiates. In her work, Gayle has helped save the lives of many people and continues to steer others towards greatly improved lives. Her heart is solid gold, but it is sheathed in a gentle firmness that is effective in getting patients to accept, enjoy and hold onto their recoveries.

Her sister, Lisa, was VP business initiative manager at Wells Fargo Bank until her sudden death due to an unforeseen stroke at age 44. Words cannot describe the unexpected loss of such a lovely, exciting and productive person. Lisa was the life of the party, a natural leader; she set the tone of every meeting she attended. Groups could get only so far in a typical discussion, before someone would look up and say, "I want to wait and see what Lisa thinks about this." The group agreed, it just seemed natural – they needed her, as we need her still. Lisa's passing left a huge hole in our world that is impossible to fill. Some tragedies are just too horrendous to make any sense. All four of our daughters have conducted their lives towards serving others, each one giving something of intrinsic value to people through creativity, artistic flair and technical skill in her chosen profession.

A Leaf of a Different Color

As I got older, I wanted to stop producing 'good, but ho-hum' wines in favor of wines that nobody else was making. I had made Cabernet and Pinot Noir wines for years. So what? A multitude of winemakers do the same thing. I wanted to do something new, exciting and different, something that also offered 'pizzazz.' By accident I encountered that very thing at a wine competition in Europe. I was judging wines at the International Wine & Spirits Competition at Ockley in Surrey, England in November 1980. The chief judge, Anton Massel, told me of the discovery in the 1950s of a single ancient grapevine growing against a stone wall in the village of Wrotham, [6] Kent not far away from our competition. The fruit clusters on that vine looked like Pinot Noir, but the vine leaves were a very different shape from Pinot Noir. Leaf color was not the yellowish-green that predominates in most other Vitis vinifera [7] grapevines; rather, it was a colder, grayish green, with a whitish cast that made the vines look as if they were covered by a light coating of flour. There was no vineyard anywhere in England that contained similar vines. Indeed, there was only the one vine to be found; it was estimated to be 200 years old, and nobody had any idea where it had come from, who had planted it or from where the seed or cutting was transplant-

---

[6] Wrotham is pronounced by locals as "Root-em." Americans pronounce it phonetically, as "Roth-em."

[7] *Vitis vinifera* is the scientific name for the primary species of the world's wine grapes.

ed. Ed Hyams, the discover of the grapevine, was a British wine enthusiast traveling through the area. He noticed the vine because it was so different, so old, and because there were no other vines that looked like it in any of the country's commercial vineyards. Obviously, residents of Wrotham village were accustomed to seeing the vine, but no one gave it any notice. If it was mentioned in conversations, it was called, "the old vine." If it were to be discovered at all, it would have to be discovered by an outsider.

Hyams finally reckoned that the vine was probably Pinot Noir, which would suggest that it may have been brought into England by the Romans, who are known to have brought the varietal into the country nearly two thousand years ago. It was presumed that the vine must have mutated naturally many times over the centuries, which could account for the changed appearance of its leaf structure over time. University scientists had guessed that the vine might be a clone of Pinot Meunier, since Meunier has a similar 'dusty leaf' appearance caused by tiny white whiskers growing on the leaf surfaces. There were differences, to be sure; new small Wrotham leaves are distinctly pink in spring, becoming white an inch or two behind the growing tip, and finally turning grey-green, as they grow larger. It is unclear whether the old Wrotham vine mutated originally from a common Pinot Noir or, perhaps, mutated directly from Pinot Meunier, itself a clone of Pinot Noir. It is often claimed that there are more clones of Pinot Noir in commerce than of any other variety. Undoubtedly, that is due to the strong tendency for Pinot Noir vines to mutate naturally, though I've never heard a theory on why that should be more true for Pinot Noir than other varieties.

After the discovery, English winemakers took cuttings from the old vine to propagate a small vineyard, and eventually produced small quantities of a pink sparkling wine using the classic champenoise method. We drank a bottle of it with dinner after our judging, and I was impressed with the wine's high quality and uniqueness. I brought two dormant vine cuttings back to California and quarantined the resultant vines to guarantee against introducing new vine diseases into the U.S. Within two weeks Professor Carole Meredith, UC Davis, confirmed for me that my vines of Wrotham Pinot were, indeed, Pinot Noir (the DNA was identical). During quarantine growth, I noticed that the new vines not only were disease free, they also appeared to be immune to our common California powdery mildew! That was a block-buster discovery, since it was believed that there is no Vitis vinifera grape vine that is immune to powdery mildew.[8] The implications were that we might copy the genetic mildew resistance from Wrotham vines into Cabernet, Pinot, Chardonnay, etc. so as to make all commercial vineyards naturally immune to the disease. It would be a stunning improvement for the industry if sulfur use could be avoided in all vineyards by future farmers.

So far, that has not been possible; it is a more difficult problem than we had hoped, and no scientist has yet solved the mildew problem. University researchers even told me that Wrotham Pinot itself is not 100% immune. However, for practical purposes, it is so close to immune that I have farmed all my vines completely free from the use of sulfur (or any other mildewcide) for nearly two decades. I planted two acres of the Wrotham Pinot vines on my farm just south of Yountville in 1995 and have been producing miniscule amounts of very high-quality Wrotham Clone Pinot Noir Red Table Wine and Blanc de Noir Sparkling Wine since 2000. Viticulturists have suggested that when the original variety was brought into England, the vines were faced with a colder and more humid climate than they were accustomed to farther south in Europe. Over time, the vines mutated, changing so as to become acclimatized to the new conditions; eventually, the story goes, one of the vines became immune to powdery mildew, which is why that vine survived. All the other vines died. It's a nice story, certainly possible, but we may never know the whole truth.

Can't Retire; Promised Mom I Wouldn't

In 1998, John Parducci, a long time friend and one of the true 'old-timers' in the wine industry, called me with a serious problem. He said the Parducci Winery had been hit by a serious amount of cork taint in one of his

---

[8] Powdery mildew can devastate commercial vineyards unless the vines are dusted with sulfur every few weeks during the first half of every growing season. Thousands of tons of sulfur dust are used on commercial vineyards all over the world to protect from the disease.

best Cabernet wines. It was so insidious that he thought it might halt all consumer demand for Parducci wines and bankrupt his company. He asked whether I could serve as an expert witness for him in a lawsuit he was filing against the cork producer. I was well aware of the chemistry of cork taint[9] and felt certain that I could explain it to a judge or jury, though I certainly was not conversant with any part of the law. "You don't have to know zilch about the law, I just want you to explain where the taint in my wines came from," he told me. "I'll need to inspect your winery and bottling room, and analyze the wines," I replied. "Only after that can I tell you where the taint came from." I knew his winery was old and any inspector could find traces of mold around sewers in the winery. The cork company was sure to claim that those were the sources of the taint in his wine. However, when I saw results of the wine analyses, I told John that he already had proof that the taint did, indeed, come from the corks, and not from somewhere in his winery.

He had analyzed a total of four random cases (48 bottles) of the wine and found four bottles with serious cork taint. More than 8% of his bottles were tainted, which is enough to destroy the winery's image and stop customers from buying Parducci wine altogether. The good news was that the untainted 91.7% of the bottles were perfect, containing no traces of TCA. I assured him that was absolute proof that the wine was clean in his wine tanks and had no TCA at the time of bottling. If the taint had come from dirty barrels, tanks or hoses there would have been taint in all the bottles, because the wine came from a single tank and passed through the same bottling equipment. Since it appeared in only 8% of the bottled wines, the taint had to have come from the corks. Three other wineries joined Parducci in the suit and the case was settled in Parducci's favor as soon as the defense attorneys heard the above argument. Most cork companies have now

---

[9] Cork taint is the name for a moldy off smell and taste that occurs in bottled wines that have been closed with a mold-infested cork. When mold grows on cork pieces, it often leaves traces of a compound called '2,4,6-trichloranisole' (TCA) on the cork. Unfortunately, the human nose can detect as little as three parts per trillion of TCA! Any wine with serious cork taint must be thrown away; the taint cannot be removed.

made major improvements in their procedures for handling cork materials. The happy result is that wineries today have much better odds of receiving TCA-free corks than was the case around year 2000.

New attorneys called repeatedly in the following months asking me to be an expert witness in various other cases. My name had appeared on some mysterious list that attorneys share with each other. Apparently, there weren't many expert witnesses on wine chemistry and viticulture. I was surprised at the large number and the individuality of the next few dozen cases. No two were alike, but most involved my figuring out what caused a certain wine to spoil, or what the vineyardist or winemaker had done wrong (if anything). I never took one side or the other; when I was hired, I promised to look at the facts honestly and to tell them exactly what I believed, regardless of which side it helped or hurt. Whether they used my evidence was up to the attorneys, but my job was to tell them the truth.

I learned something about the U.S. wine industry from several of the legal cases for which I served as expert witness. I now recognize that too many winemakers are poorly trained and yet continue to crush grapes, let them spoil, bottle their juice and brag about what a great job they've done in winemaking. They routinely produce wines that are embarrassments to their peers, often leading to insurance claims and actual lawsuits. These winemakers lack an understanding of biochemistry, but each promotes himself or herself as 'a great winemaker, ready to turn your grapes into fabulous wine for a (large) fee.' They seek those who have moved to wine country for a storybook life-style, as newcomers eagerly accept the great winemaker's claim that he/she can make a great wine for them. That is often a recipe for failure. The wines are usually flawed, though sometimes passable, and the gentle people spend months and sometimes years selling poor wines to consumers, some of whom may not distinguish great flavors from spoilage flavors. The most elementary rules of sanitation are ignored, because the winemaker doesn't know any better. In the industry today, my biggest disappointment is the lack of basic competence among some untrained, but extremely confident new commercial winemakers. Their incompetence shows up as poor wine on store shelves, standing among some truly beautiful wines from successful wineries.

I believe successes as an expert witness can be traced to two "common-sense laws." First, if good litigators are good teachers, then expert witnesses have to be good teachers. When I spoke to attorneys, judges and juries as a teacher, they appreciated hearing the facts stated clearly, and in lay terms. The second point was realizing that an expert is an expert only so long as what he says can be easily confirmed as true. In every case, the expert witness should study appropriate textbooks and other historic sources immediately prior to testifying, either at depositions, trials, arbitrations or mediations. During testimony, he/she will be certain of the facts, and that is what success is made of.

I have participated as an expert in nearly fifty cases, averaging about four or five per year, including insurance claims. Of all the benefits I received for doing this work, the greatest bonus accrued to my mental alertness; by studying the applicable chemistry, biochemistry and industry practices prior to testifying, I was forced to exercise my brain, and found that Mom was correct. I still remember every tonal inflection in her voice as she told me, "Don't you ever retire; if you retire, you just get old and die." Mom would be thrilled to know that I have avoided retirement like the plague.

Air view of caves under construction showing spoils used for roadways and as a base for the eventual winery building, which was to be built in front of the caves.

Nearly completed terraces at the highest edge of the Atlas Peak property. Dam and reservoir are visible in the distance to the right; the caves are located in the biggest hill at right edge of photo. In 1988, nearly 100 tons of grapes were crushed for the J.Wile and Atlas Peak labels. Today, this is one of the highest quality wine producing vineyards in the Foss Valley.

The Dosco drilling machine. The hard alloy drilling teeth were easily replaced as they wore out.

The long Dosco machine just beginning to drill into a hillside at Atlas Peak (drill head is at right). Spoils were conveyed all the way to back (on left of machine), where they were dropped into a waiting truck to be spread around.

The first stage of dam construction was to open a deep trench to form an impermeable base; the trench was then filled with well compacted clay soil, layer by layer, until it became a 30 foot high dam, strong enough to hold back 960 acre-feet of water.

Air view of the completed Whitbread Lake, with dam at left. Filled with rainwater, the dam (with a capacity of 313 million gallons) holds enough water to irrigate the entire property for three consecutive drought years.

A gathering of the Old Timers group for lunch in 2005. Seated in front (*from left*):
Bob Mondavi, Ernest Gallo, Liz Martini and Peter Mondavi.

The author with daughter Holly and wife Sandra, on the occasion of receiving the California
State Fair Lifetime Achievement Award in 2006. A sure sign of getting old.

Winemaker Heidi Barrett (*left*) cradling a magnum of her finest 'La Sirena' Cabernet Sauvignon wine from her vineyard in the Napa Valley. Heidi was the Screaming Eagle winemaker from 1992 to 2008. *Photo ©Rory Earnshaw.*

Holly Peterson (*above*) chef-owner of Flourish Special Events and Robin's Egg Chocolates, at the author's 75th birthday luncheon.

Autographed magnum (*left*) of 1992 Screaming Eagle given to the author as a thank you by owner Jean Phillips, along with a rare fifth of the 1991 vintage (Jean's first but never marketed label).

The author surrounded by the next generations of family (*from left*): Gayle Henry, Chelsea Barrett, Holly Peterson, Lisa Henry, Heidi Barrett and Remi Barrett. Remi and Chelsea are grandchildren (Heidi's daughters). Good thing he enjoys ladies.

Lisa Henry, former vice president for Wells Fargo private banking, and Gayle Henry, licensed clinical social worker, thinking up trouble on the steps of their parents' Napa Valley home.

The winegrower in 2010 tilling his Wrotham Pinot vineyard, using his small diesel tractor. Vines are dormant in February, but the yellow mustard is in full bloom.

The Petersons at home. Lake in background irrigates their Wrotham Pinot vines as well as the well-loved Christmas trees they also farm. *Photo by Nanci Kerby.*

Wrotham Pinot clusters ready for picking. If you were given a choice of drinking wine produced from either happy grapes or sad ones, which would you choose?

The author produces miniscule amounts of this Wrotham Pinot vintage sparkling wine. It is aged on the yeast for a full seven years prior to disgorging, which explains why this unique wine is rare and costly to produce.

Epilogue

Forks in the Road

All the wineries whose histories are related in these pages encountered forks in the road as they begged, pleaded, pushed, and stormed their way forward through business life. Some succeeded beautifully, while others failed miserably; all were steered by their owners and managers along a conventional, but shaky path. Which fork in the road to take? The choice made all the difference. I watched each decision unfold.

Industry leaders made decisions along the way, taking a left turn here and a right turn there. Ernest and Julio Gallo each made mistakes, but quickly recovered and then surged forward. Their winery today is a success because of their mutual competence. They pushed and tutored employees, the company gained, occasionally lost, then gained even more. Sometimes they had to guess which road to take; other times they were sure of themselves. After choosing a pathway, the road owned them. It wouldn't be possible to turn around. They had to push on and solve any problem the route presented, until the next fork appeared. Looking back, they can feel proud, as I am proud of the small part I played at Gallo.

On top from the beginning, Beaulieu was different. Its competitive advantage was that the owner, Georges de Latour, was French. He was not handcuffed by the attitude of American Prohibition; instead, he learned to use it to his advantage. Prohibition had retarded American winemakers, who could only react to it. Georges eschewed them and instead chose a young Russian, whose modern French winemaking established Beaulieu's preeminence in California wine. Andre Tchelistcheff was superb, and it showed in his wines. I was lucky; I was too young to have Prohibition affect my demeanor. I could learn from the European attitude on wine, and could excel because the French have excelled.

The next generation of Beaulieu ownership had no interest in wine, only in a lifestyle that accompanies it. They mauled Georges de Latour's little baby Beaulieu by selling it for a song to non-wine businessmen. The new owners completed the coup by amputating vineyards from the winery and giving them away. Their notions of 'make quality by promotion, forget substance' and 'promote & sell, promote & sell' toppled the winery's reputation. Aloof business leaders took a bite, spit it out, took another bite, and asked only the price. The company's image, followed by its wine quality, rolled steadily downhill. Eventually, more modern ideas took hold; the wines mostly recovered, but Beaulieu would never again compete effectively against newer, small wineries for the pre-eminence that was once solely its own. Purists among us shed tears for Beaulieu, but even the saddest eyes dry and we recover. All it took to guarantee the winery's steady decline was one arrogant manager who chose to avoid all branches of the road, to avoid moving Beaulieu in any direction at all. Andre correctly predicted that the winery would strangle as a result.

Monterey was a magnificent sunrise looming below the horizon, overflowing with promise. It was nearly devoid of grapevines and the wines that could be produced from them. Ready for the plucking, it attracted entrepreneurs who never bothered to find out whether the area might have its own stubborn personality. Not wanting to waste time on a meandering road to success, they took shortcuts through the hills which blinded them to the pitfalls lurking below. Believing Monterey would knuckle under to their wishes, they cut every corner possible and lost their way. In the end, their rigid scheme couldn't be modified to match the uniqueness of Monterey's climate and they lost their vineyards and winery.

A white knight appeared and studied the situation thoroughly before deciding how to rescue the winery in distress. There was room for science then; I could study Monterey carefully before deciding which path to take, and that paid off handsomely in fun and profit. Departing from the beaten path, we made TCC a winner by blending with Monterey wine - its more intense flavor made all the difference. TCC was elegant and the white knight rescued the ailing winery, avoiding mistakes of the earlier pioneers. He developed a business far more successful than his predecessors had dared to dream. We were astonished. It was as if the white knight had taken all forks in the road that had 'success' signs attached and bypassed the others. Clearly, Coca-Cola knew something the others didn't; yet in the end, he didn't know everything. He didn't know that 'even if his company performed perfectly, he couldn't accrue the same gigantic profits he would with soft drinks.' The great white knight disappeared as abruptly as he had arrived.

The white knight was replaced by a sleek and polished knight on a shiny black horse. In direct opposition to the white knight, this one took every fork in the road that had a warning sign. He'd been so successful in previous campaigns that he took pleasure in deliberately shunning the signs. It made him feel good to know that fearful followers looked at him with awe when he grinned at a warning sign, then deliberately turned his army onto that road. He ignored those who thought his company had become heavy and sluggish. He assumed that success was guaranteed (it was only a question of 'how much' success, not whether success would be likely). Failure for him was impossible, since it was so rare in his alcohol business. He didn't know, or ignored the fact, that his army was destroying itself by internal fighting and jockeying for favors from above. This knight had neither the will nor the skill to know when to avoid taking the road most heavily traveled. His head office had even established rules directing his employees never to stray from the familiar approach of marketing all products as if they were alcoholic spirits. He'd accumulated so many riches in liquor that he thought it would be a plume in his cap to devour 'that cute little second cousin of spirits they call wine.' As each of his subsidiary companies failed, his PR firm announced voluntary sell-offs, as if each sale was just another in a long series of outstanding successes.

The newest winery, Atlas Peak, overflowed with magnetic prospects for success in the beginning. Its ownership included experienced and historical wine industry families from Europe. The majority owner was a beer company with a history of direct sales of consumer beverages to the public. While this road was new, it promised to remain parallel to the paths of its partners, routes that had supported centuries-old classical European wine families. This was no fly-by-night company bent on buying cheap alcohol and selling it in shiny packages to the public. Whitbread had been producing fine ales and unique beers for longer than the U.S. had been a country. For a while its managers enjoyed the exciting wine excursion; then, unaccountably, they got cold feet. Did they fail? Not exactly, but neither did they succeed. They just didn't feel comfortable in the fine wine world. So they terminated the journey and turned back onto the pathway they knew.

Their decision was reminiscent of an aviation rule that is well-known to experienced pilots: The safest and most reliable maneuver in an airplane is often the 180 degree turn. When the sky ahead offers nothing but boiling clouds, fierce lightening and churning darkness, turn onto a more familiar road – the path directly behind you – and fly back to where you've been, for you know that is safe. That turn-around provided asylum for the beer and ale producer, but left its winery partners in states of unease. Each was forced to find a new road; perhaps the experience was best for all. Both European wineries have continued their outstanding growth, maintaining their records of producing some of the world's finest table wines and champagnes.

Forks in the road for people are sometimes inconsequential, but forks in the road for wineries tend to multiply and exaggerate the result. Wineries, like people, laugh, whimper, bite, kick and scream as the business moves forward. Each winery had leaders and managers who made choices. Most took the road more heavily traveled only because it was more familiar. They began by fighting their competitors, then chasing them, until both contestants only copied and re-copied each other; in the end, most never knew why they failed. They had missed the excitement of discovery, never delighting in the joy of newness, the thrill of invention, Karel Popper's 'flash of genius.' Many times, taking the road less traveled meant all the difference for me. When I failed, I could find out why and move on refreshed.

The Future

At the repeal of Prohibition, there were just 1,300 acres of Cabernet Sauvignon vines in Napa County; most of the grapes were shipped east. Today, Napa's Cabernet acreage is more than 20,000 and nearly all the grapes are fermented locally. Immediately after repeal, the Napa County grapes crushed for wine totaled 15,000 tons. That number grew to a total of 270,610 tons by 2013, an 18-fold increase. In 1968, when I represented Beaulieu as one of the twelve member wineries at Napa Valley Vintners luncheon meetings, I couldn't have guessed that fewer than fifty years later, that number would grow to more than 500 member wineries; in the single year between 2013 and 2014, the total actually jumped by one hundred members.

Napa is no longer California's only region producing high-quality wines. In fact, an overwhelming percentage of the wines produced in Napa County today come from non-Napa grapes. Labels on wine bottles must show the area from which the grapes were grown (the appellation) so that consumers can see and compare quality levels of wines grown in various locations. A 2012 Stonebridge report, "The Economic Impact of Napa County's Wine and Grapes" (prepared for Napa Vintners), states that in 2011, a total of nearly 50 million cases of wine were produced in Napa County, of which fewer than 8.5 million cases were Napa appellation wines!

It's easy to foresee a continuation of industry growth; today's new grape clones, yeasts and technology promise significant improvements to come. However, there are a few ominous signs as well. An astonishingly high percentage of today's table wines contain far too much alcohol and too little varietal character. Table wines historically contained 14% or less (the world's very best table wines were often between 11% and 13% alcohol). Incredibly, today we frequently see more than 15% alcohol listed on red table wine labels; those exaggerated wines are often more reminiscent of after-dinner port, a desert wine. Most do not age well in bottle and are impossible to enjoy with food. They taste hot, aggressive, rough and devoid of varietal elegance; the winemaker screams, "My wines are bigger and (therefore) better than anybody else's." Can quality be judged by weight?

At the end of Prohibition, consumers wanted only one thing: higher and higher alcohol content in their drinks. By 1958, winemaking started moving towards lower alcohol and higher quality – reversing the Prohibition attitude, as the world resumed enjoying exquisite foods and wines together. Today's alarming surge towards higher alcohol in some wines begs the question: "Are consumers coming full circle, back towards coarse and harsher drinks?" Alternatively, will the excitement of finesse, subtlety and excellence in wine and food reverse what appears to be a misstep? Perhaps so; already, increasing numbers of voices are speaking out to promote the virtues of delicacy, smoothness and more elegance in table wines.[1]

Today, even those superb Napa Valley varietal wines of 1968 are routinely surpassed by wines from more than a few wineries. Many of today's outstanding wines are neither grown nor produced in Napa Valley; indeed, they are not even produced in California. Every one of the fifty states now grows grapes and produces wines, and each produces gold medal wines. Judges often notice that the biggest winners in various competitions now come from New York, Michigan, Missouri, New Mexico, Washington, Oregon and other states, as well as California.

The list of outstanding smaller wineries producing great wines continues to explode. Larger wineries, like Gallo and Bronco, produce outstanding quality table wines that sell at bargain prices. Small wineries also excel in giving high quality bargains to the public. Labels like Scott Harvey, Hawk and Horse, Tondré and others are difficult to find, but worth the search. Equally valuable new names are appearing regularly. The outlook for wine consumers is more exciting today than it ever was. Despite taking wrong turns, the wine industry adjusts, recovers and moves forward with

---

[1] The alcohol content must be printed on wine labels, either the front or back. It is usually hidden in unreadably small type, but I believe it is worthwhile to search for it. Make your own decision whether the European preference for lower-alcohol table wines is correct for you as well. It makes all the difference for me.

more zeal, competence and confidence than ever before. What fun it is for consumers to search for the best wines at great prices today. As Sandra tells me, "Trust that time will cure the frailties of human nature, it always has." The future is bright, indeed.

WHO'S WHO

Amaral, Bill	Beaulieu Maintenance Manager
Amerine, Maynard	U.C. Davis Enology Professor
Andersen, John	Atlas Peak Vineyard Chairman
Andrew, Dorothy	Beaulieu Secretary (wife of Andre Tchelistcheff)
Antinori, Piero	Antinori Winery Owner, Whitbread Partner (Atlas Peak)
Asher, Gerald	Monterey Vineyard Wine Marketer/Sales Manager
Austin, J. Paul	Coca-Cola Company Chairman
Bachman, Pete	Monterey Vineyard Cellar Manager, Assistant Winemaker
Baird, Tony	Entrepreneur, Oak Chip Supplier
Balzer, Robert L.	Wine Writer, Author, Wine Judge
Bareuther, Jim	Paul Masson & Taylor California Cellars Sales Manager
Barnes, James	Atlas Peak Vineyard Financial Manager
Barrett, Heidi P.	La Sirena Winery Owner/Winemaker (author's daughter)
Beckstoffer, Andy	Heublein Corporate Acquisitions Manager
Beekman, Phil	Seagram President
Bizot, Christian	Bollinger Champagne Owner, Whitbread Partner (Atlas Peak)
Borchert, Ed	Consultant/Troubleshooter (distressed companies)
Bouthilet, Robert	Gallo Research Director
Boyce-Smith, John	Foremost-McKesson VP
Branch, Bob	Beaulieu Shipping Supervisor
Bronfman, Edgar	Seagram Corporation Chairman/Owner
Bronfman, Sam	Seagram Wine Manager (son of Edgar Bronfman)
Brounstein, Al	Diamond Creek Vineyards Founder/Owner
Cairney, Len	Taylor California Cellars Engineer
Cameron, Todd	Monterey Vineyard Assistant Winery Manager
Caputi, Art, Jr.	Gallo Lab Manager
Caputi, Art, Sr.	Gallo Maintenance Manager
Carpy, Chuck	Freemark Abbey Winery Partner
Carriuolo, Chris	Heublein Wine Sales Manager

Cheek, Mike	Taylor California Cellars VP, Sales Manager
Chellemi, Dan	Andre Tchelistcheff Scholarship Recipient (first)
Chodola, Randy	Paul Masson Cellar Sub-Foreman
Clancy, Terry	Allied-Lyons Wine Division President
Coleman, Jim	Gallo Assistant Production Manager Bottling/Shipping
Corti, Darrell	Wine/Food Expert, Wine Judge
Crawford, Charlie	Gallo VP, Production Manager
Crocci, Guido	Gallo Winemaker
Crowley, Jim	Atlas Peak Vineyard Dynamiter, Dosco Operator
Culhane, Bill	Taylor California Cellars Asst. Sales Manager
Dalla Valle, Gustav	Dalla Valle Winery Founder/Owner
de Latour, Georges	Beaulieu Founder/Owner
de Pins, Galcerand	Husband of Hélène de Latour de Pins
de Pins, Hélène	Beaulieu Owner (daughter of Georges de Latour)
Ellis, Duane	Grade School/High School pal
Farella, Frank	Monterey Vineyard Chief Attorney
Feller, Bob	Ace Cleveland Indians Pitcher
Fenderson, Albion	Gallo VP Sales
Fields, Jack	Gallo Cellar Supervisor
Fike, Richard	Atlas Peak Vineyard Maintenance Manager, Dosco Operator
Findlay, Martin	Whitbread London Sub-Chairman
Fortino, Luigi	Monterey Vineyard Cellar Supervisor
Franzia, Fred	Bronco Winery Partner/Owner
Gallo, Ernest	Gallo Founder/Partner
Gallo, Julio	Gallo Founder/Partner
Gibbons, Jim	Monterey Vineyard VP Finance
Gramlow, Otto	Beaulieu Chief Financial Officer
Griffin, Mel	Seagram Executive VP Manufacturing
Hamler, Ed	Taylor California Cellars President
Henrion, Marc	Barton & Gustier President
Henry, Gayle	Licensed Clinical Social Worker (author's daughter)
Henry, Lisa	Wells Fargo VP Business Initiative Manager (author's daughter)
Herrmann, Ray	Foremost-McKesson Wine Sales Chairman

Hill, William   Promoter/Entrepreneur

Hoffman, John   Christian Brothers Winery Manager

Ibsen, Gary   Monterey Vineyard Assistant Sales Manager

Jackson, Don   Heublein Costs Analyzer

Jerant, Frank   Seagram Wine Company Plant Manager

Joslyn, Maynard   U.C. Berkeley Professor, Wine & Food

Katz, Morris   Paul Masson President

Keith, Dick   Monterey Vineyard Architect

Killeen, Albert   Coca-Cola Company VP, Marketing Manager

Knowles, Legh   Beaulieu Sales Manager, General Manager

Kornell, Hans   Hans Kornell Champagne Cellars Owner

Kornell, Marylouise   Wife of Hans Kornell

Little, Dave   McFarland Vineyard Manager

Lucas, Dan   Monterey Vineyard Controller

Macumber, Bruce   TMV (Coca-Cola) Assistant Sales Manager

Maher, Dick   Seagram Wine Sales Manager

Martini, Liz   Wife of Louis P. Martini

Marx, Corny   Atlas Peak Sales Manager

McCarthy, George   Lancers (Heublein) Wine Sales Manager

McFarland, Gerry   McFarland Management Partner/Vineyard Manager

McFarland, Myron   McFarland Management Partner/Chairman

Meredith, Burgess   Radio Announcer, Actor

Meyer, Justin   Silver Oak Cellars Founder/Owner, Winemaker

Miller, Gene   Miller the Driller Owner (author's brother-in-law)

Mondavi, Peter   Charles Krug Owner/Chairman

Mondavi, Robert   Robert Mondavi Winery Founder/Owner

Moosebrugger, F.   Commander of USS Springfield, Navy Lt. Cruiser

Moramarco, Jon   Allied-Lyons Assistant to Terry Clancy

Mrak, Prof. Emil   U.C. Davis First Chancellor

Nordmann, Gary   Atlas Peak VP Finance

Nowlin, R.L.   Gallo Chief Engineer

O'Brien, Linda   Monterey Vineyard Laboratory Manager

Oster, Dick   United Vintners President

Pauling, Prof. Linus   U.C. Berkeley Biochemistry Professor

Peterson, Bob (B.K.)   High School/College Buddy

Peterson, Holly   Chef and Owner, Flourishchocolate.com (author's daughter)

Peterson, Sandra	Teacher, Editor (author's wife)
Peterson, Tom	Monterey Vineyard Assistant Plant Manager
Peynaud, Prof. Emile	Enology/Viticulture Professor in France
Phillips, Jean	Screaming Eagle Founder/Owner
Popper, Karel	Gallo Research Scientist
Raymond, Roy	Beringer Winery Manager
Rhodes, Barney & Belle	Wine/Food Judges, Social Leaders
Robinson, Gary	McFarland Vineyard Manager
Rosenbrand, Theo	Beaulieu Cellar Supervisor, Winemaker (third)
Rossi, Charlie	Gallo's 'Carlo Rossi'
Runquist, Jeff	Napa Valley Co-Op Winemaker
Salva, Glenn	Atlas Peak Vineyard Manager
Sanford, Don	Gallo Winemaker, National Guard Pilot
Seaborg, Prof. Glenn	Nuclear Physicist, U.C. Berkeley Chancellor
Stralla, Louis	St. Helena Mayor (early 1970's)
Stratton, Tom	McFarland Management Partner/Financial Manager
Sullivan, Dagmar	Daughter of Marquise Hélène de Pins
Tchelistcheff, Andre	Beaulieu Winemaker (first)
Tchelistcheff, Dimitri	Gallo Winemaker (son of Andre Tchelistcheff)
Tchelistcheff, Paul	Beaulieu Champagne Worker (son of Dimitri Tchelistcheff)
Teasley, Harry	Coca-Cola VP, Wine Spectrum Chairman (post Killeen)
Timothy, Brother	Christian Brothers Winemaker
Toeppen, Paul	Financial/Business Consultant
Travers, Bob	Mayacamas Vineyard Owner/Winemaker
Varrelman, Mel	Napa County Supervisor
Watson, Stuart	Heublein Corporation Chairman
Williams, Billy Joe	Gallo's first Microbiologist
Williams, Howard	Gallo VP Marketing

INDEX

INDEX

ABOUT THE AUTHOR

Born in Iowa during the Great Depression, Richard (Dick) Peterson has been an innovator in the California wine industry since the late 1950s. The industry was just emerging from the effects of Prohibition, and the near dormant wine trade was about to explode into life. Peterson was perfectly positioned to become a key player in that dynamic revolution.

After receiving his PhD in Agricultural Chemistry from UC Berkeley in 1958, he was with the E. & J. Gallo Winery for ten years, culminating as Research Director and Assistant Production Manager in charge of all winemaking. In 1968, he was chosen by Andre Tchelistcheff to replace him as Winemaster of Beaulieu Vineyards in Napa Valley, and remained there six vintages, moving in 1974 to become Winemaster and President of The Monterey Vineyard. From 1986 until 1990, he was Winemaker and President of Atlas Peak Vineyards in Napa Valley.

Peterson invented many wine techniques still in use today, such as 'no topping, bung-and-roll,' a practice for barrel aging red wines. He showed that winemakers do not need to 'top off' barrels to prevent oxidation because the head space inside a barrel of wine is not air, but a vacuum. He is the original designer of the steel barrel pallet, which allows wine barrels to be handled mechanically instead of by hand. The pallets are now used in most American wineries and in many around the world. He has authored numerous wine publications, including newsletters and research articles in technical journals. For many years, he wrote a column, 'Common Sense Winemaking,' in Wines & Vines magazine.

He created many successful new wines, including Lancers Vinho Branco in Portugal, the J. Wile line of varietal wines, Seagram's first wine cooler, and all the original Monterey Vineyard and Taylor California Cellars varietal and generic table and sparkling wines.

In 1977-78, he was president of the 2,000 member American Society for Enology and Viticulture, having been a member since 1959 and a director, 1973-75. He was a director of The Wine Institute for twelve years, past chairman of WITS, a Supreme Knight in the Universal Order of Knights of the Vine, and a member of most professional wine societies. He is a founding member of the

Society of Wine Educators, AWARE, American Institute of Wine and Food, and the International Wine Academy. He has judged wines professionally in Australia, Portugal, France, Argentina, and the U.K. as well as the United States.

Today he lives with his wife, Sandra, on their seven acre farm in Napa Valley where he has a two acre Wrotham Pinot vineyard from which he produces two wines for his brand, Richard G. Peterson: Brut Rose Napa Valley Sparkling Wine and Pinot Noir still wine.* He has been an expert legal witness in nearly fifty wine-related civil suit cases, and is a sought-after judge at prominent national and international wine competitions. *The Winemaker* is his first book.

ADDITIONAL INFORMATION

For more information, visit Dr. Peterson's website at

www.richardGpeterson.com

The web site provides additional information about the author, his body of work, research papers, and the winemaking process.

His helpful and informative *Glossary of Wine Terms*, too large for inclusion in this publication, can also be found there.

---

* As time marches on, they sold the Napa Valley farm and moved to a smaller property in the city of Napa in 2016. Prior to that, Dick took cuttings of his Wrotham Pinot to Monterey's 'Santa Lucia Highlands,' planting the vines there for its exceptionally cool climate. He continues making his label Wrotham Pinot Sparkling Wine and classic Burgundian Pinot Noir from the Tondre Alarid Santa Lucia Vineyard. Marketing is by Amuse Bouche, John Schwartz and Heidi P. Barrett, owners.

ACKNOWLEDGEMENTS

I am indebted to Narsai David, Tracey Hawkins, Bob Foster, Chris Cook, Doug Frost, Gene Miller, Scott Harvey, Dorothy Tchelistcheff, John Schwartz, Bob Kirk Peterson, Fred Franzia, Antonio Galloni and Jackie Wilferd for their generous time in reading, giving me criticisms, photographs and encouragement as the text was being written. I am especially thankful to Gaye Allen of Meadowlark Publishing for her many hours of guidance in bringing this book to fruition. It was she, above all others, who showed the way and made this project a fun learning experience. The editorial team of Amy Marr, Lisa Atwood and Ken della Penta also provided much appreciated advice in shaping the final text.

Special thanks to Sharon Archer, who typed my recorded voice notes into electronic form as random notes during the years I was a winemaker in Monterey County. Thanks also to my granddaughter, Remi Barrett, who recognized that the notes' true value could be seen only after careful sorting into chronological order, so that each story could find its place in the overall narrative.